AF684405

Psychology IN THE FIRST PERSON

Classic and Contemporary Readings

David T. Liebert, Ed.D.
St. Petersburg College

Bent Tree Press

Copyright © 2008 by Bent Tree Press.

All rights reserved. No part of this book may be reproduced in any form whatsoever, by photograph or xerography or by any other means, by broadcast or transmission, by translation into any kind of language, nor by recording electronically or otherwise, without permission in writing from the publisher, except by a reviewer, who may quote brief passages in critical articles and reviews.

Printed in the United States of America.

ISBN: 1-60250-014-2
978-1-60250-014-3

Bent Tree Press

59 Damonte Ranch Parkway, Suite B 284 • Reno, NV 89521 • (800) 970-1883

www.benttreepress.com

Address all correspondence and order information to the above address.

Table of Contents

Acknowledgements

Bent Tree Press gratefully acknowledges these organizations and individuals for providing reprint permissions on the following articles:

Alexander, B., Beyerstein, B., Hadaway, P., & Coambs, R. B. (1981). Effect of early and later colony housing on oral ingestion of morphine in rats. *Pharmacology, Biochemistry, and Behavior*, ***15 (4)***, 571-576.
Reprinted from Alexander, B., Beyerstein, B., Hadaway, P., & Coambs, R. B. (1981). Effect of early and later colony housing on oral ingestion of morphine in rats. *Pharmacology, Biochemistry, and Behavior*, *15 (4)*, 571-576. Copyright © 1981, with permission from Elsevier.

Angell, M. (2000). Is academic medicine for sale? *New England Journal of Medicine*, ***342 (20)***, 1516-1518.
Copyright © 2000 Massachusetts Medical Society. All rights reserved.

Bouchard, T., Lykken, D., McGue, M. Segal, N., & Tellegen, A. (1990). Sources of human psychological differences: The Minnesota study of twins reared apart. *Science*, ***250***, 223-229.
Reprinted with permission from Bouchard, T., Lykken, D., McGue, M., Segal, N., & Tellegen, A. (1990). Sources of human psychological differences: The Minnesota study of twins reared apart. *Science*, *250*. Copyright 1990 AAAS.

Caballero, J., & Nahata, M. C. (2005). Selective serotonin-reuptake inhibitors and suicidal ideation and behavior in children. *American Journal of Health-System Pharmacy*, ***62 (8)***, 864-868.
Originally published in Caballero, J., & Nahata, M. C. (2005). Selective serotonin-reuptake inhibitors and suicidal ideation and behavior in children. *American Journal of Health-System Pharmacy*, *62 (8)*. © 2005, American Society of Health-System Pharmacists, Inc. All rights reserved. Reprinted with permission. (R0703).

Darley, J. M., & Latane, B. (1968). Bystander intervention in emergencies: Diffusion of responsibility. *Journal of Personality and Social Psychology*, ***8 (4)***, 377-383.
Copyright © 1968 by the American Psychological Association. Reproduced with permission.

Gazzaniga, M. S. (1967). The split brain in man. *Scientific American*, ***217***, 24-29.
Reprinted with permission from Scientific American, http://www.sciam.com/page.cfm?section=repub_text. Illustrations by Eric O. Mose and Dr. Michael S. Gazzaniga. Reprinted by permission of The Estate of Eric Mose and Dr. Michael S. Gazzaniga.

Gibson, E. J. & Walk, R. D. (1960). The "visual cliff." *Scientific American*, ***202***, 67-71,
Reprinted with permission from Scientific American, http://www.sciam.com/page.cfm?section=repub_text.

Hobson, J. A., & McCarley, R. W. (1977). The brain as a dream-state generator: An activation-synthesis hypothesis of the dream process. *American Journal of Psychiatry*, ***134***, 1335-1348.
Reprinted with permission from the American Journal of Psychiatry, (Copyright 1977). American Psychiatric Association.

Langer, E. J., & Rodin, J. (1966). The effects of choice and enhanced personal responsibility for the aged: A field experiment in an institutional setting. *Journal of Personality and Social Psychology*, ***34***, 191-198.
Copyright © 1966 by the American Psychological Association. Reproduced with permission.

Loftus, E. F. (1993). The reality of repressed memories. *American Psychologist*, ***48***, 518-537.
Copyright © 1993 by the American Psychological Association. Reproduced with permission.

Milgram, S. (1963). Behavioral study of obedience. *Journal of Abnormal and Social Psychology*, ***67***, 371-378.
Milgram, S. "Behavioral Study of Obedience," *Journal of Abnormal and Social Psychology*, *64*, 4, pp. 371-378 (1963). © Renewed by Alexandra Milgram 1991.

Piaget, J. (1962). The stages of intellectual development of the child. *Bulletin of the Menninger Clinical*, 26.
Reprinted by permission of Guilford Press.

Rosenhan, D. L. (1973). On being sane in insane places. *Science*, ***197***, 250-258.
Reprinted with permission from Rosenhan, D. L. (1973). On being sane in insane places. *Science*, *197*. Copyright 1973 AAAS.

Rosenthal, R., & Jacobson, L. (1968). Teachers' expectancies: Determinants of Pupils' IQ Gains. *Psychological Reports*, ***19***, 115-118.
Rosenthal, R., & Jacobson, L. Teachers' expectancies: Determinants of Pupils' IQ Gains. *Psychological Reports*, 1966, *19*, 115-118. © Southern Universities Press 1966.

Seligman, M. E. P., & Maier, S. F. (1967). Failure to escape traumatic shock. *Journal of Experimental Psychology*, ***74***, 1-9.
Copyright © 1967 by the American Psychological Association. Reproduced with permission.

Shiffrin, R. M., & Atkinson, R. C. (1969). Storage and retrieval processes in long-term memory. *Psychological Review*, ***76***, 179-193.
Copyright © 1969 by the American Psychological Association. Reproduced with permission.

The illustrations and photos accompanying the articles by E. J. Gibson and R. D. Walk, "The Visual Cliff"; H. F. Harlow, "The Nature of Love"; and J. A. Hobson and R. W. McCarley, "The Brain as a Dream-State Generator: An Activation Synthesis Hypothesis of the Dream Process" are reprinted here without permissions of the owners. While we worked diligently to secure these permissions, we were unable to locate the rights owners due to the age of the images. If you own the rights to these images, please contact Bent Tree Press at www.benttreepress.com, or call 1-800-970-1883.

1 Effect of Early and Later Colony Housing on Oral Ingestion of Morphine in Rats

Bruce K. Alexander, Barry L. Beyerstein, Patricia F. Hadaway and Robert B. Coambs

Department of Psychology, Simon Fraser University • Burnaby, B.C. V5A 1S6 Canada • Received 5 December 1980

ALEXANDER, B. K., B. L. BEYERSTEIN, P. F. HADAWAY AND R. B. COAMBS. *Effects of early and later colony housing on oral ingestion of morphine in rats.* PHARMAC. BIOCHEM. BEHAV. 15(4) 571-576, 1981.—Male and female rats were raised from weaning either in isolation or in a large colony. At 65 days of age, half the rats in each environment were moved to the other. At 80 days, the animals were given continuous access to water and to a sequence of 7 solutions: 3 sweet or bitter-sweet control solutions and 4 different concentrations of morphine hydrochloride (MHCl) in 10% sucrose solution. Rats housed in the colony at the time of testing drank less MHCl solution than isolated rats, but no less of the control solutions. Colony-dwelling rats previously housed in isolation tended to drink more MHCl solution than those housed in the colony since weaning, but this effect reached statistical significance only at the lowest concentration of MHCl. These data were related to the hypothesis that colony rats avoid morphine because it interferes with complex, species-specific behavior.

Morphine   Self-administration
Environment   Isolation

UNDER appropriate conditions, laboratory animals drink opiate drug solutions in preference to water [3,14,16], and self-inject opiates through indwelling catheters [19,20]. These findings are sometimes taken to suggest that mammals, in general, have a natural affinity for opiates [2,7,8]. However, recent data indicate that laboratory housing may itself increase opiate intake. Rats housed in a quasi-natural colony drank much less morphine hydrochloride (MHCl) solution than rats isolated in standard laboratory cages. This was found both in rats which had been pre-treated with morphine [1] and in untreated rats [10].

The present experiment is designed to analyse this housing effect more fully by separating the effect of early housing from that of housing contemporaneous with intake testing. We have proposed [10] that colony housed rats avoid morphine because its ingestion interferes with species-specific behaviors which can occur only in a colony, such as nest building, mating, and fighting. This speculation implicates housing contemporaneous with testing as the cause of the housing effect, and is compatible with recent demonstrations that relatively small doses of morphine significantly reduce sexual behavior and "social cohesion" in rats [15,17], and with the evidence that species-specific behaviors are self-reinforcing [6]. Another plausible explanation for the housing effect, that morphine reinforces isolated rats because it relieves the stress of isolation, also would implicate the contemporaneous environment.

On the other hand, complexity of the very early post-weaning environment has major effects on development of the central nervous system (e.g., [9,11]), some of which have been related to drug use [18]. Many of the widely accepted personality theories of human addiction (e.g., [13]) also stress very early experience. Early rather than contemporaneous housing could clearly be responsible for the housing effect observed in our previous experiments [1,10].

METHOD

Subjects

Sixteen male and sixteen female albino rats of Wistar origin (University of British Columbia Breeding Stock) were obtained at weaning (21 ± 2 days of age). Eight males and eight females were placed in individual housing; eight males and eight females were housed in a colony.

Apparatus and Procedure

Individual housing was in standard wire mesh cages (18 x 25 x 18 cm). During intake testing, fluid consumption was monitored by weighing the two drinking bottles affixed to each cage daily. An approximate correction for leakage and evaporation was made by subtracting the mean weight loss from two similar bottles mounted on empty cages in the same rack.

Colony housing was in a large (8.8 m^2), open-topped plywood enclosure containing cedar shavings, empty canisters, and small boxes for hiding and nesting. Fluids were available at the end of a short transparent tunnel attached to an opening in the wall. Inside dimensions of the tunnel were just sufficient to accommodate one adult rat at a time (4.4 x 5.8 cm). At the far end of the tunnel were two fluid dispensers (Lafayette Instruments, catalogue no. 80201), each positioned over a shallow well, with a photoelectric beam running across each well. Drinking from a well required a rat to break a light beam with its head. Withdrawing its head re-instated the beam, automatically releasing another drop of fluid into the well. The number of drops released from each dispenser was displayed on digital counters. This device is described in greater detail elsewhere [5].

When a rat entered the tunnel, a photoelectrically activated video camera recorded the dye mark on its back and the number of drops released by the previous rat as displayed on the digital counters. Any overflow from a well was drawn off by a vacuum pump into separate containers for each fluid. This loss (usually less than 10% of total intake) was subtracted proportionately to each rat's intake for the day.

Other environmental variables were controlled by situating both housing environments in the same large room, with a 12-hr light-dark cycle. Food was available ad lib throughout.

At 60 days of age all rats were weighed and dye marked for identification. At 65 days of age, half the colony rats were transferred to individual cages and half the isolated rats were placed in the colony, producing four housing conditions each containing four rats of each sex (see Table 1). The rats were then left undisturbed for two weeks. During this period colony rats drank their water from the dispensing device, a skill which each rat learned readily.

Intake testing began at 80 days of age. In each phase rats were given 24 hr access to a drug-sucrose solution and a tap water alternative. The concentrations of the drug-sucrose solutions, sequence and length of the seven phases, and phase abbreviations appear in Table 1. Phase PRE provided access to tap water and to a 10% sucrose solution to determine if housing conditions had affected preference for sweet solutions. Next, Phase Q entailed access to water and to a solution of 0.06 mg quinine sulfate/ml 10% sucrose solution to check for effects of housing on preference for bitter-sweet solutions. To the human palate, this quinine-sucrose solution tasted the same as the morphine-sucrose solution used later in Phase 0.3. In a pilot experiment, rats given 8 hours exposure to these two solutions ingested approximately equal amounts.

The next 4 phases each entailed continuous access to water and to progressively decreasing concentrations of MHCl in 10% sucrose. In Phase 1, the drug solution contained 1 mg MHCl/ml of vehicle; in Phase 0.5, 0.5 mg MHCl/ml vehicle; in Phase 0.3, 0.3 mg MHCl/ml vehicle, and in Phase 0.15, 0.15 mg MHCl/ml vehicle. Finally, Phase POST entailed the same water vs sugar-water alternatives as Phase PRE. Left-right positions of water and drug-sucrose solution were reversed after each phase in both environments.

The "days" column in Table 1 indicates the number of days in each phase. A persistent electronic malfunction caused the loss of several days' data from the colony rats. On these days, data for isolated rats was also dropped from the ANOVA. The "usable days" column indicates the number of days actually analysed for each phase. The lost days were 1, 2, and 4 from Phase Q; 2 from Phase 1; 1, 3, and 4 from Phase 0.5; and 1 from Phase POST. Fortunately, no days were lost from 2 of the 3 phases which provided the critical test of the housing effect, but the lost data from the Q Phase may have contributed some ambiguity to the results for females, as reported below.

TABLE 1

HOUSING CONDITIONS AND SEQUENCE OF DRUG-SUCROSE SOLUTIONS PRESENTED IN EXPERIMENTAL PHASES

Housing Conditions			
Designation	Early (22-65 Days)	Contemporaneous (65 Days Onwards)	N
II	Isolated	Isolated	4M,4F
CI	Colony	Isolated	4M,4F
IC	Isolated	Colony	4M,4F
CC	Colony	Colony	4M,4F

Phases			
Phase Name	Morphine or Quinine/Sucrose Solution	Days	Usable Days
PRE	water+10% sucrose	3	3
Q	0.06 mg QSO4/ml water+10% sucrose	5	2
1	1.00 mg MHCl/ml water+10% sucrose	5	4
0.5	0.50 mg MHCl/ml water+10% sucrose	5	2
0.3	0.30 mg MHCl/ml water+10% sucrose	5	5
0.15	0.15 mg MHCl/ml water+10% sucrose	5	5
POST	water+10% sucrose	3	2

Repeated measures analyses of variance (ANOVAs) were run separately for each phase for grams drug-sucrose solution ingested, mg quinine sulphate or MHCl/kg body weight, and proportion of drug-sucrose solution to total fluid intake. Death of a female in group CC after completion of Phase 0.3 and a female in group IC after Phase 0.15 reduced the number to 3 for these groups in the analyses for the final phases. ANOVAs were run separately for males and females and for all animals together. Because of differences in outcome, the data relating to housing effects are reported below separately for males and females.

RESULTS

Housing Effects: Males

Males living in the colony at the time of testing ingested much less MHCl solution than isolated males, but no less of the control solutions. Early isolation appeared to increase morphine intake in the colony-dwelling males, but the effect reached significance only in Phase 0.15.

No males drank much of the extremely bitter MHCl solution in Phase 1, however, in Phases 0.5, 0.3, and 0.15, colony males (conditions CC and IC) drank less of the morphine-sucrose solution than isolated males (conditions II and CI) on all three measures (see Fig. 1). Eight of nine Fs for contemporaneous environment in these three phases were statistically significant, five beyond the 0.0001 level. Significance levels for each phase appear in Fig. 1. The effect was greatest in Phases 0.5 and 0.3, in which the isolated males drank 19 times and 6 times as much MHCl solution as the colony males respectively (based on mg/kg data).

There were no significant Fs due to early environment alone, but the early by contemporaneous environment interactions in Phase 0.15 were significant for g MHCl solution and mg MHCl/kg body weight. On both measures, colony males which had been isolated early in life (IC condition) drank more MHCl solution than males reared from weaning in the colony (CC). Differences between II and CI males, however, were not consistent between measures (see Fig. 1).

The variance was large, both between individuals and between the same individuals' scores on different days. The influence of the large variance on the significance tests was reduced by basing inter-condition comparisons on 5-day totals.

To illustrate the nature of the variability, Table 2 presents day-by-day individual data for a representative phase (Phase 0.3, males, mg/kg) and an abbreviated ANOVA summary table.

TABLE 2

SAMPLE DATA AND ANOVA SUMMARY. DATA FROM PHASE 0.3, MALES, mg MHCl CONSUMED /kg BODY WEIGHT

	Day					
Condition	1	2	3	4	5	Mean
IC	8.862	15.821	29.077	13.368	27.601	18.946
	2.679	2.673	7.401	25.189	33.615	14.311
	0.0	0.728	1.436	1.239	3.650	1.411
	3.238	22.107	22.553	35.376	36.964	24.048
CC	0.000	0.000	0.793	6.268	0.000	1.412
	1.070	4.026	2.825	4.644	5.276	3.568
	2.857	1.695	0.767	2.066	1.133	1.704
	0.0	2.742	3.575	4.160	5.096	3.115
II	66.414	59.085	68.021	79.144	61.335	66.800
	77.167	3.565	82.269	34.320	20.270	43.518
	56.932	28.466	5.790	17.550	19.782	25.704
	87.166	12.612	2.233	14.714	25.815	28.508
CI	93.244	64.880	21.740	28.109	78.723	57.335
	68.999	84.104	24.489	41.918	47.102	53.322
	88.335	3.198	5.356	26.860	70.668	38.883
	111.561	131.539	78.699	37.156	62.549	84.301

Analysis of Variance for Housing Conditions

	df	MS	F	*p*
Contemporaneous Environment (C)	1	34002	33.64	<0.0001
Early Environment (E)	1	130	0.13	N.S.
C X E	1	4368	4.32	0.06
Error	12	1011		

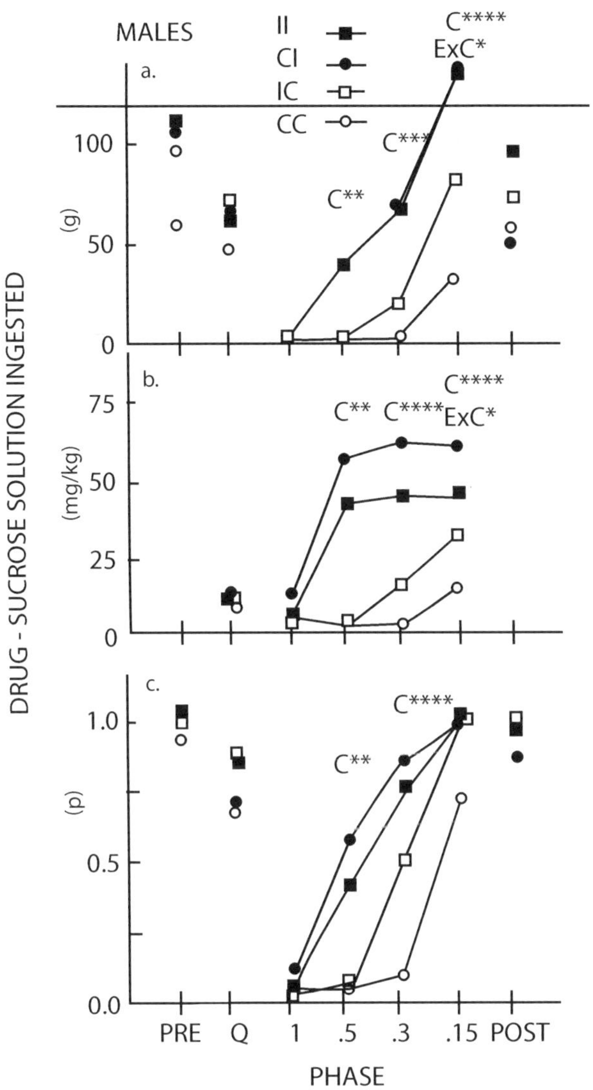

Fig. 1. Ingestion of drug-sucrose solutions by male rats measured as g drug-sucrose solution, mg MHCl or quinine sulfate/kg body weight, and proportion of drug-sucrose solution to total fluid intake. C signifies that the F for the effect of contemporaneous environment was significant, E indicates that early environment was significant, and ExC indicates a significant interaction. *, **, *** and **** signify significance at the 0.05, 0.01 0.001 and 0.0001 levels, respectively.

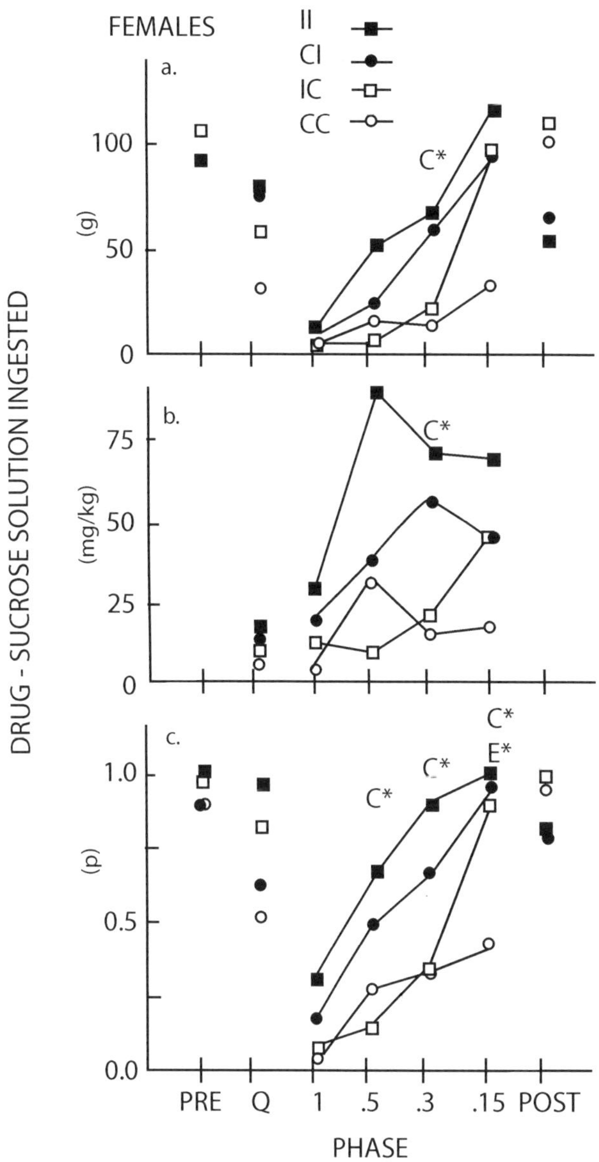

Fig. 2. Consumption of drug-sucrose solutions by female rats. Notation is the same as for Fig. 1.

Housing Effects: Females

Results were similar for females, but less conclusive. Females housed in the colony consumed less MHCl in Phases 0.5, 0.3, and 0.15 on all three measures. Fs for contemporaneous environment were significant for g MHCl solution and mg MHCl/kg in Phase 0.3 and for proportion of MHCl solution to total fluid intake in Phases 0.5, 0.3, and 0.15 (see Fig. 2 for significance levels). IC females appeared to consume much more MHCl than CC females in Phase 0.15 in all three measures, but the only significant F was for early environment for the proportion measure in Phase 0.15.

Although no differences reached statistical significance in control Phases PRE, Q, or POST, the colony females (CC and IC) tended to drink less quinine-sucrose solution in Phase Q than the isolated (II and CI) females (Fig. 2a-c). The F values for contemporaneous environment approached significance for g MHCl solution and mg MHCl/kg, $F(1,12)=2.45$, $p=0.143$, and $F(1,12)=2.58$, $p=0.134$, respectively.

The loss of three days' data from the Q Phase may have increased the intra-group variance, thus reducing the likelihood of statistical significance in this phase.

Because of the possibility of an effect of housing on preference for bitter-sweet solutions in females, which could have affected their intake of the drug-bearing solutions, the female data from Phases 0.5, 0.3, and 0.15 were subjected to analysis of covariance. For each measure, the covariate was mean consumption by the same measure in Phase Q. Of the 5 significant Fs for contemporaneous environment, 3 were also significant in the analysis of covariance, all 3 for the proportion measure (Phase 0.5; $F(1,11)=5.53$, $p<0.05$: Phase 0.3; $F(1,11)=8.91$, $p<0.05$: Phase 0.15; $F(1,10)=6.52$, $p<0.05$). The Fs for g MHCl solution and mg MHCl/kg in Phase 0.3, both significant in the original ANOVA, narrowly missed significance, $F(1,11)=3.71$, $p=0.08$, and $F(1,11)=3.65$, $p=0.08$, respectively.

No Fs for early housing conditions reached significance in the analysis of covariance, but three early by contemporaneous interactions did. For the proportion measure in Phase 0.15, the adjusted cell means were similar in the II, CI, and IC females and much lower in the CC females, indicating that early isolation had increased MHCl consumption in the colony females, but not in the isolated females. For g MHCl solution in Phase 0.15, and for mg MHCl/kg in Phase 0.5, the adjusted cell means were highest in the II females followed by the CC, CI, and IC females, in that order. Overall, the adjusted means for the isolation housed females were higher than those of the colony housed females, in spite of the relatively high adjusted means of the CC group.

Gender Differences

Analyses of variance performed on data for both sexes revealed that neither the ingestion of morphine nor of control solutions was affected by gender. Of 76 F tests for the gender main effect plus all its interactions with early and contemporaneous environment in the 7 phases, only 1 was significant at the 0.05 level.

DISCUSSION

Rats living in a colony at the time of testing consumed less MHCl than isolated rats, whatever their early housing condition, even though they had been exposed to the early environment for 44 days and to the contemporaneous environment for only 15 days prior to the start of the experiment. Early isolation appeared to increase morphine consumption in Phase 0.15 for colony-dwelling rats, but the statistical support for this observation was weaker.

The apparently large effect of living in a colony on morphine consumption must be qualified by recognition of two facts. First, the loss of 3 days' data on Phase 0.5 reduces the confidence with which that phase's results can be accepted. This problem, however, does not apply to Phases 0.3 in which the housing effect was also large, since no data were lost. Second, there was a trend toward increasing consumption of MHCl in the IC rats and, to a lesser extent, the CC rats across the 5 days of Phases 0.3 and 0.15, suggesting that a longer period of exposure might reduce the magnitude of the housing effect. In spite of these qualifications, however, the present results and those of two previous experiments [1,10] suggest that the housing effect is both large and robust.

Two broad conclusions are suggested. First, the consumption of opiates by animals in self-administration experiments may be strongly facilitated by the typically isolated housing conditions during intake testing. Generalizations from such experiments should be qualified by this possibility. Second, some attributes which differ between the two housing environments in this experiment must affect a powerful control mechanism for opiate self-administration. Full analysis of the effect requires determining which attributes of the two environments are most critical and how their effect on opiate consumption is mediated. In addition to space and social contact, the colony environment contained cedar shavings, empty cans and boxes, and a high ceiling which allowed three-dimensional movement. Experiments underway in our laboratory should reveal the relative contributions of such factors.

The fact that housing at the time of intake testing accounts for most of the housing effect is compatible with our speculation [10] that colony rats avoid opiates because opiate consumption interferes with the performance of complex, species-specific behaviors. This speculation grew from evidence that colony rats forced to consume MHCl engage in significantly less fighting and sexual behavior [1], that relatively small doses of morphine significantly reduce sexual behavior and "social cohesion" in group caged rats [15,17], and that species-specific behaviors are self reinforcing [6].

There are, however, several other possible explanations for the housing effect. One of the most plausible is that morphine may reinforce isolated rats by relieving stress resulting from social and sensory isolation. This possibility, however, is contradicted by demonstrations that isolated, non-physically-dependent rats avoid drinking opiates, unless they are induced to by sweetening the opiate solution. Isolated, non-physically-dependent rats with sectioned lingual and glossopharyngeal nerves reject morphine solution [12], indicating an aversion to its effects rather than to its bitter taste. Isolated, non-physically-dependent rats also reject presumably tasteless solutions of etonitazene [21]. It has recently been reported [4] that rats rejected methadone when the alternative was an equally bitter quinine solution. However, when given naltrexone injections, eliminating the pharmacological effects of methadone, the rats drank equal amounts of both solutions. Therefore the initial avoidance was not to the taste or odor of the opiate, but to its effects.

These findings suggest that oral opiates are not reinforcing to isolate rats. The apparent contradiction between these findings and observations of spontaneous opiate self-administration by isolated rats in self-injection experiments remains to be explained.

The present data comprise a better controlled replication of the previously reported housing effect. Colony males ingested much less morphine solution than isolated males though there was no difference in preference for sweet or bitter-sweet solutions. The data were not as conclusive for females, since there was a trend (short of statistical significance) toward less intake of bitter-sweet control solution in colony females. Analysis of covariance generally indicated a housing effect, but a more precise measure of it for females would require ruling out taste factors, perhaps by using etonitazene.

ACKNOWLEDGEMENTS

We are grateful for help and advice from Wayne Tressel, Kathy Redmond, Joan Foster, Benjamin Staat, Ray Koopman, and Stanton Peele. This research was supported by grants from the Health Promotion Directorate, Health and Welfare, Canada, the British Columbia Ministry of Labour, and from the Steel Foundation, Simon Fraser University.

REFERENCES

1. Alexander, B. K., R. B. Coambs, and P. F. Hadaway. The effect of housing and gender on morphine self-administration in rats. *Psychopharmcology* **58**: 175-179, 1978.
2. Berot, N. Addiction to pleasure: A biological and social-Psychological theory of addiction. In: *Theories on Drug Abuse: Selected Contemporary Perspectives*, (NIDA Research Monograph 30), edited by D. J. Lettieri, M. Sayers, and H. W. Pearson. Washington, DC: National Institute of Drug Abuse, 1980, pp. 246-255.
3. Carroll, M. E., and R. A. Meisch. Concurrent etonitazene and water intake in rats: Role of taste, olfaction and auditory stimuli. *Psychopharmacology* **64**: 1-7, 1979.
4. Chipkin, R. E., and J. A. Rosecrans. Aversiveness of oral methadone in rats. *Psychopharmacology* **57**: 303-310, 1978.
5. Coambs, R. B., B. K. Alexander, C. M. Davis, P. F. Hadaway, and W. K. Tressel. A drug dispenser to measure individual drinking in rat colonies. *Pharmac. Biochem. Behav.* **13**: 593-595, 1980.
6. Glickman, S. E., and B. B. Schiff. A biological theory of reinforcement. *Psychol. Rev.* **74**: 81-109, 1967.
7. Goldstein, A. Heroin addiction and the role of methadone in its treatment. *Archs gen. Psychiat.* **26**: 291-297, 1972.
8. Goldstein, A. Heroin maintenance: A medical view. A conversation between a physician and a politician. *J. Drug Issues* **9**: 341-347, 1979.
9. Greenough, W. T. Experimental modification of the developing brain. *Am. Scient.* **63**: 37-46, 1975.
10. Hadaway, P. F., B. K. Alexander, R. B. Coambs, and B. Beyerstein. The effect of housing and gender on preference for morphine-sucrose solutions in rats. *Psychopharmacology* **66**: 87-91, 1979.
11. Horn, G., S. P. R. Rose, and P. P. G. Bateson. Experience and plasticity in the central nervous system. *Science* **203**: 75-78, 1979.
12. Huidobro, F. Studies in morphine: VI. Ingestion of morphine solutions in normal mice and rats and in animals with chronic morphinism. *Archs int. Pharmacodyn.* **151**: 299-312, 1964.

13. Khantzian, E. J. An ego/self theory of substance dependence: A contemporary psychoanalytic perspective. In: *Theories on Drug Abuse: Selected Contemporary Perspectives*, (NIDA Research Monograph 30), edited by D. J. Lettieri, M. Sayers, and H. W. Pearson. Washington, DC: National Institute of Drug Abuse, 1980, pp. 29-33.

14. Khavari, K. A., T. C. Peters, and P. L. Baity. Voluntary morphine ingestion, morphine dependence, and recovery from withdrawal signs. *Pharmac. Biochem. Behav.* **3**: 1093-1096, 1975.

15. McIntosh, T. K., M. L. Vallano, and R. J. Barfield. Effects of Morphine, ß-endorphine and naloxone on catecholamine levels and sexual behavior in the male rat. *Pharmac. Biochem. Behav.* **13**: 435-441, 1980.

16. Nichols, J. R., C. P. Headlee, and H. W. Coppock. Drug Addiction. I. Addiction by escape training. J. *Am. pharm. Ass.* **45:** 788-791, 1956.

17. Panksepp, J., N. Najam, and F. Scares. Morphine reduces cohesion in rats. *Pharmac. Biochem. Behav.* **11**: 131-134, 1979.

18. Prescott, J. W. Somatosensory affectional deprivation (SAD) theory of drug and alcohol use. In: *Theories on Drug Abuse: Selected Contemporary Perspectives*, (NIDA Research Monograph 30), edited by D. J. Lettieri, M. Sayers, and H. W. Pearson. Washington, DC: National Institute of Drug Abuse, l980, pp. 286-296.

19. Weeks, J. R., and R. J. Collins. Factors affecting voluntary morphine intake in self-maintained addicted rats. *Psychopharmacology* **6**: 267-279, 1964.

20. Weeks, J. R., and R. J. Collins. Dose and physical dependence as factors in the self-administration of morphine by rats. *Psychopharmacology* **65**: 171-177, 1979.

21. Wikler, A., and F. T. Pescor. Classical conditioning of a morphine abstinence phenomenon, reinforcement of opioid drinking behavior and 'relapse' in morphine addicted rats. *Psychopharmacologia* **10**: 255-284, 1967.

2 Is Academic Medicine for Sale?

Marcia Angell, MD

Originally Published: (2000). *The New England Journal of Medicine, 342 (20), 1516-1518*

In 1984 the *Journal* became the first of the major medical journals to require authors of original research articles to disclose any financial ties with companies that make products discussed in papers submitted to us.[1] We were aware that such ties were becoming fairly common, and we thought it reasonable to disclose them to readers. Although we came to this issue early, no one could have foreseen at the time just how ubiquitous and manifold such financial associations would become. The article by Keller et al.[2] in this issue of the *Journal* provides a striking example. The authors' ties with companies that make antidepressant drugs were so extensive that it would have used too much space to disclose them fully in the *Journal.* We decided merely to summarize them and to provide the details on our Web site.

Finding an editorialist to write about the article presented another problem. Our conflict-of-interest policy for editorialists, established in 1990,[3] is stricter than that for authors of original research papers. Since editorialists do not provide data, but instead selectively review the literature and offer their judgments, we require that they have no important financial ties to companies that make products related to the issues they discuss. We do not believe disclosure is enough to deal with the problem of possible bias. This policy is analogous to the requirement that judges recuse themselves from hearing cases if they have financial ties to a litigant. Just as a judge's disclosure would not be sufficiently reassuring to the other side in a court case, so we believe that a policy of caveat emptor is not enough for readers who depend on the opinion of editorialists.

But as we spoke with research psychiatrists about writing an editorial on the treatment of depression, we found very few who did not have financial ties to drug companies that make antidepressants. (Fortunately, Dr. Jan Scott, who is eminently qualified to write the editorial,[4] met our standards with respect to conflicts of interest.) The problem is by no means unique to psychiatry. We routinely encounter similar difficulties in finding editorialists in other specialties, particularly those that involve the heavy use of expensive drugs and devices.

In this editorial, I wish to discuss the extent to which academic medicine has become intertwined with the pharmaceutical and biotechnology industries, and the benefits and risks of this state of affairs. Bodenheimer, in his Health Policy Report elsewhere in this issue of the *Journal,*[5] provides a detailed view of an overlapping issue — the relations between clinical investigators and the pharmaceutical industry.

The ties between clinical researchers and industry include not only grant support, but also a host of other financial arrangements. Researchers serve as consultants to companies whose products they are studying, join advisory boards and speakers' bureaus, enter into patent and royalty arrangements, agree to be the listed authors of articles ghostwritten by interested companies, promote drugs and devices at company-sponsored symposiums, and allow themselves to be plied with expensive gifts and trips to luxurious settings. Many also have equity interest in the companies.

Although most medical schools have guidelines to regulate financial ties between their faculty members and industry, the rules are generally quite relaxed and are likely to become even more so. For some years, Harvard Medical School prided itself on having unusually strict guidelines. For example, Harvard has prohibited researchers from having more than $20,000 worth of stock in companies whose products they are studying.[6] But now the medical school is in the process of softening its guidelines. Those reviewing the Harvard policy claim that the guidelines need to be modified to prevent the loss of star faculty members to other schools. The executive dean for academic programs was reported to say, "I'm not sure what will come of the proposal. But the impetus is to make sure our faculty has reasonable opportunities."[7]

Academic medical institutions are themselves growing increasingly beholden to industry. How can they justify rigorous conflict-of-interest policies for individual researchers when their own ties are so extensive? Some academic institutions have entered into partnerships with drug companies to set up research centers and teaching programs in which students and faculty members essentially carry out industry research. Both sides see great benefit in this arrangement. For financially struggling medical centers, it means cash. For the companies that make the drugs and devices, it means access to research talent, as well as affiliation with a prestigious "brand." The time-honored custom of drug companies' gaining entry into teaching hospitals by bestowing small gifts on house officers has reached new levels of munificence. Trainees now receive free meals and other substantial favors from drug companies virtually daily, and they are often invited to opulent dinners and other quasi-social events to hear lectures on various medical topics. All of this is done with the acquiescence of the teaching hospitals.

What is the justification for this large-scale breaching of the boundaries between academic medicine and for-profit industry? Two reasons are usually offered, one emphasized more than the other. The first is that ties to industry are necessary to facilitate technology transfer — that is, the movement of new drugs and devices from the laboratory to the marketplace. The term "technology transfer" entered the lexicon in 1980, with the passage of federal legislation, called the Bayh–Dole Act,[8] that encouraged academic institutions supported by federal grants to patent and license new products developed by their faculty members and to share royalties with the researchers. The Bayh–Dole Act is now frequently invoked to justify the ubiquitous ties between academia and industry. It is argued that the more contacts there are between academia and industry, the better it is for clinical medicine; the fact that money changes hands is considered merely the way of the world.

A second rationale, less often invoked explicitly, is simply that academic medical centers need the money. Many of the most prestigious institutions in the country are bleeding red ink as a result of the reductions in Medicare reimbursements contained in the 1997 Balanced Budget Act and the hard bargaining of other third-party payers to keep hospital costs down. Deals with drug companies can help make up for the shortfall, so that academic medical centers can continue to carry out their crucial missions of education, research, and the provision of clinical care for the sickest and neediest. Under the circumstances, it is not surprising that institutions feel justified in accepting help from any source.

I believe the claim that extensive ties between academic researchers and industry are necessary for technology transfer is greatly exaggerated, particularly with regard to clinical research. There may be some merit to the claim for basic research, but in most clinical research, including clinical trials, the "technology" is essentially already developed. Researchers are simply testing it. Furthermore, whether financial arrangements facilitate technology transfer depends crucially on what those arrangements are. Certainly grant support is constructive, if administered properly. But it is highly doubtful whether many of the other financial arrangements facilitate technology transfer or confer any other social benefit. For example, there is no conceivable social benefit in researchers' having equity interest in companies whose products they are studying. Traveling around the world to appear at industry-sponsored symposiums has much more to do with marketing than with technology transfer. Consulting arrangements may be more likely to further the development of useful products, but even this is arguable. Industry may ask clinical researchers to become consultants more to obtain their goodwill than to benefit from their expertise. The goodwill of academic researchers is a very valuable commodity for drug and device manufacturers. Finally, it is by no means necessary for technology transfer that researchers be personally rewarded. One could imagine a different system for accomplishing the same purpose. For example, income from consulting might go to a pool earmarked to support research or any other mission of the medical center.

What is wrong with the current situation? Why shouldn't clinical researchers have close ties to industry? One obvious concern is that these ties will bias research, both the kind of work that is done and the way it is reported. Researchers might undertake studies on the basis of whether they can get industry funding, not whether the studies are scientifically important. That would mean more research on drugs and devices and less designed to gain insights into the causes and mechanisms of disease. It would also skew research toward finding trivial differences between drugs, because those differences can be exploited for marketing. Of even greater concern is the possibility that financial ties may influence the outcome of research studies.

As summarized by Bodenheimer,[5] there is now considerable evidence that researchers with ties to drug companies are indeed more likely to report results that are favorable to the products of those companies than researchers without such ties. That does not conclusively prove that researchers are influenced by their financial ties to industry. Conceivably, drug companies seek out researchers who happen to be getting positive results. But I believe bias is the most likely explanation, and in either case, it is clear that the more enthusiastic researchers are, the more assured they can be of industry funding.

Many researchers profess that they are outraged by the very notion that their financial ties to industry could affect their work. They insist that, as scientists, they can remain objective, no matter what the blandishments. In short, they cannot be bought. What is at issue is not whether researchers can be "bought," in the sense of a quid pro quo. It is that close and remunerative collaboration with a company naturally creates goodwill on the part of researchers and the hope that the largesse will continue. This attitude can subtly influence scientific judgment in ways that may be difficult to discern. Can we really believe that clinical researchers are more immune to self-interest than other people?

When the boundaries between industry and academic medicine become as blurred as they now are, the business goals of industry influence the mission of the medical schools in multiple ways. In terms of education, medical students and house officers, under the constant tutelage of industry representatives, learn to rely on drugs and devices more than they probably should. As the critics of medicine so often charge, young physicians learn that for every problem, there is a pill (and a drug company representative to explain it). They also become accustomed to receiving gifts and favors from an industry that uses these courtesies to influence their continuing education. The academic medical centers, in allowing themselves to become research outposts for industry, contribute to the overemphasis on drugs and devices. Finally, there is the issue of conflicts of commitment. Faculty members who do extensive work for industry may be distracted from their commitment to the school's educational mission.

All of this is not to gainsay the importance of the spectacular advances in therapy and diagnosis made possible by new drugs and devices. Nor is it to deny the value of cooperation between academia and industry. But that cooperation should be at arm's length, with both sides maintaining their own standards and ethical norms. The incentives of the marketplace should not become woven into the fabric of academic medicine. We need to remember that for-profit businesses are pledged to increase the value of their investors' stock. That is a very different goal from the mission of medical schools.

What needs to be done — or undone? Softening its conflict-of-interest guidelines is exactly the wrong thing for Harvard Medical School to do. Instead, it should seek to encourage other institutions to adopt stronger ones. If there were general agreement among the major medical schools on uniform and rigorous rules, the concern about losing faculty to more lax schools — and the consequent race to the bottom — would end. Certain financial ties should be prohibited altogether, including equity interest and many of the writing and speaking arrangements. Rules regarding conflicts of commitment should also be enforced. It is difficult to believe that full-time faculty members can generate outside income greater than their salaries without shortchanging their institutions and students.

As Rothman urges, teaching hospitals should forbid drug-company representatives from coming into the hospital to promote their wares and offer gifts to students and house officers.[2] House officers should buy their own pizza, and hospitals should pay them enough to do so. To the argument that these gifts are too inconsequential to constitute bribes, the answer is that the drug companies are not engaging in charity. These gifts are intended to buy the goodwill of young physicians with long prescribing lives ahead of them. Similarly, academic medical centers should be wary of partnerships in which they make available their precious resources of talent and prestige to carry out research that serves primarily the interests of the companies. That is ultimately a Faustian bargain.

It is well to remember that the costs of the industry-sponsored trips, meals, gifts, conferences, and symposiums and the honorariums, consulting fees, and research grants are simply added to the prices of drugs and devices. The Clinton administration and Congress are now grappling with the serious problem of escalating drug prices in this country. In these difficult times, academic medicine depends more than ever on the public's trust and goodwill. If the public begins to perceive academic medical institutions and clinical researchers as gaining inappropriately from cozy relations with industry — relations that create conflicts of interest and contribute to rising drug prices — there will be little sympathy for their difficulties. Academic institutions and their clinical faculty members must take care not to be open to the charge that they are for sale.

REFERENCES

Relman AS. Dealing with conflicts of interest. N Engl J Med 1984;310:1182-1183.

Keller MB, McCullough JP, Klein DN, et al. A comparison of nefazodone, the cognitive behavioral-analysis system of psychotherapy, and their combination for the treatment of chronic depression. N Engl J Med 2000;342:1462-1470.

Relman AS. New "Information for Authors" — and readers. N Engl J Med 1990;323:56-56.

Scott J. Treatment of chronic depression. N Engl J Med 2000;342:1518-1520.

Bodenheimer T. Uneasy alliance — clinical investigators and the pharmaceutical industry. N Engl J Med 2000;342:1539-1544.

Faculty policies on integrity in science. Cambridge, Mass.: Harvard University, February 1996.

Abel D. Harvard mulls easing rules on research. Boston Globe. February 10, 2000:A1.

University and Small Business Patent Procedures Act of 1980.

Rothman DJ. Medical professionalism — focusing on the real issues. N Engl J Med 2000;342:1284-1286.

3 Transmission of Aggression Through Imitation of Aggressive Models[1]

Albert Bandura, Dorothea Ross, and Sheila A. Ross [2] *(1961)*

First published in *Journal of Abnormal and Social Psychology,* 63, 575-582

A previous study, designed to account for the phenomenon of identification in terms of incidental learning, demonstrated that children readily imitated behavior exhibited by an adult model in the presence of the model (Bandura & Huston, 1961). A series of experiments by Blake (1958) and others (Grosser, Polansky, & Lippitt, 1951; Rosenblith, 1959; Schachter & Hall, 1952) have likewise shown that mere observation responses of a model has a facilitating effect on subjects' reactions in the immediate social influence setting.

While these studies provide convincing evidence for the influence and control exerted on others by the behavior of a model, a more crucial test of imitative learning involves the generalization of imitative response patterns in new settings in which the model is absent.

In the experiment reported in this paper children were exposed to aggressive and nonaggressive adult models and were then tested on amount of imitative learning in a new situation in the absence of the model. According to the prediction, subjects exposed to aggressive models would reproduce aggressive acts resembling those of their models and would differ in this respect both from subjects who served as nonaggressive models and from those who had no prior exposure to any models. This hypothesis assumed that subjects had learned imitative habits as a result of prior reinforcement, and that these tendencies would generalize to some extent to adult experimenters (Miller & Dollard, 1941).

It was further predicted that observation of subdued nonaggressive models would have a generalized inhibiting effect on the subjects' subsequent behavior, and this effect would be reflected in a difference between the nonaggressive and the control groups, with subjects in the latter group displaying significantly more aggression.

Hypotheses were also advanced concerning the influence of the sex of model and sex of subjects on imitation. Fauls and Smith (1956) have shown that preschool children perceive their parents as having distinct preferences regarding sex appropriate modes of behavior for their children. Their findings, as well as informal observation, suggest that parents reward imitation of sex appropriate behavior and discourage or punish sex inappropriate imitative responses, e.g., a male child is unlikely to receive much reward for performing female appropriate activities, such as cooking, or for adopting other aspects of the maternal role, but these same behaviors are typically welcomed if performed by females. As a result of differing reinforcement histories, tendencies to imitate male and female models thus acquire differential habit strength. One would expect, on this basis, subjects to imitate the behavior of a same-sex model to a greater degree than a model of the opposite sex.

Since aggression, however, is a highly masculine-typed behavior, boys should be more predisposed than girls toward imitating aggression, the difference being most marked for subjects exposed to the male aggressive model.

METHOD

Subjects

The subjects were 36 boys and 36 girls enrolled in the Stanford University Nursery School. They ranged in age from 37 to 69 months, with a mean age of 52 months.

Two adults, a male and a female, served in the role of model, and one female experimenter conducted the study for all 72 children.

Experimental Design

Subjects were divided into eight experimental groups of six subjects each and a control group consisting of 24 subjects. Half the experimental subjects were exposed to aggressive models and half were exposed to models that were subdued and nonaggressive in their behavior. These groups were further subdivided into male and female subjects. Half the subjects in the aggressive and nonaggressive conditions observed [p. 576] same-sex models, while the remaining subjects in each group viewed models of the opposite sex. The control group had no prior exposure to the adult models and was tested only in the generalization situation.

It seemed reasonable to expect that the subjects' level of aggressiveness would be positively related to the readiness with which they imitated aggressive modes of behavior. Therefore, in order to increase the precision of treatment comparisons, subjects in the experimental and control groups were matched individually on the basis of ratings of their aggressive behavior in social interactions in the nursery school.

The subjects were rated on four five-point rating scales by the experimenter and a nursery school teacher, both of whom were well acquainted with the children. These scales measured the extent to which subjects displayed physical aggression, verbal aggression, aggression toward inanimate objects, and aggressive inhibition. The latter scale, which dealt with the subjects' tendency to inhibit aggressive reactions in the face of high instigation, provided a measure of aggression anxiety.

Fifty-one subjects were rated independently by both judges so as to permit an assessment of interrater agreement. The reliability of the composite aggression score, estimated by means of the Pearson product-moment correlation, was .89.

The composite score was obtained by summing the ratings on the four aggression scales; on the basis of these scores, subjects were arranged in triplets and assigned at random to one of two treatment conditions or to the control group.

Experimental Conditions

In the first step in the procedure subjects were brought individually by the experimenter to the experimental room and the model who was in the hallway outside the room, was invited by the experimenter to come and join in the game. The experimenter then escorted the subject to one corner of the room, which was structured as the subject's play area. After seating the child at a small table, the experimenter demonstrated how the subject could design pictures with potato prints and picture stickers provided. The potato prints included a variety of geometrical forms; the stickers were attractive multicolor pictures of animals, flowers, and Western figures to be pasted on a pastoral scene. These activities were selected since they had been established, by previous studies in the nursery school, as having high interest value for the children.

After having settled the subject in his corner, the experimenter escorted the model to the opposite corner of the room which contained a small table and chair, a tinker toy set, a mallet, and a 5-foot inflated Bobo doll. The experimenter explained that these were the materials provided for the model to play with and, after the model was seated, the experimenter left the experimental room.

With subjects in the *nonaggressive condition*, the model assembled the tinker toys in a quiet subdued manner totally ignoring the Bobo doll.

In contrast, with subjects in the *aggressive condition*, the model began by assembling the tinker toys but after approximately a minute had elapsed, the model turned to the Bobo doll and spent the remainder of the period aggressing toward it.

Imitative learning can be clearly demonstrated if a model performs sufficiently novel patterns of responses which are unlikely to occur independently of the observation of the behavior of a model and if a subject reproduces these behaviors in substantially identical form. For this reason, in addition to punching the Bobo doll, a response that is likely to be performed by children independently of a demonstration, the model exhibited distinctive aggressive acts which were to be scored as imitative responses. The model laid the Bobo doll on its side, sat on it and punched it repeatedly in the nose. The model then raised the Bobo doll, picked up the mallet and struck the doll on the head. Following the mallet aggression, the model tossed the doll up in the air aggressively and kicked it about the room. This sequence of physically aggressive acts was repeated approximately three times, interspersed with verbally aggressive responses such as, "Sock him in the nose...," "Hit him down...," "Throw him in the air...," "Kick him...," "Pow...," and two non-aggressive comments, "He keeps coming back for more" and "He sure is a tough fella."

Thus in the exposure situation, subjects were provided with a diverting task which occupied their attention while at the same time insured observation of the model's behavior in the absence of any instructions to observe or to learn the responses in question. Since subjects could not perform the model's aggressive behavior, any learning that occurred was purely on an observational or covert basis.

At the end of 10 minutes, the experimenter entered the room, informed the subject that he would now go to another game room, and bid the model goodbye.

Aggression Arousal

Subjects were tested for the amount of imitative learning in a different experimental room that was set off from the main nursery school building, The two experimental situations were thus clearly differentiated; in fact, many subjects were under the impression that they were no longer on the nursery school grounds.

Prior to the test for imitation, however, all subjects, experimental and control, were subjected to mild aggression arousal to insure that they were under some degree of instigation to aggression. The arousal experience was included for two main reasons. In the first place, observation of aggressive behavior exhibited by others tends to reduce the probability of aggression on the part of the observer (Rosenbaum & deCharms, 1960). Consequently, subjects in the aggressive condition, in relation both to the nonaggressive and control groups, would be under weaker instigation following exposure to the models. Second, if subjects in the nonaggressive condition expressed little aggression in the face of appropriate instigation, the presence of an inhibitory process would seem to be indicated.

Following the exposure experience, therefore, the experimenter brought the subject to an anteroom that contained these relatively attractive toys: a fire engine, a locomotive, a jet fighter plane, a cable car, a colorful spinning top, and a doll set complete with wardrobe, doll carriage, and baby crib. The experimenter [p. 577] explained that the toys were for the subject to play with but, as soon as the subject became sufficiently involved with the play material (usually in about 2 minutes), the experimenter remarked that these were her very best toys, that she did not let just anyone play with them, and that she had decided to reserve these toys for the other children. However, the subject could play with any of the toys that were in the next room. The experimenter and the subject then entered the adjoining experimental room.

It was necessary for the experimenter to remain in the room during the experimental session; otherwise a number of the children would either refuse to remain alone or would leave before the termination of the session. However, in order to minimize any influence her presence might have on the subject's behavior, the experimenter remained as inconspicuous as possible by busying herself with paper work at a desk in the far corner of the room and avoiding any interaction with the child.

Test for Delayed Imitation

The experimental room contained a variety of toys including some that could be used in imitative or nonimitative aggression, and others that tended to elicit predominantly nonaggressive forms of behavior. The aggressive toys included a 3-foot Bobo doll, a mallet and peg board, two dart guns, and a tether ball with a face painted on it which hung from the ceiling. The nonaggressive toys, on the other hand, included a tea set, crayons and coloring paper, a ball, two dolls, three bears, cars and trucks, and plastic farm animals.

In order to eliminate any variation in behavior due to mere placement of the toys in the room, the play material was arranged in a fixed order for each of the sessions.

The subject spent 20 minutes in this experiments room during which time his behavior was rated in terms of predetermined response categories by judges who observed the session though a one-way mirror in an adjoining observation room. The 20-minute session was divided into 5-second intervals by means of at electric interval timer, thus yielding a total number of 240 response units for each subject.

The male model scored the experimental sessions for all 72 children. Except for the cases in which he served as the model, he did hot have knowledge of the subjects' group assignments. In order to provide an estimate of interscorer agreement, the performance of half the subjects were also scored independently by a second observer. Thus one or the other of the two observers usually had no knowledge of the conditions to which the subjects were assigned. Since, however, all but two of the subjects in the aggressive condition performed the models' novel aggressive responses while subjects in the other conditions only rarely exhibited such reactions, subjects who were exposed to the aggressive models could be readily identified through the distinctive behavior.

The responses scored involved highly specific concrete classes of behavior and yielded high interscorer reliabilities, the product-moment coefficients being in the .90s.

Response Measures

Three measures of imitation were obtained:

Imitation of physical aggression: This category included acts of striking the Bobo doll with the mallet, sitting on the doll and punching it in the nose, kicking the doll, and tossing it in the air.

Imitative verbal aggression: Subject repeats the phrases, "Sock him," "Hit him down," "Kick him," "Throw him in the air," or "Pow."

Imitative nonaggressive verbal responses: Subject repeats, "He keeps coming back for more," or "He sure is a tough fella."

During the pretest, a number of the subjects imitated the essential components of the model's behavior but did not perform the complete act, or they directed the imitative aggressive response to some object other than the Bobo doll. Two responses of this type were therefore scored and were interpreted as partially imitative behavior.

Mallet aggression: Subject strikes objects other than the Bobo doll aggressively with the mallet.

Sits on Bobo doll: Subject lays the Bobo doll on its side and sits on it, but does not aggress toward it.

The following additional nonimitative aggressive responses were scored:

Punches Bobo doll: Subject strikes, slaps, or pushes the doll aggressively.

Nonimitative physical and verbal aggression: This category included physically aggressive acts directed toward objects other than the Bubo doll and any hostile remarks except for those in the verbal imitation category; e.g., "Shoot the Bobo," "Cut him," "Stupid ball," "Knock over people," "Horses fighting, biting."

Aggressive gun play: Subject shoots darts or aims the guns and fires imaginary shots at objects in the room.

Ratings were also made of the number of behavior units in which subjects played nonaggressively or sat quietly and did not play with any of the material at all.

RESULTS

Complete Imitation of Models' Behavior

Subjects in the aggression condition reproduced a good deal of physical and verbal aggressive behavior resembling that of the models, and their mean scores differed markedly from those of subjects in the nonaggressive and control groups who exhibited virtually no imitative aggression (See Table 1).

Since there were only a few scores for subjects in the nonaggressive and control conditions (approximately 70% of the subjects had zero scores), and the assumption of homogeneity of variance could not be made, the Friedman two-way analysis of variance by ranks was employed to test the significance of the obtained differences.

The prediction that exposure of subjects to aggressive models increases the probability [p. 578] of aggressive behavior is clearly confirmed (see Table 2). The main effect of treatment conditions is highly significant both for physical and verbal imitative aggression. Comparison of pairs of scores by the sign test shows that the obtained over-all differences were due almost

TABLE 1

MEAN AGGRESSION SCORES FOR EXPERIMENTAL AND CONTROL SUBJECTS

Response category	Experimental groups				Control groups
	Aggressive		Nonaggressive		
	F Model	M Model	F Model	M Model	
Imitative physical aggression					
Female subjects	5.5	7.2	2.5	0.0	1.2
Male subjects	12.4	25.8	0.2	1.5	2.0
Imitative verbal aggression					
Female subjects	13.7	2.0	0.3	0.0	0.7
Male subjects	4.3	12.7	1.1	0.0	1.7
Mallet aggression					
Female subjects	17.2	18.7	0.5	0.5	13.1
Male subjects	15.5	28.8	18.7	6.7	13.5
Punches Bobo doll					
Female subjects	6.3	16.5	5.8	4.3	11.7
Male subjects	18.9	11.9	15.6	14.8	15.7
Nonimitative aggression					
Female subjects	21.3	8.4	7.2	1.4	6.1
Male subjects	16.2	36.7	26.1	22.3	24.6
Aggressive gun play					
Female subjects	1.8	4.5	2.6	2.5	3.7
Male subjects	7.3	15.9	8.9	16.7	14.3

TABLE 2

SIGNIFICANCE OF THE DIFFERENCES BETWEEN EXPERIMENTAL AND CONTROL GROUPS IN THE EXPRESSION OF AGGRESSION

Response category	χ^2_r	Q	p	Comparison of pairs of treatment conditions: Aggressive vs. Nonaggressive p	Aggressive vs. Control p	Nonaggressive vs. Control p
Imitative responses						
Physical aggression	27.17		<.001	<.001	<.001	.09
Verbal aggression	9.17		<.02	.004	.048	.09
Nonaggressive verbal responses		17.50	<.001	.004	.004	*ns*
Partial imitation						
Mallet aggression	11.06		<.01	.026	*ns*	.005
Sits on Bobo		13.44	<.01	.018	.059	*ns*
Nonimitative aggression						
Punches Bobo doll	2.87		*ns*			
Physical and verbal	8.96		<.02	.026	*ns*	*ns*
Aggressive gun play	2.75		*ns*			

entirely to the aggression displayed by subjects who had been exposed to the aggressive models. Their scores were significantly higher than those of either the nonaggressive or control groups, which did not differ from each other (Table 2).

Imitation was not confined to the model's aggressive responses. Approximately one-third of the subjects in the aggressive condition also repeated the model's nonaggressive verbal responses while none of the subjects in either the nonaggressive or control groups made such remarks. This difference, tested by means of the Cochran *Q* test, was significant well beyond the .001 level (Table 2).

Partial Imitation of Models' Behavior

Differences in the predicted direction were also obtained on the two measures of partial imitation.

Analysis of variance of scores based on the subjects' use of the mallet aggressively toward objects other than the Bobo doll reveals that treatment conditions are a statistically significant source of variation (Table 2). In addition, individual sign tests show that both the aggressive and the control groups, relative to subjects in the nonaggressive condition, produced significantly more mallet aggression, the difference being particularly marked with regard to female subjects. Girls who observed nonaggressive models performed a mean number of 0.5 mallet aggression responses as compared to mean values of 18.0 and 13.1 for girls in the aggressive and control groups, respectively.

Although subjects who observed aggressive models performed more mallet aggression (M = 20.0) than their controls (M = 13.3), the difference was not statistically significant.

[p. 579] With respect to the partially imitative response of sitting on the Bobo doll, the over-all group differences were significantly beyond the .01 level (Table 2). Comparison of pairs of scores by the sign test procedure reveals that subjects in the aggressive group reproduced this aspect of the models' behavior to a greater extent than did the nonaggressive (p = .018) or the control (p = .059) subjects. The latter two groups, on the other hand, did not differ from each other.

Nonimitative Aggression

Analyses of variance of the remaining aggression measures (Table 2) show that treatment conditions did not influence the extent to which subjects engaged in aggressive gun play or punched the Bobo doll. The effect of conditions is highly significant (c $^2{}_r$ = 8.96, $p < .02$), however in the case of the subjects' expression of nonimitative physical and verbal aggression. Further comparison of treatment pairs reveals that the main source of the over-all difference was the aggressive and nonaggressive groups which differed significantly from each other (Table 2), with subjects exposed to the aggressive models displaying the greater amount of aggression.

Influence of Sex of Model and Sex of Subjects on Imitation

The hypothesis that boys are more prone than girls to imitate aggression exhibited by a model was only partially confirmed. t tests computed for the subjects in the aggressive condition reveal that boys reproduced more imitative physical aggression than girls (t = 2.50 $p < .01$). The groups do not differ, however, in their imitation of verbal aggression.

The use of nonparametric tests, necessitated by the extremely skewed distributions of scores for subjects in the nonaggressive and control conditions, preclude an over-all test of the influence of sex of model per se, and of the various interactions between the main effects. Inspection of the means presented in Table 1 for subjects in the aggression condition, however, clearly suggests the possibility of a Sex x Model interaction. This interaction effect is much more consistent and pronounced for the male model than for the female model. Male subjects, for example, exhibited more physical (t = 2.07, $p < .05$) and verbal imitative aggression (t = 2.51, $p < .05$), more non-imitative aggression (t = 3.15, $p < .025$), and engaged in significantly more aggressive gun play (t = 2.12, $p < .05$) following exposure to the aggressive male model than the female subjects. In contrast, girls exposed to the female model performed considerably more imitative verbal aggression and more non-imitative aggression than did the boys (Table 1). The variances, however, were equally large and with only a small N in each cell the mean differences did not reach statistical significance.

Data for the nonaggressive and control subjects provide additional suggestive evidence that the behavior of the male model exerted a greater influence than the female model on the subjects' behavior in the generalization situation.

It will be recalled that, except for the greater amount of mallet aggression exhibited by the control subjects, no significant differences were obtained between the nonaggressive and control groups. The data indicate, however, that the absence of significant differences between these two groups was due primarily to the fact that subjects exposed to the nonaggressive female model did not differ from the controls on any of the measures of aggression. With respect to the male model, on the other hand, the differences between the groups are striking. Comparison of the sets of scores by means of the sign test reveals that, in relation to the control group, subjects exposed to the nonaggressive male model performed significantly less imitative physical aggression ($p = .06$), less imitative verbal aggression ($p = .002$), less mallet aggression ($p = .003$), less nonimitative physical and verbal aggression ($p = .03$), and they were less inclined to punch the Bobo doll ($p = .07$).

While the comparison of subgroups, when some of the over-all tests do not reach statistical significance, is likely to capitalize on chance differences, nevertheless the consistency of the findings adds support to the interpretation in terms of influence by the model.

Nonaggressive Behavior

With the exception of expected sex differences, Lindquist (1956) Type III analyses of variance of the nonaggressive response scores yielded few significant differences.

Female subjects spent more time than boys [p. 580] playing with dolls ($p < .001$), with the tea set ($p < .001$), and coloring ($p < .05$). The boys, on the other hand, devoted significantly more time than the girls to exploratory play with the guns ($p < .01$). No sex differences were found in respect to the subjects [*sic*] use of the other stimulus objects, i.e., farm animals, cars, or tether ball.

Treatment conditions did produce significant differences on two measures of nonaggressive behavior that are worth mentioning. Subjects in the nonaggressive condition engaged in significantly more nonaggressive play with dolls than either subjects in the aggressive group ($t = 2.67$, $p < .02$), or in the control group ($t = 2.57$, $p < .02$).

Even more noteworthy is the finding that subjects who observed nonaggressive models spent more than twice as much time as subjects in the aggressive condition ($t = 3.07$, $p < .01$) in simply sitting quietly without handling any of the play material.

DISCUSSION

Much current research on social learning is focused on the shaping of new behavior through rewarding and punishing consequences. Unless responses are emitted, however, they cannot be influenced. The results of this study provide strong evidence that observation of cues produced by the behavior of others is one effective means of eliciting certain forms of responses for which the original probability is very low or zero. Indeed, social imitation may hasten or short-cut the acquisition of new behaviors without the necessity of reinforcing successive approximations as suggested by Skinner (1953).

Thus subjects given an opportunity to observe aggressive models later reproduced a good deal of physical and verbal aggression (as well as nonaggressive responses) substantially identical with that of the model. In contrast, subjects who were exposed to nonaggressive models and those who had no previous exposure to any models only rarely performed such responses.

To the extent that observation of adult models displaying aggression communicates permissiveness for aggressive behavior, such exposure may serve to weaken inhibitory responses and thereby to increase the probability of aggressive reactions to subsequent frustrations. The fact, however, that subjects expressed their aggression in ways that clearly resembled the novel patterns exhibited by models provides striking evidence for the occurrence of learning by imitation.

In the procedure employed by Miller and Dollard (1941) for establishing imitative behavior, adult or peer models performed discrimination responses following which they were consistently rewarded, and the subjects were similarly reinforced whenever they matched the leaders' choice responses. While these experiments have been widely accepted as demonstrations of learning by means of imitation, in fact, they simply involve a special case of discrimination learning in which the behavior of others serves as discriminative stimuli for responses that are already part of the subject's repertoire. Auditory or visual environmental cues could easily have been substituted for the social stimuli to facilitate the discrimination learning. In contrast, the process of imitation studied in the present experiment differed in several important respects from the one investigated by Miller and Dollard in that subjects learned to combine fractional responses into relatively complex novel patterns solely by observing the performance of social models without any opportunity to perform the models' behavior in the exposure setting, and without any reinforcers delivered either to the models or to the observers.

An adequate theory of the mechanisms underlying imitative learning is lacking. The explanations that have been offered (Logan, Olmsted, Rosner, Schwartz, & Stevens, 1955; Maccoby, 1959) assume that the imitator performs the model's responses covertly. If it can be assumed additionally that rewards and punishments are self-administered in conjunction with the covert responses, the process of imitative learning could be accounted for in terms of the same principles that govern instrumental trial-and-error learning. In the early stages of the developmental process, however, the range of component responses in the organism's repertoire is probably increased through a process of classical conditioning (Bandura & Huston, 1961; Mowrer, 1950).

The data provide some evidence that the male model influenced the subjects' behavior [p. 581] outside the exposure setting to a greater extent than was true for the female model. In the analyses of the Sex x Model interactions, for example, only the comparisons involving the male model yielded significant differences. Similarly, subjects exposed to the nonaggressive male model performed less aggressive behavior than the controls, whereas comparisons involving the female model were consistently nonsignificant.

In a study of learning by imitation, Rosenblith (1959) has likewise found male experimenters more effective than females in influencing childrens' [*sic*] behavior. Rosenblith advanced the tentative explanation that the school setting may involve some social deprivation in respect to adult males which, in turn, enhances the male's reward value.

The trends in the data yielded by the present study suggest an alternative explanation. In the case of a highly masculine-typed behavior such as physical aggression, there is a tendency for both male and female subjects to imitate the male model to a greater degree than the female model. On the other hand, in the case of verbal aggression, which is less clearly sex linked, the greatest amount of imitation occurs in relation to the same-sex model. These trends together with the finding that boys in relation to girls are in general more imitative of physical aggression but do not differ in imitation of verbal aggression, suggest that subjects may be differentially affected by the sex of the model but that predictions must take into account the degree to which the behavior in question is sex-typed.

The preceding discussion has assumed that maleness-femaleness rather than some other personal characteristics of the particular models involved, is the significant variable — an assumption that cannot be tested directly with the data at hand. It was clearly evident, however, particularly from boys' spontaneous remarks about the display of aggression by the female model, that some subjects at least were responding in terms of sex discrimination and their prior learning about what is sex appropriate behavior (e.g., "Who is that lady? That's not the way for a lady to behave. Ladies are supposed to act like ladies. . ." "You should have seen what that girl did in there. She was just acting like a man. I never saw a girl act like that before. She was punching and fighting but no swearing."). Aggression by the male model, on the other hand, was more likely to be seen as appropriate and approved by both the boys ("Al's a good socker, he beat up Bobo. I want to sock like Al.") and the girls ("That man is a strong fighter, he punched and punched and he could hit Bobo right down to the floor and if Bobo got up he said, 'Punch your nose.' He's a good fighter like Daddy.").

The finding that subjects exposed to the quiet models were more inihibited and unresponsive than subjects in the aggressive condition, together with the obtained difference on the aggression measures, suggests that exposure to inhibited models not only decreases the probability of occurrence of aggressive behavior but also generally restricts the range of behavior emitted by the subjects.

"Identification with aggressor" (Freud, 1946) or "defensive identification" (Mowrer, 1950), whereby a person presumably transforms himself from object to agent of aggression by adopting the attributes of an aggressive threatening model so as to allay anxiety, is widely accepted as an explanation of the imitative learning of aggression.

The development of aggressive modes of response by children of aggressively punitive adults, however, may simply reflect object displacement without involving any such mechanism of defensive identification. In studies of child training antecedents of aggressively antisocial adolescents (Bandura & Walters, 1959) and of young hyperaggressive boys (Bandura, 1960), the parents were found to be nonpermissive and punitive of aggression directed toward themselves. On the other hand, they actively encouraged and reinforced their son's aggression toward persons outside the home. This pattern of differential reinforcement of aggressive behavior served to inhibit the boys' aggression toward the original instigators and fostered the displacement of aggression toward objects and situations eliciting much weaker inhibitory responses.

Moreover, the findings from an earlier study (Baudura & Huston, 1961), in which children imitated to an equal degree aggression exhibited by a nurturant and a nonnurturant model, together with the results [p. 582] of the present experiment in which subjects readily imitated aggressive models who were more or less neutral figures suggest that mere observation of aggression, regardless of the quality of the model-subject relationship, is a sufficient condition for producing imitative aggression in children. A comparative study of the subjects' imitation of aggressive models who are feared, who are liked and esteemed, or who are essentially neutral figures would throw some light on whether or not a more parsimonious theory than the one involved in "identification with the aggressor" can explain the modeling process.

SUMMARY

Twenty-four preschool children were assigned to each of three conditions. One experimental group observed aggressive adult models; a second observed inhibited non-aggressive models; while subjects in a control group had no prior exposure to the models. Half the subjects in the experimental conditions observed same-sex models and half viewed models of the opposite sex. Subjects were then tested for the amount of imitative as well as nonimitative aggression performed in a new situation in the absence of the models.

Comparison of the subjects' behavior in the generalization situation revealed that subjects exposed to aggressive models reproduced a good deal of aggression resembling that of the models, and that their mean scores differed markedly from those of subjects in the nonaggressive and control groups. Subjects in the aggressive condition also exhibited significantly more partially imitative and nonimitative aggressive behavior and were generally less inhibited in their behavior than subjects in the nonaggressive condition.

Imitation was found to be differentially influenced by the sex of the model with boys showing more aggression than girls following exposure to the male model, the difference being particularly marked on highly masculine-typed behavior.

Subjects who observed the nonaggressive models, especially the subdued male model, were generally less aggressive than their controls.

The implications of the findings based on this experiment and related studies for the psychoanalytic theory of identification with the aggressor were discussed.

REFERENCES

Bandura, A. Relationship of family patterns to behavior disorders. Progress Report, 1960, Stanford University, Project No. M-1734, United States Public Health Service.

Bandura, A., & Huston, Aletha C. Identification as a process of incidental learning. *J. abnorm. soc. Psychol.,* 1961, **63**, 311-318.

Bandura, A., & Walters, R. H. *Adolescent aggrersion.* New York: Ronald, 1959.

Blake, R. R. The other person in the situation. In R. Tagiuri & L. Petrullo (Eds.), *Person perception and interpersonal behavior.* Stanford, Calif: Stanford Univer. Press, 1958. Pp. 229-242.

Fauls, Lydia B., & Smith, W. D. Sex-role learning of five-year olds. *J. genet. Psychol.,* 1956, **89**, 105-117.

Freud, Anna. *The ego and the mechanisms of defense.* New York: International Univer. Press, 1946.

Grosser, D., Polansky, N., & Lippit, R. A laboratory study of behavior contagion. *Hum. Relat.* 1951, **4**, 115-142.

Lindquist, E. F. *Design and analysis of experiments.* Boston: Houghton Mifflin, 1956.

Logan, F., Opmsted, O. L., Rosner, B. S., Shwartz, R. D., & Stevens, C. M. *Behavior theory and social science.* New Haven: Yale Univer. Press, 1955.

Maccoby, Elanor E. Role-taking in childhood and its consequences for social learning. *Child Develpm.,* 1959, **30**, 239-252.

Miller, N. F., & Dollard, J. *Social learning and imitation.* New Haven: Yale Univer. Press, 1941.

Mowrer, O. H. (Ed.) Identification: A link between learning theory and psychotherapy. In, *Learning theory and personality dynamics.* New York: Ronald, 1950. Pp.69-94.

Rosenbaum, M. E., & Dercharms, R. Direct and vicarious reduction of hostility. *J. abnorm. soc. Psychol.,* 1960, **60**, 105-111.

Rosenblith, Judy F. Learning by imitation in kindergarten children. *Child Develpm.,* 1959, **30**, 69-80.

Schacter, S., & Hall, R. Group-derived restraints and audience persuasion. *Hum. Relat.*, 1952, 5, 397-406.

Skinner, B. F. *Science and human behavior.* New York: Macmillan, 1953. (Received December 2, 1960)

FOOTNOTES

[1.] This investigation was supported by Research MA398 from the National Institute of Health, United States Public Health Service.

[2.] The authors wish to express their appreciation to Edith Dowley, Director, and Patricia Rowe, Head Teacher, Stanford University Nursery School for their assistance throughout this study.

4 Sources of Human Psychological Differences: The Minnesota Study of Twins Reared Apart

Thomas J. Bouchard, Jr., David T. Lykken, Matthew McGue, Nancy L. Segal, Auke Tellegen*

Since 1979, a continuing study of monozygotic and dizygotic twins, separated in infancy and reared apart, has subjected more than 100 sets of reared-apart twins or triplets to a week of intensive psychological and physiological assessment. Like the prior, smaller studies of monozygotic twins reared apart, about 70% of the variance in IQ was found to be associated with genetic variation. On multiple measures of personality and temperament, occupational and leisure-time interests, and social attitudes, monozygotic twins reared apart are about as similar as are monozygotic twins reared together. These findings extend and support those from numerous other twin, family, and adoption studies. It is a plausible hypothesis that genetic differences affect psychological differences largely indirectly, by influencing the effective environment of the developing child. This evidence for the strong heritability of most psychological traits, sensibly construed, does not detract from the value or importance of parenting, education, and other propaedeutic interventions.

Monozygotic and dizygotic twins who were separated early in life and reared apart (MZA and DZA twin pairs) are a fascinating experiment of nature. They also provide the simplest and most powerful method for disentangling the influence of environmental and genetic factors on human characteristics. The rarity of twins reared apart explains why only three previous studies of modest scope are available in the literature (1-4).

More than 100 sets of reared-apart twins or triplets from across the United States and the United Kingdom have participated in the Minnesota Study of Twins Reared Apart since it began in 1979. Participants have also come from Australia, Canada, China, New Zealand, Sweden, and West Germany. The study of these reared-apart twins has led to two general and seemingly remarkable conclusions concerning the sources of the psychological differences—behavioral variation—between people: (i) genetic factors exert a pronounced and pervasive influence on behavioral variability, and (ii) the effect of being reared in the same home is negligible for many psychological traits. These conclusions will not come as revelations to the many behavioral geneticists who have observed similar results and drawn similar conclusions (5).This study and the broader behavioral genetic literature, nevertheless, challenge prevailing psychological theories on the origins of individual differences in ability, personality, interests, and social attitudes (6). Here we summarize our procedures and review our results and interpretations of them.

Participants complete approximately 50 hours of medical and psychological assessment. Two or more test instruments are used in each major domain of psychological assessment to ensure adequate coverage (for example, four personality trait inventories, three occupational interest inventories, and two mental ability batteries). A systematic assessment of aspects of the twins' rearing environments that might have had causal roles in their psychological development is also carried out. Separate examiners administer the IQ test, life history interview, psychiatric interview, and sexual life history interview. A comprehensive mental ability battery is administered as a group test. The twins also complete questionnaires independently, under the constant supervision of a staff member.

Reared-apart twins have been ascertained in several ways, such as: (i) friends, relatives, or the reunited twins themselves, having learned of the project, contact the Minnesota Center for Twin and Adoption Research (MICTAR); (ii) members of the adoption movement, social workers, and other professionals who encounter reared-apart twins serve as intermediaries; (iii) twins who are, or become aware of, a separated co-twin solicit assistance from the MICTAR staff in locating this individual. Selection on the basis of similarity is minimized by vigorously recruiting all reared-apart twins, regardless of known or presumed zygosity and similarity. We have been unable to recruit to the study six pairs of twins reared apart whom we believe to be monozygotic.

Zygosity diagnosis is based on extensive serological comparisons, fingerprint ridge count, and anthropometric measurements. The probability of misclassification is less than 0.001 (7). Where appropriate, our data are corrected for age and sex effects (8). Due to space limitations and the smaller size of the DZA sample (30 sets), in this article we focus on the MZA data (56 sets). The results reported here are, for the most part, based on previously reported findings, so that the sample sizes do not include the most recently assessed pairs and vary depending on when in the course of this ongoing study the analyses were conducted.

As shown in Table 1, the sample consists of adult twins, separated very early in life, reared apart during their formative years, and reunited as adults. Circumstances of adoption were sometimes informal, and the adoptive parents, in comparison to parents who volunteer to participate in most adoption studies, have a lower level of education (mean equals 2 years of high school), and are quite heterogeneous in educational attainment and socioeconomic status (SES). Because our sample includes no subjects with IQs in the retardate range (≤ 70), the mean IQ is higher and the standard deviation lower than for the general population.

COMPONENTS OF PHENOTYPIC VARIANCE

If genetic and environmental factors are uncorrelated and combine additively (points we return to later), the total observed variance, V_t, of a trait within a population can be expressed as

$$V_t = V_g + V_e + V_m \qquad (1)$$

where V_g is variance due to genetic differences among people, V_e is variance due to environmental or experiential factors, and V_m is variance due to measurement error and unsystematic temporal fluctuations. For measures of psychological traits, V_m ranges from approximately 10% (of V_t) for the most reliably measured and stable of traits (for example, IQ) to as high as 50 to 60% for traits that are less reliable or that show considerable secular instability (for example,

TABLE 1. Means, standard deviations (SD), and ranges for age, measures of contact, IQ, and parental educational level for MZA twins. Two MZA male triplet sets were each entered as one set. Data are based on the first 56 sets of MZAs recruited, although the sample size varies slightly from measure to measure, data are not always available or relevant (for example, rearing mother died very early in twins' life or twins could not be tested with an English language WAIS).

Statistic	Age (years)	Time together prior to separation (months)	Time apart to first reunion (years)	Total contact time (weeks)	IQ (WAIS)	Rearing father's education level (years)	Rearing mother's education level (years)
Mean SD Range	41.0 12.0 19.0-68.0	5.1 8.5 0—48.7	30.0 14.3 0.5—64.7	112.5 230.7 1—1233	108.1 10.8 79—133	10.7 4.5 0—20	10.3 3.7 0—19

some social attitudes). The environmental component, V_e, can be divided into variance due to experiences that are shared, V_{es}, and experiences that are unshared, V_{eu}. Shared events may be experienced differently by two siblings (for example, a roller coaster ride or a family vacation), in which case they contribute to the V_{eu} component. If the total variance, V_t, is set at unity, the correlation between MZ twins, R_{mz}, equals $V_g + V_{es}$. The heritability of a trait equals V_g; the heritability of the stable component of a trait (for example, the mean value around which one's aggressiveness varies) equals $V_g/(V_t - Vm)$. V_t and Vm can be estimated from studies of singletons, but V_g is more elusive: for monozygotic twins reared together (MZT), some of the within-pair correlation might be due to effects of shared experience, V_{es}. The power of the MZA design is that for twins reared apart from early infancy and randomly placed for adoption, V_{es} is negligible, so that V_g can be directly estimated from the MZA correlation.

SIMILARITY IN THE IQ OF MZA TWINS

The study of IQ is paradigmatic of human behavior genetic research. There are more than 100 relevant twin, adoptee, and family studies of IQ, and IQ has been at the center of the nature-nurture debate (9). The analysis of IQ is also paradigmatic of the approach taken by this study. It illustrates our use of replicated measures, evaluation of rearing environmental effects, and analysis of environmental similarity. We obtain three independent measures of IQ: (i) the Wechsler Adult Intelligence Scale (WAIS); (ii) a Raven, Mill-Hill composite; and (iii) the first principal component (PC) of two multiple abilities batteries. The WAIS consists of a set of six verbal and five performance subtests that are individually administered, requiring about 1.5 hours, and that yield an age-corrected estimate of IQ (10). To avoid examiner bias, we administer the WAIS simultaneously to the twins in different rooms by professional psychometrists. The Raven Progressive Matrices (Standard Set) is a widely used nonverbal measure of problem-solving ability often paired with the Mill-Hill Vocabulary Test, a multiple-choice word knowledge test (11). In this study, the Raven and Mill-Hill are both administered and scored by computer. The two age- and sex-corrected scores are transformed to have a mean equal to 50 and a standard deviation of 10. The sum of these transformed scores (which intercorrelate about 0.57) provides a separate estimate of IQ. The first major ability battery included in our assessment is an expanded version of the battery used in the Hawaii Family Study of Cognition (12). The second major ability battery is the Comprehensive Ability Battery (13). Detailed results from analysis of both tests are reported elsewhere (14).

In each of the three prior studies of MZA twins, two independent estimates of intelligence were obtained. The sample sizes and intraclass correlations for all four studies are compared in Table 2. The table illustrates the remarkable consistency of the MZA correlations on IQ across measurement instrument, country of origin, and time period. These correlations vary within a narrow range (0.64 to 0.74) and suggest, under the assumption of no environmental similarity, that genetic factors account for approximately 70% of the variance in IQ.

This estimate of the broad heritability of IQ is higher than the recent estimates (0.47 to 0.58) based on a

TABLE 2. Sample sizes and intraclass correlations (± standard error) for all IQ measures and weighted averages for four studies of MZA twins.

Study and test used (primary/secondary/tertiary)	*n* for each test	Primary test	Secondary test	Tertiary test	Mean of multiple test *(43)*
Newman *et al. (1)* (Stanford-Binet/Otis)	19/19	0.68 ± 0.12	0.74 ± 0.10		0.71
Juel-Nielsen *(1)* (Wechsler-Bellevue/Raven)	12/12	0.64 ± 0.17	0.73 ± 0.13		0.69
Shields *(1)* (Mill-Hill/Dominoes)	38/37	0.74 ± 0.07	0.76 ± 0.07		0.75
Bouchard *et al. (42)* (WAIS/Raven, Mill-Hill/first principal component)	48/42/43	0.69 ± 0.07	0.78 ± 0.07	0.78 ± 0.07	0.75

review of the literature that includes all kinship pairings (9, 15). Virtually the entire literature on IQ similarity in twins and siblings is limited, however, to studies of children and adolescents. It has been demonstrated (16) that heritability of cognitive ability increases with age. A heritability estimate of approximately 70% from these four studies of mainly middle-aged adults is not inconsistent with the previous literature.

DO ENVIRONMENTAL SIMILARITIES IN REARING ENVIRONMENTS EXPLAIN MZA IQ SIMILARITY?

Such marked behavioral similarities between reared-apart MZA twins raise the question of correlated placement: were the twins' adoptive homes selected to be similar in trait-relevant feature which, in turn, induced psychological similarity? If so, given that the total variance equals 1.0, then V_{es} will equal at least $R_{ff} \times r^2_{ft}$, when R_{ff} is the within-pair correlation for a given feature, *f*, of the adoptive homes (the placement coefficient), and r_{ft} is the product moment correlation between the feature and the trait in question, *t*.

A checklist of available household facilities (for example, power tools, sailboat, telescope, unabridged dictionary, and original artwork) provides an index of the cultural and intellectual resources in the adoptive home (17). Each twin completes the Moos Family Environment Scale (FES), a widely used instrument with scales describing the individual's retrospective impression of treatment and rearing provided by the adoptive parents during childhood and adolescence (18). The age- and sex-corrected placement coefficients for these and other measures are shown in Table 3, together with the correlations between twins' IQ and the environmental measure (r_{ft}) and the total estimated contribution to MZA twin similarity. The maximum contribution to MZA trait correlations that could be explained by measured similarity of the adoptive rearing environments on a single variable is about 0.03 (19). The absence of any significant effect due to SES or other environmental measures on the IQ scores of these adult adopted twins is consistent with the findings of other investigators (20). Rearing SES effects on IQ in adoption studies have been found for young children but not in adult samples (21), suggesting that although parents may be able to affect their children's rate of cognitive skill acquisition, they may have relatively little influence on the ultimate level attained.

HAS PRE- AND POST-REUNION CONTACT CONTRIBUTED TO MZA TWIN SIMILARITY IN IQ?

MZA twins share prenatal and perinatal environments, but except for effects of actual trauma, such as fetal alcohol syndrome, there is little evidence that early shared environment significantly contributes to the variance of psychological traits. Twins are especially vulnerable to prenatal and perinatal trauma, but these effects are most likely to decrease, rather than increase, within-pair similarity (22). There is evidence that twins who maintain closer contact with each other later in life tend to be more similar in some respects than twins who engage in infrequent contact (23). It appears, however, that it is the similarity that leads to increased contact, rather than the other way around (24). MZA twins in this study vary widely in the amount of contact they have had prior to assessment. All twin pairs spent their formative years apart. Some had their first adult reunion at the time of assessment, whereas others met as much as 20 years earlier and had experienced varying degrees of contact. A small number of the pairs actually met at intervals during childhood. As shown in Table 1, total contact time for the MZA twins ranges from 1 to 1233 weeks. In the one case of 1233 weeks of contact, the twins met as teenagers and lived near each other until assessment when they were adults. Since they met on a regular basis, most of this time was coded as contact time. Degree of social contact between two members of a reared-apart twin pair accounts for virtually none of their similarity. The correlations with the within-pair absolute WAIS IQ difference are 0.06 ± 0.15 for time together prior to separation, 0.08 ± 0.15 for time apart to first reunion, -0.14 ± 0.15 for total contact time, and 0.17 ± 0.15 for percentage of lifetime spent apart (25).

The absolute within-pair difference in WAIS IQ of co-twins as a function of degree of contact are plotted in Fig. 1. Also shown are the expected absolute IQ differences between randomly paired individuals and between two testings of the same individual (26). Although the MZA average difference approximates the absolute difference expected between two testings of a single individual, we do observe a wide range of

TABLE 3. Placement coefficients for environmental variables, correlations between IQ and the environmental variables, and estimates of the contribution of placement to twin similarity in WAIS IQ.

Placement variable	MZA similarity (R_{ff})	Correlation between IQ and placement variable (r_{ft})	Contribution of placement to the MZA correlation ($R_{ff} \times r^2_{ft}$)
SES indicators			
Father's education	0.134	0.100	0.001
Mother's education	0.412	-0.001	0.000
Father's SES	0.267	0.174	0.008
Physical facilities			
Material possessions	0.402	0.279**	0.032
Scientific/technical	0.151	-0.090	0.001
Cultural	-0.085	-0.279**	-0.007
Mechanical	0.303	0.077	0.002
Relevant FES scales			
Achievement	0.11	-0.103	0.001
Intellectual orientation	0.27	0.106	0.003

**r_{ft} significantly different from zero at $P < 0.01$.

differences. It is not that we have found no evidence of environmental influence; in individual cases environmental factors have been highly significant (for example, the 29 IQ point difference in Fig. 1). Rather, we find little support for the types of environmental influences on which psychologists have traditionally focused (27).

SIMILARITY OF MZA TWINS ON A VARIETY OF DIMENSIONS

Table 4 (28) gives the MZA correlations, most previously published, on variables ranging from anthropometry and psychophysiology, to aptitudes, personality and temperament, leisure-time and vocational interests, to social attitudes. Correlations for MZT twins and retest stability coefficients are also provided for comparison. Stable, reliably measured variables like fingerprint ridge count and stature show the highest correlations. Brain wave spectra are highly reproducible (29) and are strongly correlated in both MZA and MZT twins. Most other psychophysiological variables (for example, blood pressure and electrodermal response) vary considerably across time so that the retest correlations between repeated measurements on the same persons range from 0.5 to 0.8 (30). These retest correlations set the upper limit of similarity that might be found between MZ co-twins. The retest stability of aptitude measures, such as IQ, is rather better, ranging from 0.8 to 0.9 (10), whereas stability of personality and interest measures ranges from 0.6 to 0.7.

With these upper limits in mind, the findings in Table 4 demonstrate remarkable similarity between MZA twins. In terms of standardized tests and measures, the MZA twin similarities are often nearly equal to those for MZT twins (last column) and constitute a substantial portion of the reliable variance (column 5) of each trait.

THE MINIMAL EFFECT OF BEING REARED TOGETHER

Some of the MZA twins have had considerable contact as adults, but all of them were reared apart throughout the formative periods of childhood and adolescence. If being reared together enhances similarity in twins, within-pair correlations for MZA twins are expected to be smaller than those for MZT twins. For example, the mean MZT correlation for IQ, based on 34 studies of primarily children or adolescents, is 0.86 (9) as compared to 0.72 for all, primarily adult, MZA twins. If the mean MZT correlation were maintained into adulthood, its difference from the MZA correlation would suggest that common rearing increases the similarity of IQ in twins (and siblings). However, the MZT correlation apparently declines with age (for example, as a result of the accumulation of nonshared environmental effects) (16), in which event the small MZT-MZA correlation difference would suggest little influence of common rearing on adult IQ. In any case, a significant contribution of shared environment is found for the personality trait of social closeness (31), and possibly religious interests and values (32).

TABLE 4. Interclass correlations (R), sample sizes, and MZA/MZT ratio for monozygotic twins reared apart and together for nine classes of variables. NA, not available.

Variables (reference)	Minnesota MZAs R	Pairs (no.)	MZTs R	Pairs (no.)	Reliability*	R_{MZA}/R_{MZT}
Anthropometric variables (28)						
Fingerprint ridge count	0.97	54	0.96	274	0.99	1.01
Height	0.86	56	0.93	274	0.98	0.925
Weight	0.73	56	0.83	274	NA	0.880
Electroencephalographic (brainwave) variables (28)						
Amount of 8- to 12-Hz (alpha) activity	0.80	35	0.81	42	NA	0.987
Midfrequency of alpha activity	0.80	35	0.82	42	NA	0.975
Psychophysiologic variables (29)						
Systolic blood pressure	0.64	56	0.70	34	0.70	0.914
Heart rate	0.49	49	0.54	160	0.58-0.80	0.907
Electrodermal response (EDR) amplitude †						
Males	0.82	20	0.70	17	NA	0.17
Females	0.30	23	0.54	19	NA	0.555
Trials to habituation EDR	0.43	43	0.42	36	NA	1.02
Information processing ability factors (17)						
Speed of response	0.56	40	0.73	50	NA	0.767
Acquisition speed	0.20	40	NA	NA	NA	NA
Speed of spatial processing	0.36	40	NA	NA	NA	NA
Mental ability—general factor (44)						
WAIS IQ—full scale	0.69	48	0.88	40	0.90	0.784
WAIS IQ—verbal	0.64	48	0.88	40	0.84	0.727
WAIS IQ—performance	0.71	48	0.79	40	0.86	0.899
Raven, Mill-Hill composite	0.78	42	0.76	37	NA	1.03
First principal component of special mental abilities	0.78	43	NA	NA	NA	NA
Special mental abilities (14)						
Mean of 15 Hawaii-battery scales	0.45	45	NA	NA	0.80	NA
Mean of 13 Comprehensive Ability Battery scales	0.48	41	NA	NA	0.78	NA
Personality variables (31)						
Mean of 11 Multidimensional Personality Questionnaire (MPQ) scales	0.50	44	0.49	217	0.88	1.02
Mean of 18 California Psychological Inventory (CPI) scales	0.48	38	0.49	99	0.65	0.979
Psychological interests (45)						
Mean of 23 Strong Campbell Interest Inventory scales (SCII)	0.39	52	0.48	116‡	0.82	0.813
Mean of 34 Jackson Vocational Interest Survey scales (JVIS)	0.43	45	NA	NA	0.84	NA
Mean of 17 Minnesota Occupational Interest scales	0.40	40	0.49	376	0.75	0.816
Social attitudes (32)						
Mean of 2 religiosity scales	0.49	31	0.51	458	0.80	0.961
Mean of 14 nonreligious social attitude items	0.34	42	0.28	421	0.48	1.21
MPQ traditionalism scale	0.53	44	0.50	217	0.49	1.06

*The correlation between two testings of the same individual. These estimates of the stable component of the observed trait variance also estimate the upper limit for R_{MZ}. †The marked difference in EDR amplitude between males and females is discussed in Lykken *et al.* (29). ‡This value is for 116 studies, not pairs.

As illustrated in Table 4, however, adult MZ twins are about equally similar on most physiological and psychological traits, regardless of rearing status. This finding and the failure to find significant r_{ft} effects for cognitive abilities (17) or personality (31), together with findings from numerous studies of MZT and DZT twins, sibs, and foster sibs, implies that common rearing enhances familial resemblance during adulthood only slightly and on relatively few behavioral dimensions. This conclusion is given detailed discussion by Plomin and Daniels (5).

WHY ARE MZA TWINS SO SIMILAR?

It is well known to naturalists and to animal breeders that there are wide and heritable differences in behavior within other species, but there is a curious reluctance among some scientists (33) to acknowledge the contribution of genetic variation to psychological differences within the human species. Our findings support and extend those from many family, twin, and adoption studies (15), a broad consilience of findings leading to the following generalization: For almost every behavioral trait so far investigated, from reaction time to religiosity, an important fraction of the variation among people turns out to be associated with genetic variation. This fact need no longer be subject to debate (34); rather, it is time instead to consider its implications. We suggest the following:

1) *General intelligence or IQ is strongly affected by genetic factors.* The IQs of the adult MZA twins assessed with various instruments in four independent studies correlate about 0.70, indicating that about 70% of the observed variation in IQ in this population can be attributed to genetic variation. Since only a few of these MZA twins were reared in real poverty or by illiterate parents and none were retarded, this heritability estimate should not be extrapolated to the extremes of environmental disadvantage still encountered in society. Moreover, these findings do not imply that traits like IQ cannot be enhanced. Flynn (35), in a survey covering 14 countries, has shown that the average IQ test score has significantly increased in recent years. This increase may be limited to that part of the population with low IQs (36). The present findings, therefore, do not define or limit what might be conceivably achieved in an optimal environment. They do indicate that, in the current environments of the broad middle-class, in industrialized societies, two-thirds of the observed variance of IQ can be traced to genetic variation.

2) *The institutions and practices of modern Western society do not greatly constrain the development of individual differences in psychological traits.* The heritability of a psychological trait reveals as much about the culture as it does about human nature. Heritability must increase as V_e, the variance affected by the environment, decreases. Where the culture's influence is relatively homogeneous and efficacious, V_e will decrease and heritability will increase; most American boys, for example, have similar opportunities to play baseball, so that one expects heritability of baseball skill in American young men to be high. Where culture is efficacious, but heterogeneous, V_e (and total phenotypic variance) will increase; thus, one would expect the heritability of specific linguistic or religious behaviors in the United States or in the Soviet Union to be low. Individuals in Western societies are heterogeneous with respect to personality traits, interests, and attitudes, yet the heritabilities of these traits are relatively high. We infer that the diverse cultural agents of our society, in particular most parents, are less effective in imprinting their distinctive stamp on the children developing within their spheres of influence—or are less inclined to do so—than has been supposed.

Psychologists have been surprised by the evidence that being reared by the same parents in the same physical environment does not, on average, make siblings more alike as adults than they would have been if reared separately in adoptive homes. It is obvious that parents can produce shared effects if they grossly deprive or mistreat all their children. It seems reason-

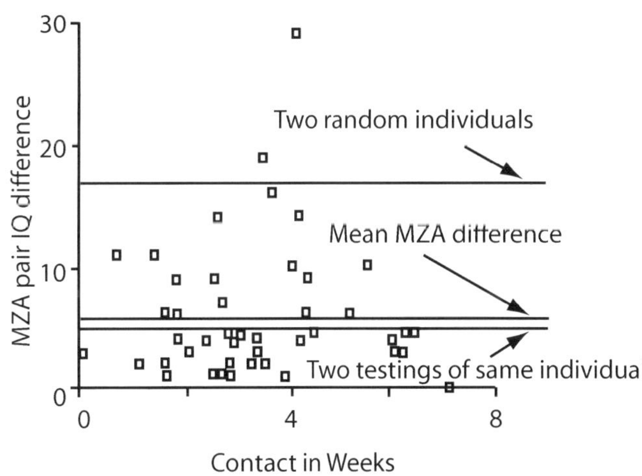

FIG. 1. The absolute value of the MZA within-pair IQ difference as a function of the natural logarithm of pair contact in weeks. The horizontal lines are the expected absolute IQ difference between two randomly selected individuals, the observed average MZA absolute difference, and the expected IQ difference between two testings of the same individual.

able that charismatic, dedicated parents, determined to make all their children share certain personal qualities, interests, or values, may sometimes succeed. Our findings, and those of others (37), do not imply that parenting is without lasting effects. The remarkable similarity in MZA twins in social attitudes (for example, traditionalism and religiosity) does not show that parents cannot influence those traits, but simply that this does not tend to happen in most families.

3) *MZA twins are so similar in psychological traits because their identical genomes make it probable that their effective environments are similar.* Specific mechanisms by which genetic differences in human behavior are expressed in phenotypic differences are largely unknown. It is a plausible conjecture that a key mechanism by which the genes affect the mind is indirect, and that genetic differences have an important role in determining the effective psychological environment of the developing child (38).

Infants with different temperaments elicit different parenting responses. Toddlers who are active and adventurous undergo different experiences than their more sedentary or timid siblings. In addition, children and adolescents seek out environments that they find congenial. These are forms of gene-environment covariance, C_{ge}. Moreover, different individuals pay different attention to or respond differently to the same objective experience, or both. These are forms of gene-environment interaction, V_{ge}. From infancy onwards, genetic individuality helps to steer the developing organism through the multitude of possible experiences and choices. That is, Eq. 1 must be elaborated to include these indirect and modifiable ways in which the genome exerts its influence.

$$V_t = V_g + V_e + C_{ge} + V_{ge} + V_m \qquad (2)$$

The proximal cause of most psychological variance probably involves learning through experience, just as radical environmentalists have always believed. The effective experiences, however, to an important extent are self-selected, and that selection is guided by the steady pressure of the genome (a more distal cause). We agree with Martin *et al.* (39) who see "humans as exploring organisms whose innate abilities and predispositions help them select what is relevant and adaptive from the range of opportunities and stimuli presented in the environment. The effects of mobility and learning, therefore, augment rather than eradicate the effects of the genotype on behavior" (p. 4368).

If this view is correct, the developmental experiences of MZ twins are more similar than those of DZ twins, again as environmentalist critics of twin research have contended. However, even MZA twins tend to elicit, select, seek out, or create very similar effective environments and, to that extent, the impact of these experiences is counted as a genetic influence. Finally, if the genome impresses itself on the psyche largely by influencing the character, selection, and impact of experiences during development—if the correct formula is nature via nurture—then intervention is not precluded even for highly heritable traits, but should be the more effective when tailored to each specific child's talents and inclinations.

RELEVANCE TO EVOLUTIONARY PSYCHOLOGY AND SOCIOBIOLOGY

This research focuses on individual differences, but like other animals we share certain species-specific tendencies by virtue of our being human. Whereas behavioral geneticists study variations within a species, evolutionary psychologists or sociobiologists attempt to delineate species-typical proclivities or instincts and to understand the relevant evolutionary developments that took place in the Pleistocene epoch and were adaptive in the lives of tribal hunter-gatherers. The genes sing a prehistoric song that today should sometimes be resisted but which it would be foolish to ignore.

At the interface of behavioral genetics and sociobiology is the question of the origin and function, if any, of the within-species variability we have been discussing. One view is that it represents evolutionary debris (40), unimportant to fitness and not expressed in prehistoric environments. Another view is that variability has an adaptive function and has been selected for. Whether sociobiologists can make evolutionary sense of the varieties of human genetic variation we have discussed here remains to be seen (41).

Whatever the ancient origins and functions of genetic variability, its repercussions in contemporary society are pervasive and important. A human species whose members did not vary genetically with respect to significant cognitive and motivational attributes, and who were uniformly average by current standards, would have created a very different society than the one we know. Modern society not only augments the influence of genotype on behavioral variability, as we have suggested, but permits this variability to reciprocally contribute to the rapid pace of cultural change. If generic variation was evolutionary debris at the end of the Pleistocene, it is now a salient and essential feature of the human condition.

REFERENCES AND NOTES

1. H. H. Newman, F. N. Freeman, K. J. Holzinger, *Twins: A Study of Heredity and Environment* (Univ. of Chicago Press, Chicago, 1937); N. Juel-Nielson, *Acta Psychiatr. Neural. Scand. Suppl.* 183, (1965); J. Shields, *Monozygotic Twins: Brought up Apart and Brought up Together* (Oxford Univ. Press, London, 1962). There are two other ongoing studies of twins reared apart, one in Sweden (2) and one in Finland (3). The questionable study by Burt (4) has been omitted.

2. N. Pedersen, G. E. McClearn, R. Plomin, L. Friberg, *Behav. Genet.* 15, 407 (1985); R. Plomin, P. Lichtenstein, N. L. Pedersen, G. E. McClearn, J. R. Nesselroade, *Psychol. Aging* 5, 25 (1990).

3. H. Langainvainio, J. Kaprio, M. Koskenvuo, J. Lonnqvist, *Acta Genet. Med. Gemellol.* 33, 259 (1984).

4. L. Hearnshaw, *Cyril Burt: Psychologist* (Hodder & Stoughten, London, 1979); but see R. B. Joynson, *The Burt Affair* (Routledge, London, 1990).

5. R. Plomin and D. Daniels, *Behav. Brain Sci.* 10, 1 (1987); L. J. Eaves, H. J. Eysenck, N. G. Martin, *Genes Culture and Personality: An Empirical Approach* (Academic Press, New York, 1989).

6. T. J. Bouchard, Jr., in *The Chemical and Biological Bases of Individuality,* S. Fox, Ed. (Plenum, New York, 1984), p. 147; N. L. Segal, W. M. Grove, T. J. Bouchard, Jr., in *Genetic Issues in Psychosocial Epidemiology,* M. Tsuang, K. Kendler, M. Lyons, Eds. (Rutgers Univ. Press, New Brunswick, NJ, in press).

7. D. T. Lykken, *Behav. Genet.* 8, 437 (1978).

8. M. McGue and T. J. Bouchard, Jr., *ibid.* 14, 325 (1984).

9. T. J. Bouchard, Jr., and M. McGue, *Science* 212, 1055 (1981).

10. J. D. Matarazzo, *Wechsler's Measurement and Appraisal of Adult Intelligence* (Williams and Wilkins, Baltimore, ed. 5, 1972).

11. J. Raven, *Manual for Raven's Progressive Matrices and Vocabulary Scales* (Lewis, London, 1986).

12. J. C. DeFries *et al., Behav. Genet.* 9, 23 (1979).

13. A. R. Hakstian and R. B. Cattell, *J. Educ. Psychol.* 70, 657 (1978).

14. T. J. Bouchard, Jr., N. L. Segal, D. T. Lykken, *Acta Genet. Med. Gemellol.* 39, 193 (1990).

15. J. C. Loehlin, *Am. Psychol.* 44, 1285 (1989); R. Plomin and J. C. Loehlin, *Behav. Genet.* 19, 331 (1989).

16. K. McCartney, M. J. Harris, F. Bernieri, *Psychol. Bull.* 107, 26 (1990).

17. M. McGue and T. J. Bouchard, Jr., in *Advances in the Psychology of Human Intelligence,* R. J. Sternberg, Ed. (Erlbaum, New York, 1989), vol. 5, p. 7. This checklist yields four relatively independent scales: scientific or technical, cultural, mechanical, and material possessions.

18. R. H. Moos and B. S. Moos, *Manual: Family Environment Scale* (Consulting Psychologists Press, Palo Alto, CA, 1986).

19. Formally, this is the maximum linear contribution; nonlinear effects are, of course, possible. For these data, however, investigation of higher-ordered relationships (quadratic and cubic) showed no associations that did not exist at the linear level and there was no discernible nonlinearity detected in visual inspection of the scatterplots.

20. T. J. Bouchard, Jr., *Intelligence* 7, 175 (1983).

21. C. Capron and M. Duyme [*Nature* 340, 552

(1989)] have shown an SES effect in an adoption study of young children; S. Scarr and R. Weinberg [*Amer. Social. Rev.* 43, 674 (1978)] did not find an SES effect in a study of young adult adoptees.

22. B. Price, *Am. J. Hum. Genet.* 2, 293 (1950).

23. R. J. Rose and J. Kaprio, *Behav. Genet.* 18, 309 (1988).

24. D. T. Lykken, T. J. Bouchard, Jr., M. McGue, A. Tellegen, *Behav. Genet.,* in press.

25. As in our earlier analysis, nonlinear relationships were tested for and found not to exist. Additionally, deletion of a single outlier (IQ difference of 29 points) did not appreciably change the correlation estimates.

26. Expected difference *(D)* can be expressed as a function of the correlation *(r)* and standard deviation as $D = 1.13\,\sigma\sqrt{1 - r}$ [R. Plomin and J. C. DeFries, *Intelligence* 4, 15 (1980)].

27. K. R. White, *Psychol. Bull.* 86, 461 (1982).

28. D. T. Lykken, T. J . Bouchard, Jr., M. McGue, A. Tellegen, *Acta Genet. Med. Gemellol.* 39, 35 (1990); and (6).

29. H. H. Stassen, D. T. Lykken, G. Bomben, *Eur. Arch. Psychiatry Neurol. Sci.* 237, 244 (1988).

30. Systolic blood pressure from Minnesota twin studies. Heart rate from B. Hanson *et al., Am. J. Cardiol.* 63, 606 (1989). Electrodermal and habituation data from D. T. Lykken, W. G. Iacono, K. Haroian, M. McGue, T. J. Bouchard, Jr., *Psychophysiology* 25, 4 (1988). Reliability data from K. Matthews, C. Rakczky, C. Stoney, S. Manuck, *ibid.* 24, 464 (1987); M. Llabre *et al., ibid.* 25, 97 (1988).

31. MPQ data from A. Tellegen *et al., J. Pers. Soc. Psychol.* 54, 1031 (1988); CPI data from T. J. Bouchard, Jr., and M. McGue, *J. Pers.* 58, 263 (1990). Reliability data from test manuals.

32. MZA and MZT Religiosity data from N. G. Waller, B. A. Kojetin, T. J. Bouchard, Jr., D. T. Lvkken, A. Tellegen. *Psychol. Sci.* 1, 138 (1990). Reliability of religious leisure time interests and religious occupational interests and mean of 14 nonreligious social attitude items from Minnesota twin study data base (28). Reliability of other scales from test manuals. For a general discussion of the reliability of traits such as those measured in this study, see K. C. H. Parker, R. K. Hanson, J. Hunsley [*Psychol. Bull.* 103, 367 (1988)] and J. J. Conley [*Pers. Individ. Differ.* 5, 11 (1984)].

33. R. C. Lewontin, S. Rose, L. J. Kamin, *Not in Our Genes; Biology, Ideology, and Human Nature* (Pantheon, New York, 1984).

34. S. Scarr, *Behav. Genet.* 17, 219 (1987).

35. J. R. Flynn. *Psychol. Bull.* 101, 171 (1987).

36. R. Lynn, *Pers. Individ. Differ.* 11, 273 (1990); T. W. Teasedale and D. R. Owen, *Intelligence* 13, 255 (1989).

37. R. Wilson, *Child Dev.* 54, 298 (1983).

38. K. J. Hayes, *Psychol. Rep.* 10, 299 (1962); C. J. Lumsden and E. O. Wilson, *Genes, Mind and Culture* (Harvard Univ. Press, Cambridge, MA, 1981); S. Scarr and K. McCartney, *Child Dev.* 54, 424 (1983).

39. N. G. Martin *et al., Proc. Nat. Acad. Sci. U.S.A.* 83, 4364 (1986).

40. M. W. Feldman and R. C. Lewontin, *Science* 190, 1163 (1975); D. Symonds, *The Evolution of Human Sexuality* (Oxford Univ. Press, New York, 1979).

41. D. M. Buss, *J. Pers.* 58, 1 (1990).

42. T. J. Bouchard, Jr., D. T. Lykken, M. McGue, N. L. Segal, A. Tellegen, this article.

43. The MZA correlation of 0.771 reported by the late Sir Cyril Burt and questioned for its authenticity after his death (4) falls within the range of findings reviewed here.

44. WAIS data for MZTs from K. Tambs, J. M. Sundet, P. Magnus, *Intelligence* 8, 283 (1984). Reliabilities from (10). Raven, Mill-Hill, and composite data from Minnesota twin studies (6, 42).

45. MZA data on SCII and JVIS from D. Moloney, unpublished thesis (University of Minnesota, Minneapolis, 1990). Minnesota Occupational Interest Scale data from N. Waller, D. T. Lykken, A. Tellegen, in *Wise Counsel Essays* in *Honor of Lloyd Lofquist,* R. Dawis and D. Lubinski, Eds. (Univ. of Minnesota Press, Minneapolis, in press). SCII MZT data from Nichols [*Homo* 29, 158 (1978)]. Reliability data from test manuals.

46. We thank our colleagues E. D. Eckert, L. L. Heston, and I. I. Gottesman for their help on the medical and psychiatric portions of the study and H. Polesky, director, for the blood testing. This research has been supported by grants from The Pioneer Fund, The Seaver Institute, The University of Minnesota Graduate School, The Koch Charitable Foundation, The Spencer Foundation, The National Science Foundation (BNS-7926654), The National Institute of Mental Health (MH37860), The National Institute on Aging (AG06886), and the Harcourt Brace Jovanovich Publishing Company.

FOOTNOTE

[*] T. J. Bouchard, Jr, and M. McGue are in the Department of Psychology and the Institute of Human Genetics, University of Minnesota, Minneapolis, MN, 55455. D. T. Lykken, N. L. Segal, and A. Tellegen are in the Department of Psychology, University of Minnesota, Minneapolis, MN, 55455.

*To whom reprint requests should be addressed.

5 Selective Serotonin-Reuptake Inhibitors and Suicidal Ideation and Behavior in Children

Joshua Caballero and Milap C. Nahata

Am J Health-Syst Pharm. 2005; 62:864-7

Depression is one of the most common mood disorders among children and adolescents, occurring in approximately 2% of children and 6.5% of adolescents in the United States.[1,2] Between 20% and 40% of these patients may have a relapse within two years. Each episode usually lasts about eight months, and symptoms may include irritability, apathy, hopelessness, decreased concentration, and, in some cases, suicidal thoughts and behaviors. Suicide is one of the leading causes of death in the pediatric population, especially among adolescents.[3] Of children and adolescents who committed suicide, 50–75% suffered from a mood disorder, most frequently depression.[4] Therefore, health care providers must be able to recognize the signs and symptoms of depression in the pediatric population and manage their therapy accordingly.

Psychotherapy and antidepressants have been the primary methods of treating depression in children but are often underused. Less than 50% of adolescent females and under 20% of adolescent males received psychotherapy or antidepressants within the year before their suicide.[5] Thus far, cognitive behavioral therapy (CBT) and interpersonal therapy have led to significant improvements in adolescents with depression and are considered the preferred psychotherapies in this patient population.[6-9] These therapies may help children and adolescents with mild or moderate depression and serve as adjunct therapy for patients with severe depression.[1,9] Antidepressants may be most beneficial to those who do not have access to a psychotherapist, lack the time or interest to attend the sessions, or do not respond adequately to psychotherapy alone.

Antidepressants, including tricyclics, selective serotonin-reuptake inhibitors (SSRIs), and atypical agents (e.g., venlafaxine, mirtazapine), have been used to treat depression in children and adolescents. Tricyclics, however, have not been shown to be superior to placebo,[10,11] perhaps because children have an underdeveloped noradrenergic system.[12] Tricyclics have more intolerable adverse effects, such as anticholinergic complications, confusion, cardiotoxicity, and drowsiness, than do other antidepressants and are more likely to cause death in the event of an overdose. Safety and efficacy data are lacking for newer agents, such as venlafaxine, which was shown to be ineffective in treating pediatric patients with depression.[13,14] Also, it may increase the risk of suicide-related events. SSRIs have shown greater efficacy in treating depression than placebo and caused more tolerable adverse effects than tricyclics,[9,15-17] making SSRIs the antidepressants of choice. However, there has been an increased concern that SSRIs and other antidepressants may increase the occurrence of suicidal ideation and suicide in children and adolescents.

Early reports and recent regulatory action. In 1990, the case reports of six patients who developed suicidal ideation after starting fluoxetine were published.[18] One patient was an adolescent, had recently been hospitalized for depression, and demonstrated psychotic behavior, including paranoia, dissociation, and mild suicidal behavior, before antidepressant therapy. The patient displayed an increased frequency of self-injurious behavior (i.e., head banging, mutilation) and attempted suicide after fluoxetine was initiated and when the daily dosage was increased from 20 to 80 mg over six weeks. In June 2003, the United Kingdom's Committee on Safety and Medicines stated that paroxetine and venlafaxine should not be given to children under 18 years of age. Shortly afterward, the Food and Drug Administration (FDA) recommended against treating with paroxetine adolescents and children under age 18 and warned against abrupt discontinuation of the drug.

In March 2004, FDA asked manufacturers of SSRIs and atypical antidepressants to include warning statements in their labeling recommending close observation for the possibility of worsening depression or the emergence of suicidal ideation, self-injurious behavior, and suicide attempts. FDA also urged health care professionals to reevaluate drug therapy should anxiety, mania, agitation, hostility, or akathisia develop in patients.

The data were further analyzed by an FDA advisory committee, which issued a statement in September 2004 that fluoxetine was the only one of the seven products evaluated (fluoxetine, sertraline, paroxetine, citalopram, venlafaxine, nefazodone, and mirtazapine) that showed efficacy in the treatment of depression. However, the committee did acknowledge the increased risk of suicidality associated with antidepressant therapy and recommended that warnings about this increased risk should be placed on all antidepressant labeling. The advisory committee agreed that a patient information sheet should be distributed with every antidepressant prescription. It also voted (15 to 8) to add a black-box warning to all antidepressants' labeling to alert prescribers that children taking these medications are at increased risk for suicidality. It recommended the drugs not be contraindicated in children and adolescents because access to antidepressants is necessary for those who benefit from them.

Overview of clinical trials. Depending on how and which data are analyzed, different authors have arrived at different conclusions regarding SSRI-induced suicidal behavior.[14,19-21] One study involving patients 10–19 years of age demonstrated a decrease in the incidence of suicide after initiation of SSRI therapy.[22] For every 1% increase in SSRI use in adolescents, a decrease of 0.23 suicides per 100,000 adolescents per year was found. On the contrary, a study of approximately 2800 acts of self-injurious behavior demonstrated by adults and adolescents found a higher incidence of self-injurious behavior in patients receiving SSRIs versus other antidepressants.[23] However, these results should be viewed with caution. The presence of confounding factors, such as cultural background, selective prescribing, comorbid psychiatric conditions, drug–drug interactions, and adherence to antidepressant therapy, may reduce the possibility of a causal relationship between SSRIs and suicidal behavior.

SSRIs have shown efficacy in a few randomized controlled studies of children and adolescents.[9,15-17] In one study, patients treated with paroxetine (mean dose, 28 mg daily) demonstrated significantly greater improvements when compared with those who received placebo.[15] Of the 93 patients receiving paroxetine, 5 had suicidal ideations or behaviors, compared with 1 of 87 in the placebo group. Fluoxetine (20 mg daily) has also shown greater efficacy than placebo after two months.[16,17] In one study, 56% of patients showed improvements with fluoxetine versus 33% who received placebo.[16] However, adverse effects were not clearly identified. In another study, fluoxetine demonstrated greater remission rates for depression compared with placebo (41% versus 20%, respectively).[17] Three of 109 patients receiving fluoxetine discontinued therapy because of agitation, hyperkinesia, and mania, compared with 1 of 101 patients who discontinued placebo because of anxiety.

In another study, 439 patients were randomly assigned to receive fluoxetine alone (10–40 mg daily), CBT alone, fluoxetine (10–40 mg daily) with CBT, or placebo.[9] Results over 12 weeks demonstrated greater efficacy with fluoxetine and CBT (71%) than with monotherapy with fluoxetine (61%), CBT (43%), or placebo (35%). All treatment groups had a decrease in suicidal ideation, and there was no difference between fluoxetine and placebo in the exacerbations of suicidal thoughts. Also, those patients treated with both CBT and fluoxetine had a lower frequency of psychiatric symptoms compared with those who received fluoxetine alone.[9] However, this study did not have a sufficient sample size to determine a statistical difference in suicide attempts between treatment groups.

Whittington and colleagues[14] performed a meta-analysis of published and unpublished data regarding the use of antidepressants in patients 5–18 years old. Five randomized controlled studies were included in their analysis. Paroxetine, sertraline, citalopram, and venlafaxine demonstrated an increased relative risk for suicidal ideation or suicide attempts, ranging between 1.5 and 13.8. Fluoxetine was the only drug that did not cause an increase in the relative risk of suicidal ideation and behavior and demonstrated no increase in suicidal behavior compared with placebo. While it is important to note these results, the studies analyzed were not intended to identify attempted suicide and may not have had the statistical power to determine suicide risk because of their small sample size. Another meta-analysis found that the rate of suicidal acts with fluoxetine did not significantly differ from placebo.[24] Retrospective analysis of 17 double-blind studies, including over 3,000 patients, found that fluoxetine (20–80 mg daily) did not increase patients' risk for suicide. This study mostly evaluated adults; therefore, these conclusions cannot be extrapolated to pediatric patients.

Mechanisms of SSRI-induced suicidal behavior. Several hypotheses have attempted to explain the increased risk of suicidal ideation, self-injurious behavior, and suicide attempts caused by SSRIs, including inadequate dosing, activating adverse effects, and nonadherence to drug therapy.

Inadequate dosing. Data about the optimal initial and maintenance dosages of antidepressants in children are unclear. *The Pediatric Dosage Handbook*, a widely used reference, generally suggests that children should receive half the initial adult dosage of SSRIs, and the maintenance dosage should be adjusted to achieve efficacy.[25] However, this recommendation may not apply to all children. Pharmacokinetic parameters differ between children and adults. SSRIs are largely metabolized by the cytochrome P-450 (CYP) isoenzymes 2D6 or 3A4, and their clearance may vary among patients. The concentration of these isoforms may be elevated during childhood and approach adult concentrations by puberty. This suggests that greater-than-normal adult doses may be required for children (per kilogram of their body weight) but not for adolescents.[26] It is also unclear if serotonin concentrations and serotonergic-receptor binding rates differ among the pediatric populations. Recent studies suggest that gene variations between serotonin transporters may also play a role in individualizing therapy.[27,28] Inappropriate initial dosing or adjustment of SSRIs may lead to inadequate response or adverse effects. Plasma concentrations below or above the target level may contribute to self-injurious behavior. Insufficient plasma concentrations of these agents may be associated with suicidal ideation as a result of undertreated depression. Overdoses may cause adverse effects, such as mania or aggression, which may lead to suicide. Thus, careful adjustment of these agents is warranted. The availability of a liquid formulation may improve adherence, as some caregivers may have difficulty administering tablets or capsules to young children.

Activating adverse effects. Currently, fluoxetine is the only SSRI approved by FDA for the treatment of depression in children and adolescents, but other SSRIs are commonly prescribed for this population. Adverse events associated with SSRIs (e.g., sedation, gastrointestinal distress, fatigue, dizziness, and headache) are usually regarded as mild and transient. However, SSRIs have also been associated with hypomania, agitation, insomnia, and akathisia, which some believe may lead to suicidal ideation.[29-31]

Activating adverse effects (e.g., hypomania, agitation, and hyperkinesia) associated with SSRIs may increase suicidal thoughts, self-injurious behavior, and suicide attempts.[20,32] However, this theory has not been proven. Among the SSRIs, fluoxetine is one of the most activating agents.[33] Thus, it would seem that patients receiving fluoxetine should have the highest rate of suicide attempts. However, that idea has been contradicted by two meta-analyses.[14,24] As previously mentioned, other underlying diseases may increase the chance of suicide in patients receiving SSRIs. For example, in patients with undiagnosed comorbid illnesses, such as bipolar disorder, the addition of an SSRI may lead to mania and increase the chance of suicidal thoughts and self-injurious behavior.

Nonadherence. Nonadherence with antidepressant therapy may lead to plasma concentrations below the target level or withdrawal syndrome (with abrupt discontinuation), both of which may lead to suicide. A statement from the American Academy of Child and Adolescent Psychiatry reported that 12 of 49 adolescents who committed suicide had been prescribed antidepressants, but none had detectable plasma concentrations of SSRIs at the time of death.[34] Withdrawal effects seen with abrupt discontinuation of antidepressants include mania, nervousness, and agitation. Withdrawal effects may be less of an issue with fluoxetine because of the drug's long elimination half-life (approximately three days), which is about three times higher than the half-lives of other SSRIs. Therefore, adequate concentrations may remain in the body despite nonadherence for a few days.

Conclusion. Clinicians must be cautious when initiating antidepressant therapy in children and adolescents. Patients should be monitored closely for any possible adverse effects (including suicidal thoughts and behavior) and adherence to therapy. Antidepressants may increase the risk for suicidal behaviors (i.e., self-injurious behavior, suicide attempts), but clinicians should be cautious in accepting that as a rationale for not using treatment when it is clearly indicated.

REFERENCES

1. Birmaher B, Brent DA, Benson RS. Summary of the practice parameters for the assessment and treatment of children and adolescents with depressive disorders. *J Am Acad Child Adolesc Psychiatry.* 1998; 37:1234-8.
2. Jellinek MS, Snyder JB. Depression and suicide in children and adolescents. *Pediatr Rev.* 1998; 19:255-64.
3. World Health Organization. WHO Statistical Information System. www3.who.int/whosis/menu.cfm (accessed 2004 Sep).
4. Marttunen MJ, Pelkonen M. Psychiatric risk factors for adolescent suicide: a review. *Psychiatr Fenn.* 2000; 31:110-25.
5. Marttunen MJ, Aro HM, Lonnqvist JK. Adolescent suicide: endpoint of long-term difficulties. *J Am Acad Child Adolesc Psychiatry.* 1992; 31:649-54.
6. Clarke GN, Rohde P, Lewinsohn PM et al. Cognitive-behavioral treatment of adolescent depression: efficacy of acute group treatment and booster sessions. *J Am Acad Child Adolesc Psychiatry.* 1999; 38:272-9.
7. Rossello J, Bernal G. The efficacy of cognitive-behavioral and interpersonal treatments for depression in Puerto Rican adolescents. *J Consult Clin Psychol.* 1999; 67:734-45.
8. Brent DA, Holder D, Kolko D et al. A clinical psychotherapy trial for adolescent depression comparing cognitive, family, and supportive therapy. *Arch Gen Psychiatry.* 1997; 54:877-85.
9. March J, Silva S, Petrycki S et al. Fluoxetine, cognitive-behavioral therapy, and their combination for adolescents with depression: Treatment for Adolescents With Depression Study (TADS) randomized controlled trial. *JAMA.* 2004; 292:807-20.
10. Hazell P, O'Connell D, Heathcote D et al. Efficacy of tricyclic drugs in treating child and adolescent depression: a meta-analysis. *Br Med J.* 1995; 310: 897-901.
11. Geller B, Cooper TB, McCombs HG et al. Double-blind, placebo-controlled study of nortriptyline in depressed children using a "fixed plasma level" design. *Psychopharmacol Bull.* 1989; 25:101-8.
12. Ryan ND, Varma D. Child and adolescent mood disorders—experience with serotonin-based therapies. *Biol Psychiatry.* 1998; 44:336-40.
13. Mandoki MW, Tapia MR, Tapia MA et al. Venlafaxine in the treatment of children and adolescents with major depression. *Psychopharmacol Bull.* 1997; 33:149-54.

14. Whittington CJ, Kendall T, Fonagy P et al. Selective serotonin reuptake inhibitors in childhood depression: systematic review of published versus unpublished data. *Lancet.* 2004; 363:1341-5.

15. Keller MB, Ryan ND, Strober M et al. Efficacy of paroxetine in the treatment of adolescent major depression: a randomized, controlled trial. *J Am Acad Child Adolesc Psychiatry.* 2001; 40:762-72.

16. Emslie GJ, Rush AJ, Weinberg WA et al. A double-blind, randomized, placebo-controlled trial of fluoxetine in children and adolescents with depression. *Arch Gen Psychiatry.* 1997; 54:1031-7.

17. Emslie GJ, Heiligenstein JH, Wagner KD et al. Fluoxetine for acute treatment of depression in children and adolescents: a placebo-controlled, randomized clinical trial. *J Am Acad Child Adolesc Psychiatry.* 2002; 41:1205-15.

18. Teicher MH, Glod C, Cole JO. Emergence of intense suicidal preoccupation during fluoxetine treatment. *Am J Psychiatry.* 1990; 147:207-10.

19. Khan A, Khan S, Kolts R et al. Suicide rates in clinical trials of SSRIs, other antidepressants, and placebo: analysis of FDA reports. *Am J Psychiatry.* 2003; 160:790-2.

20. Healy D, Whitaker C. Antidepressants and suicide: risk-benefit conundrums. *J Psychiatry Neurosci.* 2003; 28:331-7.

21. Balon R. Selective serotonin reuptake inhibitors and suicide: is the evidence, as with beauty, in the eye of the beholder? *Psychother Psychosom.* 2003; 72:293-9.

22. Olfson M, Shaffer D, Marcus SC et al. Relationship between antidepressant medication treatment and suicide in adolescents. *Arch Gen Psychiatry.* 2003; 60:978-82.

23. Donovan S, Clayton A, Beeharry M et al. Deliberate self-harm and antidepressant drugs. Investigation of a possible link. *Br J Psychiatry.* 2000; 177:551-6.

24. Beasley CM Jr, Dornseif BE, Bosomworth JC et al. Fluoxetine and suicide: a meta-analysis of controlled trials of treatment for depression. *Br Med J.* 1991; 303:685-92.

25. Taketomo CK, Hodding JH, Kraus DM. Pediatric dosage handbook. 10th ed. Hudson, OH: Lexi-Comp Inc.; 2003:507,1017.

26. Leeder S. Pediatric pharmacogenetics. In: Louis A, Pagliaro AM, eds. Problems in pediatric drug therapy. 4th ed. Washington, DC: American Pharmaceutical Association; 2002:475-91.

27. Zanardi R, Benedetti F, Di Bella D et al. Efficacy of paroxetine in depression is influenced by a functional polymorphism within the promoter of the serotonin transporter gene. *J Clin Psychopharmacol.* 2000; 20:105-7. Letter.

28. Arias B, Catalan R, Gasto C et al. 5-HTTLPR polymorphism of the serotonin transporter gene predicts nonremission in major depression patients treated with citalopram in a 12-week follow-up study. *J Clin Psychopharmacol.* 2003; 23:563-7.

29. Teicher MH, Glod CA, Cole JO. Antidepressant drugs and the emergence of suicidal tendencies. *Drug Saf.* 1993; 8:186- 212.

30. Healy D. Lines of evidence on the risks of suicide with selective serotonin reuptake inhibitors. *Psychother Psychosom.* 2003; 72:71-9.

31. Healy D, Langmaak C, Savage M. Suicide in the course of the treatment of depression. *J Psychopharmacol.* 1999; 13:94-9.

32. Vitiello B, Swedo S. Antidepressant medications in children. *N Engl J Med.* 2004; 350:1489-91.

33. Finley PR. Selective serotonin reuptake inhibitors: pharmacologic profiles and potential therapeutic distinctions. *Ann Pharmacother.* 1994; 28:1359-69.

34. American Academy of Child and Adolescent Psychiatry. Children and antidepressant medication, 2004. www.aacap.org/Announcements/antidepressants.htm (accessed 2004 May 1).

6 Bystander Intervention in Emergencies: Diffusion of Responsibility[1]

John M. Darley, New York University
Bibb Latan, Columbia University

Journal of Personality and Social Psychology 1968, Vol. 8 , No. 4, 377-383 (Received July 8, 1967)

Ss overheard an epileptic seizure. They believed either that they alone heard the emergency, or that 1 or 4 unseen others were also present. As predicted the presence of other bystanders reduced the individual's feelings of personal responsibility and lowered his speed of reporting ($p < .01$). In groups of size 3, males reported no faster than females, and females reported no slower when the 1 other bystander was a male rather than a female. In general, personality and background measures were not predictive of helping. Bystander inaction in real-life emergencies is often explained by "apathy" "alienation," and "anomie." This experiment suggests that the explanation may lie more in the bystander's response to other observers than in his indifference to the victim.

Several years ago, a young woman was stabbed to death in the middle of a street in a residential section of New York City. Although such murders are not entirely routine, the incident received little public attention until several weeks later when the New York Times disclosed another side to the case: at least 38 witnesses had observed the attack and none had even attempted to intervene. Although the attacker took more than half an hour to kill Kitty Genovese, not one of the 38 people who watched from the safety of their own apartments came out to assist her. Not one even lifted the telephone to call the police (Rosenthal, 1964).

Preachers, professors, and news commentators sought the reasons for such apparently conscienceless and inhumane lack of intervention. Their conclusions ranged from "moral decay," to "dehumanization produced by the urban environment," to "alienation," "anomie," and "existential despair." An analysis of the situation, however, suggests that factors other than apathy and indifference were involved.

A person witnessing an emergency situation, particularly such a frightening and dangerous one as a stabbing, is in conflict. There are obvious humanitarian norms about helping the victim, but there are also rational and irrational fears about what might happen to a person who does intervene (Milgram & Hollander, 1964). "I didn't want to get involved," is a familiar comment, and behind it lies fears of physical harm, public embarrassment, involvement with police procedures, lost work days and jobs, and other unknown dangers.

In certain circumstances, the norms favoring intervention may be weakened, leading bystanders to resolve the conflict in the direction of nonintervention. One of these circumstances may be the presence of other onlookers. For example, in the case above, each observer, by seeing lights and figures in other apartment house windows, knew that others were also watching. However, there was no way to tell how the other observers were reacting. These two facts provide several reasons why any individual may have delayed or failed to help. The responsibility for helping was diffused among the observers; there was also diffusion of any potential blame for not taking action; and finally, it was possible that somebody, unperceived, had already initiated helping action.

When only one bystander is present in an emergency, if help is to come, it must come from him. Although he may choose to ignore it (out of concern for his personal safety, or desires "not to get involved"), any pressure to intervene focuses uniquely on him. When there are several observers present, however, the pressures to intervene do not focus on any one of the observers; instead the responsibility for intervention is shared among all the onlookers and is not unique to any one. As a result, no one helps.

A second possibility is that potential blame may be diffused. However much we may wish to think that an individual's moral behavior is divorced from considerations of personal punishment or reward, there is both theory and evidence to the contrary (Aronfreed, 1964; Miller & Dollard, 1941; Whiting & Child, 1953). It is perfectly reasonable to assume that, under circumstances of group responsibility for a punishable act, the punishment or blame that accrues to any one individual is often slight or nonexistent.

Finally, if others are known to be present, but their behavior cannot be closely observed, any one bystander can assume that one of the other observers is already taking action to end the emergency. Therefore, his own intervention would be only redundant—perhaps harmfully or confusingly so. Thus, given the presence of other onlookers whose behavior cannot be observed, any given bystander can rationalize his own inaction by convincing himself that "somebody else must be doing something."

These considerations lead to the hypothesis that the more bystanders to an emergency, the less likely, or the more slowly, any one will intervene to provide aid. To test this proposition it would be necessary to create a situation in which a realistic "emergency" could plausibly occur. Each subject should also be blocked from communicating with others to prevent his getting information about their behavior during the emergency. Finally, the experimental situation should allow for the assessment of the speed and frequency of the subjects' reaction to the emergency. The experiment reported below attempted to fulfill these conditions.

PROCEDURE

Overview. A college student arrived in the laboratory and was ushered into an individual room from which a communication system would enable him to talk to the other participants. It was explained to him that he was to take part in a discussion about personal problems associated with college life and that the discussion would be held over the intercom system, rather than face-to-face, in order to avoid embarrassment by preserving the anonymity of the subjects. During the course of the discussion, one of the other subjects underwent what appeared to be a very serious nervous seizure similar to epilepsy. During the fit it was impossible for the subject to talk to the other discussants or to find out what, if anything, they were doing about the emergency. The dependent variable was the speed with which the subjects reported the emergency to the experimenter. The major independent variable was the number of people the subject thought to be in the discussion group.

Subjects. Fifty-nine female and thirteen male students in introductory psychology courses at New York University were contacted to take part in an unspecified experiment as part of a class requirement.

Method. Upon arriving for the experiment, the subject found himself in a long corridor with doors opening off it to several small rooms. An experimental assistant met him, took him to one of the rooms, and seated him at a table. After filling out a background information form, the subject was given a pair of headphones with an attached microphone and was told to listen for instructions.

Over the intercom, the experimenter explained that he was interested in learning about the kinds of personal problems faced by normal college students in a high pressure, urban environment. He said that to avoid possible embarrassment about discussing personal problems with strangers several precautions had been taken. First, subjects would remain anonymous, which was why they had been placed in individual rooms rather than face-to-face. (The actual reason for this was to allow tape recorder simulation of the other subjects and emergency.) Second, since the discussion might be inhibited by the presence of outside listeners, the experimenter would not listen to the initial discussion, but would get the subject's reactions later, by questionnaire. (The real purpose of *this* was remove the obviously responsible experimenter from the scene of the emergency.)

The subjects were told that since the experimenter was not present, it was necessary to impose some organization. Each person would talk in turn, presenting his problems to the group. Next, each person in turn would comment on what the others had said, and finally, there would be a free discussion. A mechanical switching device would regulate this discussion sequence and each subject's microphone would be on for about 2 minutes. While any microphone was on, all other microphones would be off. Only one subject, therefore, could be heard over the network at any given time. The subjects were thus led to realize when they later heard the seizure that only the victim's microphone was on and there was no way of determining what any of the other witnesses were doing, nor of discussing the event and its possible solution with the others. When these instructions had been given, the discussion began.

In the discussion the victim said that he found it difficult to get adjusted to New York City and to his studies. Very hesitantly, and with obvious embarrassment, he mentioned that he was prone to seizures, particularly when studying hard or taking exams. The other people, including the real subject, took their turns and discussed problems (minus, of course, the proneness to seizures). The naive subject talked last in the series, after the last prerecorded voice was played.[2]

When it was again the victim's turn to talk, he made a few relatively calm comments, and then, increasingly louder and incoherent, he continued:

I-er-um-I think I-I need-er-if-if could-er-er-somebody er-er-er-er-er-er-er give me a little-er-give me a little help here because-er-I-er-I'm-er-er-h-having a-a-a real problem-er-right now and I-er-if somebody could help me out it would-it would-er-er s-s-sure be-sure be good . . . because-er-there-er-er-a cause I-er-I-uh-I've got a-a one of the-er-sei——-er-er-things coming on and-and-and I could really-er-use some help so if somebody would-er-give me a little h-help-uh-er-er-er-er-er c-could somebody-er-er-help-er-uh-uh-uh (choking sounds). . . . I'm gonna die-er-er-I'm . . . gonna die-er-help-er-er-seizure-er-[chokes, then quiet].

The experimenter began timing the speed of the real subject's response at the beginning of the victim's speech. Informed judges listening to the tape have estimated that the victim's increasingly louder and more disconnected ramblings clearly represented a breakdown about 70 seconds after the signal for the victim's second speech. The victim's speech was abruptly cut off 125 seconds after this signal, which could be interpreted by the subject as indicating that the time allotted for that speaker had elapsed and the switching circuits had switched away from him. Times reported in the results are measured from the start of the fit.

Group size variable. The major independent variable of the study was the number of other people that the subject believed also heard the fit. By the assistant's comments before the experiment, and also by the number of voices heard to speak in the first round of the group discussion, the subject was led to believe that the discussion group was one of three sizes: either a two-person group (consisting of a person who would later have a fit and the real subject), a three-person group (consisting of the victim, the real subject, and one confederate voice), or a six-person group (consisting of the victim, the subject, and four confederate voices). All the confederates' voices were tape-recorded.

Variations in group composition. Varying the kind as well as the number of bystanders present at an emergency [illegible] responsibility felt by any single bystander. To test this, several variations of the three-person group were run. In one three-person condition, the taped bystander voice was that of a female, in another a male, and in the third a male who said that he was a premedical student who occasionally worked in the emergency wards at Bellevue hospital.

In the above conditions, the subjects were female college students. In a final condition males drawn from the same introductory psychology subject pool were tested in a three-person female-bystander condition.

Time to help. The major dependent variable was the time elapsed from the start of the victim's fit until the subject left her experimental cubicle. When the subject left her room, she saw the experimental assistant seated at the end of the hall, and invariably went to the assistant. If 6 minutes elapsed without the subject having emerged from her room, the experiment was terminated.

As soon as the subject reported the emergency, or after 6 minutes had elapsed, the experimental assistant disclosed the true nature of the experiment, and dealt with any emotions aroused in the subject. Finally the subject filled out a questionnaire concerning her thoughts and feelings during the emergency, and completed scales of Machiavellianism, anomie, and authoritarianism (Christie, 1964), a social desirability scale (Crowne & Marlowe, 1964), a social responsibility scale (Daniels & Berkowitz, 1964), and reported vital statistics and socioeconomic data.

RESULTS

Plausibility of Manipulation

Judging by the subjects' nervousness when they reported the fit to the experimenter, by their surprise when they discovered that the fit was simulated, and by comments they made during the fit (when they thought their microphones were off), one can conclude that almost all of the subjects perceived the fit as real. There were two exceptions in different experimental conditions, and the data for these subjects were dropped from the analysis.

Effect of Group Size on Helping

The number of bystanders that the subject perceived to be present had a major effect on the likelihood with which she would report the emergency (Table 1). Eighty-five percent of the subjects who thought they alone knew of the victim's plight reported the seizure before the victim was cut off, only 31% of those who thought four other bystanders were present did so.

Every one of the subjects in the two-person groups, but only 62% of the subjects in the six-person groups, ever reported the emergency. The cumulative distributions of response times for groups of different perceived size (Figure 1) indicates that, by any point in time, more subjects from the two-person groups had responded than from the three-person groups, and more from the three-person groups than from the six-person groups.

Ninety-five percent of all the subjects who ever responded did so within the first half of the time available to them. No subject who had not reported within 3 minutes after the fit began ever did so. The shape of these distributions suggests that had the experiment been allowed to run for a considerably longer time, few additional subjects would have responded.

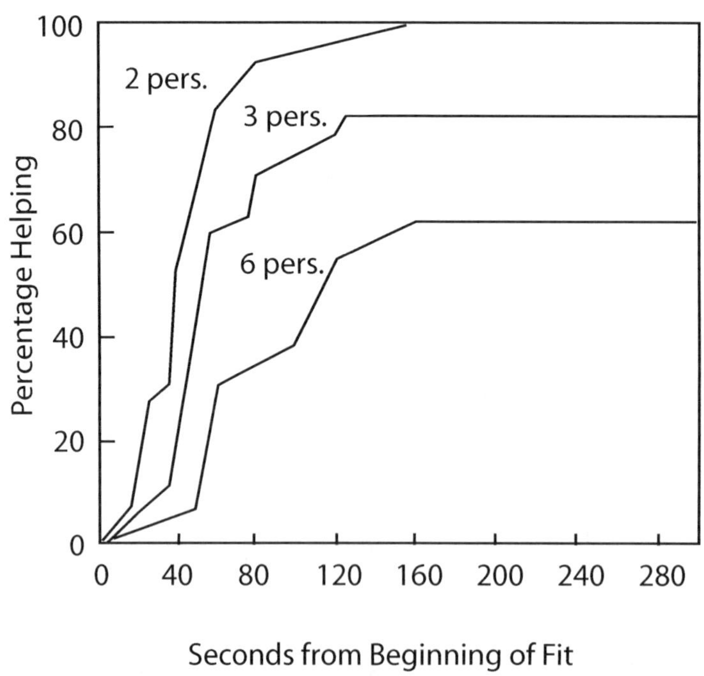

Figure 1

TABLE 1
EFFECTS OF GROUP SIZE ON LIKELIHOOD AND SPEED OF RESPONSE

Group size	*N*	% responding by end of fit	Time in sec.	Speed score
2 (*S* & victim)	13	85	52	.87
3 (*S*, victim, & 1 other)	26	62	93	.72
6 (*S*, victim, & 4 others)	13	31	166	.51

Note—p value of differences: $x^2 = 7.91$, $p < .02$; $F = 8.09$, $p < .01$, for speed scores.

Speed of Response

To achieve a more detailed analysis of the results, each subject's time score was transformed into a "speed" score by taking the reciprocal of the response time in seconds and multiplying by 100. The effect of transformation was to deemphasize differences between longer time scores, thus reducing the contribution to the results of the arbitrary 6-minute limit on scores. A high speed score indicates a fast response.

An analysis of variance indicates that effect of group size is highly significant ($p < .01$). Duncan multiple-range tests indicate that all but the two- and three-person groups differ significantly from one another ($p < .05$).

Victim's Likelihood of Being Helped

An individual subject is less likely to respond if he thinks that others are present. But what of the victim? Is the inhibition of the response of each individual strong enough to counteract the fact that with five onlookers there are five times as many people available to help? From the data of this experiment, it is possible mathematically to create hypothetical groups with one, two, or five observers.[3] The calculations indicate that the victim is about equally likely to get help from one bystander as from two. The victim is considerably more likely to have gotten help from one or two observers than from five during the first minute of the fit. For instance, by 45 seconds after the start of the fit, the victim's chances of having been helped by the single bystanders were about 50%, compared to none in the five observer condition. After the first minute, the likelihood of getting help from at least one person is high in all three conditions.

Effect of Group Composition on Helping the Victim

Several variations of the three-person group were run. In one pair of variations, the female subject thought the other bystander was either male or female; in another, she thought the other bystander was a premedical student who worked in an emergency ward at

TABLE 2
EFFECTS OF GROUP COMPOSITION ON LIKELIHOOD AND SPEED OF RESPONSE*

Group composition	*N*	% responding by end of fit	Time in sec.	Speed score
Female *S*, male other	13	62	94	74
Female *S*, female other	13	62	92	71
Female *S*, male medic other	5	100	60	77
Male *S*, female other	13	69	110	68

*Three-person group, male victim.

Bellevue hospital. As Table 2 shows, the variations in sex and medical competence of the other bystander had no important or detectable affect on speed of response. Subjects responded equally frequently and fast whether the other bystander was female, male, or medically experienced.

Sex of the Subject and Speed of Response

Coping with emergencies is often thought to be the duty of males, especially when females are present, but there was no evidence that this was the case in this study. Male subjects responded to the emergency with almost exactly the same speed as did females (Table 2).

Reasons for Intervention or Nonintervention

After the debriefing at the end of the experiment each subject was given a 15-item checklist and asked to check those thoughts which had "crossed your mind when you heard Subject 1 calling for help." Whatever the condition, each subject checked very few thoughts, and there were no significant differences in number or kind of thoughts in the different experimental groups. The only thoughts checked by more than a few subjects were "I didn't know what to do" (18 out of 65 subjects), or "I thought it must be some sort of fake" (20 out of 65), and "I didn't know exactly what was happening" (26 out of 65).

It is possible that subjects were ashamed to report socially undesirable rationalizations, or, since the subjects checked the list *after* the true nature of the experiment had been explained to them, their memories might have been blurred. It is our impression, however, that most subjects checked few reasons because they had few coherent thoughts during the fit.

We asked all subjects whether the presence or absence of other bystanders had entered their minds during the time that they were hearing the fit. Subjects in the three- and six-person groups reported that they were aware that other people were present, but they felt that this made no difference to their own behavior.

Individual Difference Correlates of Speed of Report

The correlations between speed of report and various individual differences on the personality and background measures were obtained by normalizing the distribution of report speeds within each experimental condition and pooling these scores across all conditions (n = 62-65). Personality measures showed no important or significant correlations with speed of reporting the emergency. In fact, only one of the 16 individual difference measures, the size of the community in which the subject grew up, correlated ($r = -.26$, $p < .05$) with the speed of helping.

DISCUSSION

Subjects, whether or not they intervened, believed the fit to be genuine and serious. "My God, he's having a fit," many subjects said to themselves (and were overheard via their microphones) at the onset of the fit. Others gasped or simply said "Oh." Several of the male subjects swore. One subject said to herself, "It's just my kind of luck, something has to happen to me!" Several subjects spoke aloud of their confusion about what course of action to take, "Oh God, what should I do?"

When those subjects who intervened stepped out of their rooms, they found the experimental assistant down the hall. With some uncertainty, but without panic, they reported the situation. "Hey, I think Number 1 is very sick. He's having a fit or something." After ostensibly checking on the situation, the experimenter returned to report that "everything is under control." The subjects accepted these assurances with obvious relief.

Subjects who failed to report the emergency showed few signs of the apathy and indifference thought to characterize "unresponsive bystanders." When the experimenter entered her room to terminate the situation, the subject often asked if the victim was "all right." "Is he being taken care of?" "He's all right, isn't he?" Many of these subjects showed physical signs of nervousness; they often had trembling hands and sweating palms. If anything, they seemed more emotionally aroused than did the subjects who reported the emergency.

Why, then, didn't they respond? It is our impression that nonintervening subjects had not decided *not* to respond. Rather they were still in a state of indecision and conflict concerning whether to respond or not. The emotional behavior of these nonresponding subjects was a sign of their continuing conflict, a conflict that other subjects resolved by responding.

The fit created a conflict situation of the avoidance-avoidance type. On the one hand, subjects worried about the guilt and shame they would feel if they did not help the person in distress. On the other hand, they were concerned not to make fools of themselves by overreacting, not to ruin the ongoing experiment by leaving their intercom, and not to destroy the anonymous nature of the situation, which the experimenter had earlier stressed as important. For subjects in the two-person condition, the obvious distress of the victim and his need for help were so important that their conflict was easily resolved. For the subjects who knew there were other bystanders present, the cost of not helping was reduced and the conflict they were in more acute. Caught between the two negative alternatives of letting the victim continue to suffer or the costs of rushing in to help, the nonresponding bystanders vacillated between them rather than choosing not to respond. This distinction may be academic for the victim, since he got no help in either case, but it is an extremely important one for arriving at an understanding of the causes of bystanders' failures to help.

Although the subjects experienced stress and conflict during the experiment, their general reactions to it were highly positive. On a questionnaire administered after the experimenter had discussed the nature and purpose of the experiment, every single subject found the experiment either "interesting" or "very interesting" and was willing to participate in similar experiments in the future. All subjects felt they understood what the experiment was about and indicated that they thought the deceptions were necessary and justified. All but one felt they were better informed about the nature of psychological research in general.

Male subjects reported the emergency faster than did females. These results (or lack of them) seem to conflict with Berkowitz, Klanderman, and Harris (1964) finding that males tend to assume more responsibility and take more initiative than females in giving help to dependent others. Also, females reacted equally fast when the other bystander was another female, a male, or even a person practiced in dealing with medical emergencies. The ineffectiveness of these manipulations of group composition cannot be explained by general insensitivity of the speed measure, since the group-size variable had a marked effect on report speed.

It might be helpful in understanding this lack of difference to distinguish two general classes of intervention in emergency situations: direct and reportorial. Direct intervention (breaking up a fight, extinguishing a fire, swimming out to save a drowner) often requires skill, knowledge, or physical power. It may involve danger. American cultural norms and Berkowitz's results seem to suggest that males are more responsible than females for this kind of direct intervention.

A second way of dealing with an emergency is to report it to someone qualified to handle it, such as the police. For this kind of intervention, there seem to be no norms requiring male action. In the present study, subjects clearly intended to report the emergency rather than take direct action. For indirect intervention, sex or medical competence does not appear to affect one's qualifications or responsibilities. Anybody, male or female, medically trained or not, can find the experimenter.

In this study, no subject was able to tell how the other subjects reacted to the fit. (Indeed, there were no other subjects actually present.) The effects of group size on speed of helping, therefore, are due simply to the perceived presence of others rather than to the influence of their actions. This means the experimental situation is unlike emergencies, such as a fire, in which bystanders interact with each other. It is, however, similar to emergencies, such as the Genovese murder, in which spectators knew others were also watching but were prevented by walls between them from communication that might have counteracted the diffusion of responsibility.

The present results create serious difficulties for one class of commonly given explanations for the failure of bystanders to intervene in actual emergencies, those involving apathy or indifference. These explanations generally assert that people who fail to intervene are somehow different in kind from the rest of us, that they are "alienated by industrialization," "dehumanized by urbanization," "depersonalized by living in the cold society," or "psychopaths." These explanations serve a dual function for people who adopt them. First, they explain (if only in a nominal way) the puzzling and frightening problem of why people watch others die. Second, they give individuals reason to deny that they too might fail to help in a similar situation.

The results of this experiment seem to indicate that such personality variables may not be as important as these explanations suggest. Alienation, Machiavellianism, acceptance of social responsibility, need for approval, and authoritarianism are often cited in these explanations. Yet they did not predict the speed or likelihood of help. In sharp contrast, the perceived number of bystanders did. The explanation of bystander "apathy" may lie more in the bystander's response to other observers than in presumed personality deficiencies of "apathetic" individuals. Although this realization may force us to face the guilt-provoking possibility that we too might fail to intervene, it also suggests that individuals are not, of necessity, "noninterveners" because of their personalities. If people understand the situational forces that can make them hesitate to intervene, they may better overcome them.

REFERENCES

Aronfreed, J. The origin of self-criticism. *Psychological Review*, 1964, 71, 193-219.

Berkowitz, L., Klanderman, S., & Harris, R. Effects of experimenter awareness and sex of subject on reactions to dependency relationships. *Sociometry*, 1964, 27, 327-329.

Christie, R. *The prevalence of machiavellian orientations.* Paper presented at the meeting of the American Psychological Association, Los Angeles, 1964.

Crowne, D., & Marlowe, D. *The approval motive.* New York: Wiley, 1964.

Daniels, L., & Berkowitz, L. Liking and response to dependency relationships. *Human Relations*, 1963, 16, 141-148.

Milgram, S., & Hollander, P. Murder they heard. *Nation*, 1964, 198, 602-604.

Miller, N., & Dollard, J. *Social learning and imitation.* New Haven: Yale University Press, 1941.

Rosenthal, A. M. *Thirty-eight witnesses.* New York: McGraw-Hill, 1964.

Whiting, J. W. M., & Child, I. *Child training and personality.* New Haven: Yale University Press, 1953.

FOOTNOTES

[1.] This research was supported in part by National Science Foundation Grants GS1238 and GS1239. Susan Darley contributed materially to the design of the experiment and ran the subjects, and she and Thomas Moriarty analyzed the data. Richard Nisbett, Susan Millman, Andrew Gordon, and Norma Neiman helped in preparing the tape recordings.

[2.] To test whether the order in which the subjects spoke in the first discussion round significantly affected the subjects' speed of report, the order in which the subjects spoke was varied (in the six-person group). This had no significant or noticeable effect on the speed of the subjects' reports.

[3.] The formula for the probability that at least one person will help by a given time is $1 - (1 - P)^n$ where n is the number of observers and P is the probability of a single individual (who thinks he is one of n observers) helping by that time.

7 The Origin and Development of Psychoanalysis[1]

Sigmund Freud (1910)

First published in *American Journal of Psychology*, 21, 181-218

FIRST LECTURE

Ladies and Gentlemen: It is a new and somewhat embarrassing experience for me to appear as lecturer before students of the New World. I assume that I owe this honor to the association of my name with the theme of psychoanalysis, and consequently it is of psychoanalysis that I shall aim to speak. I shall attempt to give you in very brief form an historical survey of the origin and further development of this new method of research and cure.

Granted that it is a merit to have created psychoanalysis, it is not my merit. I was a student, busy with the passing of my last examinations, when another physician of Vienna, Dr. Joseph Breuer,[2] made the first application of this method to the case of an hysterical girl (1880-82). We must now examine the history of this case and its treatment, which can be found in detail in "Studien über Hysterie," later published by Dr. Breuer and myself.[3]

But first one word. I have noticed, with considerable satisfaction, that the majority of my hearers do not belong to the medical profession. Now do not fear that a medical education is necessary to follow what I shall have to say. We shall now accompany the doctors a little way, but soon we shall take leave of them and follow Dr. Breuer on a way which is quite his own.

Dr. Breuer's patient was a girl of twenty-one, of a high degree of intelligence. She had developed in the course of her two years' illness a series of physical and mental disturbances which well deserved to be taken seriously. She had a severe paralysis of both right extremities, with anasthesia [sic], and at times the same affection of the members of the left side of the body; disturbance of eye-movements, and much impairment of vision; difficulty in maintaining the position of the head, an intense *Tussis nervosa,* nausea when she attempted to take nourishment, and at one time for several weeks a loss of the power to drink, in spite of tormenting thirst. Her power of speech was also diminished, and this progressed so far that she could neither speak nor understand her mother tongue; and, finally, she was subject to states of "absence," of confusion, delirium, alteration of her whole personality. These states will later claim our attention.

When one hears of such a case, one does not need to be a physician to incline to the opinion that we are concerned here with a serious injury, probably of the brain, for which there is little hope of cure and which will probably lead to the early death of the patient. The doctors will tell us, however, that in one type of case with just as unfavorable symptoms, another, far more favorable, opinion is justified. When one finds such a series of symptoms in the case of a young girl, whose vital organs (heart, kidneys), are shown by objective tests to be normal, but who has suffered from strong emotional disturbances, and when the symptoms differ in certain finer characteristics from what one might logically expect, in a case like this the doctors are not too much disturbed. They consider that there is present no organic lesion of the brain, but that enigmatical state, known since the time of the Greek physicians as hysteria, which can simulate a whole series of symptoms of various diseases. They consider in such a case that the life of the patient is not in danger and that a restoration to health will probably come about of itself. The differentiation of such an hysteria from a severe organic lesion is not always very easy. But we do not need to know how a differential diagnosis of this kind is made; you may be sure that the case of Breuer's patient was such that no skillful physician could fail to diagnose an hysteria. We may also add a word here from the history of the case. The illness first appeared while the patient was caring for her father, whom she tenderly loved, during the severe illness which led to his death, a task which she was compelled to abandon because she herself fell ill.

So far it has seemed I best to go with the doctors, but we shall soon part company with them. You must not think that the outlook of a patient with regard to medical aid is essentially bettered when the diagnosis points to hysteria rather than to organic disease of the brain. Against the serious brain diseases medical skill is in most cases powerless, but also in the case of hysterical affections the doctor can do nothing. He must leave it to benign nature, when and how his hopeful prognosis will be realized.[4] Accordingly, with the recognition of the disease as hysteria, little is changed in the situation of the patient, but there is a great change in the attitude of the doctor. We can observe that he acts quite differently toward hystericals than toward patients suffering from organic diseases. He will not bring the same interest to the former as to the latter, since their suffering is much less serious and yet seems to set up the claim to be valued just as seriously.

But there is another motive in this action. The physician, who through his studies has learned so much that is hidden from the laity, can realize in his thought the causes and alterations of the brain disorders in patients suffering from apoplexy or dementia, a representation which must be right up to a certain point, for by it he is enabled to understand the nature of each symptom. But before the details of hysterical symptoms, all his knowledge, his anatomical-physiological and pathological education, desert him. He cannot understand hysteria. He is in the same position before it as the layman. And that is not agreeable to any one, who is in the habit of setting such a high valuation upon his knowledge. Hystericals, accordingly, tend to lose his sympathy; he considers them persons who overstep the laws of his science, as the orthodox regard heretics; he ascribes to them all possible evils, blames them for exaggeration and intentional deceit, "simulation," and he punishes them by withdrawing his interest.

Now Dr. Breuer did not deserve this reproach in this case; he gave his patient sympathy and interest, although at first he did not understand how to help her. Probably this was easier for him on account of those superior qualities of the patient's mind and character, to which he bears witness in his account of the case.

His sympathetic observation soon found the means which made the first help possible. It had been noticed that the patient, in her states of "absence," of psychic alteration, usually mumbled over several words to herself. These seemed to spring from associations with which her thoughts were busy. The doctor, who was able to get these words, put her in a sort of hypnosis and repeated them to her over and over, in order to bring up any associations that they might have. The patient yielded to his suggestion and reproduced for him those psychic creations which controlled her thoughts during her "absences," and which betrayed themselves in these single spoken words. These were fancies, deeply sad, often poetically beautiful, day dreams, we might call them, which commonly took as their starting point the situation of a girl beside the sick-bed of her father. Whenever she had related a number of such fancies, she was, as it were, freed and restored to her normal mental life. This state of health would last for several hours, and then give place on the next day to a new "absence," which was removed in the same way by relating the newly-created fancies. It was impossible not to get the impression that the psychic alteration which was expressed in the "absence" was a consequence of the excitations originating from these intensely emotional fancy-images. The patient herself, who at this time of her illness strangely enough understood and spoke only English, gave this new kind of treatment the name "talking care," or jokingly designated it as "chimney sweeping."

The doctor soon hit upon the fact that through such cleansing of the soul more could be accomplished than a temporary removal of the constantly recurring mental "clouds." Symptoms of the disease would disappear when in hypnosis the patient could be made to remember the situation and the associative connections under which they first appeared, provided free vent was given to the emotions which they aroused.

"There was in the summer a time of intense heat, and the patient had suffered very much from thirst; for, without any apparent reason, she had suddenly become unable to drink. She would take a glass of water in her hand, but as soon as it touched her lips she would push it away as though suffering from hydrophobia. Obviously for these few seconds she was in her absent state. She ate only fruit, melons and the like, in order to relieve this tormenting thirst. When this had been going on about six weeks, she was talking one day in hypnosis about her English governess, whom she disliked, and finally told, with every sign of disgust, how she had come into the room of the governess, and how that lady's little dog, that she abhorred, had drunk out of a glass. Out of respect for the conventions the patient had remained silent. Now, after she had given energetic expression to her restrained anger, she asked for a drink, drank a large quantity of water without trouble, and woke from hypnosis with the glass at her lips. The symptom thereupon vanished permanently.[5]

Permit me to dwell for a moment on this experience. No one had ever cured an hysterical symptom by such means before, or had come so near understanding its cause. This would be a pregnant discovery if the expectation could be confirmed that still other, perhaps the majority of symptoms, originated in this way and could be removed by the same method. Breuer spared no pains to convince himself of this and investigated the pathogenesis of the other more serious symptoms in a more orderly way. Such was indeed the case; almost all the symptoms originated in exactly this way, as remnants, as precipitates, if you like, of affectively-toned experiences, which for that reason we later called "psychic traumata." The nature of the symptoms became clear through their relation to the scene which caused them. They were, to use the technical term, "determined" (*determiniert*) by the scene whose memory traces they embodied, and so could no longer be described as arbitrary or enigmatical functions of the neurosis.

Only one variation from what might be expected must be mentioned. It was not always a single experience which occasioned the symptom, but usually several, perhaps many similar, repeated traumata cooperated in this effect. It was necessary to repeat the whole series of pathogenic memories in chronological sequence, and of course in reverse order, the last first and the first last. It was quite impossible to reach the first and often most essential trauma directly, without first clearing away those coming later.

You will of course want to hear me speak of other examples of the causation of hysterical symptoms beside this of inability to drink on account of the disgust caused by the dog drinking from the glass. I must, however, if I hold to my programme, limit myself to very few examples. Breuer relates, for instance, that his patient's visual disturbances could be traced back to external causes, in the following way. "The patient, with tears in her eyes, was sitting by the sick-bed when her father suddenly asked her what time it was. She could not see distinctly, strained her eyes to see, brought the watch near her eyes so that the dial seemed very large (macropia and strabismus conv.), or else she tried hard to suppress her tears, so that the sick man might not see them."[6]

All the pathogenic impressions sprang from the time when she shared in the care of her sick father. "Once she was watching at night in the greatest anxiety for the patient, who was in a high fever, and in suspense, for a surgeon was expected from Vienna, to operate on the patient. Her mother had gone out for a little while, and Anna sat by the sick-bed, her right arm hanging over the back of her chair. She fell into a revery [sic] and saw a black snake emerge, as it were, from the wall and approach the sick man as though to bite him. (It is very probable that several snakes had actually been seen in the meadow behind the house, that she had already been frightened by them, and that these former experiences furnished the material for the hallucination.) She tried to drive off the creature, but was as though paralyzed. Her right arm, which was hanging over the back of the chair, had 'gone to sleep,' become anasthetic [sic] and paretic, and as she was looking at it, the fingers changed into little snakes with deaths-heads. (The nails.) Probably she attempted to drive away the snake with her paralyzed right hand, and so the anasthesia [sic] and paralysis of this member formed associations with the snake hallucination. When this had vanished, she tried in her anguish to speak, but could not. She could not express herself in any language, until finally she thought of the words of an English nursery song, and thereafter she could think and speak only in this language."[7] When the memory of this scene was revived in hypnosis the paralysis of the right arm, which had existed since the beginning of the illness, was cured and the treatment ended.

When, a number of years later, I began to use Breuer's researches and treatment on my own patients, my experiences completely coincided with his. In the case of a woman of about forty, there was a tic, a peculiar smacking noise which manifested itself whenever she was laboring under any excitement, without any obvious cause. It had its origin in two experiences which had this common element, that she attempted to make no noise, but that by a sort of counter-will this noise broke the stillness. On the first occasion, she had finally after much trouble put her sick child to sleep, and she tried to be very quiet so as not to awaken it. On the second occasion, during a ride with both her children in a thunderstorm the horses took fright, and she carefully avoided any noise for fear of frightening them still more.[8] I give this example instead of many others which are cited in the "Studien über Hysterie."

Ladies and gentlemen, if you will permit me to generalize, as is indispensable in so brief a presentation, we may express our results up to this point in the formula: *Our hysterical patients suffer from reminiscences.* Their symptoms are the remnants and the memory symbols of certain (traumatic) experiences.

A comparison with other memory symbols from other sources will perhaps enable us better to understand this symbolism. The memorials and monuments with which we adorn our great cities, are also such memory symbols. If you walk through London you will find before one of the greatest railway stations of the city a richly decorated Gothic pillar — "Charing Cross." One of the old Plantagenet kings, in the thirteenth century, caused the body of his beloved queen Eleanor to be borne to Westminster, and had Gothic crosses erected at each of the stations where the coffin was set down. Charing Cross is the last of these monuments, which preserve the memory of this sad journey.[9] In another part of the city, you will see a high pillar of more modern construction, which is merely called "the monument." This is in memory of the great fire which broke out in the neighborhood in the year 1666, and destroyed a great part of the city. These monuments are memory symbols like the hysterical symptoms; so far the comparison seems justified. But what would you say to a Londoner who today stood sadly before the monument to the funeral of Queen Eleanor, instead of going about his business with the haste engendered by modern industrial conditions, or rejoicing with the young queen of his own heart? Or to another, who before the "monument" bemoaned the burning of his loved native city, which long since has arisen again so much more splendid than before?

Now hystericals and all neurotics behave like these two unpractical Londoners, not only in that they remember the painful experiences of the distant past, but because they are still strongly affected by them. They cannot escape from the past and neglect present reality in its favor. This fixation of the mental life on the pathogenic traumata is an essential, and practically a most significant characteristic of the neurosis. I will willingly concede the objection which you are probably formulating, as you think over the history of Breuer's patient. All her traumata originated at the time when she was caring for her sick father, and her symptoms could only be regarded as memory symbols of his sickness and death. They corresponded to mourning, and a fixation on thoughts of the dead so short a time after death is certainly not pathological, but rather corresponds to normal emotional behavior. I concede this: there is nothing abnormal in the fixation of feeling on the trauma shown by Breuer's patient. But in other cases, like that of the tic that I have mentioned, the occasions for which lay ten and fifteen years back, the characteristic of this abnormal clinging to the past is very clear, and Breuer's patient would probably have developed it, if she had not come under the "cathartic treatment" such a short time after the traumatic experiences and the beginning of the disease.

We have so far only explained the relation of the hysterical symptoms to the life history of the patient; now by considering two further moments which Breuer observed, we may get a hint as to the processes of the beginning of the illness and those of the cure. With regard to the first, it is especially to be noted that Breuer's patient in almost all pathogenic situations had to suppress a strong excitement, instead of giving vent to it by appropriate words and deeds. In the little experience with her governess' dog, she suppressed, through regard for the conventions, all manifestations of her very intense disgust. While she was seated by her father's sick bed, she was careful to betray nothing of her anxiety and her painful depression to the patient. When, later, she reproduced the same scene before the physician, the emotion which she had suppressed on the occurrence of the scene burst out with especial strength, as though it had been pent up all along. The symptom which had been caused by that scene reached its greatest intensity while the doctor was striving to revive the memory of the scene, and vanished after it had been fully laid bare. On the other hand, experience shows that if the patient is reproducing the traumatic scene to the physician, the process has no curative effect if, by some peculiar chance, there is no development of emotion. It is apparently these emotional processes upon which the illness of the patient and the restoration to health are dependent. We feel justified in regarding "emotion" as a quantity which may become increased, derived and displaced. So we are forced to the conclusion that the patient fell ill because the emotion developed in the pathogenic situation was prevented from escaping normally, and that the essence of the sickness lies in the fact that these "imprisoned" *(dingeklemmt)* emotions undergo a series of abnormal changes. In part they are preserved as a lasting charge and as a source of constant disturbance in psychical life; in part they undergo a change into unusual bodily innervations [sic] and inhibitions, which present themselves as the physical symptoms of the case. We have coined the name "hysterical conversion" for the latter process. Part of our mental energy is, under normal conditions, conducted off by way of physical innervation [sic] and gives what we call "the expression of emotions." Hysterical conversion exaggerates this part of the course of a mental process which is emotionally colored; it corresponds to a far more intense emotional expression, which finds outlet by new paths. If a stream flows in two channels, an overflow of one will take place as soon as the current in the other meets with an obstacle.

You see that we are in a fair way to arrive at a purely psychological theory of hysteria, in which we assign the first rank to the affective processes. A second observation of Breuer compels us to ascribe to the altered condition of consciousness a great part in determining the characteristics of the disease. His patient showed many sorts of mental states, conditions of "absence," confusion and alteration of character, besides her normal state. In her normal state she was entirely ignorant of the pathogenic scenes and of their connection with her symptoms. She had forgotten those scenes, or at any rate had dissociated them from their pathogenic connection. When the patient was hypnotized, it was possible, after considerable difficulty, to recall those scenes to her memory, and by this means of recall the symptoms were removed. It would have been extremely perplexing to know how to interpret this fact, if hypnotic practice and experiments had not pointed out the way. Through the study of hypnotic phenomena, the conception, strange though it was at first, has become familiar, that in one and the same individual several mental groupings are possible, which may remain relatively independent of each other, "know nothing" of each other, and which may cause a splitting of consciousness along lines which they lay down. Cases of such a sort, known as "double personality" ("*double conscience*"), occasionally appear spontaneously. If in such a division of personality consciousness remains constantly bound up with one of the two states, this is called the *conscious* mental state, and the other the *unconscious.* In the well-known phenomena of so-called post hypnotic suggestion, in which a command given in hypnosis is later executed in the normal state as though by an imperative suggestion, we have an excellent basis for understanding how the unconscious state can influence the conscious, although the latter is ignorant of the existence of the former. In the same way it is quite possible to explain the facts in hysterical cases. Breuer came to the conclusion that the hysterical symptoms originated in such peculiar mental states, which he called "hypnoidal states." (*hypnoide Zustände.*) Experiences of an emotional nature, which occur during such hypnoidal states easily become pathogenic, since such states do not present the conditions for a normal draining off of the emotion of the exciting processes. And as a result there arises a peculiar product of this exciting process, that is, the symptom, and this is projected like a foreign body into the normal state. The latter has, then, no conception of the significance of the hypnoidal pathogenic situation. Where a symptom arises, we also find an amnesia, a memory gap, and the filling of this gap includes the removal of the conditions under which the symptom originated.

I am afraid that this portion of my treatment will not seem very clear, but you must remember that we are dealing here with new and difficult views, which perhaps could not be made much clearer. This all goes to show that our knowledge in this field is not yet very far advanced. Breuer's idea of the hypnoidal states has, moreover, been shown to be superfluous and a hindrance to further investigation, and has been dropped from present conceptions of psychoanalysis. Later I shall at least suggest what other influences and processes have been disclosed besides that of the hypnoidal states, to which Breuer limited the causal moment.

You have probably also felt, and rightly, that Breuer's investigations gave you only a very incomplete theory and insufficient explanation of the phenomena which we have observed. But complete theories do not fall from Heaven, and you would have had still greater reason to be distrustful, had any one offered you at the beginning of his observations a well-rounded theory, without any gaps; such a theory could only be the child of his speculations and not the fruit of an unprejudiced investigation of the facts.

SECOND LECTURE

Ladies and Gentlemen: At about the same time that Breuer was using the "talking-cure" with his patient, M. Charcot began in Paris, with the hystericals of the Salpetrière, those researches which were to lead to a new understanding of the disease. These results were, however, not yet known in Vienna. But when about ten years later Breuer and I published our preliminary communication on the psychic mechanism of hysterical phenomena, which grew out of the cathartic treatment of Breuer's first patient, we were both of us under the spell of Charcot's investigations. We made the pathogenic experiences of our patients, which acted as psychic traumata, equivalent to those physical traumata whose influence on hysterical paralyses Charcot had determined; and Breuer's hypothesis of hypnoidal states is itself only an echo of the fact that Charcot had artificially reproduced those traumatic paralyses in hypnosis.

The great French observer, whose student I was during the years 1885-86, had no natural bent for creating psychological theories. His student, P. Janet, was the first to attempt to penetrate more deeply into the psychic processes of hysteria, and we followed his example, when we made the mental splitting and the dissociation of personality the central points of our theory. Janet propounds a theory of hysteria which draws upon the principal theories of heredity and degeneration which are current in France. According to his view hysteria is a form of degenerative alteration of the nervous system, manifesting itself in a congenital "weakness" of the function of psychic synthesis. The hysterical patient is from the start incapable of correlating and unifying the manifold of his mental processes, and so there arises the tendency to mental dissociation. If you will permit me to use a banal but clear illustration, Janet's hysteria reminds one of a weak woman who has been shopping, and is now on her way home, laden with packages and bundles of every description. She cannot manage the whole lot with her two arms and her ten fingers, and soon she drops one. When she stoops to pick this up, another breaks loose, and so it goes on.

Now it does not agree very well, with this assumed mental weakness of hystericals, that there can be observed in hysterical cases, besides the phenomena of lessened functioning, examples of a partial increase of functional capacity, as a sort of compensation. At the time when Breuer's patient had forgotten her mother-tongue and all other languages save English, her control of English attained such a level that if a German book was put before her she could give a fluent, perfect translation of its contents at sight. When later I undertook to continue on my own account the investigations begun by Breuer, I soon came to another view of the origin of hysterical dissociation (or splitting of consciousness). It was inevitable that my views should diverge widely and radically, for my point of departure was not, like that of Janet, laboratory researches, but attempts at therapy. Above everything else, it was practical needs that urged me on. The cathartic treatment, as Breuer had made use of it, presupposed that the patient should be put in deep hypnosis, for only in hypnosis was available the knowledge of his pathogenic associations, which were unknown to him in his normal state. Now hypnosis, as a fanciful, and so to speak, mystical, aid, I soon came to dislike; and when I discovered that, in spite of all my efforts, I could not hypnotize by any means all of my patients, I resolved to give up hypnotism and to make the cathartic method independent of it.

Since I could not alter the psychic state of most of my patients at my wish, I directed my efforts to working with them in their normal state. This seems at first sight to be a particularly senseless and aimless undertaking. The problem was this: to find out something from the patient that the doctor did not know and the patient himself did not know. How could one hope to make such a method succeed? The memory of a very noteworthy and instructive proceeding came to my aid, which I had seen in Bernheim's clinic at Nancy. Bernheim showed us that persons put in a condition of hypnotic somnambulism, and subjected to all sorts of experiences, had only apparently lost the memory of those somnambulic experiences, and that their memory of them could be awakened even in the normal state. If he asked them about their experiences during somnambulism, they said at first that they did not remember, but if he persisted, urged, assured them that they did know, then every time the forgotten memory came back.

Accordingly I did this with my patients. When I had reached in my procedure with them a point at which they declared that they knew nothing more, I would assure them that they did know, that they must just tell it out, and I would venture the assertion that the memory which would emerge at the moment that I laid my hand on the patient's forehead would be the right one. In this way I succeeded, without hypnosis, in learning from the patient all that was necessary for a construction of the connection between the forgotten pathogenic scenes and the symptoms which they had left behind. This was a troublesome and in its length an exhausting proceeding, and did not lend itself to a finished technique. But I did not give it up without drawing definite conclusions from the data which I had gained. I had substantiated the fact that the forgotten memories were not lost. They were in the possession of the patient, ready to emerge and form associations with his other mental content, but hindered from becoming conscious, and forced to remain in the unconscious by some sort of a force. The existence of this force could be assumed with certainty, for in attempting to drag up the unconscious memories into the consciousness of the patient, in opposition to this force, one got the sensation of his own personal effort striving to overcome it. One could get an idea of this force, which maintained the pathological situation, from the resistance of the patient.

It is on this idea of *resistance* that I based my theory of the psychic processes of hystericals. It had been found that in order to cure the patient it was necessary that this force should be overcome. Now with the mechanism of the cure as a starting point, quite a definite theory could be constructed. These same forces, which in the present situation as resistances opposed the emergence of the forgotten ideas into consciousness, must themselves have caused the forgetting, and repressed from consciousness the pathogenic experiences. I called this hypothetical process "repression" (*Verdrängung*), and considered that it was proved by the undeniable existence of resistance.

But now the question arose: what were those forces, and what were the conditions of this repression, in which we were now able to recognize the pathogenic mechanism of hysteria? A comparative study of the pathogenic situations, which the cathartic treatment has made possible, allows us to answer this question. In all those experiences, it had happened that a wish had been aroused, which was in sharp opposition to the other desires of the individual, and was not capable of being reconciled with the ethical, aesthetic and personal pretensions of the patient's personality. There had been a short conflict, and the end of this inner struggle was the repression of the idea which presented itself to consciousness as the bearer of this irreconcilable wish. This was, then, repressed from consciousness and forgotten. The incompatibility of the idea in question with the "ego" of the patient was the motive of the repression, the ethical and other pretensions of the individual were the repressing forces. The presence of the incompatible wish, or the duration of the conflict, had given rise to a high degree of mental pain; this pain was avoided by the repression. This latter process is evidently in such a case a device for the protection of the personality.

I will not multiply examples, but will give you the history of a single one of my cases, in which the conditions and the utility of the repression process stand out clearly enough. Of course for my purpose I must abridge the history of the case and omit many valuable theoretical considerations. It is that of a young girl, who was deeply attached to her father, who had died a short time before, and in whose care she had shared — a situation analogous to that of Breuer's patient. When her older sister married, the girl grew to feel a peculiar sympathy for her new brother-in-law, which easily passed with her for family tenderness. This sister soon fell ill and died, while the patient and her mother were away. The absent ones were hastily recalled, without being told fully of the painful situation. As the girl stood by the bedside of her dead sister, for one short moment there surged up in her mind an idea, which might be framed in these words: "Now he is free and can marry me." We may be sure that this idea, which betrayed to her consciousness her intense love for her brother-in-law, of which she had not been conscious, was the next moment consigned to repression by her revolted feelings. The girl fell ill with severe hysterical symptoms, and, when I came to treat the case, it appeared that she had entirely forgotten that scene at her sister's bedside and the unnatural, egoistic desire which had arisen in her. She remembered it during the treatment, reproduced the pathogenic moment with every sign of intense emotional excitement, and was cured by this treatment.[10]

Perhaps I can make the process of repression and its necessary relation to the resistance of the patient, more concrete by a rough illustration, which I will derive from our present situation.

Suppose that here in this hall and in this audience, whose exemplary stillness and attention I cannot sufficiently commend, there is an individual who is creating a disturbance, and, by his ill-bred laughing, talking, by scraping his feet, distracts my attention from my task. I explain that I cannot go on with my lecture under these conditions, and thereupon several strong men among you get up, and, after a short struggle, eject the disturber of the peace from the hall. He is now "repressed," and I can continue my lecture. But in order that the disturbance may not be repeated, in case the man who has just been thrown out attempts to force his way back into the room, the gentlemen who have executed my suggestion take their chairs to the door and establish themselves there as a "resistance," to keep up the repression. Now, if you transfer both locations to the psyche, calling this "consciousness," and the outside the "unconscious," you have a tolerably good illustration of the process of repression.

We can see now the difference between our theory and that of Janet. We do not derive the psychic fission from a congenital lack of capacity on the part of the mental apparatus to synthesize its experiences, but we explain it dynamically by the conflict of opposing mental forces; we recognize in it the result of an active striving of each mental complex against the other.

New questions at once arise in great number from our theory. The situation of psychic conflict is a very frequent one; an attempt of the ego to defend itself from painful memories can be observed everywhere, and yet the result is not a mental fission. We cannot avoid the assumption that still other conditions are necessary, if the conflict is to result in dissociation. I willingly concede that with the assumption of "repression" we stand, not at the end, but at the very beginning of a psychological theory. But we can advance only one step at a time, and the completion of our knowledge must await further and more thorough work.

Now do not attempt to bring the case of Breuer's patient under the point of view of repression. This history cannot be subjected to such an attempt, for it was gained with the help of hypnotic influence. Only when hypnosis is excluded can you see the resistances and repressions and get a correct idea of the pathogenic process. Hypnosis conceals the resistances and so makes a certain part of the mental field freely accessible. By this same process the resistances on the borders of this field are heaped up into a rampart, which makes all beyond inaccessible.

The most valuable things that we have learned from Breuer's observations were his conclusions as to the connection of the symptoms with the pathogenic experiences or psychic traumata, and we must not neglect to evaluate this result properly from the standpoint of the repression-theory. It is not at first evident how we can get from the repression to the creation of the symptoms. Instead of giving a complicated theoretical derivation, I will return at this point to the illustration which I used to typify repression.

Remember that with the ejection of the rowdy and the establishment of the watchers before the door, the affair is not necessarily ended. It may very well happen that the ejected man, now embittered and quite careless of consequences, gives us more to do. He is no longer among us, we are free from his presence, his scornful laugh, his half-audible remarks, but in a certain sense the repression has miscarried, for he makes a terrible uproar outside, and by his outcries and by hammering on the door with his fists interferes with my lecture more than before. Under these circumstances it would be hailed with delight if possibly our honored president, Dr. Stanley Hall, should take upon himself the role of peacemaker and mediator. He would speak with the rowdy on the outside, and then turn to us with the recommendation that we let him in again, provided he would guarantee to behave himself better. On Dr. Hall's authority we decide to stop the repression, and now quiet and peace reign again. This is in fact a fairly good presentation of the task devolving upon the physician in the psychoanalytic therapy of neuroses. To say the same thing more directly: we come to the conclusion, from working with hysterical patients and other neurotics, that they have not fully succeeded in repressing the idea to which the incompatible wish is attached. They have, indeed, driven it out of consciousness and out of memory, and apparently saved themselves a great amount of psychic pain, *but in the unconscious the suppressed wish still exists,* only waiting for its chance to become active, and finally succeeds in sending into consciousness, instead of the repressed idea, a disguised and unrecognizable surrogate-creation (*Ersatzbildung*), to which the same painful sensations associate themselves that the patient thought he was rid of through his repression. This surrogate of the suppressed idea — the symptom — is secure against further attacks from the defenses of the ego, and instead of a short conflict there originates now a permanent suffering. We can observe in the symptom, besides the tokens of its disguise, a remnant of traceable similarity with the originally repressed idea; the way in which the surrogate is built up can be discovered during the psychoanalytic treatment of the patient, and for his cure the symptom must be traced back over the same route to the repressed idea. If this repressed material is once more made part of the conscious mental functions — a process which supposes the overcoming of considerable resistance — the psychic conflict which then arises, the same which the patient wished to avoid, is made capable of a happier termination, under the guidance of the physician, than is offered by repression. There are several possible suitable decisions which can bring conflict and neurosis to a happy end; in particular cases the attempt may be made to combine several of these. Either the personality of the patient may be convinced that he has been wrong in rejecting the pathogenic wish, and he may be made to accept it either wholly or in part; or this wish may itself be directed to a higher goal which is free from objection, by what is called sublimation (*Sublimierung*); or the rejection may be recognized as rightly motivated, and the automatic and therefore insufficient mechanism of repression be reinforced by the higher, more characteristically human mental faculties: one succeeds in mastering his wishes by conscious thought.

Forgive me if I have not been able to present more clearly these main points of the treatment which is today known as "psychoanalysis." The difficulties do not lie merely in the newness of the subject.

Regarding the nature of the unacceptable wishes, which succeed in making their influence felt out of the unconscious, in spite of repression; and regarding the question of what subjective and constitutional factors must be present for such a failure of repression and such a surrogate or symptom creation to take place, we will speak in later remarks.

THIRD LECTURE

Ladies and Gentlemen: It is not always easy to tell the truth, especially when one must be brief, and so today I must correct an incorrect statement that I made in my last lecture.

I told you how when I gave up using hypnosis I pressed my patients to tell me what came into their minds that had to do with the problem we were working on. I told them that they would remember what they had apparently forgotten, and that the thought which irrupted into consciousness (*Einfall*) would surely embody the memory for which we were seeking. I claimed that I substantiated the fact that the first idea of my patients brought the right clue and could be shown to be the forgotten continuation of the memory. Now this is not always so; I represented it as being so simple only for purposes of abbreviation. In fact, it would only happen the first times that the right forgotten material would emerge through simple pressure on my part. If the experience was continued, ideas emerged in every case which could not be the right ones, for they were not to the purpose, and the patients themselves rejected them as incorrect. Pressure was of no further service here, and one could only regret again having given up hypnosis. In this state of perplexity I clung to a prejudice which years later was proved by my friend C. G. Jung of the University of Zürich, and his pupils to have a scientific justification. I must confess that it is often of great advantage to have prejudices. I put a high value on the strength of the determination of mental processes, and I could not believe that any idea which occurred to the patient, which originated in a state of concentrated attention, could be quite arbitrary and out of all relation to the forgotten idea that we were seeking. That it was not identical with the latter, could be satisfactorily explained by the hypothetical psychological situation. In the patients whom I treated there were two opposing forces: on the one hand the conscious striving to drag up into consciousness the forgotten experience which was present in the unconscious; and on the other hand the resistance which we have seen, which set itself against the emergence of the suppressed idea or its associates into consciousness. In case this resistance was nonexistent or very slight, the forgotten material could become conscious without disguise (*Enstellung*). It was then a natural supposition that the disguise would be the more complete, the greater the resistance to the emergence of tbe idea. Thoughts which broke into the patient's consciousness instead of the ideas sought for, were accordingly made up just like symptoms; they were new, artificial, ephemeral surrogates for the repressed ideas, and differed from these just in proportion as they had been more completely disguised under the influence of the resistances. These surrogates must, however, show a certain similarity with the ideas which are the object of our search, by virtue of their nature as symptoms; and when the resistance is not too intensive it is possible from the nature of these irruptions to discover the hidden object of our search. This must be related to the repressed thought as a sort of allusion, as a statement of the same thing in *indirect* terms.

We know cases in normal psychology in which analogous situations to the one which we have assumed give rise to similar experiences. Such a case is that of wit. By my study of psychoanalytic technique I was necessarily led to a consideration of the problem of the nature of wit. I will give one example of this sort, which, too, is a story that originally appeared in English.

The anecdote runs: [11]Two unscrupulous business men had succeeded by fortunate speculations in accumulating a large fortune, and then directed their efforts to breaking into good society. Among other means they thought it would be of advantage to be painted by the most famous and expensive artist of the city, a man whose paintings were considered as events. The costly paintings were first shown at a great soirée and both hosts led the most influential connoisseur and art critic to the wall of the salon on which the portraits were hung, to elicit his admiring judgment. The artist looked for a long time, looked about as though in search of something, and then merely asked, pointing out the vacant space between the two pictures, "And where is the Saviour?"

I see that you are all laughing over this good example of wit, which we will now attempt to analyse. We understand that the critic means to say; "You are a couple of malefactors, like those between whom the Saviour was crucified." But he does not say this, he expresses himself instead in a way that at first seems not to the purpose and not related to the matter in hand, but which at the next moment we recognize as an *allusion* to the insult at which he aims, and as a perfect surrogate for it. We cannot expect to find in the case of wit all those relations that our theory supposes for the origin of the irruptive ideas of our patients, but it is my desire to lay stress on the similar motivation of wit and irruptive idea. Why does not the critic say directly what he has to say to the two rogues? Because, in addition to his desire to say it straight out, he is actuated by strong opposite motives. It is a proceeding which is liable to be dangerous to offend people who are one's hosts, and who can call to their aid the strong arms of numerous servants. One might easily suffer the same fate that I used in the previous lecture to illustrate repression. On this ground, the critic does not express the particular insult directly, but in a disguised form, as an allusion with omission. The same constellation comes into play, according to our hypothesis, when our patient produces the irruptive idea as a surrogate for the forgotten idea which is the object of the quest.

Ladies and gentlemen, it is very useful to designate a group of ideas which belong together and have a common emotive tone, according to the custom of the Zürich school (Bleuler, Jung and others), as a "complex." So we can say that if we set out from the last memories of the patient to look for a repressed complex, that we have every prospect of discovering it, if only the patient will communicate to us a sufficient number of the ideas which come into his head. So we let the patient speak along any line that he desires, and cling to the hypothesis that nothing can occur to him except what has some indirect bearing on the complex that we are seeking. If this method of discovering the repressed complexes seems too circumstantial, I can at least assure you that it is the only available one.

In practicing this technique, one is further bothered by the fact that the patient often stops, is at a standstill, and considers that he has nothing to say; nothing occurs to him. If this were really the case and the patient were right, our procedure would again be proven inapplicable. Closer observation shows that such an absence of ideas never really occurs, and that it only appears to when the patient holds back or rejects the idea which he perceives, under the influence of the resistance, which disguises itself as critical judgment of the value of the idea. The patient can be protected from this if he is warned in advance of this circumstance, and told to take no account of the critical attitude. He must say anything that comes into his mind, fully laying aside such critical choice, even though he may think it unessential, irrelevant, nonsensical, especially when the idea is one which is unpleasant to dwell on. By following this prescription we secure the material which sets us on the track of the repressed complex.

These irruptive ideas, which the patient himself values little, if he is under the influence of the resistance and not that of the physician, are for the psychologist like the ore, which by simple methods of interpretation he reduces from its crude state to valuable metal. If one desires to gain in a short time a preliminary knowledge of the patient's repressed complexes, without going into the question of their arrangement and associations, this examination may be conducted with the help of the association experiments, as Jung [12] and his pupils have perfected them. This procedure is to the psychologist what qualitative analysis is to the chemist; it may be dispensed with in the therapy of neurotic patients, but is indispensable in the investigations of the psychoses, which have been begun by the Zürich school with such valuable results.

This method of work with whatever comes into the patient's head when he submits to psychoanalytic treatment, is not the only technical means at our disposal for the widening of consciousness. Two other methods of procedure serve the same purpose, the interpretation of his dreams and the evaluation of acts which he bungles or does without intending to *(Fehl- und Zufallshandlungen).*

I might say, esteemed hearers, that for a long time I hesitated whether instead of this hurried survey of the whole field of psychoanalysis, I should not rather offer you a thorough consideration of the analysis of dreams; a purely subjective and apparently secondary motive decided me against this. It seemed rather an impropriety that in this country, so devoted to practical pursuits, I should pose as "interpreter of dreams," before you had a chance to discover what significance the old and despised art can claim.

Interpretation of dreams is in fact the *via regia* to the interpretation of the unconscious, the surest ground of psychoanalysis and a field in which every worker must win his convictions and gain his education. If I were asked how one could become a psychoanalist [sic], I should answer, through the study of his own dreams. With great tact all opponents of the psychoanalytic theory have so far either evaded any criticism of the "*Traumdeutung*" [13] or have attempted to pass over it with the most superficial objections. If, on the contrary, you will undertake the solution of the problems of dream life, the novelties which psychoanalysis present to your thoughts will no longer be difficulties.

You must remember that our nightly dream productions show the greatest outer similarity and inner relationship to the creations of the insane, but on the other hand are compatible with full health during waking life. It does not sound at all absurd to say that whoever regards these normal sense illusions, these delusions and alterations of character as matter for amazement instead of understanding, has not the least prospect of understanding the abnormal creations of diseased mental states in any other than the lay sense. You may with confidence place in this lay group all the psychiatrists of today. Follow me now on a brief excursion through the field of dream problems.

In our waking state we usually treat dreams with as little consideration as the patient treats the irruptive ideas which the psychoanalyst demands from him. It is evident that we reject them, for we forget them quickly and completely. The slight valuation which we place on them is based, with those dreams that are not confused and nonsensical, on the feeling that they are foreign to our personality, and, with other dreams, on their evident absurdity and senselessness. Our rejection derives support from the unrestrained shamelessness and the immoral longings which are obvious in many dreams. Antiquity, as we know, did not share this light valuation of dreams. The lower classes of our people today stick close to the value which they set on dreams; they, however, expect from them, as did the ancients, the revelation of the future. I confess that I see no need to adopt mystical hypotheses to fill out the gaps in our present knowledge, and so I have never been able to find anything that supported the hypothesis of the prophetic nature of dreams. Many other things, which are wonderful enough, can be said about them.

And first, not all dreams are so foreign to the character of the dreamer, are incomprehensible and confused. If you will undertake to consider the dreams of young children from the age of a year and a half on, you will find them quite simple and easy to interpret. The young child always dreams of the fulfillment of wishes which were aroused in him the day before and were not satisfied. You need no art of interpretation to discover this simple solution, you only need to inquire into the experiences of the child on the day before (the "dream day"). Now it would certainly be a most satisfactory solution of the dream-riddle, if the dreams of adults, too, were the same as those of children, fulfillments of wishes which had been aroused in them during the dream day. This is actually the fact; the difficulties which stand in the way of this solution can be removed step by step by a thorough analysis of the dream.

There is, first of all, the most weighty objection, that the dreams of adults generally have an incomprehensible content, which shows wish-fulfillment least of anything. The answer is this: these dreams have undergone a process of disguise, the psychic content which underlies them was originally meant for quite different verbal expression. You must differentiate between the *manifest dream-content*, which we remember in the morning only confusedly, and with difficulty clothe in words which seem arbitrary, and the *latent dream-thoughts*, whose presence in the unconscious we must assume. This distortion of the dream *(Traumentstellung)* is the same process which has been revealed to you in the investigations of the creations (*symptoms*) of hysterical subjects; it points to the fact that the same opposition of psychic forces has its share in the creation of dreams as in the creation of symptoms.

The manifest dream-content is the disguised surrogate for the unconscious dream thoughts, and this disguising is the work of the defensive forces of the ego, of the resistances. These prevent the repressed wishes from entering consciousness during the waking life, and even in the relaxation of sleep they are still strong enough to force them to hide themselves by a sort of masquerading. The dreamer, then, knows just as little the sense of his dream as the hysterical knows the relation and significance of his symptoms. That there are latent dream-thoughts and that between them and the manifest dream-content there exists the relation just described, of this you may convince yourselves by the analysis of dreams, a procedure the technique of which is exactly that of psychoanalysis. You must abstract entirely from the apparent connection of the elements in the manifest dream and seek for the irruptive ideas which arise through free association, according to the psychoanalytic laws, from each separate dream element. From this material the latent dream thoughts may be discovered, exactly as one divines the concealed complexes of the patient from the fancies connected with his symptoms and memories. From the latent dream thoughts which you will find in this way, you will see at once how thoroughly justified one is in interpreting the dreams of adults by the same rubrics as those of children. What is now substituted for the manifest dream-content is the real sense of the dream, is always clearly comprehensible, associated with the impressions of the day before, and appears as the fulfilling of an unsatisfied wish. The manifest dream, which we remember after waking, may then be described as a *disguised* fulfillment of *repressed* wishes.

It is also possible by a sort of synthesis to get some insight into the process which has brought about the disguise of the unconscious dream thoughts as the manifest dream-content. We call this process "dream-work" *(Traumarbeit)*. This deserves our fullest theoretical interest, since here as nowhere else we can study the unsuspected psychic processes which are existent in the unconscious, or, to express it more exactly, *between* two such separate systems as the conscious and the unconscious. Among these newly discovered psychic processes, two, condensation (*Verdichtung*) and displacement or transvaluation, change of psychic accent (*Verschiebung*), stand out most prominently. Dream work is a special case of the reaction of different mental groupings on each other, and as such is the consequence of psychic fission. In all essential points it seems identical with the work of disguise, which changes the repressed complex in the case of failing repression into symptoms.

You will furthermore discover by the analysis of dreams, most convincingly your own, the unsuspected importance of the role which impressions and experiences from early childhood exert on the development of men. In the dream life the child, as it were, continues his existence in the man, with a retention of all his traits and wishes, including those which he was obliged to allow to fall into disuse in his later years. With irresistible might it will be impressed on you by what processes of development, of repression, sublimation and reaction there arises out of the child, with its peculiar gifts and tendencies, the so-called normal man, the bearer and partly the victim of our painfully acquired civilization. I will also direct your attention to the fact that we have discovered from the analysis of dreams that the unconscious makes use of a sort of symbolism, especially in the presentation of sexual complexes. This symbolism in part varies with the individual, but in part is of a typical nature, and seems to be identical with the symbolism which we suppose to lie behind our myths and legends. It is not impossible that these latter creations of the people may find their explanation from the study of dreams.

Finally, I must remind you that you must not be led astray by the objection that the occurrence of anxiety-dreams (*Angsttraüme*) contradicts our idea of the dream as a wish-fulfillment. Apart from the consideration that anxiety-dreams also require interpretation before judgment can be passed on them, one can say quite generally that the anxiety does not depend in such a simple way on the dream content as one might suppose without more knowledge of the facts, and more attention to the conditions of neurotic anxiety. Anxiety is one of the ways in which the ego relieves itself of repressed wishes which have become too strong, and so is easy to explain in the dream, if the dream has gone too far towards the fulfilling of the objectionable wish.

You see that the investigation of dreams was justified by the conclusions which it has given us concerning things otherwise hard to understand. But we came to it in connection with the psychoanalytic treatment of neurotics. From what has been said you can easily understand how the interpretation of dreams, if it is not made too difficult by the resistance of the patient, can lead to a knowledge of the patient's concealed and repressed wishes and the complexes which he is nourishing. I may now pass to that group of everyday mental phenomena whose study has become a technical help for psychoanalysis.

These are the bungling of acts *(Feldhandlungen)* among normal men as well as among neurotics, to which no significance is ordinarily attached; the forgetting of things which one is supposed to know and at other times really does know (for example the temporary forgetting of proper names); mistakes in speaking (*Versprechen*), which occur so frequently; analogous mistakes in writing (*Verschreiben*) and in reading (*Verlesen*), the automatic execution of purposive acts in wrong situations (*Vergreifen*) and the loss or breaking of objects, etc. These are trifles, for which no one has ever sought a psychological determination, which have passed unchallenged as chance experiences, as consequences of absent-mindedness, inattention and similar conditions. Here, too, are included the acts and gestures executed without being noticed by the subject, to say nothing of the fact that he attaches no psychic importance to them; as playing and trifling with objects, humming melodies, handling one's person and clothing and the like.[14]

These little things, the bungling of acts, like the symptomatic and chance acts (*Symptom und Zufallshandlungen*) are not so entirely without meaning as is generally supposed by a sort of tacit agreement. They have a meaning, generally easy and sure to interpret from the situation in which they occur, and it can be demonstrated that they either express impulses and purposes which are repressed, hidden if possible from the consciousness of the individual, or that they spring from exactly the same sort of repressed wishes and complexes which we have learned to know already as the creators of symptoms and dreams.

It follows that they deserve the rank of symptoms, and their observation, like that of dreams, can lead to the discovery of the hidden complexes of the psychic life. With their help one will usually betray the most intimate of his secrets. If these occur so easily and commonly among people in health, with whom repression has on the whole succeeded fairly well, this is due to their insignificance and their inconspicuous nature. But they can lay claim to high theoretic value, for they prove the existence of repression and surrogate creations even under the conditions of health. You have already noticed that the psychoanalyst is distinguished by an especially strong belief in the determination of the psychic life. For him there is in the expressions of the psyche nothing trifling, nothing arbitrary and lawless, he expects everywhere a widespread motivation, where customarily such claims are not made; more than that, he is even prepared to find a manifold motivation of these psychic expressions, while our supposedly inborn causal need is satisfied with a single psychic cause.

Now keeping in mind the means which we possess for the discovery of the hidden, forgotten, repressed things in the soul life: the study of the irruptive ideas called up by free association, the patient's dreams, and his bungled and symptomatic acts; and adding to these the evaluation of other phenomena which emerge during the psychoanalytic treatment, on which I shall later make a few remarks under the heading of "transfer" (*Uebertragung*), you will come with me to the conclusion that our technique is already sufficiently efficacious for the solution of the problem of how to introduce the pathogenic psychic material into consciousness, and so to do away with the suffering brought on by the creation of surrogate symptoms.

The fact that by such therapeutic endeavors our knowledge of the mental life of the normal and the abnormal is widened and deepened, can of course only be regarded as an especial attraction and superiority of this method.

I do not know whether you have gained the impression that the technique through whose arsenal I have led you is a peculiarly difficult one. I consider that on the contrary, for one who has mastered it, it is quite adapted for use. But so much is sure, that it is not obvious, that it must be learned no less than the histological or the surgical technique.

You may be surprised to learn that in Europe we have heard very frequently judgments passed on psychoanalysis by persons who knew nothing of its technique and had never practised it, but who demanded scornfully that we show the correctness of our results. There are among these people some who are not in other things unacquainted with scientific methods of thought, who for example would not reject the result of a microscopical research because it cannot be confirmed with the naked eye in anatomical preparations, and who would not pass judgment until they had used the microscope. But in matters of psychoanalysis circumstances are really more unfavorable for gaining recognition. Psychoanalysis will bring the repressed in mental life to conscious acknowledgment, and every one who judges it is himself a man who has such repressions perhaps only maintained with difficulty. It will consequently call forth the same resistances from him as from the patient, and this resistance can easily succeed in disguising itself as intellectual rejection, and bring forward arguments similar to those from which we protect our patients by the basic principles of psychoanalysis. It is not difficult to substantiate in our opponents the same impairment of intelligence produced by emotivity which we may observe every day with our patients.

The arrogance of consciousness which for example rejects dreams so lightly, belongs — quite generally — to the strongest protective apparatus which guards us against the breaking through of the unconscious complexes, and as a result it is hard to convince people of the reality of the unconscious, and to teach them anew, what their conscious knowledge contradicts.

FOURTH LECTURE

Ladies and Gentlemen: At this point you will be asking what the technique which I have described has taught us of the nature of the pathogenic complexes and repressed wishes of neurotics.

One thing in particular: psychoanalytic investigations trace back the symptoms of disease with really surprising regularity to impressions from the sexual life, show us that the pathogenic wishes are of the nature of erotic impulse-components (*Triebkomponente*), and necessitate the assumption that to disturbances of the erotic sphere must be ascribed the greatest significance among the etiological factors of the disease. This holds of both sexes.

I know that this assertion will not willingly be credited. Even those investigators who gladly follow my psychological labors, are inclined to think that I overestimate the etiological share of the sexual moments. They ask me why other mental excitations should not lead to the phenomena of repression and surrogate-creation which I have described. I can give them this answer; that I do not know why they should not do this, I have no objection to their doing it, but experience shows that they do not possess such a significance, and that they merely support the effect of the sexual moments, without being able to supplant them. This conclusion was not a theoretical postulate; in the *Studien über Hysterie,* published in 1895 with Dr. Breuer, I did not stand on this ground. I was converted to it when my experience was richer and had led me deeper into the nature of the case. Gentlemen, there are among you some of my closest friends and adherents, who have travelled to Worcester with me. Ask them, and they will tell you that they all were at first completely sceptical of the assertion of the determinative significance of the sexual etiology, until they were compelled by their own analytic labors to come to the same conclusion.

The conduct of the patients does not make it any easier to convince one's self of the correctness of the view which I have expressed. Instead of willingly giving us information concerning their sexual life, they try to conceal it by every means in their power. Men generally are not candid in sexual matters. They do not show their sexuality freely, but they wear a thick overcoat — a fabric of lies — to conceal it, as though it were bad weather in the world of sex. And they are not wrong; sun and wind are not favorable in our civilized society to any demonstration of sex life. In truth no one can freely disclose his erotic life to his neighbor. But when your patients see that in your treatment they may disregard the conventional restraints, they lay aside this veil of lies, and then only are you in a position to formulate a judgment on the question in dispute. Unfortunately physicians are not favored above the rest of the children of men in their personal relationship to the questions of the sex life. Many of them are under the ban of that mixture of prudery and lasciviousness which determines the behaviour of most *Kulturmenschen* in affairs of sex.

Now to proceed with the communication of our results. It is true that in another series of cases psychoanalysis at first traces the symptoms back not to the sexual, but to banal traumatic experiences. But the distinction loses its significance through other circumstances. The work of analysis which is necessary for the thorough explanation and complete cure of a case of sickness does not stop in any case with the experience of the time of onset of the disease, but in every case it goes back to the adolescence and the early childhood of the patient. Here only do we hit upon the impressions and circumstances which determine the later sickness. Only the childhood experiences can give the explanation for the sensitivity to later traumata and only when these memory traces, which almost always are forgotten, are discovered and made conscious, is the power developed to banish the symptoms. We arrive here at the same conclusion as in the investigation of dreams — that it is the incompatible, repressed wishes of childhood which lend their power to the creation of symptoms. Without these the reactions upon later traumata discharge normally. But we must consider these mighty wishes of childhood very generally as sexual in nature.

Now I can at any rate be sure of your astonishment. Is there an infantile sexuality? you will ask. Is childhood not rather that period of life which is distinguished by the lack of the sexual impulse? No, gentlemen, it is not at all true that the sexual impulse enters into the child at puberty, as the devils in the gospel entered into the swine. The child has his sexual impulses and activities from the beginning, he brings them with him into the world, and from these the so-called normal sexuality of adults emerges by a significant development through manifold stages. It is not very difficult to observe the expressions of this childish sexual activity; it needs rather a certain art to overlook them or to fail to interpret them.[15]

As fate would have it, I am in a position to call a witness for my assertions from your own midst. I show you here the work of one Dr. Sanford Bell, published in 1902 in the *American Journal of Psychology.* The author was a fellow of Clark University, the same institution within whose walls we now stand. In this thesis, entitled "A Preliminary Study of the Emotion of Love between the Sexes," which appeared three years before my "Drei Abhandlungen zur Sexualtheorie, " the author says just what I have been saying to you: "The emotion of sex love . . . does not make its appearance for the first time at the period of adolescence as has been thought." He has, as we should say in Europe, worked by the American method, and has gathered not less than 2,500 positive observations in the course of fifteen years, among them 800 of his own. He says of the signs by which this amorous condition manifests itself: "The unprejudiced mind, in observing these manifestations in hundreds of couples of children, cannot escape referring them to sex origin. The most exacting mind is satisfied when to these observations are added the confessions of those who have as children experienced the emotion to a marked degree of intensity, and whose memories of childhood are relatively distinct." Those of you who are unwilling to believe in infantile sexuality will be most astonished to hear that among those children who fell in love so early not a few are of the tender ages of three, four, and five years.

It would not be surprising if you should believe the observations of a fellow-countryman rather than my own. Fortunately a short time ago from the analysis of a five-year-old boy who was suffering from anxiety, an analysis undertaken with correct technique by his own father,[16] I succeeded in getting a fairly complete picture of the bodily expressions of the impulse and the mental productions of an early stage of childish sexual life. And I must remind you that my friend, Dr. C. G. Jung, read you a few hours ago in this room an observation on a still younger girl who from the same cause as my patient — the birth of a little child in the family — betrayed certainly almost the same secret excitement, wish and complex-creation. Accordingly I am not without hope that you may feel friendly toward this idea of infantile sexuality that was so strange at first. I might also quote the remarkable example of the Zürich psychiatrist, E. Bleuler, who said a few years ago openly that he faced my sexual theories incredulous and bewildered, and since that time by his own observations had substantiated them in their whole scope.[17] If it is true that most men, medical observers and others, do not want to know anything about the sexual life of the child, the fact is capable of explanation only too easily. They have forgotten their own infantile sexual activity under the pressure of education for civilization and do not care to be reminded now of the repressed material. You will be convinced otherwise if you begin the investigation by a self-analysis, by an interpretation of your own childhood memories.

Lay aside your doubts and let us evaluate the infantile sexuality of the earliest years.[18] The sexual impulse of the child manifests itself as a very complex one; it permits of an analysis into many components, which spring from different sources. It is entirely disconnected from the function of reproduction which it is later to serve. It permits the child to gain different sorts of pleasure sensations, which we include, by the analogues and connections which they show, under the term sexual pleasures. The great source of infantile sexual pleasure is the auto-excitation of certain particularly sensitive parts of the body; besides the genitals are included the rectum and the opening of the urinary canal, and also the skin and other sensory surfaces. Since in this first phase of child sexual life the satisfaction is found on the child's own body and has nothing to do with any other object, we call this phase after a word coined by Havelock Ellis, that of "auto-erotism." The parts of the body significant in giving sexual pleasure we call "erogenous zones." The thumb-sucking (*Ludeln*) or passionate sucking (*Wonnesaugen*) of very young children is a good example of such an auto-erotic satisfaction of an erogenous zone. The first scientific observer of this phenomenon, a specialist in children's diseases in Budapest by the name of Lindner, interpreted these rightly as sexual satisfaction and described exhaustively their transformation into other and higher forms of sexual gratification.[19] Another sexual satisfaction of this time of life is the excitation of the genitals by masturbation, which has such a great significance for later life and, in the case of many individuals, is never fully overcome. Besides this and other auto-erotic manifestations we see very early in the child the impulse-components of *sexual pleasure*, or, as we may say, of the *libido*, which presupposes a second person as its object. These impulses appear in opposed pairs, as active and passive. The most important representatives of this group are the pleasure in inflicting pain (sadism) with its passive opposite (masochism) and active and passive exhibition pleasure (*Schaulust*). From the first of these later pairs splits off the curiosity for knowledge, as from the latter the impulse toward artistic and theatrical representation. Other sexual manifestations of the child can already be regarded from the view-point of object-choice, in which the second person plays the prominent part. The significance of this was primarily based upon motives of the impulse of self-preservation. The difference between the sexes plays, however, in the child no very great role. One may attribute to every child, without wronging him, a bit of the homosexual disposition.

The sexual life of the child, rich, but dissociated, in which each single impulse goes about the business of arousing pleasure independently of every other, is later correlated and organized in two general directions, so that by the close of puberty the definite sexual character of the individual is practically finally determined. The single impulses subordinate themselves to the overlordship of the genital zone, so that the whole sexual life is taken over into the service of procreation, and their gratification is now significant only so far as they help to prepare and promote the true sexual act. On the other hand, object-choice prevails over auto-erotism, so that now in the sexual life all components of the sexual impulse are satisfied in the loved person. But not all the original impulse components are given a share in the final shaping of the sexual life. Even before the advent of puberty certain impulses have undergone the most energetic repression under the impulse of education, and mental forces like shame, disgust and morality are developed, which, like sentinels, keep the repressed wishes in subjection. When there comes, in puberty, the high tide of sexual desire it finds dams in this creation of reactions and resistances. These guide the outflow into the so-called normal channels, and make it impossible to revivify the impulses which have undergone repression.

The most important of these repressed impulses are koprophilism, that is, the pleasure in children connected with the excrements; and, further, the tendencies attaching themselves to the persons of the primitive object-choice.

Gentlemen, a sentence of general pathology says that every process of development brings with it the germ of pathological dispositions in so far as it may be inhibited, delayed, or incompletely carried out. This holds for the development of the sexual function, with its many complications. It is not smoothly completed in all individuals, and may leave behind either abnormalities or disposition to later diseases by the way of later falling back or *regression.* It may happen that not all the partial impulses subordinate themselves to the rule of the genital zone. Such an impulse which has remained disconnected brings about what we call a perversion, which may replace the normal sexual goal by one of its own. It may happen, as has been said before, that the auto-erotism is not fully overcome, as many sorts of disturbances testify. The originally equal value of both sexes as sexual objects may be maintained and an inclination to homosexual activities in adult life result from this, which, under suitable conditions, rises to the level of exclusive homosexuality. This series of disturbances corresponds to the direct inhibition of development of the sexual function, it includes the perversions and the general *infantilism* of the sex life that are not seldom met with.

The disposition to neuroses is to be derived in another way from an injury to the development of the sex life. The neuroses are related to the perversions as the negative to the positive; in them we find the same impulse-components as in perversions, as bearers of the complexes and as creators of the symptoms; but here they work from out of the unconscious. They have undergone a repression, but in spite of this they maintain themselves in the unconscious. Psychoanalysis teaches us that overstrong expression of the impulse in very early life leads to a sort of fixation *(Fixirung),* which then offers a weak point in the articulation of the sexual function. If the exercise of the normal sexual function meets with hindrances in later life, this repression, dating from the time of development, is broken through at just that point at which the infantile fixation took place.

You will now perhaps make the objection: "But all that is not sexuality." I have used the word in a very much wider sense than you are accustomed to understand it. This I willingly concede. But it is a question whether you do not rather use the word in much too narrow a sense when you restrict it to the realm of procreation. You sacrifice by that the understanding of perversions; of the connection between perversion, neurosis and normal sexual life; and have no means of recognizing, in its true significance, the easily observable beginning of the somatic and mental sexual life of the child. But however you decide about the use of the word, remember that the psychoanalyst understands sexuality in that full sense to which he is led by the evaluation of infantile sexuality.

Now we turn again to the sexual development of the child. We still have much to say here, since we have given more attention to the somatic than to the mental expressions of the sexual life. The primitive object-choice of the child, which is derived from his need of help, demands our further interest. It first attaches to all persons to whom he is accustomed, but soon these give way in favor of his parents. The relation of the child to his parents is, as both direct observation of the child and later analytic investigation of adults agree, not at all free from elements of sexual accessory excitation *(Miterregung).* The child takes both parents, and especially one, as an object of his erotic wishes. Usually he follows in this the stimulus given by his parents, whose tenderness has very clearly the character of a sex manifestation, though inhibited so far as its goal is concerned. As a rule, the father prefers the daughter, the mother the son; the child reacts to this situation, since, as son, he wishes himself in the place of his father, as daughter, in the place of the mother. The feelings awakened in these relations between parents and children, and, as a resultant of them, those among the children in relation to each other, are not only positively of a tender, but negatively of an inimical sort. The complex built up in this way is destined to quick repression, but it still exerts a great and lasting effect from the unconscious. We must express the opinion that this with its ramifications presents the *nuclear complex* of every neurosis, and so we are prepared to meet with it in a not less effectual way in the other fields of mental life. The myth of King Oedipus, who kills his father and wins his mother as a wife is only the slightly altered presentation of the infantile wish, rejected later by the opposing barriers of incest. Shakespeare's tale of Hamlet rests on the same basis of an incest complex, though better concealed. At the time when the child is still ruled by the still unrepressed nuclear complex, there begins a very significant part of his mental activity which serves sexual interest. He begins to investigate the question of where children come from and guesses more than adults imagine of the true relations by deduction from the signs which he sees. Usually his interest in this investigation is awakened by the threat to his welfare through the birth of another child in the family, in whom at first he sees only a rival. Under the influence of the partial impulses which are active in him he arrives at a number of "infantile sexual theories," as that the same male genitals belong to both sexes, that children are conceived by eating and born through the opening of the intestine, and that sexual intercourse is to be regarded as an inimical act, a sort of overpowering.

But just the unfinished nature of his sexual constitution and the gaps in his knowledge brought about by the hidden condition of the feminine sexual canal, cause the infant investigator to discontinue his work as a failure. The facts of this childish investigation itself as well as the infant sex theories created by it are of determinative significance in the building of the child's character, and in the content of his later neuroses.

It is unavoidable and quite normal that the child should make his parents the objects of his first object-choice. But his *libido* must not remain fixed on these first chosen objects, but must take them merely as a prototype and transfer from these to other persons in the time of definite object-choice. The breaking loose (*Ablösung*) of the child from his parents is thus a problem impossible to escape if the social virtue of the young individual is not to be impaired. During the time that the repressive activity is making its choice among the partial sexual impulses and later, when the influence of the parents, which in the most essential way has furnished the material for these repressions, is lessened, great problems fall to the work of education, which at present certainly does not always solve them in the most intelligent and economic way.

Gentlemen, do not think that with these explanations of the sexual life and the sexual development of the child we have too far departed from psychoanalysis and the cure of neurotic disturbances. If you like, you may regard the psychoanalytic treatment only as a continued education for the overcoming of childhood-remnants (*Kindheitsresten*).

FIFTH LECTURE

Ladies and Gentlemen: With the discovery of infantile sexuality and the tracing back of the neurotic symptoms to erotic impulse-components we have arrived at several unexpected formulae for expressing the nature and tendencies of neurotic diseases. We see that the individual falls ill when in consequence of outer hindrances or inner lack of adaptability the satisfaction of the erotic needs in the sphere of reality is denied. We see that he then flees to sickness, in order to find with its help a surrogate satisfaction for that denied him. We recognize that the symptoms of illness contain fractions of the sexual activity of the individual, or his whole sexual life, and we find in the turning away from reality the chief tendency and also the chief injury of the sickness. We may guess that the resistance of our patients against the cure is not a simple one, but is composed of many motives. Not only does the ego of the patient strive against the giving up of the repressions by which it has changed itself from its original constitution into its present form, but also the sexual impulses may not renounce their surrogate satisfaction so long as it is not certain that they can be offered anything better in the sphere of reality.

The flight from the unsatisfying reality into what we call, on account of its biologically injurious nature, disease, but which is never without an individual gain in pleasure for the patient, takes place over the path of regression, the return to earlier phases of the sexual life, when satisfaction was not lacking. This regression is seemingly a twofold one, a *temporal*, in so far as the *libido* or erotic need falls back to a temporally earlier stage of development, and a *formal*, since the original and primitive psychic means of expression are applied to the expression of this need. Both sorts of regression focus in childhood and have their common point in the production of an infantile condition of sexual life.

The deeper you penetrate into the pathogenesis of neurotic diseases, the more the connection of neuroses with other products of human mentality, even the most valuable, will be revealed to you. You will be reminded that we men, with the high claims of our civilization and under the pressure of our repressions, find reality generally quite unsatisfactory and so keep up a life of fancy in which we love to compensate for what is lacking in the sphere of reality by the production of wish-fulfillments. In these phantasies is often contained very much of the particular constitutional essence of personality and of its tendencies, repressed in real life. The energetic and successful man is he who succeeds by dint of labor in transforming his wish fancies into reality. Where this is not successful in consequence of the resistance of the outer world and the weakness of the individual, there begins the turning away from reality. The individual takes refuge in his satisfying world of fancy. Under certain favorable conditions it still remains possible for him to find another connecting link between these fancies and reality, instead of permanently becoming a stranger to it through the regression into the infantile. If the individual who is displeased with reality is in possession of that *artistic talent* which is still a psychological riddle, be can transform his fancies into artistic creations. So he escapes the fate of a neurosis and wins back his connection with reality by this round-about way.[20] Where this opposition to the real world exists, but this valuable talent fails or proves insufficient, it is unavoidable that the *libido*, following the origin of the fancies, succeeds by means of regression in revivifying the infantile wishes and so producing a neurosis. The neurosis takes, in our time, the place of the cloister, in which were accustomed to take refuge all those whom life had undeceived or who felt themselves too weak for life. Let me give at this point the main result at which we have arrived by the psychoanalytic investigation of neurotics, namely, that neuroses have no peculiar psychic content of their own, which is not also to be found in healthy states; or, as C. G. Jung has expressed it, neurotics fall ill of the same complexes with which we sound, people struggle. It depends on quantitative relationships, on the relations of the forces wrestling with each other, whether the struggle leads to health, to a neurosis, or to compensatory over-functioning (*Ueberleistung*).

Ladies and gentlemen, I have still withheld from you the most remarkable experience which corroborates our assumptions of the sexual impulse-forces of neurotics. Every time that we treat a neurotic psychoanalytically, there occurs in him the so-called phenomenon of *transfer* (Uebertragung), that is, he applies to the person of the physician a great amount of tender emotion, often mixed with enmity, which has no foundation in any real relation, and must be derived in every respect from the old wish-fancies of the patient which have become unconscious. Every fragment of his emotive life, which can no longer be called back into memory, is accordingly lived over by the patient in his relations to the physician, and only by such a living of them over in the "transfer" is he convinced of the existence and the power of these unconscious sexual excitations. The symptoms, which, to use a simile from chemistry, are the precipitates of earlier love experiences (in the widest sense), can only be dissolved in the higher temperature of the experience of transfer and transformed into other psychic products. The physician plays in this reaction, to use an excellent expression of S. Ferenczi,[21] the role of a *catalytic ferment*, which temporarily attracts to itself the affect which has become free in the course of the process.

The study of transfer can also give you the key to the understanding of hypnotic suggestion, which we at first used with our patients as a technical means of investigation of the unconscious. Hypnosis showed itself at that time to be a therapeutic help, but a hindrance to the scientific knowledge of the real nature of the case, since it cleared away the psychic resistances from a certain field, only to pile them up in an unscalable wall at the boundaries of this field. You must not think that the phenomenon of transfer, about which I can unfortunately say only too little here, is created by the influence of the psychoanalytic treatment. The transfer arises spontaneously in all human relations and in the relations of the patient to the physician; it is everywhere the especial bearer of therapeutic influences, and it works the stronger the less one knows of its presence. Accordingly psychoanalysis does not create it, it merely discloses it to consciousness, and avails itself of it, in order to direct the psychic processes to the wished for goal. But I cannot leave the theme of transfer without stressing the fact that this phenomenon is of decisive importance to convince not only the patient, but also the physician. I know that all my adherents were first convinced of the correctness of my views through their experience with transfer, and I can very well conceive that one may not win such a surety of judgment so long as he makes no psychoanalysis, and so has not himself observed the effects of transfer.

Ladies and gentlemen, I am of the opinion that there are, on the intellectual side, two hindrances to acknowledging the value of the psychoanalytic viewpoint: first, the fact that we are not accustomed to reckon with a strict determination of mental life, which holds without exception, and second, the lack of knowledge of the peculiarities through which unconscious mental processes differ from those conscious ones with which we are familiar. One of the most widespread resistances against the work of psychoanalysis with patients as with persons in health reduces to the latter of the two moments. One is afraid of doing harm by psychoanalysis, one is anxious about calling up into consciousness the repressed sexual impulses of the patient, as though there were danger that they could overpower the higher ethical strivings and rob him of his cultural acquisitions. One can see that the patient has sore places in his soul life, but one is afraid to touch them, lest his suffering be increased. We may use this analogy. It is, of course, better not to touch diseased places when one can only cause pain. But we know that the surgeon does not refrain from the investigation and reinvestigation of the seat of illness, if his invasion has as its aim the restoration of lasting health. Nobody thinks of blaming him for the unavoidable difficulties of the investigation or the phenomena of reaction from the operation, if these only accomplish their purpose, and gain for the patient a final cure by temporarily making his condition worse. The case is similar in psychoanalysis; it can lay claim to the same things as surgery; the increase of pain which takes place in the patient during the treatment is very much less than that which the surgeon imposes upon him, and especially negligible in comparison with the pains of serious illness. But the consequence which is feared, that of a disturbance of the cultural character by the impulse which has been freed from repression, is wholly impossible. In relation to this anxiety we must consider what our experiences have taught us with certainty, that the somatic and mental power of a wish, if once its repression has not succeeded, is incomparably stronger when it is unconscious than when it is conscious, so that by being made conscious it can only be weakened. The unconscious wish cannot be influenced, is free from all strivings in the contrary direction, while the conscious is inhibited by those wishes which are also conscious and which strive against it. The work of psychoanalysis accordingly presents a better substitute, in the service of the highest and most valuable cultural strivings, for the repression which has failed.

Now what is the fate of the wishes which have become free by psychoanalysis, by what means shall they be made harmless for the life of the individual? There are several ways. The general consequence is, that the wish is consumed during the work by the correct mental activity of those better tendencies which are opposed to it. The repression is supplanted by a condemnation carried through with the best means at one's disposal. This is possible, since for the most part we have to abolish only the effects of earlier developmental stages of the ego. The individual for his part only repressed the useless impulse, because at that time he was himself still incompletely organized and weak; in his present maturity and strength he can, perhaps, conquer without injury to himself that which is inimical to him. A second issue of the work of psychoanalysis may be that the revealed unconscious impulses can now arrive at those useful applications which, in the case of undisturbed development, they would have found earlier. The extirpation of the infantile wishes is not at all the ideal aim of development. The neurotic has lost, by his repressions, many sources of mental energy whose contingents would have been very valuable for his character building and his life activities. We know a far more purposive process of development, the so-called *sublimation* (*Sublimirung*), by which the energy of infantile wish-excitations is not secluded, but remains capable of application, while for the particular excitations, instead of becoming useless, a higher, eventually no longer sexual, goal is set up. The components of the sexual instinct are especially distinguished by such a capacity for the sublimation and exchange of their sexual goal for one more remote and socially more valuable. To the contributions of the energy won in such a way for the functions of our mental life we probably owe the highest cultural consequences. A repression taking place at an early period excludes the sublimation of the repressed impulse; after the removal of the repression the way to sublimation is again free.

We must not neglect, also, to glance at the third of the possible issues. A certain part of the suppressed libidinous excitation has a right to direct satisfaction and ought to find it in life. The claims of our civilization make life too hard for the greater part of humanity, and so further the aversion to reality and the origin of neuroses, without producing an excess of cultural gain by this excess of sexual repression. We ought not to go so far as to fully neglect the original animal part of our nature, we ought not to forget that the happiness of individuals cannot be dispensed with as one of the aims of our culture. The plasticity of the sexual-components, manifest in their capacity for sublimation, may cause a great temptation to accomplish greater culture-effects by a more and more far reaching sublimation. But just as little as with our machines we expect to change more than a certain fraction of the applied heat into useful mechanical work, just as little ought we to strive to separate the sexual impulse in its whole extent of energy from its peculiar goal. This cannot succeed, and if the narrowing of sexuality is pushed too far it will have all the evil effects of a robbery.

I do not know whether you will regard the exhortation with which I close as a presumptuous one. I only venture the indirect presentation of my conviction, if I relate an old tale, whose application you may make yourselves. German literature knows a town called Schilda, to whose inhabitants were attributed all sorts of clever pranks. The wiseacres, so the story goes, had a horse, with whose powers of work they were well satisfied, and against whom they had only one grudge, that he consumed so much expensive oats. They concluded that by good management they would break him of this bad habit, by cutting down his rations by several stalks each day, until he had learned to do without them altogether. Things went finely for a while, the horse was weaned to one stalk a day, and on the next day he would at last work without fodder. On the morning of this day the malicious horse was found dead; the citizens of Schilda could not understand why he had died. We should be inclined to believe that the horse had starved, and that without a certain ration of oats no work could be expected from an animal.

I thank you for calling me here to speak, and for the attention which you have given me.

FOOTNOTES

[1.] Lectures delivered at the Celebration of the Twentieth Anniversary of the opening of Clark University, Sept., 1909; translated from the German by Harry W. Chase, Fellow in Psychology, Clark University, and revised by Prof. Freud.

[2.] Dr. Joseph Breuer, born 1842, corresponding member of the "Kaiserliche Akademie der Wissenschaften," is known by works on respiration and the physiology of the sense of equilibrium.

[3.] "Studien über Hysterie," 1895, Deuticke, Vienna. Second edition, 1909. Parts of my contributions to this book have been translated into English by Dr. A. A. Brill, of New York. ("Selected Papers on Hysteria and other Psychoneuroses," by S. Freud.)

[4.] I know that this view no longer holds today, but in the lecture I take myself and my hearers back to the time before 1880. If things have become different since that time it has been largely due to the work the history of which I am sketching.

[5.] "Studien über Hysterie," 2d edition, p. 26.

[6.] ["]Studien über Hysterie," 2d edition, p. 31.

[7.] "Studien über Hysterie," 2d edition, p. 30.

[8.] *Loc Cit.*, 2d ed. Pp. 43-46. A selection from this book, augmented by several later treatises on hysteria, lies before me, in an English translation by Dr. A. A. Brill, of New York. It bears the title "Selected Papers on Hysteria and other Psychoneuroses," 1909. (No. 4 of the Nervous and Mental Disease Monograph Series, New York.]

[9.] Or rather the later copy of such a monument. The name "Charing" is itself, as Dr. E. Jones tells me, derived from the words *"chère reine."*

[10.] This case has been translated by Dr. Brill in "Selected papers on hysteria," etc., p. 31— F 4.

[11.] Der Witz und seine Beziehung zum Unbewussten. Deuticke, Vienna, 1905, p. 59.

[12.] C. G. Jung: Diagnostische Assoziationsstudien, B. 1, 1906.

[13.] Die Traumdeutung: 2d edition. Deuticke, Vienna, 1909.

[14.] Zur Psychopathologie des Alltagslebens- 3d edition, 1910. S. Kargar, Berlin.

[15.] Drei Abhandlungen zur Sexualtheorie. Wien, F. Deuticke, 1908, 2d ed.

[16.] Analyse der Phobie eines 5-jährigen Knaben. Jahrbuch f. Psychoanalytische u. psychopathologische Forschungen. B. 1, H. 1., 1909. [In the original, this footnote is cited in the text as note 2 on page 208, but is given as note 3 at the bottom of the page.]

[17.] Bleuler: Sexuelle Abnormitäten der Kinder. Jahrbuch der schweizer, Gesellschaft für Schulgesundheitspflege. IX, 1908.

[18.] Drei Abhandlungen zur Sexualtheorie, Vienna, 1910, 2d ed.

[19.] Jahıbuch f. Kinderheilkunde, 1879.

[20.] Compare, Rank, Otto: Der Künstler, Ansätze zu einer Sexual-Psychologie. 56 p. Heller & Co., Wien, 1907.

[21.] S. Ferenczi: Introduction und Uebertragung. Jahrbuch f. psychoanal. u. psychopath. Forschungen, Bd. 1, H. 2., 1909.

8 The Split Brain in Man

by Michael S. Gazzaniga

The human brain is actually two brains, each capable of advanced mental functions. When the cerebrum is divided surgically, it is as if the cranium contained two separate spheres of consciousness.

The brain of the higher animals, including man, is a double organ, consisting of right and left hemispheres connected by an isthmus of nerve tissue called the corpus callosum. Some 15 years ago Ronald E. Myers and R.W. Speny, then at the University of Chicago, made a surprising discovery: When this connection between the two halves of the cerebrum was cut, each hemisphere functioned independently as if it were a complete brain. The phenomenon was first investigated in a cat in which not only the brain but also the optic chiasm, the crossover of the optic nerves, was divided, so that visual information from the left eye was dispatched only to the left brain and information from the right eye only to the right brain. Working on a problem with one eye, the animal could respond normally and learn to perform a task; when that eye was covered and the same problem was presented to the other eye, the animal evinced no recognition of the problem and had to learn it again from the beginning with the other half of the brain.

The finding introduced entirely new questions in the study of brain mechanisms. Was the corpus callosum responsible for integration of the operations of the two cerebral hemispheres in the intact brain? Did it serve to keep each hemisphere informed about what was going on in the other? To put the question another way, would cutting the corpus callosum literally result in the right hand not knowing what the left was doing? To what extent were the two half-brains actually independent when they were separated? Could they have separate thoughts, even separate emotions?

Such questions have been pursued by Sperry and his co-workers in a wide-ranging series of animal studies at the California Institute of Technology over the past decade [see "The Great Cerebral Commissure," by R.W. Sperry; SCIENTIFIC AMERICAN, January, 1964]. Recently these questions have been investigated in human patients who underwent the brain-splitting operation for medical reasons. The demonstration in experimental animals that sectioning of the corpus callosum did not seriously impair mental faculties had encouraged surgeons to resort to this operation for people afflicted with uncontrollable epilepsy. The hope was to confine a seizure to one hemisphere. The operation proved to be remarkably successful; curiously there is an almost total elimination of all attacks, including unilateral ones. It is as if the intact callosum had served in these patients to facilitate seizure activity.

This article is a brief survey of investigations Sperry and I have carried out at Cal Tech over the past five years with some of these patients. The operations were performed by P. J. Vogel and J. E. Bogen of the California College of Medicine. Our studies date back to 1961, when the first patient, a 48-year-old war veteran, underwent the operation: cutting of the corpus callosum and other commissure structures connecting the two halves of the cerebral cortex [see illustration on page 76]. As of today 10 patients have had the operation, and we have examined four thoroughly over a long period with many tests.

From the beginning one of the most striking observations was that the operation produced no noticeable change in the patients' temperament, personality or general intelligence. In the first case the patient could not speak for 30 days after the operation, but he then recovered his speech. More typical was the third case: on awaking from the surgery the patient quipped that he had a "splitting headache," and in his still drowsy state he was able to repeat the tongue twister "Peter Piper picked a peck of pickled peppers."

Close observation, however, soon revealed some changes in the patients' everyday behavior. For example, it could be seen that in moving about and responding to sensory stimuli the patients favored the right side of the body, which is controlled by the dominant left half of the brain. For a considerable period after the operation the left side of the body rarely showed spontaneous activity, and the patient generally did not respond to stimulation of that side: when he brushed against something with his left side he did not notice that he had done so, and when an object was placed in his left hand he generally denied its presence.

More specific tests identified the main features of the bisected-brain syndrome. One of these tests examined responses to visual stimulation. While the patient fixed his gaze on a central point on a board, spots of light were flashed (for a tenth of a second) in a row across the board that spanned both the left and the right half of his visual field. The patient was asked to tell what he had seen. Each patient reported that lights had been flashed in the right half of the visual field. When lights were flashed only in the left half of the field, however, the patients generally denied having seen any lights. Since the right side of the visual field is normally projected to the left hemisphere of the brain and the left field to the right hemisphere, one might have concluded that in these patients with divided brains the right hemisphere was in effect blind. We found, however, that this was not the case when the patients were directed to point to the lights that had flashed instead of giving a verbal report. With this manual response they were able to indicate when lights had been flashed in the left visual field, and perception with the brain's right hemisphere proved to be almost equal to perception with the left. Clearly, then, the patient's failure to report the right hemisphere's perception verbally was due to the fact that the speech centers of the brain are located in the left hemisphere.

Our tests of the patient's ability to recognize objects by touch at first resulted in the same general finding. When the object was held in the right hand, from which sensory information is sent to the left hemisphere, the patient was able to name and describe the object. When it was held in the left hand (from which information goes primarily to the right hemisphere), the patient could not describe the object verbally, but was able to identify it in a nonverbal test—matching it, for example, to the same object in a varied collection of things. We soon realized, however, that each hemisphere receives, in addition to the main input from the opposite side of the body, some input from the same side. This "ipsilateral" input is crude; it is apparently good mainly for "cuing in" the hemisphere as to the presence or absence of stimulation and relaying fairly gross information about the location of a stimulus on the surface of the body. It is unable, as a rule, to relay information concerning the qualitative nature of an object.

Tests of motor control in these split-brain patients revealed that the left hemisphere of the brain exercised normal control over the right hand but had less than full control of the left hand (for instance, it was poor at directing individual movements of fingers). Similarly, the right hemisphere had full control of the left hand but not of the right hand. When the two hemispheres were in conflict, dictating different movements for the same hand, the hemisphere on the side opposite the hand generally took charge and overruled the orders of the side of the brain with the weaker control. In general the motor findings in the human patients were much the same as those in split-brain monkeys.

We come now to the main question on which we centered our studies, namely how the separation of the hemispheres affects the mental capacities of the human brain. For these psychological tests we used two different devices. One was visual: a picture or written information was flashed (for a tenth of a second) in either the right or the left visual field, so that the information was transmitted only to the left or to the right brain hemisphere [see illustration on page 75]. The other type of test was tactile: an object was placed out of view in the patient's right or left hand,

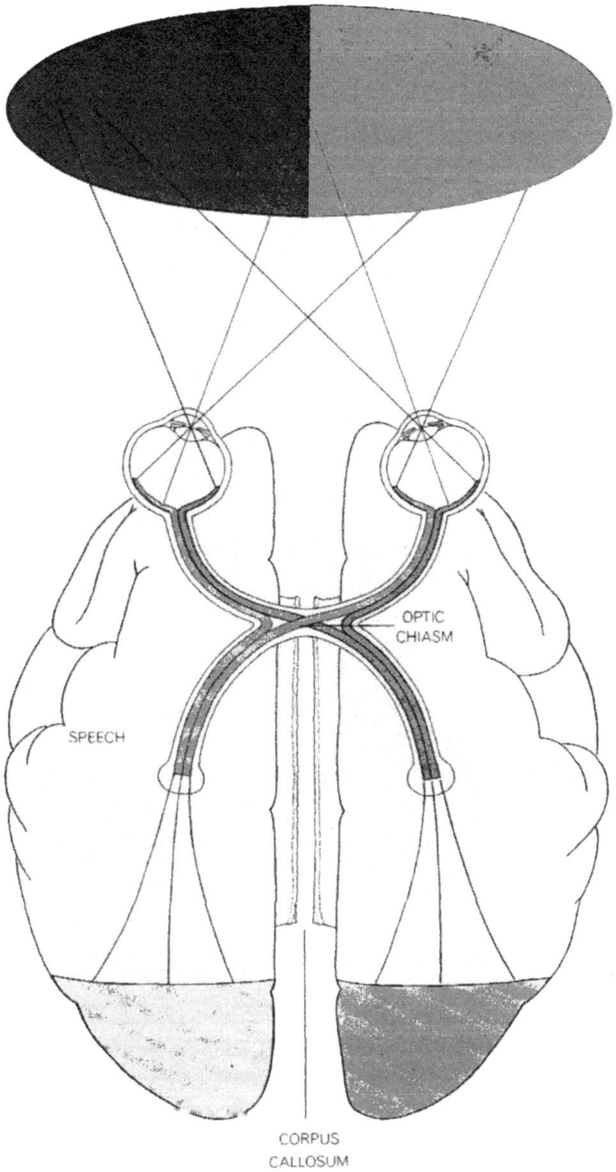

CORPUS CALLOSUM
VISUAL INPUT to bisected brain, was limited to one hemisphere by presenting information only in one visual field. The right and left fields of view are projected, via the optic chiasm, to the left and right hemispheres of the brain respectively. If a person fixes his gaze on a point, therefore, information to the left of the point goes only to the right hemisphere and information to the right of the point goes to the left hemisphere. Stimuli in the left visual field cannot be described by a split-brain patient because of the disconnection between the right hemisphere and the speech center, which is in the left hemisphere.

again for the purpose of conveying the information to just one hemisphere—the hemisphere on the side opposite the hand.

When the information (visual or tactile) was presented to the dominant left hemisphere, the patients were able to deal with and describe it quite normally, both orally and in writing. For example, when a picture of a spoon was shown in the right visual field or a spoon was placed in the right hand, all the patients readily identified and described it. They were able to read out written messages and to perform problems in calculation that were presented to the left hemisphere.

In contrast, when the same information was presented to the right hemisphere, it failed to elicit such spo-

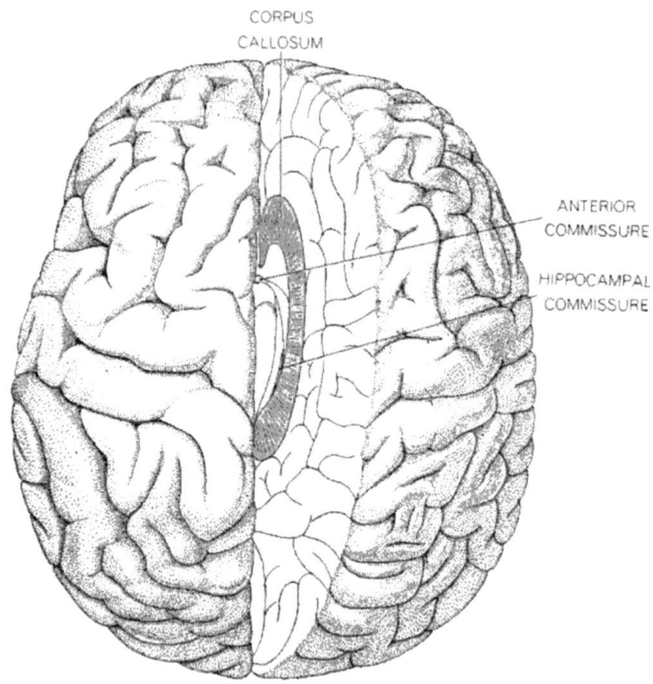

CORPUS CALLOSUM

TWO HEMISPHERES of the human brain are divided by neurosurgeons to control epileptic seizures. In this top view of the brain the right hemisphere is retracted and the corpus callosum and other commissures, or connectors, that are generally cut are shown in color.

ken or written responses. A picture transmitted to the right hemisphere evoked either a haphazard guess or no verbal response at all. Similarly, a pencil placed in the left hand (behind a screen that cut off vision) might be called a can opener or a cigarette lighter, or the patient might not even attempt to describe it. The verbal guesses presumably came not from the right hemisphere but from the left, which had no perception of the object but might attempt to identify it from indirect clues.

Did this impotence of the right hemisphere mean that its surgical separation from the left had reduced its mental powers to an imbecilic level? The earlier tests of its nonverbal capacities suggested that this was almost certainly not so. Indeed, when we switched to asking for nonverbal answers to the visual and tactile information presented in our new psychological tests, the right hemisphere in several patients showed considerable capacity for accurate performance. For example, when a picture of a spoon was presented to the right hemisphere, the patients were able to feel around with the left hand among a varied group of objects (screened from sight) and select a spoon as a match for the picture. Furthermore, when they were shown a picture of a cigarette they succeeded in selecting an ashtray, from a group of 10 objects that did not include a cigarette, as the article most closely related to the picture. Oddly enough however, even after their correct response, and while they were holding the spoon or the ashtray in their left hand, they were unable to name or describe the object or the picture. Evidently the left hemisphere was completely divorced, in perception and knowledge, from the right.

Other tests showed that the right hemisphere did possess a certain amount of language comprehension. For example, when the word "pencil" was flashed to the right hemisphere, the patients were able to pick out a pencil from a group of unseen objects with the left hand. And when a patient held an object in the left hand (out of view), although he could not say its name or describe it, he was later able to point to a card on which the name of the object was written. In one particularly interesting test the word "heart" was flashed across the center of the visual field, with the "he" portion to the left of the center and "art" to the right. Asked to tell what the word was, the patients would say they had seen "art"—the portion projected to the left brain hemisphere (which is responsible for speech). Curiously when, after "heart" had been flashed in the same way, the patients were asked to point with the left hand to one of two cards—"art" or "he"—to identify the word they had seen, they invariably pointed to "he." The experiment showed clearly that both hemispheres had simultaneously observed the portions of the word available to them and that in this particular case the right hemisphere, when it had had the opportunity to express itself, had prevailed over the left.

Because an auditory input to one ear goes to both sides of the brain, we conducted tests for the comprehension of words presented audibly to the right hemisphere not by trying to limit the original input but by limiting the ability to answer to the right hemisphere. This was done most easily by having a patient use his left hand to retrieve, from a grab bag held out of view, an object named by the examiner. We found that the patients could easily retrieve such objects as a watch, comb, marble or coin. The object to be retrieved did not even have to be named; it might simply be described or alluded to. For example, the command "Retrieve the fruit monkeys like best" results in the patients' pulling out a banana from a grab bag full of plastic fruit; at the command "Sunkist sells a lot of them" the patients retrieve an orange. We knew that touch information from the left hand was going exclusively to the right hemisphere because moments later, when the patients were asked to name various pieces of fruit placed in the left hand, they were unable to score above a chance level.

The upper limit of linguistic abilities in each hemisphere varies from subject to subject. In one case there was little or no evidence for language abilities in the right hemisphere, whereas in the other three the amount and extent of the capacities varied. The most adept patient showed some evidence of even being able to spell simple words by placing plastic letters on a table with his left hand. The subject was told to spell a word such as "pie," and the examiner then placed the three appropriate letters, one at a time in a random order, in his left hand to be arranged on the table. The patient was able to spell such words as "cup" and "love." Yet after he had completed this task, the patient was unable to name the word he had just spelled!

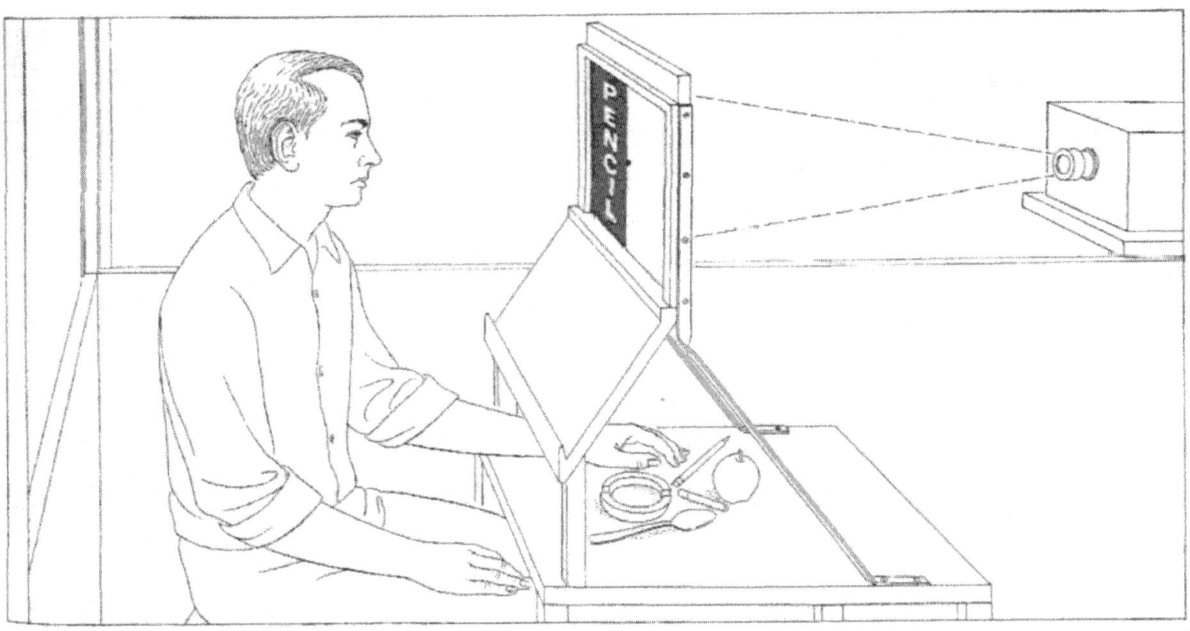

RESPONSE TO VISUAL STIMULUS is tested by flashing a word or a picture of an object on a translucent screen. The examiner first checks the subject's gaze to be sure it is fixed on a dot that marks the center of the visual field. The examiner may call for a verbal response—reading the flashed word, for example—or for a nonverbal one, such as picking up the object that is named from among a number of things spread on the table. The objects are hidden from the subject's view so that they can be identified only by touch.

The possibility that the right hemisphere has not only some language but even some speech capabilities cannot be ruled out, although at present there is no firm evidence for this. It would not be surprising to discover that the patients are capable of a few simple exclamatory remarks, particularly when under emotional stress. The possibility also remains, of course, that speech of some type could be trained into the right hemisphere. Tests aimed at this question, however, would have to be closely scrutinized and controlled.

The reason is that here, as in many of the tests, "cross-cuing" from one hemisphere to the other could be held responsible for any positive findings. We had a case of such cross-cuing during a series of tests of whether the right hemisphere could respond verbally to simple red or green stimuli. At first, after either a red or a green light was flashed to the right hemisphere, the patient would guess the color at a chance level, as might be expected if the speech mechanism is solely represented in the left hemisphere. After a few trials, however, the score improved whenever the examiner allowed a second guess.

We soon caught up on the strategy the patient used. If a red light was flashed and the patient by chance guessed red, he would stick with that answer. If the flashed light was red and the patient by chance guessed green, he would frown, shake his head and then say, "Oh no, I meant red." What was happening was that the right hemisphere saw the red light and heard the left hemisphere make the guess "green." Knowing that the answer was wrong, the right hemisphere precipitated a frown and a shake of the head, which in turn cued in the left hemisphere to the fact that the answer was wrong and that it had better correct itself! We have learned that this cross-cuing mechanism can become extremely refined. The realization that the neurological patient has various strategies at his command emphasizes how difficult it is to obtain a clear neurological description of a human being with brain damage.

Is the language comprehension by the right hemisphere that the patients exhibited in these tests a normal capability of that hemisphere or was it acquired by learning after their operation, perhaps during the course of the experiments themselves? The issue is difficult to decide. We must remember that we are examining a half of the human brain, a system easily capable of learning from a single trial in a test. We do know that the right hemisphere is decidedly inferior to the left in its overall command of language. We have established, for instance, that although the right hemisphere can respond to a concrete noun such as "pencil," it cannot do as well with verbs; patients are unable to respond appropriately to simple printed instructions, such as "smile" or "frown," when these words are flashed to the right hemisphere, nor can they point to a picture that corresponds to a flashed verb. Some of our recent studies at the University of California at Santa Barbara also indicate that the right hemisphere has a very poorly developed grammar; it seems to be incapable of forming the plural of a given word, for example.

In general, then, the extent of language present in the adult right hemisphere in no way compares with that present in the left hemisphere or, for that matter, with the extent of language present in the child's right hemisphere. Up to the age of four or so, it would appear from a variety of neurological observations, the right hemisphere is about as proficient in handling language as the left. Moreover, studies of the child's development of language, particularly with respect to grammar strongly suggest that the foundations of grammar—a ground plan for language, so to speak—are somehow inherent in the human organism and are fully realized between the ages of two and three. In other words, in the young child each hemisphere is about equally developed with respect to language and speech function. We are thus faced with the interesting question of why the right hemisphere at an early age and stage of development possesses substantial language capacity whereas at a more adult stage it possesses a rather poor capacity. It is difficult indeed to conceive of the underlying neurological mechanism that would allow for the establishment of a capacity of a high order in a particular hemisphere on a temporary basis. The implication is that during maturation the processes and systems active in making this capacity manifest are somehow inhibited and dismantled in the right hemisphere and allowed to side only in the dominant left hemisphere.

Yet the right hemisphere is not in all respects inferior or subordinate to the left. Tests have demonstrated that it excels the left in some specialized functions. As an example, tests by us and by Bogen have shown that in these patients the left hand is capable of arranging

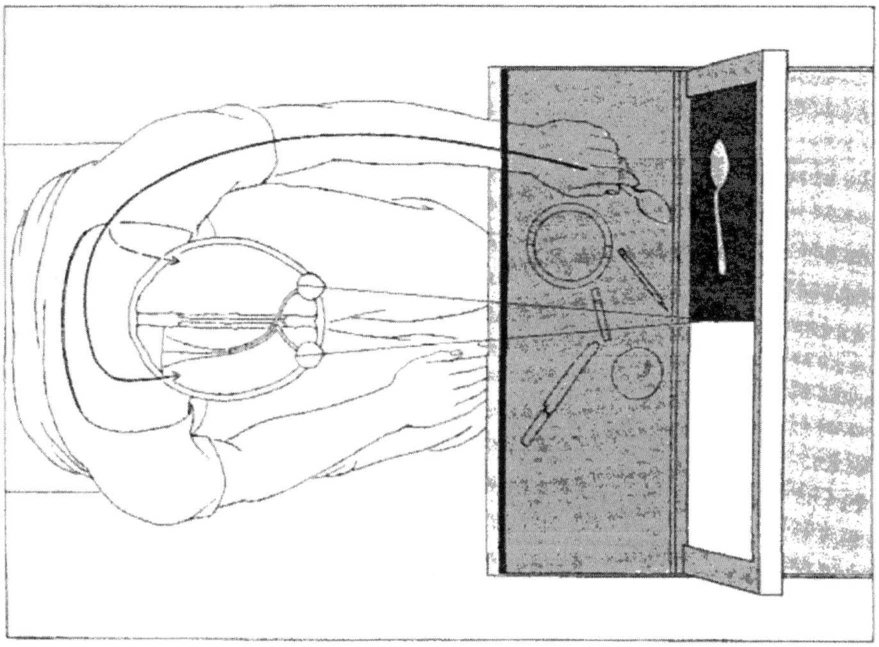

VISUAL-TACTILE ASSOCIATION is performed by a split-brain patient. A picture of a spoon is flashed to the right hemisphere; with the left hand he retrieves a spoon from behind the screen. The touch information from the left hand projects (color) mainly to the right hemisphere, but a weak "ipsilateral" component goes to the left hemisphere. This is usually not enough to enable him to say (using the left hemisphere) what he has picked up.

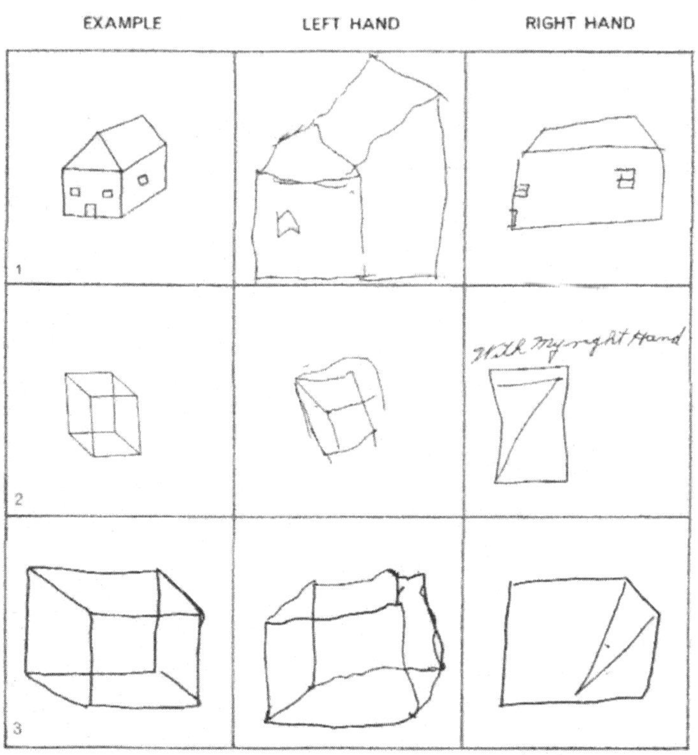

"VISUAL CONSTRUCTIONAL" tasks are handled better by the right hemisphere. This was seen most clearly in the first patient, who had poor ipsilateral control of his right hand. Although right-handed, he could copy the examples only with his left hand.

blocks to match a pictured design and of drawing a cube in three dimensions, whereas the right hand, deprived of instructions from the right hemisphere, could not perform either of these tasks.

It is of interest to note, however, that although the patients (our first subject in particular) could not execute such tasks with the right hand, they were capable of matching a test stimulus to the correct design when it appeared among five related patterns presented in their right visual field. This showed that the dominant left hemisphere is capable of discriminating between correct and incorrect stimuli. Since it is also true that the patients have no motor problems with their right hand, the patients' inability to perform these tasks must reflect a breakdown of an integrative process somewhere between the sensory system and the motor system.

We found that in certain other mental processes, the right hemisphere is on a par with the left. In particular, it can independently generate an emotional reaction. In one of our experiments exploring the matter we would present a series of ordinary objects and then suddenly flash a picture of a nude woman. This evoked an amused reaction regardless of whether the picture was presented to the left hemisphere or to the right. When the picture was flashed to the left hemisphere of a female patient, she laughed and verbally identified the picture as a nude. When it was later presented to the right hemisphere, she said in reply to a question that she saw nothing, but almost immediately a sly smile spread over her face and she began to chuckle. Asked what she was laughing at, she said: "I don't know...nothing...oh—that funny machine." Although the right hemisphere could not describe what it had seen, the sight nevertheless elicited an emotional response like the one evoked from the left hemisphere.

Taken together, our studies seem to demonstrate conclusively that in a split-brain situation we are really dealing with two brains, each capable of mental functions of a high order. This implies that the two brains should have twice as large a span of attention—that is, should be able to handle twice as much information—as a normal whole brain. We have not yet tested this precisely in human patients, but E. D. Young and I have found that a split-brain monkey can indeed deal with nearly twice as much information as a normal animal [see illustration below]. We have so far determined also that brain-bisected patients can carry out two tasks as fast as a normal person can do one.

Just how does the corpus callosum of the intact brain combine and integrate the perceptions and knowledge of the two cerebral hemispheres? This has been investigated recently by Giovanni Berlucchi, Giacomo Rizzolati and me at the Istituto di Fisiologia Umana in Pisa. We made recordings of neural activity in the posterior part of the callosum of the cat with the hope of relating the responses of that structure to stimulation

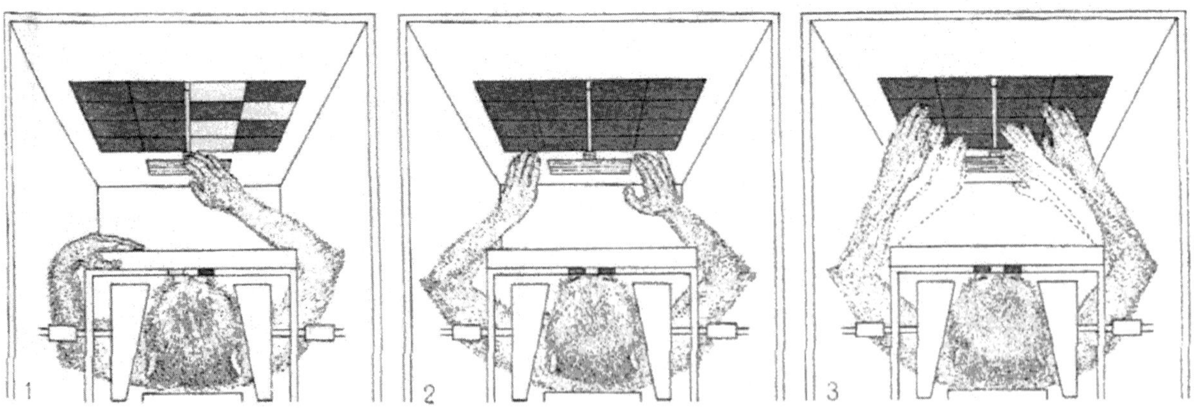

SPLIT-BRAIN MONKEYS can handle more visual information than normal animals. When the monkey pulls a knob (1), eight of the 16 panels light momentarily. The monkey must then start at the bottom and punch the lights that were lit and no others (2). With the panels lit for 600 milliseconds normal monkeys get up to the third row from the bottom before forgetting which panels were lit (3). Split-brain monkeys complete the entire task with the panels lit only 200 milliseconds. The monkeys look at the panels through filters; since the optic chiasm is cut in these animals, the filters allow each hemisphere to see the colored panels on one side only.

of the animal's visual fields. The kinds of responses recorded turned out to be similar to those observed in the visual cortext of the cat. In other words, the results suggest that visual pattern information can be transmitted through the callosum. This finding militates against the notion that learning and memory are transferred across the callosum, as has usually been suggested. Instead, it looks as though in animals with an intact callosum a copy of the visual world as seen in one hemisphere is sent over to the other, with the result that both hemispheres can learn together a discrimination presented to just one hemisphere. In the split-brain animal this extension of the visual pathway is cut off; this would explain rather simply why no learning proceeds in the visually isolated hemisphere and why it has to learn the discrimination from scratch.

Curiously, however, the neural activity in the callosum came only in response to stimuli at the midline of the visual field. This finding raises difficult questions. How can it be reconciled with the well-established observation that the left hemisphere of a normal person can give a running description of all the visual information presented throughout the entire half-field projected to the right hemisphere? For this reason alone one is wearily driven back to the conclusion that somewhere and somehow all or part of the callosum transmits not only a visual scene but also a complicated neural code of a lusher order.

All the evidence indicated that separation of the hemispheres creates two independent spheres of consciousness within a single cranium, that is to say, within a single organism. This conclusion is disturbing to some people who view consciousness as an indivisible property of the human brain. It seems premature to others, who insist that the capacities revealed thus far for the right hemisphere are at the level of an automaton. There is, to be sure, hemispheric inequality in the present cases, but it may well be a characteristic of the individuals we have studied. It is entirely possible that if a human brain were divided in a very young person, both hemispheres could as a result separately and independently develop mental functions of a high order at the level attained only in the left hemisphere of normal individuals.

9 The "Visual Cliff"

by Eleanor J. Gibson and Richard D. Walk

This simple apparatus is used to investigate depth perception in different animals. All species thus far tested seem able to perceive and avoid a sharp drop as soon as they can move about.

Human infants at the creeping and toddling stage are notoriously prone to falls from more or less high places. They must be kept from going over the brink by side panels on their cribs, gates on stairways and the vigilance of adults. As their muscular coordination matures they begin to avoid such accidents on their own. Common sense might suggest that the child learns to recognize falling-off places by experience—that is, by falling and hurting himself. But is experience really the teacher? Or is the ability to perceive and avoid a brink part of the child's original endowment?

Answers to these questions will throw lights on the genesis of space perception in general. Height perception is a special case of distance perception: information in the light reaching the eye provides stimuli that can be utilized for the discrimination both of depth and of receding distance on the level. At what stage of development can an animal respond effectively to these stimuli? Does the onset of such response vary with animals of different species and habitats?

At Cornell University we have been investigating these problems by means of a simple experimental setup that we call a visual cliff. The cliff is a simulated one and hence makes it possible not only to control the optical and other stimuli (auditory and tactual, for instance) but also to protect the experimental subjects. It consists of a board laid across a large sheet of heavy glass which is supported a foot or more above the floor. On one side of the board a sheet of patterned material is placed flush against the undersurface of the glass, giving the glass the appearance as well as the substance of solidity. On the other side a sheet of the same material is laid upon the floor; this side of the board thus becomes the visual cliff.

We tested 36 infants ranging in age from six months to 14 months on the visual cliff. Each child was placed upon the center board, and his mother called him to her from the cliff side and the shallow side successively. All of the 27 infants who moved off the board crawled out on the shallow side at least once; only three of them crept off the brink onto the glass suspended above the pattern on the floor. Many of the infants crawled away from the mother when she called to them from the cliff side; others cried when she stood there, because they could not come to her without crossing an apparent chasm. The experiment thus demonstrated that most human infants can discriminate depth as soon as they can crawl.

The behavior of the children in this situation gave clear evidence of their dependence on vision. Often they would peer down through the glass on the deep side and then back away. Others would pat the glass with their hands, yet despite this tactual assurance of solidity would refuse to cross. It was equally clear that their perception of depth had matured more rapidly than had their locomotor abilities. Many supported

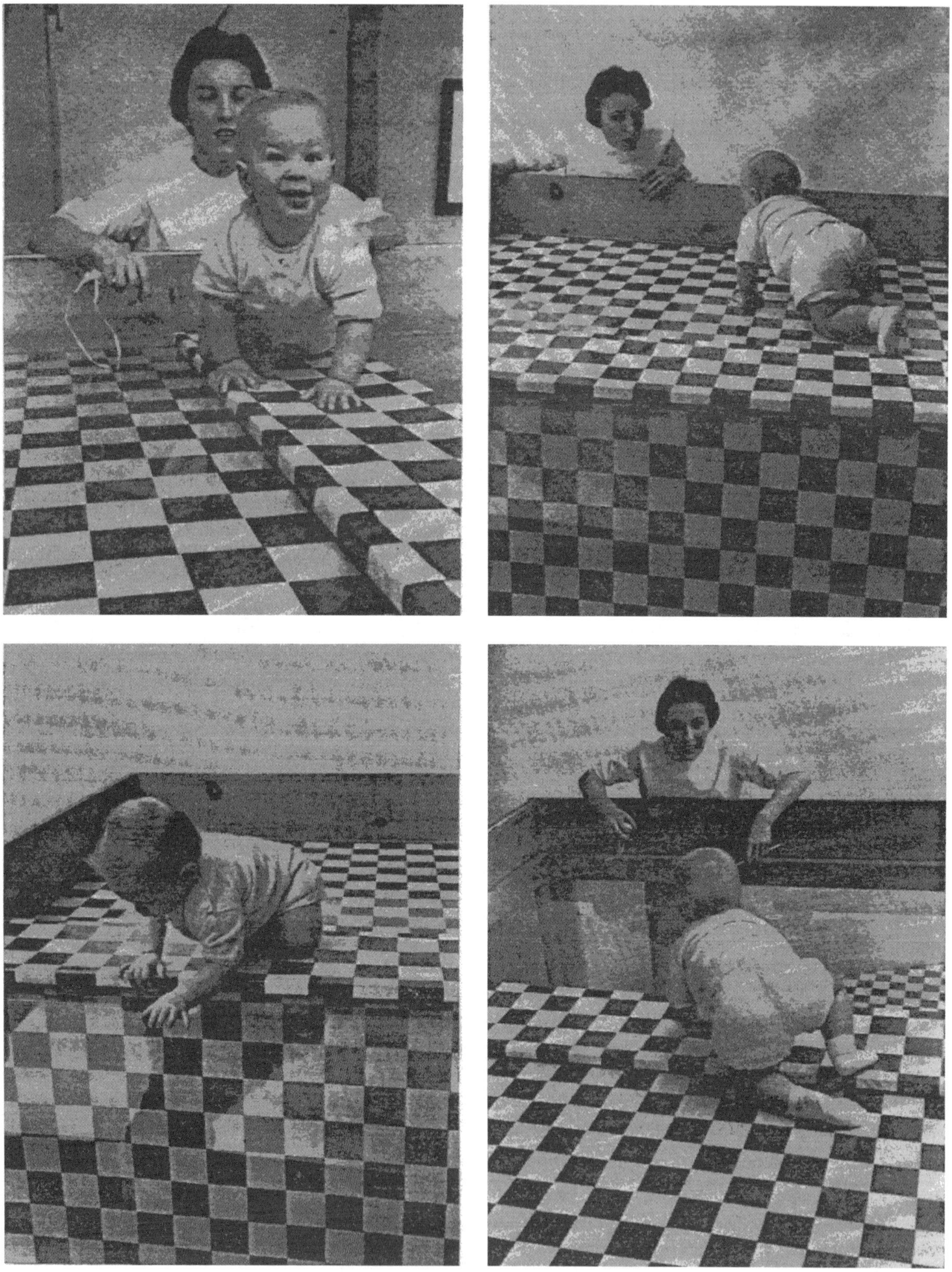

CHILD'S DEPTH PERCEPTION is tested on the visual cliff. The apparatus consists of a board laid across a sheet of heavy glass, with a patterned material directly beneath the glass on one side and several feet below it on the other. Placed in the center of the board (top left), the child crawls to its mother across the "shallow" side (top right). Called from the "deep" side, he pats the glass (bottom left), but despite this tactual evidence that the "cliff" is in fact a solid surface he refuses to cross over to the mother (bottom right).

themselves on the glass over the deep side as they maneuvered awkwardly on the board; some even backed out onto the glass as they started toward the mother on the shallow side. Were it not for the glass some of the children would have fallen off the board. Evidently infants should not be left close to a brink, no matter how well they may discriminate depth.

This experiment does not prove that the human infant's perception and avoidance of the cliff are

KITTEN'S DEPTH PERCEPTION also manifests itself at an early age. Though the animal displays no alarm on the shallow side (top), it "freezes" when placed on the glass over the deep side (bottom); in some cases it will crawl aimlessly backward in a circle.

innate. Such an interpretation is supported, however, by the experiments with nonhuman infants. On the visual cliff we have observed the behavior of chicks, turtles, rats, lambs, kids, pigs, kittens and dogs. These animals showed various reactions, each of which proved to be characteristic of their species. In each case the reaction is plainly related to the role of vision in the survival of the species, and the varied patterns of behavior suggest something about the role of vision in evolution.

In the chick, for example, depth perception manifests itself with special rapidity. At an age of less than 24 hours, the chick can be tested on the visual cliff. It never makes a "mistake" and always hops off the board on the shallow side. Without a doubt this finding is related to the fact that the chick, unlike many other young birds must scratch for itself a few hours after it is hatched.

Kids and lambs, like chicks, can be tested on the visual cliff as soon as they can stand. The response of these animals is equally predictable. No goat or lamb ever stepped onto the glass of the deep side, even at one day of age. When one of these animals was placed upon the glass on the deep side, it displayed characteristic stereotyped behavior. It would refuse to put its feet down and would back up into a posture of defense, its front legs rigid and its hind legs limp. In this state of immobility it could be pushed forward across the glass until its head and field of vision crossed the edge of the surrounding solid surface, whereupon it would relax and spring forward upon the surface.

At the Cornell Behavior Farm a group of experimenters has carried these experiments with kids and goats a step further. They fixed the patterned material to a sheet of plywood and were thus able to adjust the "depth" of the deep side. With the pattern held immediately beneath the glass, the animal would move about the glass freely. With the optical floor dropped more than a foot below the glass, the animal would immediately freeze into its defensive posture. Despite repeated experience of the tactual solidity of the glass, the animals never learned to function without optical support. Their sense of security or danger continued to depend upon the visual cues that give them their perception of depth.

GOATS SHOW DEPTH PERCEPTION at an age of only one day. A kid walks freely on the shallow side (top); on the deep side (middle) it leaps the "chasm" to safety (bottom).

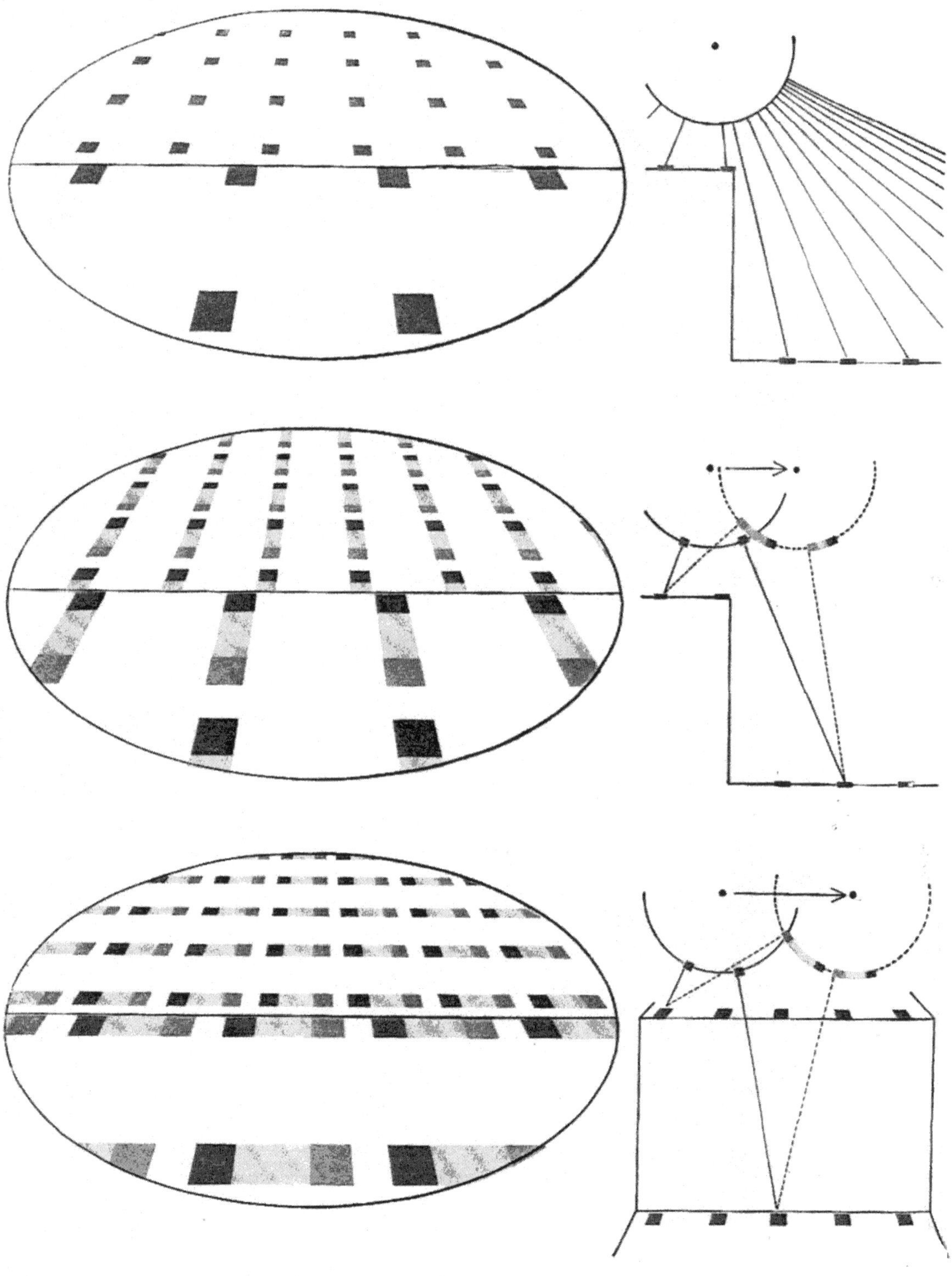

TWO TYPES OF VISUAL DEPTH-CUE are diagrammed schematically on this page. Ellipses approximate the visual field of an animal standing near the edge of the cliff and looking toward it; diagrams at right give the geometrical explanation of differences in the fields. The spacing of the pattern elements (solid color) decreases sharply beyond the edge of the cliff (top). The optical motion (shaded color) of the elements as the animal moves forward (center) or sideways (bottom) shows a similar drop-off.

The rat, in contrast, does not depend predominantly upon visual cues. Its nocturnal habits lead it to seek food largely by smell. When moving about in the dark, it responds to tactual cues from the stiff whiskers (vibrissae) on its snout. Hooded rats tested on the visual cliff show little preference for the shallow side so long as they can feel the glass with their vibrissae. Placed upon the glass over the deep side, they move about normally. But when we raise the center board several inches, so that the glass is out of reach of their whiskers, they evince good visual depth-discrimination: 95 to 100 per cent of them descend on the shallow side.

Cats, like rats, are nocturnal animals, sensitive to tactual cues from their vibrissae. But the cat, as a predator, must rely more strongly on its sight. Kittens proved to have excellent depth-discrimination. At four weeks—about the earliest age that a kitten can move about with any facility—they invariably choose the shallow side of the cliff. On the glass over the deep side, they either freeze or circle aimlessly backward until they reach the center board [see illustrations on page 85].

The animals that showed the poorest performance in our series were the turtles. The late Robert M. Yerkes of Harvard University found in 1904 that aquatic turtles have somewhat poorer depth-discrimination than land turtles. On the visual cliff one might expect an aquatic turtle to respond to the reflections from the glass as it might to water and so prefer the deep side. They showed no such preference: 76 per cent of the aquatic turtles crawled off the board on the shallow side. The relatively large minority that choose the deep side suggests either that this turtle has poorer depth-discrimination than other animals, or that its natural habitat gives it less occasion to "fear" a fall.

All of these observations square with what is known about the life history and ecological niche of each of the animals tested. The survival of a species requires that its members develop discrimination of depth by the time they take up independent locomotion, whether at one day (the chick and the goat), three to four weeks (the rat and the cat) or six to 10 months (the human infant). That such a vital capacity does not depend on possibly fatal accidents of learning in the lives of individuals is consistent with evolutionary theory.

To make sure that no hidden bias was concealed in the design of the visual cliff we conducted a number of control experiments. In one of them we eliminated reflections from the glass by lighting the patterned surfaces from below the glass (to accomplish this we dropped the pattern below the glass on both sides, but more on one side than on the other). The animals—hooded rats—still consistently chose the shallow side. As a test of the role of the patterned surface we replaced it on either side of the centerboard with a homogeneous gray surface. Confronted with this choice, the rats showed no preference for either the shallow or the deep side. We also eliminated the optical difference between the two sides of the board by placing the patterned surface directly against the undersurface of the glass on each side. The rats then descended without preference to either side. When we lowered the pattern 10 inches below the glass on each side, they stayed on the board.

We set out next to determine which of two visual cues plays the decisive role in depth perception. To an eye above the center board the optical pattern on the two sides differs in at least two important respects. On the deep side distance decreases the size and spacing of the pattern elements projected on the retina. "Motion parallax," on the other hand, causes the pattern elements on the shallow side to move more rapidly across the field of vision when the animal moves its position on the board or moves its head, just as nearby objects seen from a moving car appear to pass by more quickly than distant ones [see illustration, page 89]. To eliminate the potential distance cue provided by pattern density we increased the size and spacing of the pattern elements on the deep side in proportion to its distance from the eye [see top illustration, page 90]. With only the cue of motion parallax to guide them, adult rats still preferred the shallow side, though not so strongly as in the standard experiment. Infant rats chose the shallow side nearly 100 per cent of the time under both conditions, as did day-old chicks. Evidently both species can discriminate depth by differential motion alone, with no aid from texture density and probably little help from other cues. The perception of distance by binocular parallax, which doubtless plays an important part in human behavior, would not seem to have a significant role, for example, in the depth perception of chicks and rats.

To eliminate the cue of motion parallax we placed the patterned material directly against the glass on either side of the board but used smaller and more densely spaced pattern-elements on the cliff side. Both young

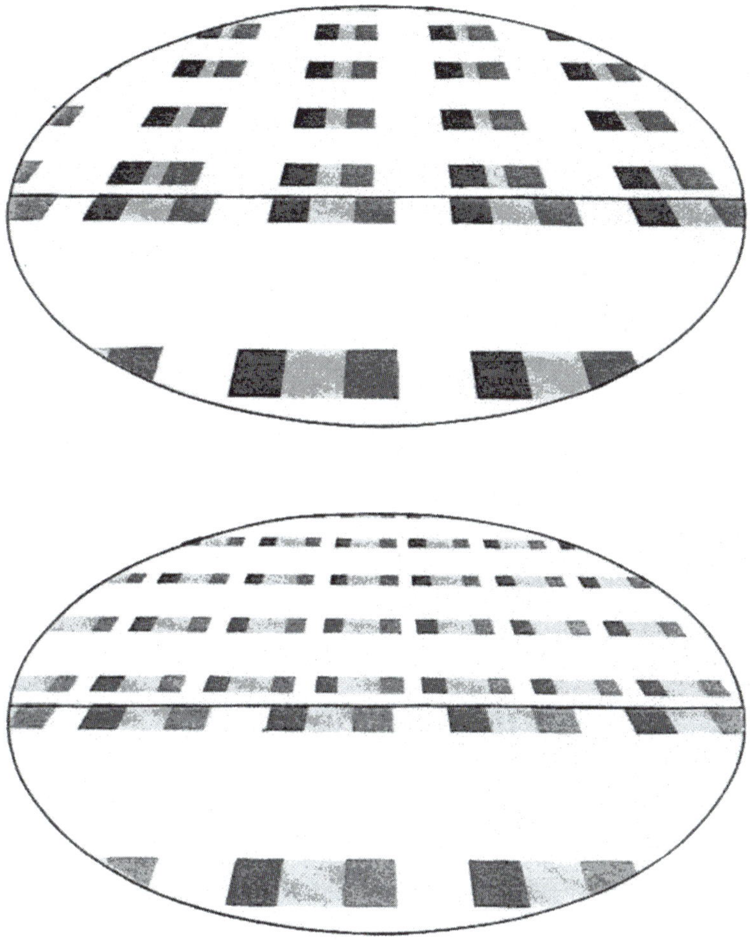

SEPARATION OF VISUAL CUES is shown in these diagrams. Pattern density is held constant (top) by using a larger pattern on the low side of the cliff; the drop in optical motion (motion parallax) remains. Motion parallax is equalized (bottom) by placing patterns at the same level; the smaller pattern on one side preserves difference in spacing.

and adult hooded rats preferred the side with the larger pattern, which evidently "signified" a nearer surface. Day-old chicks, however, showed no preference for the larger pattern. It may be that learning plays some part in the preference exhibited by the rats, since the young rats were tested at a somewhat older age than the chicks. This supposition is supported by the results of our experiments with animals reared in the dark.

The effects of early experience and of such deprivations as dark-rearing represent important clues to the relative roles of maturation and learning in animal behavior. The first experiments along this line were performed by K. S. Lashley and James T. Russell at the University of Chicago in 1934. They tested light-reared and dark-reared rats on a "jumping stand" from which they induced animals to leap toward a platform placed at varying distances. Upon finding that both groups of animals jumped with a force closely correlated with distance, they concluded that depth perception in rats is innate. Other investigators have pointed out, however, that the dark-reared rats required a certain amount of "pretraining" in the light before they could be made to jump. Since the visual-cliff technique requires no pretraining, we employed it to test groups of light-reared and dark-reared hooded rats. At the age of 90 days both groups showed the same preference for the shallow side of the apparatus, confirming Lashley's and Russell's conclusion.

Recalling our findings in the young rat, we then took up the question of whether the dark-reared rats relied upon motion parallax or upon contrast in texture density to discriminate depth. When the animals were confronted

IMPORTANCE OF PATTERN in depth perception is shown in these photographs. Of two patterns set at the same depth, normal rats almost invariably preferred the larger (top row and bottom left), presumably because it "signified" a nearer and therefore safer surface. Confronted with two patternless surfaces set at different depths, the animals displayed no preference (bottom right).

with the visual cliff, cued only by motion parallax, they preferred the shallow side, as had the light-reared animals. When the choice was cued by pattern density, however, they departed from the pattern of the normal animals and showed no significant preference [see bottom illustration at right]. The behavior of dark-reared rats thus resembles that of the day-old chicks, which also lack visual experience. It seems likely, therefore, that of the two cues only motion parallax is an innate cue for depth discrimination. Responses to differential pattern-density may be learned later.

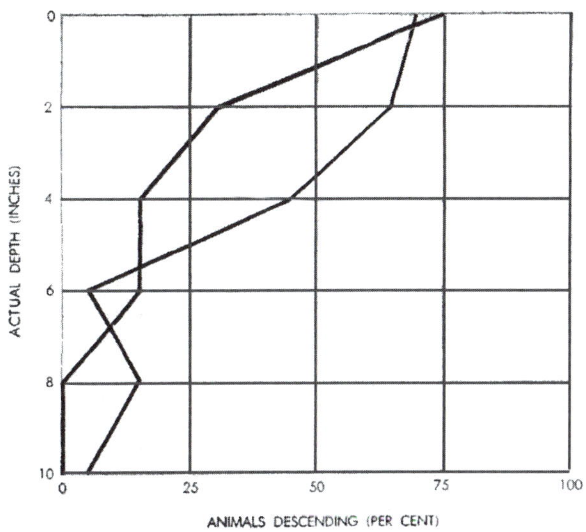

CONTROL EXPERIMENT measured the effect on rats of reflections on the glass of the apparatus. The percentage of animals leaving the center board decreased with increasing depth in much the same way, whether glass was present (top curve) or not (bottom curve).

One cannot automatically extrapolate these results to other species. But experiments with dark-reared kittens indicate that in these animals, too, depth perception matures independently of trial and error learning. In the kitten, however, light is necessary for normal visual maturation. Kittens reared in the dark to the age of 27 days at first crawled or fell of the center board equally often on the deep and shallow sides. Placed upon the glass over the deep side, they did not back in a circle like normal kittens but showed the same behavior that they had exhibited on the shallow side. Other investigators have observed equivalent behavior in dark-reared kittens; they bump into obstacles, lack normal eye movement and appear to "stare" straight ahead. These difficulties pass after a few days in the light. We accordingly tested the kittens every day. By the end of a week they were performing in every respect like normal kittens. They showed the same unanimous preference for the shallow side. Placed upon the glass over the deep side, they balked and circled backward to a visually secure surface. Repeated descents to the deep side, and placement upon the glass during their "blind" period, had not taught them that the deep side was "safe." Instead they avoided it more and more consistently. The initial blindness of dark-reared kittens makes them ideal subjects for studying the maturation of depth perception. With further study it should be possible to determine which cues they respond to first and what kinds of visual experience accelerate or retard the process of maturation.

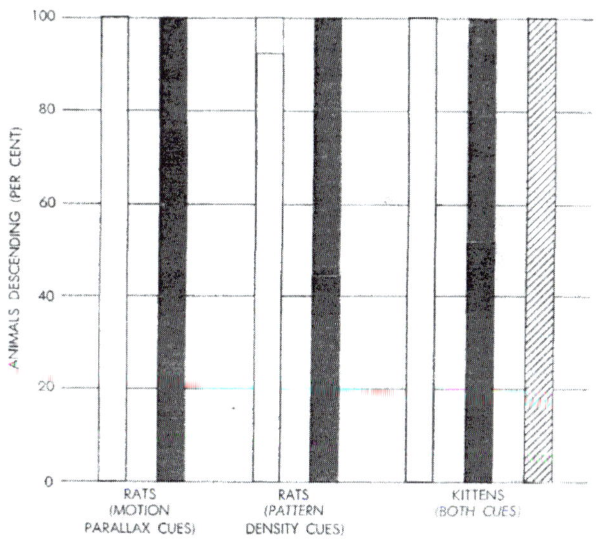

DARK-REARING EXPERIMENTS reveal the order in which different depth-cues are utilized as animals mature. Animals reared in the light (open bars) all strongly preferred the shallow side (color) to the deep side (gray). Dark-reared rats (solid bars), utilizing motion parallax alone, still preferred the shallow side; pattern density alone elicited no preference. Dark-reared kittens also showed no preference, because of temporary blindness. After seven days in the light all of them chose the shallow side (hatched bar).

From our first few years of work with the visual cliff we are ready to venture the rather broad conclusion that a seeing animal will be able to discriminate depth when its locomotion begins at birth. But many experiments remain to be done, especially on the role of different cues and on the effects of different kinds of early visual experience.

10 The Nature of Love

Harry F. Harlow (1958)[1], University of Wisconsin

First published in *American Psychologist,* 13, 673-685 • Posted March 2000

Address of the President at the sixty-sixth Annual Convention of the American Psychological Association, Washington, D.C., August 31, 1958. First published in American Psychologist, 13, 573-685.

Love is a wondrous state, deep, tender, and rewarding. Because of its intimate and personal nature it is regarded by some as an improper topic for experimental research. But, whatever our personal feelings may be, our assigned mission as psychologists is to analyze all facets of human and animal behavior into their component variables. So far as love or affection is concerned, psychologists have failed in this mission. The little we know about love does not transcend simple observation, and the little we write about it has been written better by poets and novelists. But of greater concern is the fact that psychologists tend to give progressively less attention to a motive which pervades our entire lives. Psychologists, at least psychologists who write textbooks, not only show no interest in the origin and development of love or affection, but they seem to be unaware of its very existence.

The apparent repression of love by modem psychologists stands in sharp contrast with the attitude taken by many famous and normal people. The word "love" has the highest reference frequency of any word cited in Bartlett's book of *Familiar Quotations.* It would appear that this emotion has long had a vast interest and fascination for human beings, regardless of the attitude taken by psychologists; but the quotations cited, even by famous and normal people, have a mundane redundancy. These authors and authorities have stolen love from the child and infant and made it the exclusive property of the adolescent and adult.

Thoughtful men, and probably all women, have speculated on the nature of love. From the developmental point of view, the general plan is quite clear: The initial love responses of the human being are those made by the infant to the mother or some mother surrogate. From this intimate attachment of the child to the mother, multiple learned and generalized affectional responses are formed.

Unfortunately, beyond these simple facts we know little about the fundamental variables underlying the formation of affectional responses and little about the mechanisms through which the love of the infant for the mother develops into the multifaceted response patterns characterizing love or affection in the adult. Because of the dearth of experimentation, theories about the fundamental nature of affection have evolved at the level of observation, intuition, and discerning guesswork, whether these have been proposed by psychologists, sociologists, anthropologists, physicians, or psychoanalysts.

The position commonly held by psychologists and sociologists is quite clear: The basic motives are, for the most part, the primary drives — particularly hunger, thirst, elimination, pain, and sex — and all other motives, including love or affection, are derived or secondary drives. The mother is associated with the reduction of the primary drives — particularly hunger, thirst, and pain — and through learning, affection or love is derived.

It is entirely reasonable to believe that the mother through association with food may become a secondary-reinforcing agent, but this is an inadequate mechanism to account for the persistence of the infant-maternal ties. There is a spate of researches on the formation of secondary reinforcers to hunger and thirst reduction. There can be no question that almost any external stimulus can become a secondary reinforcer if properly associated with tissue-need reduction, but the fact remains that this redundant literature demonstrates unequivocally that such derived drives suffer relatively rapid experimental extinction. Contrariwise, human affection does not extinguish when the mother ceases to have intimate association with the drives in question. Instead, the affectional ties to the mother show a lifelong, unrelenting persistence and, even more surprising, widely expanding generality.

Oddly enough, one of the few psychologists who took a position counter to modern psychological dogma was John B. Watson, who believed that love was an innate emotion elicited by cutaneous stimulation of the erogenous zones. But experimental psychologists, with their peculiar propensity to discover facts that are not true, brushed this theory aside by demonstrating that the human neonate had no differentiable emotions, and they established a fundamental psychological law that prophets are without honor in their own profession.

The psychoanalysts have concerned themselves with the problem of the nature of the development of love in the neonate and infant, using ill and aging human beings as subjects. They have discovered the overwhelming importance of the breast and related this to the oral erotic tendencies developed at an age preceding their subjects' memories. Their theories range from a belief that the infant has an innate need to achieve and suckle at the breast to beliefs not unlike commonly accepted psychological theories. There are exceptions, as seen in the recent writings of John Bowlby, who attributes importance not only to food and thirst satisfaction, but also to "primary object-clinging," a need for intimate physical contact, which is initially associated with the mother.

As far as I know, there exists no direct experimental analysis of the relative importance of the stimulus variables determining the affectional or love responses in the neonatal and infant primate. Unfortunately, the human neonate is a limited experimental subject for such researches because of his inadequate motor capabilities. By the time the human infant's motor responses can be precisely measured, the antecedent determining conditions cannot be defined, having been lost in a jumble and jungle of confounded variables.

Many of these difficulties can be resolved by the use of the neonatal and infant macaque monkey as the subject for the analysis of basic affectional variables. It is possible to make precise measurements in this primate beginning at two to ten days of age, depending upon the maturational status of the individual animal at birth. The macaque infant differs from the human infant in that the monkey is more mature at birth and grows more rapidly; but the basic responses relating to affection, including nursing, contact, clinging, and even visual and auditory exploration, exhibit no fundamental differences in the two species. Even the development of perception, fear, frustration, and learning capability follows very similar sequences in rhesus monkeys and human children.

Three years' experimentation before we started our studies on affection gave us experience with the neonatal monkey. We had separated more than 60 of these animals from their mothers 6 to 12 hours after birth and suckled them on tiny bottles. The infant mortality was only a small fraction of what we would have obtained had we let the monkey mothers raise their infants. Our bottle-fed babies were healthier and heavier than monkey-mother-reared infants. We know that we are better monkey mothers than are real monkey mothers thanks to synthetic diets, vitamins, iron extracts, penicillin, chloromycetin, 5% glucose, and constant, tender, loving care.

During the course of these studies we noticed that the laboratory raised babies showed strong attachment to the cloth pads (folded gauze diapers) which were used to cover the hardware-cloth floors of their cages. The infants clung to these pads and engaged in violet temper tantrums when the pads were removed and replaced for sanitary reasons. Such contact-need or responsiveness had been reported previously by Gertrude van Wagenen for the monkey and by Thomas McCulloch and George Haslerud for the

Figure 1. Response to cloth pad by one-day-old monkey.

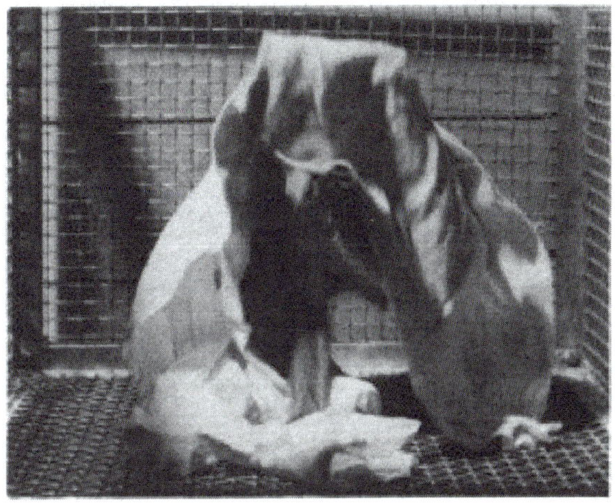

Figure 2. Response to gauze pad by six-month-old monkey used in earlier study.

chimpanzee and is reminiscent of the devotion often exhibited by human infants to their pillows, blankets, and soft, cuddly stuffed toys. Responsiveness by the one-day old infant monkey to the cloth pad is shown in Figure 1, and an unusual and strong attachment of a six-month-old infant to the cloth pad is illustrated in Figure 2. The baby, human or monkey, if it is to survive, must clutch at more than a straw.

We had also discovered during some allied observational studies that a baby monkey raised on a bare wire-mesh cage floor survives with difficulty, if at all, during the first five days of life. If a wire-mesh cone is introduced, the baby does better; and, if the cone is covered with terry cloth, husky, healthy, happy babies evolve. It takes more than a baby and a box to make a normal monkey. We were impressed by the possibility that, above and beyond the bubbling fountain of breast or bottle, contact comfort might be a very important variable in the development of the infant's affection for the mother.

At this point we decided to study the development of affectional responses of neonatal and infant monkeys to an artificial, inanimate mother, and so we built a surrogate mother which we hoped and believed would be a good surrogate mother. In devising this surrogate mother we were dependent neither upon the capriciousness of evolutionary processes nor upon mutations produced by chance radioactive fallout. Instead, we designed the mother surrogate in terms of modern human engineering principles (Figure 3). We produced a perfectly proportioned, streamlined body stripped of unnecessary bulges and appendices. Redundancy in the surrogate mother's system was avoided by reducing the number of breasts from two to one and placing this unibreast in an upper-thoracic, sagittal position, thus maximizing the natural and known perceptual-motor capabilities of the infant operator. The surrogate was made from a block of wood, covered with sponge rubber, and sheathed in tan cotton terry cloth. A light bulb behind her radiated heat. The result was a mother, soft, warm, and tender, a mother with infinite patience, a mother available twenty-four hours a day, a mother that never scolded her infant and never struck or bit her baby in anger. Furthermore, we designed a mother-machine with maximal maintenance efficiency since failure of any system or function could be resolved by the simple substitution of black boxes and new component parts. It is our opinion that we engineered a very superior monkey mother, although this position is not held universally by the monkey fathers.

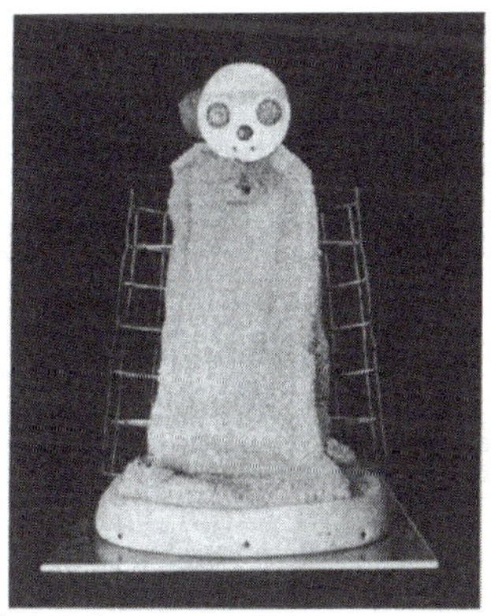

Figure 3. Cloth mother surrogate.

Before beginning our initial experiment we also designed and constructed a second mother surrogate, a surrogate in which we deliberately built less than the maximal capability for contact comfort. This surrogate mother is illustrated in Figure 4. She is made of wire-mesh, a substance entirely adequate to provide postural support and nursing capability, and she is warmed by radiant heat. Her body differs in no essential way from that of the cloth mother surrogate other than in the quality of the contact comfort which she can supply. In our initial experiment, the dual mother-surrogate condition, a cloth mother and a wire mother were placed in different cubicles attached to the infant's living cage as shown in Figure 4. For four newborn monkeys the cloth mother lactated and the wire mother did not; and, for the other four, this condition was reversed. In either condition the infant received all its milk through the mother surrogate as soon as it was able to maintain itself in this way, a capability achieved within two or three days except in the case of very immature infants. Supplementary feedings were given until the milk intake from the mother surrogate was adequate. Thus, the experiment was designed as a test of the relative importance of the variables of contact comfort and nursing comfort. During the first 14 days of life the monkey's cage floor was covered with a heating pad wrapped in a folded gauze diaper, and thereafter the cage floor was bare. The infants were always free to leave the heating pad or cage floor to contact either mother, and the time spent on the surrogate mothers was automatically recorded. Figure 5 shows the total time spent with cloth and wire mothers under the two conditions of feeding. These data make it obvious that contact comfort is a variable of overwhelming importance in the development of affectional response, whereas lactation is a variable of negligible importance. With age and opportunity to learn, subjects with the lactating wire mother showed decreasing responsiveness to her and increasing responsiveness to the nonlactating cloth mother, a finding completely contrary to any interpretation of derived drive in which the mother-form becomes conditioned to hunger-thirst reduction. The persistence of these differential responses throughout 165 consecutive days of testing is evident in Figure 6.

One control group of neonatal monkeys was raised on a single wire mother, and a second control group was raised on a single cloth mother. There were no differences between these two groups in amount of milk ingested or in weight gain. The only difference between the two groups lay in the composition of the feces, the softer stools of the wire-mother infants suggesting psychosomatic involvement. The wire mother is biologically adequate but psychologically inept.

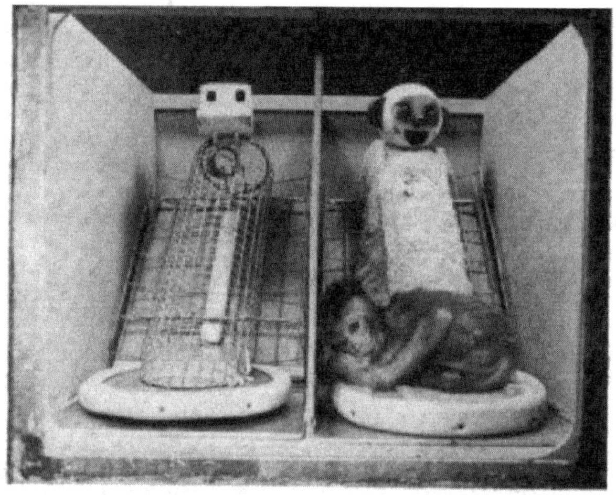

Figure 4. Wire and cloth mother surrogates.

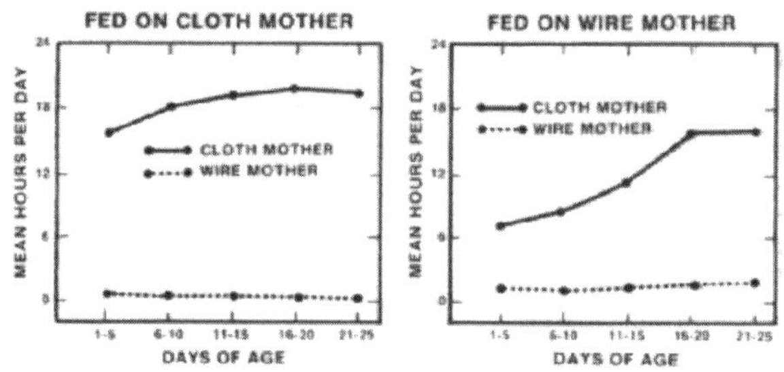

Figure 5. Time spent on cloth and wire mother surrogates.

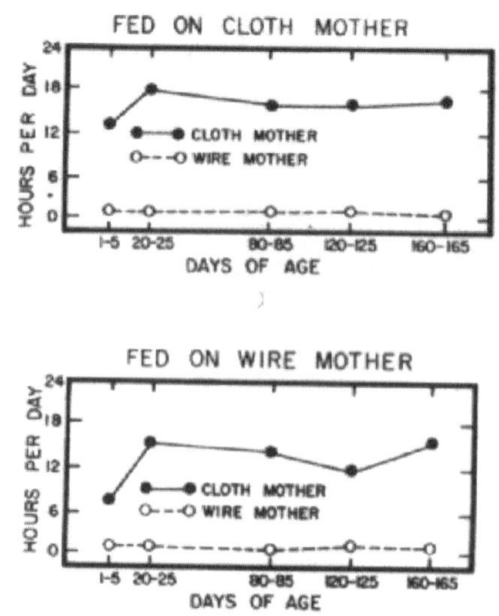

Figure 6. Long-term contact time on cloth and wire mother surrogates.

We were not surprised to discover that contact comfort was an important basic affectional or love variable, but we did not expect it to overshadow so completely the variable of nursing; indeed, the disparity is so great as to suggest that the primary function of nursing as an affectional variable is that of insuring frequent and intimate body contact of the infant with the mother. Certainly, man cannot live by milk alone. Love is an emotion that does not need to be bottle- or spoon-fed, and we may be sure that there is nothing to be gained by giving lip service to love.

A charming lady once heard me describe these experiments and, when I subsequently talked to her, her face brightened with sudden insight: "Now I know what's wrong with me," she said, "I'm just a wire mother." Perhaps she was lucky. She might have been a wire wife.

We believe that contact comfort has long served the animal kingdom as a motivating agent for affectional responses. Since at the present time we have no exper-

The Snake

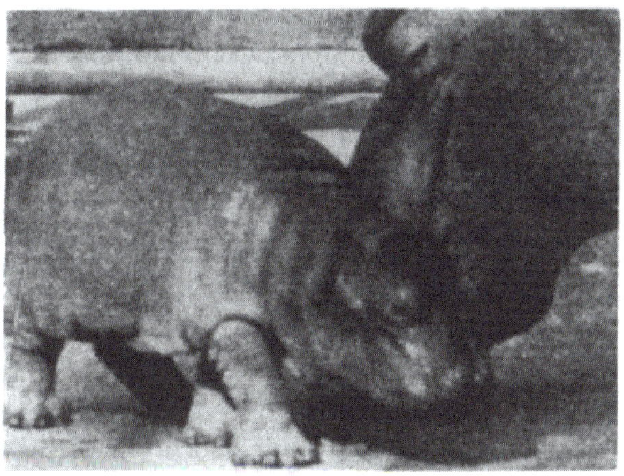

The Hippopotamus

The Elephant

The Rhinoceros

The Crocodile

imental data to substantiate this position, we supply information which must be accepted, if at all, on the basis of face validity:

One function of the real mother, human or subhuman, and presumably of a mother surrogate, is to provide a haven of safety for the infant in times of fear and danger. The frightened or ailing child clings to its mother, not its father; and this selective responsiveness in times of distress, disturbance, or danger may be used as a measure of the strength of affectional bonds. We have tested this kind of differential responsiveness by presenting to the infants in their cages, in the presence of the two mothers, various fear-producing stimuli such as the moving toy bear illustrated in Figure 13. A typical response to a fear stimulus is shown in Figure 14, and the data on differential responsiveness are presented in Figure 15. It is apparent that the cloth mother is highly preferred over the wire one, and this differential selectivity is enhanced by age and experience. In this situation,

You see, all God's chillun's got skin.

Figure 1

Figure 13. Typical fear stimulus.

Figure 14. Typical response to cloth mother surrogate in fear test.

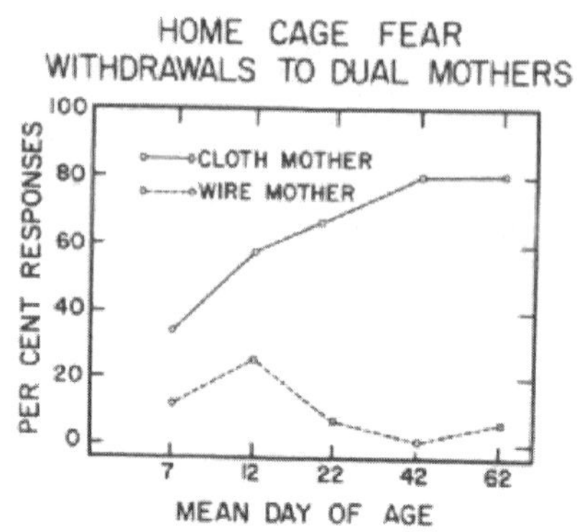

Figure 15. Differential responsiveness in fear tests.

the variable of nursing appears to be of absolutely no importance: the infant consistently seeks the soft mother surrogate regardless of nursing condition.

Similarly, the mother or mother surrogate provides its young with a source of security, and this role or function is seen with special clarity when mother and child are in a strange situation. At the present time we have completed tests for this relationship on four of our eight baby monkeys assigned to the dual mother-surrogate condition by introducing them for three minutes into the strange environment of a room measuring six feet by six feet by six feet (also called the "open-field test") and containing multiple stimuli known to elicit curiosity-manipulatory responses in baby monkeys. The subjects were placed in this situation twice a week for eight weeks with no mother surrogate present during alternate sessions and the cloth mother present during the others. A cloth diaper was always available as one of the stimuli throughout all sessions. After one or two adaptation sessions, the infants always rushed to the mother surrogate when she was present and clutched her, rubbed their bodies against her, and frequently manipulated her body and face. After a few additional sessions, the infants began to use the mother surrogate as a source of security, a base of operations. As is shown in Figures 16 and 17, they would explore and manipulate a stimulus and then return to the mother before adventuring again into the strange new world. The behavior of these infants was quite different when the mother was absent from the room. Frequently they would freeze in a crouched position, as is illustrated in Figures 18 and 19. Emotionality indices such as vocalization, crouching, rocking, and sucking increased sharply, as shown in Figure 20. Total emotionality score was cut in half when the mother was present. In the absence of the mother some of the experimental monkeys would rush to the center of the room where the mother was customarily placed and then run rapidly from object to object, screaming and crying all the while. Continuous, frantic clutching of their bodies was very common, even when not in the crouching position. These monkeys frequently contacted and clutched the cloth diaper, but this action never pacified them. The same behavior occurred in the presence of the wire mother. No difference between the cloth-mother-fed and wire-mother-fed infants was demonstrated under either condition. Four control infants never raised with a mother surrogate showed the same emotionality scores when the mother was absent as the experimental infants showed in the absence of the mother, but the controls' scores were slightly larger in the presence of the mother surrogate than in her absence.

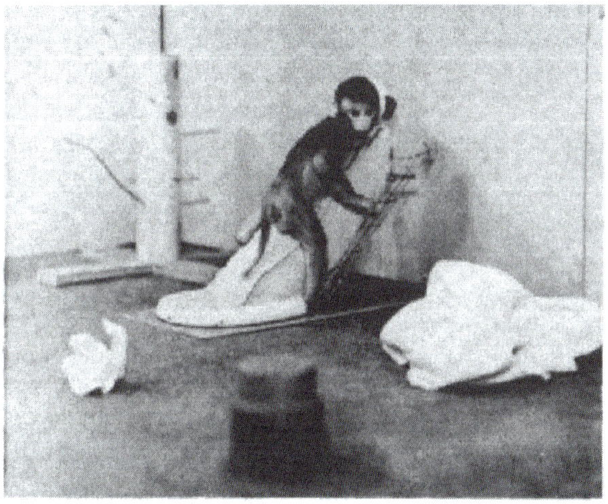

Figure 16. Response to cloth mother in the open-field test.

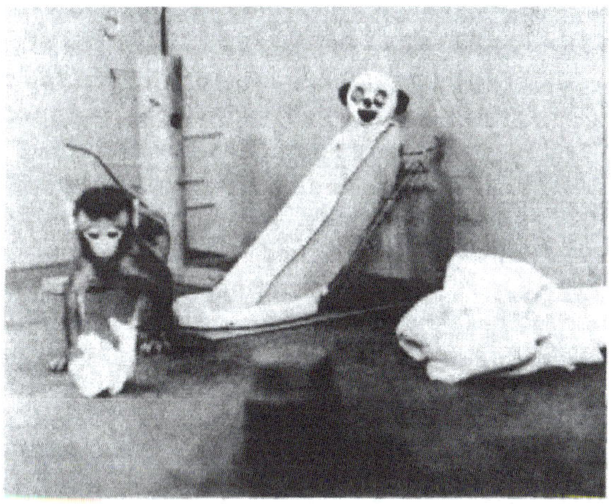

Figure 17. Object exploration in presence of cloth mother.

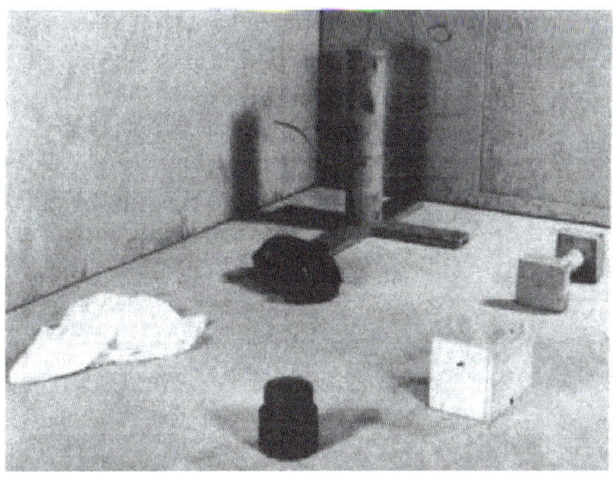

Figure 18. Response in the open-field test in the absence of the mother surrogate.

Figure 19. Response in the open-field test in the absence of the mother surrogate.

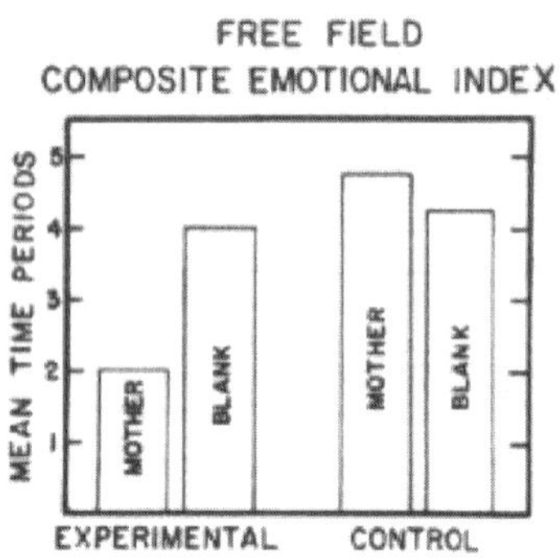

Figure 20. Emotionality index with and without the presence of the cloth mother.

Figure 21. Visual exploration apparatus.

Some years ago Robert Butler demonstrated that mature monkeys enclosed in a dimly lighted box would open and reopen a door hour after hour for no other reward than that of looking outside the box. We now have data indicating that neonatal monkeys show this same compulsive visual curiosity on their first test day in an adaptation of the Butler apparatus which we call the "love machine," an apparatus designed to measure love. Usually these tests are begun when the monkey is 10 days of age, but this same persistent visual exploration has been obtained in a three-day-old monkey during the first half-hour of testing. Butler also demonstrated that rhesus monkeys show selectivity in rate and frequency of door-opening to stimuli of differential attractiveness in the visual field outside the box. We have utilized this principle of response selectivity by the monkey to measure strength of affectional responsiveness in our infants in the baby version of the Butler box. The test sequence involves four repetitions of a test battery in which four stimuli — cloth mother, wire mother, infant monkey, and empty box — are presented for a 30-minute period on successive days. The first four subjects in the dual mother-surrogate group were given a single test sequence at 40 to 50 days of age, depending upon the availability of the apparatus, and only their data are presented. The second set of four subjects is being given repetitive tests to obtain information relating to the development of visual exploration. The apparatus is illustrated in Figure 21. The data obtained from the first four infants raised with the two mother surrogates are presented in the middle graph of Figure 22 and show approximately equal responding to the cloth mother and another infant monkey, and no greater responsiveness to the wire mother than to an empty box. Again, the results are independent of the kind of mother that lactated, cloth or wire. The same results are found for a control group raised, but not fed, on a single cloth

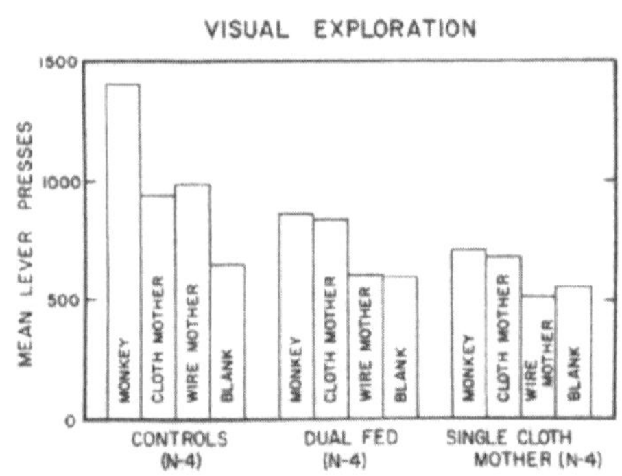

Figure 22. Differential responses to visual exploration.

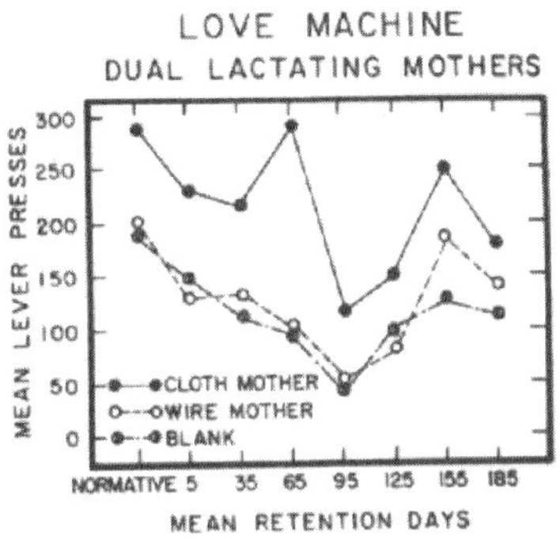

Figure 23. Retention of differential visual-exploration responses.

mother; these data appear in the graph on the right. Contrariwise, the graph on the left shows no differential responsiveness to cloth and wire mothers by a second control group, which was not raised on any mother surrogate. We can be certain that not all love is blind.

The first four infant monkeys in the dual mother-surrogate group were separated from their mothers between 165 and 170 days of age and tested for retention during the following 9 days and then at 30-day intervals for six successive months. Affectional retention as measured by the modified Butler box is given in Figure 23. In keeping with the data obtained on adult monkeys by Butler, we find a high rate of responding to any stimulus, even the empty box. But throughout the entire 185-day retention period there is a consistent and significant difference in response frequency to the cloth mother contrasted with either the wire mother or the empty box, and no consistent difference between wire mother and empty box.

Affectional retention was also tested in the open field during the first 9 days after separation and then at 30-day intervals, and each test condition was run twice at each retention interval. The infant's behavior differed from that observed during the period preceding separation. When the cloth mother was present in the post-separation period, the babies rushed to her, climbed up, clung tightly to her, and rubbed their heads and faces against her body. After this initial embrace and reunion, they played on the mother, including biting and tearing at her cloth cover; but they rarely made any attempt to leave her during the test period, nor did they manipulate or play with the objects in the room, in contrast with their behavior before maternal separation. The only exception was the occasional monkey that left the mother surrogate momentarily, grasped the folded piece of paper (one of the standard stimuli in the field), and brought it quickly back to the mother. It appeared that deprivation had enhanced the tie to the mother and rendered the contact-comfort need so prepotent that need for the mother overwhelmed the exploratory motives during the brief, three-minute test sessions. No change in these behaviors was observed throughout the 185-day period. When the mother was absent from the open field, the behavior of the infants was similar in the initial retention test to that during the preseparation tests; but they tended to show gradual adaptation to the open-field situation with repeated testing and, consequently, a reduction in their emotionality scores.

In the last five retention test periods, an additional test was introduced in which the surrogate mother was placed in the center of the room and covered with a clear Plexiglas box. The monkeys were initially disturbed and frustrated when their explorations and manipulations of the box failed to provide contact with the mother. However, all animals adapted to the situation rather rapidly. Soon they used the box as a place of orientation for exploratory and play behavior, made frequent contacts with the objects in the field, and very often brought these objects to the Plexiglas box. The emotionality index was slightly higher than in the condition of the available cloth mothers, but it in no way approached the emotionality level displayed when the cloth mother was absent. Obviously, the infant monkeys gained emotional security by the presence of the mother even though contact was denied.

Affectional retention has also been measured by tests in which the monkey must unfasten a three-device mechanical puzzle to obtain entrance into a compartment containing the mother surrogate. All the trials are initiated by allowing the infant to go through an unlocked door, and in half the trials it finds the mother present and in half, an empty compartment. The door is then locked and a ten-minute test conducted. In tests given prior to separation from the surrogate mothers, some of the infants had solved this puzzle and others had failed. The data of Figure 24 show that on the last test before separation there were no differences in total manipulation under mother-present and mother-absent conditions, but striking differences exist between the two conditions throughout the post-separation test periods. Again, there is no interaction with conditions of feeding.

The overall picture obtained from surveying the retention data is unequivocal. There is little, if any,

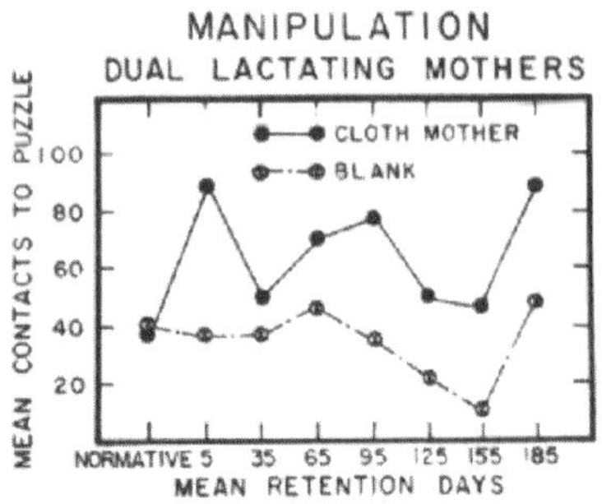

Figure 24. Retention of puzzle manipulation responsiveness.

waning of responsiveness to the mother throughout this five-month period as indicated by any measure. It becomes perfectly obvious that this affectional bond is highly resistant to forgetting and that it can be retained for very long periods of time by relatively infrequent contact reinforcement. During the next year, retention tests will be conducted at 90-day intervals, and further plans are dependent upon the results obtained. It would appear that affectional responses may show as much resistance to extinction as has been previously demonstrated for learned fears and learned pain, and such data would be in keeping with those of common human observation.

The infant's responses to the mother surrogate in the fear tests, the open-field situation, and the baby Butler box and the responses on the retention tests cannot be described adequately with words. For supplementary information we turn to the motion picture record. (At this point a 20-minute film was presented illustrating and supplementing the behaviors described thus far in the address.)

We have already described the group of four control infants that had never lived in the presence of any mother surrogate and had demonstrated no sign of affection or security in the presence of the cloth mothers introduced in test sessions. When these infants reached the age of 250 days, cubicles containing both a cloth mother and a wire mother were attached to their cages. There was no lactation in these mothers, for the monkeys were on a solid-food diet. The initial reaction of the monkeys to the alterations was one of extreme disturbance. All the infants screamed violently and made repeated attempts to escape the cage whenever the door was opened. They kept a maximum distance from the mother surrogates and exhibited a considerable amount of rocking and crouching behavior, indicative of emotionality. Our first thought was that the critical period for the development of maternally directed affection had passed and that these macaque children were doomed to live as affectional orphans. Fortunately, these behaviors continued for only 12 to 48 hours and then gradually ebbed, changing from indifference to active contact on, and exploration of, the surrogates. The home-cage behavior of these control monkeys slowly became similar to that of the animals raised with the mother surrogates from birth. Their manipulation and play on the cloth mother became progressively more vigorous to the point of actual mutilation, particularly during the morning after the cloth mother had been given her daily change of terry covering. The control subjects were now actively running to the cloth mother when frightened and had to be coaxed from her to be taken from the cage for formal testing.

Objective evidence of these changing behaviors is given in Figure 25, which plots the amount of time these infants spent on the mother surrogates. Within 10 days mean contact time is approximately nine hours, and this measure remains relatively constant throughout the next 30 days. Consistent with the results on the subjects reared from birth with dual mothers, these late-adopted infants spent less than one and one-half hours per day in contact with the wire mothers, and this activity level was relatively constant throughout the test sessions. Although the maximum time that the control monkeys spent on the cloth mother was only about half that spent by the original dual mother-surrogate group, we cannot be sure that this discrepancy is a function of differential early experience. The control monkeys were about three months older when the mothers were attached to their cages than the experimental animals had been when their mothers were removed and the retention tests begun. Thus, we do not know what the amount of contact would be for a 250-day-old animal raised from birth with surrogate mothers. Nevertheless, the magnitude of the differences and the fact that the contact-time curves for the mothered-from-birth infants had remained constant for almost 150 days suggest that early experience with the mother is a variable of measurable importance.

The control group has also been tested for differential visual exploration after the introduction of the cloth and wire mothers; these behaviors are plotted in Figure 26. By the second test session a high level of exploratory behavior had developed, and the responsiveness to the wire mother and the empty box is significantly

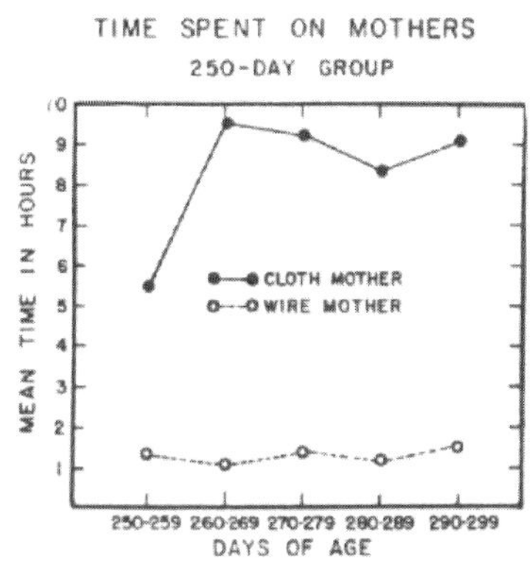

Figure 25. Differential time spent on cloth and wire mother surrogates by monkeys started at 250 days of age.

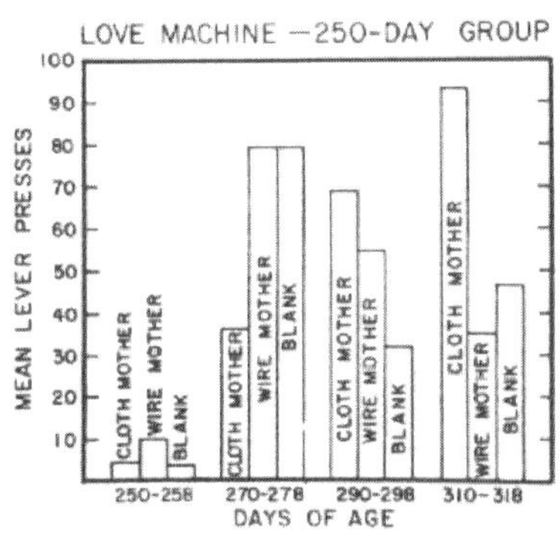

Figure 26. Differential visual exploration of monkeys started at 250 days of age.

greater than that to the cloth mother. This is probably not an artifact since there is every reason to believe that the face of the cloth mother is a fear stimulus to most monkeys that have not had extensive experience with this object during the first 40 to 60 days of life. Within the third test session a sharp change in trend occurs, and the cloth mother is then more frequently viewed than the wire mother or the blank box; this trend continues during the fourth session, producing a significant preference for the cloth mother.

Before the introduction of the mother surrogate into the home-cage situation, only one of the four control monkeys had ever contacted the cloth mother in the open-field tests. In general, the surrogate mother not only gave the infants no security, but instead appeared to serve as a fear stimulus. The emotionality scores of these control subjects were slightly higher during the mother-present test sessions than during the mother-absent test sessions. These behaviors were changed radically by the fourth post-introduction test approximately 60 days later. In the absence of the cloth mothers the emotionality index in this fourth test remains near the earlier level, but the score is reduced by half when the mother is present, a result strikingly similar to that found for infants raised with the dual mother-surrogates from birth. The control infants now show increasing object exploration and play behavior, and they begin to use the mother as a base of operations, as did the infants raised from birth with the mother surrogates. However, there are still definite differences in the behavior of the two groups. The control infants do not rush directly to the mother and clutch her violently; but instead they go toward, and orient around, her, usually after an initial period during which they frequently show disturbed behavior, exploratory behavior, or both.

That the control monkeys develop affection or love for the cloth mother when she is introduced into the cage at 250 days of age cannot be questioned. There is every reason to believe, however, that this interval of delay depresses the intensity of the affectional response below that of the infant monkeys that were surrogate-mothered from birth onward. In interpreting these data it is well to remember that the control monkeys had had continuous opportunity to observe and hear other monkeys housed in adjacent cages and that they had had limited opportunity to view and contact surrogate mothers in the test situations, even though they did not exploit the opportunities.

During the last two years we have observed the behavior of two infants raised by their own mothers. Love for the real mother and love for the surrogate mother appear to be very similar. The baby macaque spends many hours a day clinging to its real mother. If away from the mother when frightened, it rushes to her and in her presence shows comfort and composure. As far as we can observe, the infant monkey's affection for the real mother is strong, but no stronger than that of the experimental monkey for the surrogate cloth mother, and the security that the infant gains from the presence of the real mother is no greater than the security it gains from a cloth surrogate. Next year we hope to put this problem to a final, definitive, experimental test. But, whether the mother is real or a cloth surrogate, there does develop a deep and abiding bond between mother and child. In one case it may be the call of the wild and in the other the McCall of civilization, but in both cases there is "togetherness."

In spite of the importance of contact comfort, there is reason to believe that other variables of measurable importance will be discovered. Postural support may be such a variable, and it has been suggested that, when we build arms into the mother surrogate, 10 is the minimal number required to provide adequate child care. Rocking motion may be such a variable, and we are comparing rocking and stationary mother surrogates and inclined planes. The differential responsiveness to cloth mother and cloth-covered inclined plane suggests that clinging as well as contact is an affectional variable of importance. Sounds, particularly natural, maternal sounds, may operate as either unlearned or learned affectional variables. Visual responsiveness may be such a variable, and it is possible that some semblance of visual imprinting may develop in the neonatal monkey. There are indications that this becomes a variable of importance during the course of infancy through some maturational process.

John Bowlby has suggested that there is an affectional variable which he calls "primary object following," characterized by visual and oral search of the mother's face. Our surrogate-mother-raised baby monkeys are at first inattentive to her face, as are human neonates to human mother faces. But by 30 days of age ever-increasing responsiveness to the mother's face appears — whether through learning, maturation, or both — and we have reason to believe that the face becomes an object of special attention.

Our first surrogate-mother-raised baby had a mother whose head was just a ball of wood since the baby was a month early and we had not had time to design a more esthetic head and face. This baby had contact with the blank-faced mother for 180 days and was then placed with two cloth mothers, one motionless and one rocking, both being endowed with painted, ornamented faces. To our surprise the animal would compulsively rotate both faces 180 degrees so that it viewed only a round, smooth face and never the painted, ornamented face. Furthermore, it would do this as long as the patience of the experimenter in reorienting the faces persisted. The monkey showed no sign of fear or anxiety, but it showed unlimited persistence. Subsequently it improved its technique, compulsively removing the heads and rolling them into its cage as fast as they were returned. We are intrigued by this observation, and we plan to examine systematically the role of the mother face in the development of infant-monkey affections. Indeed, these observations suggest the need for a series of ethological-type researches on the two-faced female.

Although we have made no attempts thus far to study the generalization of infant-macaque affection or love, the techniques which we have developed offer promise in this uncharted field. Beyond this, there are few if any technical difficulties in studying the affection of the actual, living mother for the child, and the techniques developed can be utilized and expanded for the analysis and developmental study of father-infant and infant-infant affection.

Since we can measure neonatal and infant affectional responses to mother surrogates, and since we know they are strong and persisting, we are in a position to assess the effects of feeding and contactual schedules; consistency and inconsistency in the mother surrogates; and early, intermediate, and late maternal deprivation. Again, we have here a family of problems of fundamental interest and theoretical importance.

If the researches completed and proposed make a contribution, I shall be grateful; but I have also given full thought to possible practical applications. The socioeconomic demands of the present and the threatened socioeconomic demands of the future have led the American woman to displace, or threaten to displace, the American man in science and industry. If this process continues, the problem of proper child-rearing practices faces us with startling clarity. It is cheering in view of this trend to realize that the American male is physically endowed with all the really essential equipment to compete with the American female on equal terms in one essential activity: the rearing of infants. We now know that women in the working classes are not needed in the home because of their primary mammalian capabilities; and it is possible that in the foreseeable future neonatal nursing will not be regarded as a necessity, but as a luxury - to use Veblen's term - a form of conspicuous consumption limited perhaps to the upper classes. But whatever course history may take, it is comforting to know that we are now in contact with the nature of love.

FOOTNOTE

[1.] The researches reported in this paper were supported by funds supplied by Grant No. M-722, National Institutes of Health, by a grant from the Ford Foundation, and by funds received from the Graduate School of the University of Wisconsin.

11 The Brain as a Dream State Generator: An Activation-Synthesis Hypothesis of the Dream Process

by J. Allan Hobson, M.D. and Robert W. McCarley, M.D.

Recent research in the neurobiology of dreaming sleep provides new evidence for possible structural and functional substrates of formal aspects of the dream process. The data suggest that dreaming sleep is physiologically determined and shaped by a brain stem neuronal mechanism that can be modeled physiologically and mathematically. Formal features of the generator processes with strong implications for dream theory include periodicity and automaticity of forebrain activation, suggesting a preprogrammed neural basis for dream mentation in sleep: intense and sporadic activation of brain stem sensorimotor circuits including reticular, oculomotor, and vestibular neurons, possibly determining spatiotemporal aspects of dream imagery and shifts in transmitter ratios, possibly accounting for dream amnesia. The authors suggest that the automatically activated forebrain synthesizes the dream by comparing information generated in specific brain stem circuits with information stored in memory.

Based on the text of the Sandoz Lecture presented by Dr. Hobson at University of Edinburgh. April 23, 1975.

Dr. Hobson is Associate Professor of Psychiatry and Dr. McCarley is Assistant Professor of Psychiatry, Harvard Medical School, Boston, Mass. Dr. Hobson is also Director and Dr. McCarley is Co-Director Laboratory of Neurophysiology, Massachusetts Mental Health Center, 74 Fenwood Rd., Boston, Mass., 02115.

The research described herein was supported by Alcohol, Drug Abuse, and Mental Health Administration grant MH-13923 from the National Institute of Mental Health and by the Milton Fund of Harvard University.

The authors wish to express their appreciation to Drs. John Nemiah and John Nelson for their helpful comments on the manuscript.

SINCE THE TURN of the century, dream theory has been dominated by the psychoanalytic hypothesis that dreaming is a reactive process designed to protect consciousness and sleep from the disruptive effect of unconscious wishes that are released in sleep (1). Thus dreaming has been viewed as a psychodynamically determined state, and the distinctive formal features of dream content have been interpreted as manifestations of a defensive transformation of the unconscious wishes found unacceptable to consciousness by a hypothetical censor. A critical tenet of this wish fulfillment-disguise theory is that the transformation of the unconscious wish by the censor disguises or degrades the ideational information in forming the dream imagery. We were surprised to discover the origins of the major tenets of psychoanalytic dream theory in the neurophysiology of 1890 and have specified the transformations made by Freud in an earlier, related article (2). In detailing the neurophysiological origins of psychoanalytic dream theory, the concept of mind-body isomorphism, denoting similarity of form between psychological and physiological events, was seen as an explicit premise of Freud's thought.

Sharing Freud's conviction that mind-body isomorphism is a valid approach, we will now review modem neurophysiological evidence that we believe permits and necessitates important revisions in psychoanalytic dream theory. The activation-synthesis hypothesis that we will begin to develop in this paper asserts that many formal aspects of the dream experience may be the obligatory and relatively undistorted psychological concomitant of the regularly recurring and physiologically determined brain state called "dreaming sleep." It ascribes particular formal features of the dream experience to the particular organizational features of the brain during that state of sleep. More specifically, the theory details the mechanisms by which the brain becomes periodically activated during sleep and specifies the means by which both sensory input and motor output are simultaneously blocked, so as to account for the maintenance of sleep in the face of strong central activation of the brain. The occurrence and character of dreaming are seen as both determined and shaped by these physiological processes.

The most important tenet of the activation-synthesis hypothesis is that during dreaming the activated brain generates its own information by a pontine brain stem neuronal mechanism, which will be described in detail. We hypothesize that this internally generated sensorimotor information, which is partially random and partially specific, is then compared with stored sensorimotor data in the synthesis of dream content. The functional significance of the brain activation and the synthesis of endogenous information in dreaming sleep is not known, but we suggest that state-dependent learning is at least as likely a result of dreaming as is tension reduction or sleep maintenance.

While we believe that the two processes emphasized in this paper—activation and synthesis—are major and important advances in dream theory, we wish to state explicitly and comment on some of the things that our theory does not attempt to do. The activation-synthesis hypothesis does not exclude possible defensive distortions of the value-free sensorimotor dream stimuli, but it does deny the primacy of any such process in attempting to explain *formal* aspects of dream content or the fundamental impetus to dreaming itself. The idea that dreams reveal wishes is also beyond the direct reach of our new theory, but some specific alternatives to this interpretation of several classic dream situations can be advanced.

The new theory cannot yet account for the emotional aspects of the dream experience, but we assume that they are produced by the activation of brain regions subserving affect in parallel with the activation of the better known sensorimotor pathways. Finally, the new theory does not deny meaning to dreams, but it does suggest 1) a more direct route to their acquisition than anamnesis via free association, since dream origins are in basic physiological processes and not in disguised wishes, 2) a less complex approach to their interpretation than conversion from manifest to latent content, since unusual aspects of dreams are not seen as disguises but as results of the way the brain and mind function during sleep, and 3) a broader view of their use in therapy than that provided by the transference frame of reference, since dreams are not to be interpreted as the product of disguised unconscious (transference) wishes. Dreams offer a royal road to the mind and brain in a behavioral state, with different operating rules and principles than during waking and with the possibility of clinically useful insights from the product of these differences. These points are discussed in the last section of this paper and elsewhere (3).

WHAT IS A DREAM?

A dream may be defined as a mental experience, occurring in sleep, which is characterized by hallucinoid imagery, predominantly visual and often vivid: by bizarre elements due to such distortions as condensation, discontinuity, and acceleration; and by a delusional acceptance of these phenomena as "real" at the time that they occur. Strong emotion may or may not be associated with these distinctive formal properties of the dream, and subsequent recall of these mental events is almost invariably poor unless an immediate arousal from sleep occurs.

That this technical jargon describes a universal human experience seems certain, since the five key points in this definition are easily elicited from both naive and sophisticated individuals when they are asked to characterize their dreams. We leave aside the question of whether other less vivid and nonperceptual forms of mental activity during sleep should also be called "dreams" and confine ourselves here to the psychophysiology of the hallucinoid type of dream. In doing so, we not only simplify the immediate task at hand but may also gain insight into the mechanisms underlying the most florid symptoms of psychopathology. We mean, of course, the hallucinations and delusions of the psychotic experience, which have so often invited comparison with the dream as we have defined it here.

WHAT IS THE STATE OF THE BRAIN DURING DREAMING SLEEP?

The physiological substrate of the dream experience is the CNS in one of its three principal operating states: waking (W), synchronized sleep (S), and desynchronized sleep (D). These states can be reliably and objectively differentiated by recording the EEG, the electromyogram (EMG), and the electrooculogram (see Table 1). Hallucinoid dreaming in man occurs predominantly during the periodically recurrent phase of sleep characterized by EEG desynchronization, EMG suppression, and REMs (4). We call this kind of sleep "D" (meaning desynchronized, but also conveniently denoting dreaming).

In the systems analysis terms used in figure 1, this D brain state is characterized by the following "sensorimotor" properties: activation of the brain; relative exclusion of external input; generation of some internal input, which the activated forebrain then processes as information; and blocking of motor output, except for the oculomotor pathway. In this model the substrate of emotion is considered to be a part of the forebrain; it will not be further distinguished here because we have no specific physiological evidence as to how this part of the system might work in any brain state. Memory is not shown but is considered to be a differentiated function of the brain that operates during the D state, such that output from long-term storage is facilitated but input to long-term storage is blocked. A highly specific hypothesis about dream amnesia has previously been derived (5) from the same evidence that we will now review in our attempt to account for the general sensorimotor aspects of the dream process.

ELECTROPHYSIOLOGY OF THE BRAIN DURING THE DREAM STATE

The three major electrographic features of the D state are of obvious relevance to our attempt to answer the following three questions about the organization of the brain in the dream state.

How is the forebrain activated in the D state? Since EEG desynchronization also characterizes waking, similar mechanisms of "activation" may be involved in both instances. Physiological evidence suggests that this is so: the reticular formation of the anterior brain stem is at least as active in D sleep as it is in the waking state (see figure 2).

How is motor output blocked in the D state? Physiological evidence clearly shows that the profound EMG suppression of D sleep is a consequence

TABLE 1
Electrographic Criteria for Behavioral State Determination

State	Electromyogram	EEG	Electrooculogram
Waking	+	Low voltage, fast	+
Sleep Synchronized	+	High voltage, slow	-
Desynchronized	-	Low voltage, fast	+

FIGURE 1
Systems Model of Dream State Generation

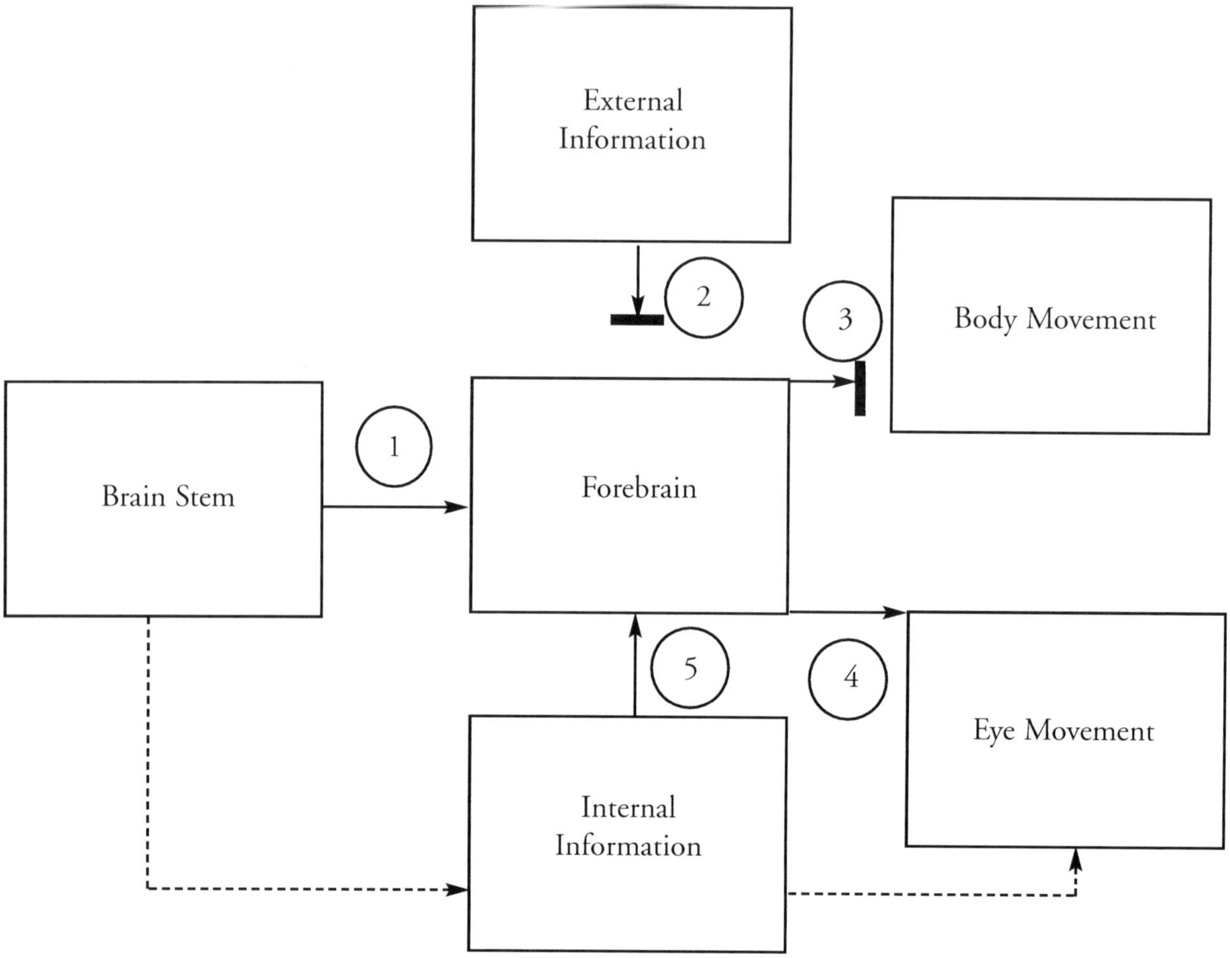

Processes Accounted for:

1 Activation of forebrain

2 Blockade of exteroceptive input

3 Blockade of motor output

4 Oculomotor activation

5 Provision of forebrain with internally generated information

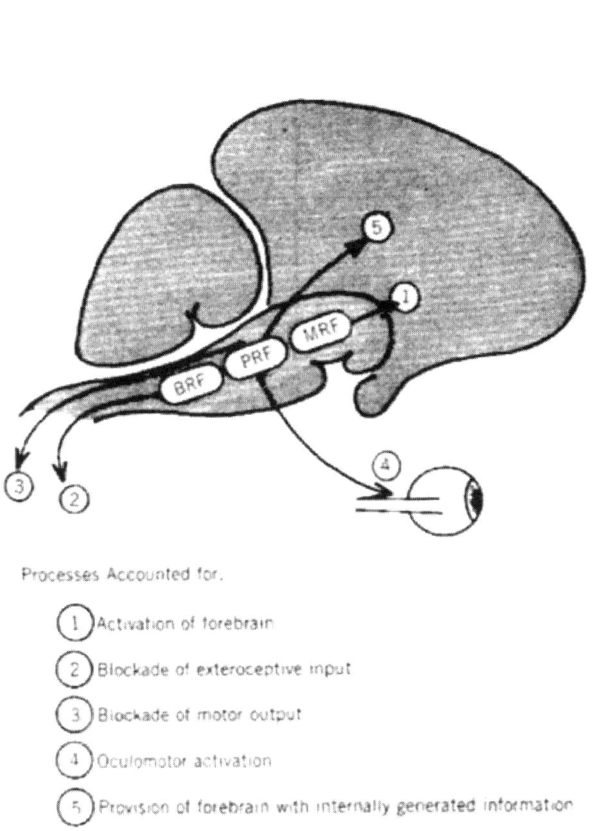

Figure 2. Physiological Model of Dream State Generation Using the Sagittal Section of the Cat Brain and Showing the Bulbar (BRF), Pontine (PRF), and Midbrain (MRF) Divisions of the Reticular Formation

of the direct inhibition of spinal cord motoneurons (6). As a consequence, any organized motor patterns that might be generated during the intense brain activation of D sleep cannot be expressed.

That organized movement patterns are in fact generated, but not expressed, in normal D sleep is dramatically demonstrated by cats with lesions of the anterodorsal pontine brain stem (7). The animals show all of the major manifestations of D sleep except the atonia; instead of the fine twitches of the digits and the limb jerks that are normally present in D, these cats display complex motor behaviors including repetitive paw movements and well-coordinated attack and defense sequences that have no apparent relationship to the environment.

How is sensory imagery generated in the D state? In waking, a corollary discharge of the oculomotor system has been shown to suppress visual transmission during saccadic eye movements, possibly contributing to the stability of the visual field during that state (8). The same mechanisms might underlie the hallucinoid dream imagery by inhibiting and exciting neurons of the lateral geniculate body (9) and the visual cortex (10) during D sleep, when retinal input is reduced and unformed.

The possibility that oculomotor impulses trigger visual imagery is particularly intriguing in view of the demonstrated quantitative correlation between eye movement intensity and dream intensity (11). More specific correlations have also been reported to relate eye movement direction to orientation of the hallucinated gaze in dreams (12). This finding has been interpreted as indicative of "scanning" the visual field—implying cortical control of the eye movements in dreaming sleep. An alternative, although not exclusive, hypothesis is that the oculomotor activity is generated at the brain stem level and that the cortex is then provided with feed-forward information about the eye movements. According to this view, we are not so much scanning dream imagery with our D sleep eye movements as we are synthesizing the visual imagery appropriate to them. We will return to the implications of this intriguing possibility in discussing the generation of eye movements in dreaming sleep, but we wish to stress here the general significance of this clue to the identity of an "internal information generator" operating at the brain stem level in the dreaming sleep state.

The eye-movement-related inhibition of sensory relays (13), as well as the possible occlusion of exogenous inputs by internally generated excitation, may also contribute to the maintenance of sleep in the face of strong central activation of the brain. In this sense the dream process is seen as having a sleep maintenance mechanism built into its physiological substrate rather than a sleep guardian function operating at the psychological level. A firm general conclusion can be reached at this point: the desynchronized phase of sleep is the physiological substrate of hallucinoid dreaming, as defined. This conclusion is of profound significance to psychophysiology, since we can now reliably and objectively characterize and measure many aspects of the brain when it is in the dream state. For example, one feature that emerges from the psychophysiological study of dreaming and one that was not at all evident from introspective, psychoanalytically oriented research, is that the brain enters the dream state at regular intervals during sleep and stays in that state for appreciable and predictable lengths of time. One clear implication of this finding is that dreaming is an automatically preprogrammed brain event and not a response to exogenous (day residue) or endogenous (visceral) stimuli. A second implication is that the dream state generator mechanism is periodic, that is, the dream state generator is a neurobiological clock (14). Since the length of the sleep cycle and, by inference, the frequency of dreaming, is a function of body size within and across mammalian species (15), the system controlling the length of the period must have a structural substrate. Thus we must account for size-related periodicity with our model of the dream state generator.

AN ANIMAL MODEL OF THE BRAIN DURING THE DREAM STATE

We said that the length of the sleep cycle varies "across species." Does that mean that nonhuman animals dream? Unfortunately we cannot know, but we are willing to assert that if they do so, it is when their brains are in the D sleep state. Because we have no direct evidence of any significant difference between the brain state of man and the brain state of other mammals in D sleep, we therefore feel justified in asserting that the brain state of our experimental animal, the cat, constitutes a reasonable subject for our study of the brain as a dream process generator, whether or not cats dream. This assertion seems justified since we are restricting our attention here to formal aspects of the dream experience; our experimental model need not dream or even possess "consciousness" to be useful as a source of physiological information. If we accept this argument and use the definition of dreaming offered above, then the presence of D sleep in cats (16) offers nothing less than an animal model in which to study the neurophysiological basis of a hallucinoidmental process in man. Such a model is as important in experimental psychiatry as it is rare. Let us now turn to the biological data upon which our sketches of the brain as a dream state generator are based.

LOCALIZATION OF THE POWER SUPPLY OR TRIGGER ZONE OF THE DREAM STATE GENERATOR

Lesion, stimulation, and recording studies pioneered by Jouvet (17) have strongly implicated the pontine brain stem as critical to the generation of the desynchronized sleep phase (see figure 3 for a summary of the neuroanatomy of this region). Important findings supporting this hypothesis include the following.

Large lesions of the pontine reticular formation prevent the occurrence of desynchronized sleep for several weeks in cats (17). This suggests that the pontine reticular formation may be the site of an executive or triggering mechanism for desynchronized sleep. Prepontine transections and forebrain ablation have no effect upon periodicity or duration of the skeletal, muscular, and oculomotor manifestations of D sleep (17). The data indicate that the trigger, the power supply, and the clock are pontine.

The pontine brain stem is thus implicated as the site of both the trigger and the clock. The periodicity of the D sleep clock in poikilothermic pontine cats lengthens as temperature declines, indicating orthodox metabolic mediation of the cycle, in contrast to the temperature independence of circadian rhythms. If we assume that the physiological substrate of consciousness is in the forebrain, these facts completely eliminate any possible contribution of ideas (or their neural substrate) to the primary driving force of the dream process.

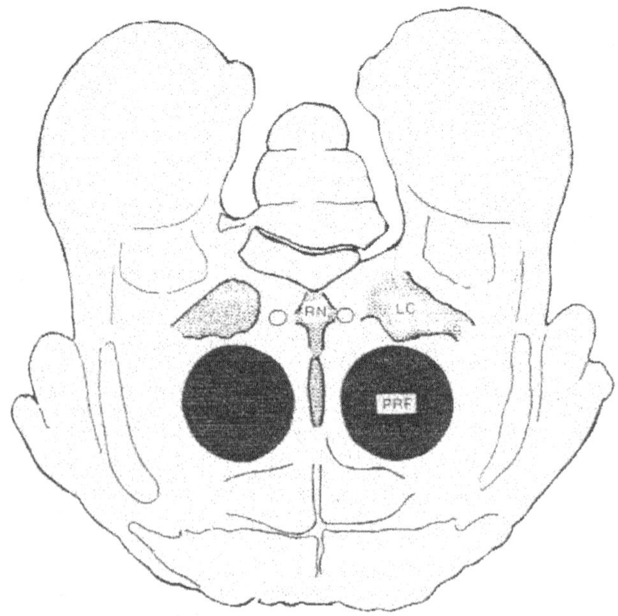

Figure 3. The Anatomy of the Pontine Brain Stem

Small lesions of the dorsal pontine brain stem, in the region of the locus coeruleus (LC), may eliminate the atonia but no other aspects of desynchronized sleep (7). This suggests that inhibition of muscle tone is somehow dependent upon the integrity of the LC. The elaborate motor behavior that characterizes the D sleep of cats with LC lesions has been described as "pseudo-hallucinatory"(7). Whether or not one accepts the sensory implications of that designation, the importance of motor inhibition in quelling the effects of central excitation during the dream state is clear.

This finding has an important bearing on mechanisms of dream paralysis and suggests that in the classic chase dream, the dreamer who has trouble fleeing from a pursuer is as much accurately reading the activated state of his motor pattern generator and the paralyzed state of his spinal neurons as he is "wishing" to be caught. This dream experience is so universal and the feeling of constrained motor action so impressive as to make its physiological basis in the descending inhibition of motoneurons seem to us inescapable. Conversely, this reasonable and adequate explanation of the paradox of the chase dream makes its interpretation as wish fulfillment less compelling. Other implications of the D sleep activation of various motor system pattern generators for movements and dream plots have been discussed elsewhere (3).

The vestibular system, as classically established, integrates head position and movement with eye position and posture. Pompeiano and Morrison (18) showed that lesions of the vestibular nuclei interfered with the bursts of REM but not with the isolated eye movements of D. This finding suggested that the vestibular system contributed to the elaboration and rhythmicity of the eye movements but that the eye movement generator was extravestibular. Magherini and associates (19) found that systemic injections of the anticholinesterase agent physostigmine produced rhythmic eye movements in decerebrate cats, suggesting that the eye movement generator may be cholinergic. Thus the central, automatic activation during sleep of the vestibular system may provide a substrate for endogenously generated, specific information about body position and movement. Flying dreams may thus be a logical, direct, and unsymbolic way of synthesizing information generated endogenously by the vestibular system in D sleep. In view of this reasonable and direct explanation, it seems gratuitous to "interpret" the sensual flying dream as sexual.

In accord with the isomorphism principle, the degree of neuronal activation in brain systems should parallel the frequency and intensity of dreams to these systems (3), and the predominance of visual sensorimotor activity in both brain and mind supports this notion. Symbol formation and the often bizarre juxtaposition of sensations in the dream may be a reflection of the heightened degree of simultaneous activation of multiple sensory channels in dreaming as compared with waking (3).

Long-term electrical stimulation of the pontine brain stem results in the earlier appearance of sleep episodes and in increases in the absolute amounts of desynchronized sleep, but it does not affect the periodicity of its occurrence (20). By implication, the delivery of electrical energy accomplishes what most psychological and behavioral treatments fail to achieve: an increase in the duration of dreaming sleep. Testing the assumption that the generator neurons are cholinoceptive, our laboratory team has recently established that injection of the cholinergic agent carbachol into the pontine reticular formation produces prolonged enhancement of D-like sleep behavior (21). In man the parenteral injection of the anticholinesterase agent physostigmine potentiates D sleep, and the pharmacologically induced episodes are associated with hallucinoid dreaming (22). The time of occurrence and duration of dreams may thus be chemically determined.

In summary, these results support the hypothesis that the pontine brain stem is the generator zone for the D sleep state. The trigger mechanism for the whole system, including the eye movement generator, may be cholinoceptive and the executive zones are probably in the reticular formation. The LC is involved, possibly in a permissive or reciprocal way, and is especially important in mediating spinal reflex inhibition. Together, these two regions may constitute the clock. We will have more to say about the hypothesis of reciprocal interaction between them later in this paper.

Although the brain stem mechanisms mediating atonia remain obscure, it is clear from the work of Pompeiano (6) that both monosynaptic and polysynaptic spinal reflexes are tonically inhibited during D sleep (see figure 4). In addition, during the bursts of REM, there is a descending presynaptic inhibition of the most rapidly conducting (group 1a), spinal afferent endings. Both presynaptic and postsynaptic inhi-

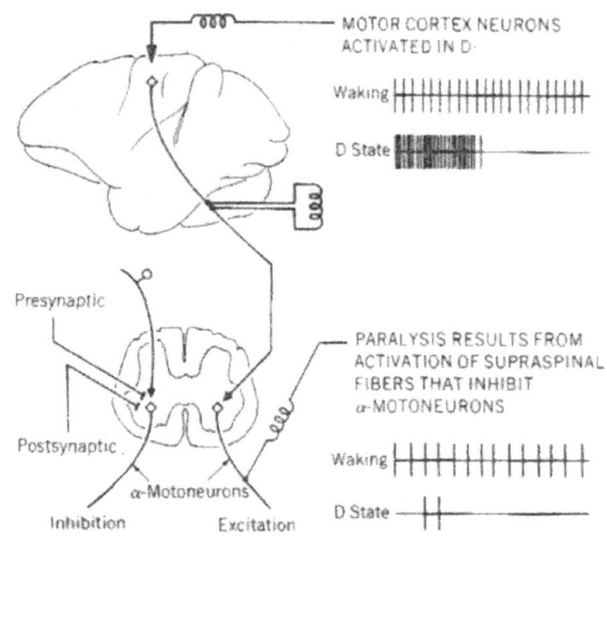

Figure 4. Mechanisms of Sleep Paralysis

bition appear to be of brain stem origin. Phasic presynaptic inhibition has also been shown to occur in sensory relays elsewhere in the brain during D sleep (6). Thus motor output is tonically damped throughout D and sensory input is phasically damped in concert with the REM bursts. In other words, we are not only paralyzed during our dreams, but the degree to which we are paralyzed fluctuates in concert with the intensity of the internally generated information and the degree to which we suppress exogenous input.

On the basis of this evidence, the systems terminology used earlier (see figure 1) can be tentatively translated into the anatomical and psychological terms of figure 2; and the activation-synthesis hypothesis of dreaming can be stated as follows: during D sleep, a cholinergic mechanism in the reticular formation of the pontine brain stem is periodically activated. The consequences of this activation are as follows:

1. The forebrain is tonically activated, probably via the midbrain reticular formation that is also responsible for its activation during waking. Thus the forebrain is made ready to process information.
2. Thc spinal reflexes are tonically inhibited, possibly via the bulbar reticular formation and LC; thus motor outflow is blocked despite high levels of activity in the brain, including the motor cortex.
3. The oculomotor and vestibular systems are phasically activated by the pontine reticular formation so as to produce eye movements. This circuitry, in its entirety, is an internal information source or generator that provides the forebrain with spatially specific but temporally disorganized information about eye velocity, relative position, and direction of movement. Information may similarly be derived from the brain stem generators of patterned motor activity.
4. At the same time that internal information feedback is being generated by the activation of various motor systems, exteroceptive input to sensory systems is phasically blocked. This may intensify the relative impact of the endogenous inputs to the brain, accounting for the intensity of dream imagery and preventing sleep disruption by the externally generated excitation.

This working sketch of the dream state generator, based on the classical localizing methods of experimental neorology, is intriguing but unsatisfying, in that it fails to specify the mechanisms by which the pontine generator is turned on, kept active for a time, and then shut off. Further, it does not say anything about the mechanism of periodicity. To provide details about the anatomy and physiology of the periodic trigger mechanisms of the generator process, we will now turn our attention to the neuronal level of analysis. In doing so, we also come full circle in our reaffirmation of isomorphism since it was the neuron that Freud recognized as the physical unit of the nervous system on which he based his dream theory (2).

HISTOLOGICAL FEATURES OF RELEVANCE TO THE PERIODIC TRIGGERING OF THE DREAMING SLEEP STATE GENERATOR

Several structural details of the pontine brain stem are notable as possible elements of a D sleep control device with rhythmic properties (see figure 3 for an illustration of the anatomy discussed). In his discussion of the histology of the pontine brain stem, Cajal (23) emphasized three points:

1. The paramedian reticular giant cells, with their rostral and caudal axonal are admirably suited to serve as output elements of the generator; when excited they could influence many other cells. The work of Brodal (24) and the Scheibels (25) shows that the spinal cord and thalamus receive projections from these elements. Although they are relatively few in number, conservative estimates of their postsynaptic domain indicate that each directly protects to nine million ($9x10^6$) postsynaptic neurons. Thus the 3,000 pontine reticular giant cells in the cat might make many billions of synapses ($2.9x10^{10}$). Since the giant cells also project to other brain stem nuclei and have recurrent axons to themselves, mutual interaction with raphetype elements (see below) and self-reexcitation are both possible. These two features could be used to create excitability variability, with powerful consequences for the whole nervous system.

2. The raphe neurons of the midline are ideally situated and connected to regulate excitability of paramedian elements, and they also have extensive projections to other brain regions. The discovery that these cells concentrate the biogenic amine serotonin (26) gives this regulatory hypothesis an attractive corollary: these cells might regulate excitability of their postsynaptic neurons via specific transmitter substances. Another brain stem cell group, in the locus coeruleus, has been shown to concentrate the amine norepinephrine (26). There are thus at least two neuronal candidates for a level setting role, and both are probably inhibitory. Since the giant cells are excitatory (and probably cholinergic; see below), a substrate for reciprocal interaction is established.

3. Cajal (23) suggested that input to the central reticular core might be via small stellate cells in the lateral zone. This input channel, which we now know to be more diffuse than was originally suspected, could be used to abort or damp the core oscillator at critical ambient stimulus levels. This is an important feature, since adaptation

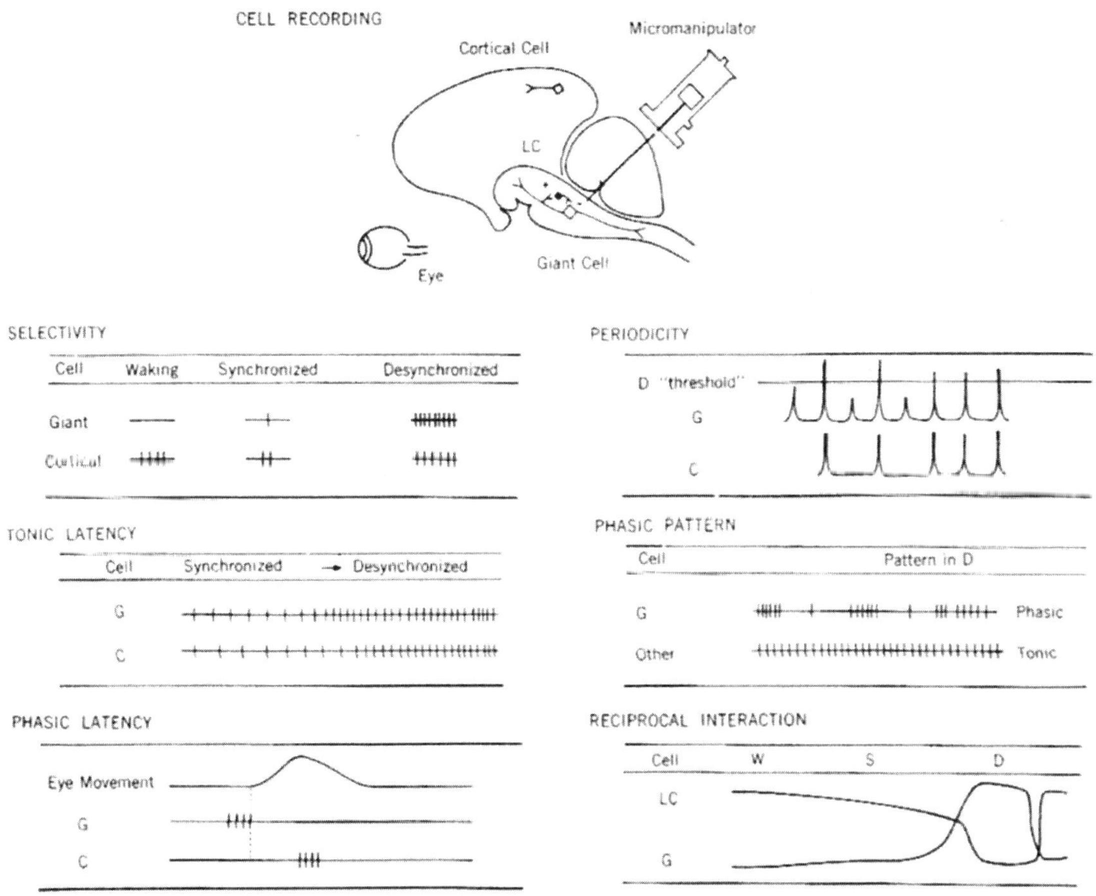

Figure 5. Cellular Neurophysiology of Dream State Generation

depends on the capacity to interrupt the cycle and not to incorporate all exogenous stimuli into the dream plot.

CELLULAR ACTIVITY IN THE PONTINE BRAIN STEM DURING THE SLEEP CYCLE

A direct experimental approach to the question of D state control has been made with cats by recording from individual neurons in many parts of the brain as the sleep cycle normally evolved. In this experimental paradigm, the frequency and pattern of extracellular action potentials, which are the signal units of nerve cells, are taken as indices of a cell's excitability; the influence of a recorded neuron upon other cells and that neuron's own control mechanism may also be inferred from the data. This method has the advantage of being relatively physiological since it does little to alter or damage the properties of the system under study. When cats are kept active at night, they will sleep under the necessary conditions of restraint during the daytime. The microelectrodes can then be stereotaxically directed at the brain stem and individual cell activity recorded for as long as 20 hours, allowing many successive sleep cycles to be studied (see figure 5).

The pontine brain stem control hypothesis has been tested in three ways at the level of single cells.

Selectivity criterion: which cells change rate most in D? We assumed that cells which showed pronounced alterations in discharge rate over the sleep cycle were more likely to be playing a controlling role than those showing minimal change. We further assumed that those cells having peaks of activity in phase with the D phase of the cycle were more likely to be specifically and actively involved in dreaming sleep state control than those with multiple peaks. We found that the giant cells of the pontine tegmentum concentrated their discharge in the D phase of sleep to a greater extent than any other group of neurons (27). They became our prime candidate for a generator function.

Tonic latency criterion: which cells change rate first in D onset? If the cells with positive discharge selectivity were driving the dreaming sleep phase of the sleep cycle, then their rates would be expected to increase in advance of the behavioral state change. Such phase leads might well be longer than those of the follower neurons under the control of the giant cells. The giant cells, when recorded over entire sleep cycles and through repeated sleep cycles, were found to change rate continuously (28). Significant rate increases occurred *as long as 5 minutes* before a desynchronized sleep phase. When the 2 minutes just prior to desynchronized sleep onset were studied, a rate increase in a pool of giant cells was observed 10 seconds before a similar increase in a pool of cerebral cortical neurons.

The rapidly accelerating limb of the giant cell activity curves at D sleep phase onset indicated that this was neurons. The goodness of fit of the data by an exponential curve indicated that reexcitation within the pool might be superimposed upon disinhibition from without. The positive tonic latency indicated that the activation of the forebrain might be a consequence of activation of the brain stem but that the converse could not be the case.

Phasic latency criterion: which cells fire before eye movements of D? Because of the proximity and direct projections to oculomotor neurons from giant cells, we tested the possibility that they might be generating the REMs so characteristic of the desynchronized phase of sleep by determining the time of occurrence of short-term rate increases by the giant cells in relation to eye movement onset. On the average, such rate increases were more prominent and anticipated eye movement by longer intervals than other brain stem neurons (29). Rate increases by presumed follower elements (in the posterolateral cerebral cortex) *followed* the eye movements by many milliseconds. It could therefore be concluded that the eye movements might be initiated by giant cells but could not be generated by cortical neurons. This finding practically wrecks the scanning hypothesis and strongly favors the idea that visual cortical events are determined by events in the oculomotor brain stem.

At this point we felt justified in concluding that the giant cells of the pontine tegmentum were critical output elements in a sleep cycle control mechanism. More particularly, we proposed that they might be generator elements for some of the tonic and phasic excitatory events in the desynchronized sleep phase of the cycles; most important to the activation-synthesis hypothesis of dreaming are the determination of EEG desynchronization (activation of the forebrain) and REMs (provision of forebrain with internally generated information). At the very least, we felt that we had found an important avenue to understanding sleep cycle control, since we could now examine the properties and possible mechanisms of giant cell excitability regulation. In this regard there are three additional points worthy of emphasis.

Periodicity criterion. Long-term recordings of giant cells revealed peaks of activity in phase with each full-blown desynchronized sleep episode (30) (see figure 6). Less prominent peaks were associated with abortive episodes and were rarely seen with no electrographic evidence of desynchronized sleep. Spectral analysis of these long-term data confirmed the impression of powerful periodicity in the discharge peaks, indicting that 1) sleep cycles are periodic, 2) underlying cell activity is probably even more so, and by definition, 3) cell excitability is under the control of a neurobiological clock. The possible mechanisms of excitability control are thus of great interest.

Phasic pattern criterion. The pattern of giant cell discharge within each D sleep episode indicated that classical pacemaker mechanisms are not involved in giant cell excitability regulation (31). Regular interspike intervals were exceptional, indicating that the rate increases were not caused by endogenous membrane depolarizations. The tendency, rather, was for giant cells to discharge in intermittent, prolonged clusters of irregularly distributed spikes as if the cells were responding to excitatory postsynaptic potentials from other neurons (see figure 7). In our view, a likely source of much of this input, especially as the longer clusters developed, was other giant cells. Once other neurons were excited, feedback from them is to be expected. It also seemed likely that the clusters of giant cell discharge were causally related to the eye movement bursts of the D sleep phase.

Reciprocal interaction criterion. If giant cell excitability change is not an intrinsic property of the giant cells, what other cell group might regulate it and in what way might that regulation be effected? Since all indices showed giant cells to discharge first in relation to both the tonic and phasic events of desynchronized sleep, we considered the possible contribution of

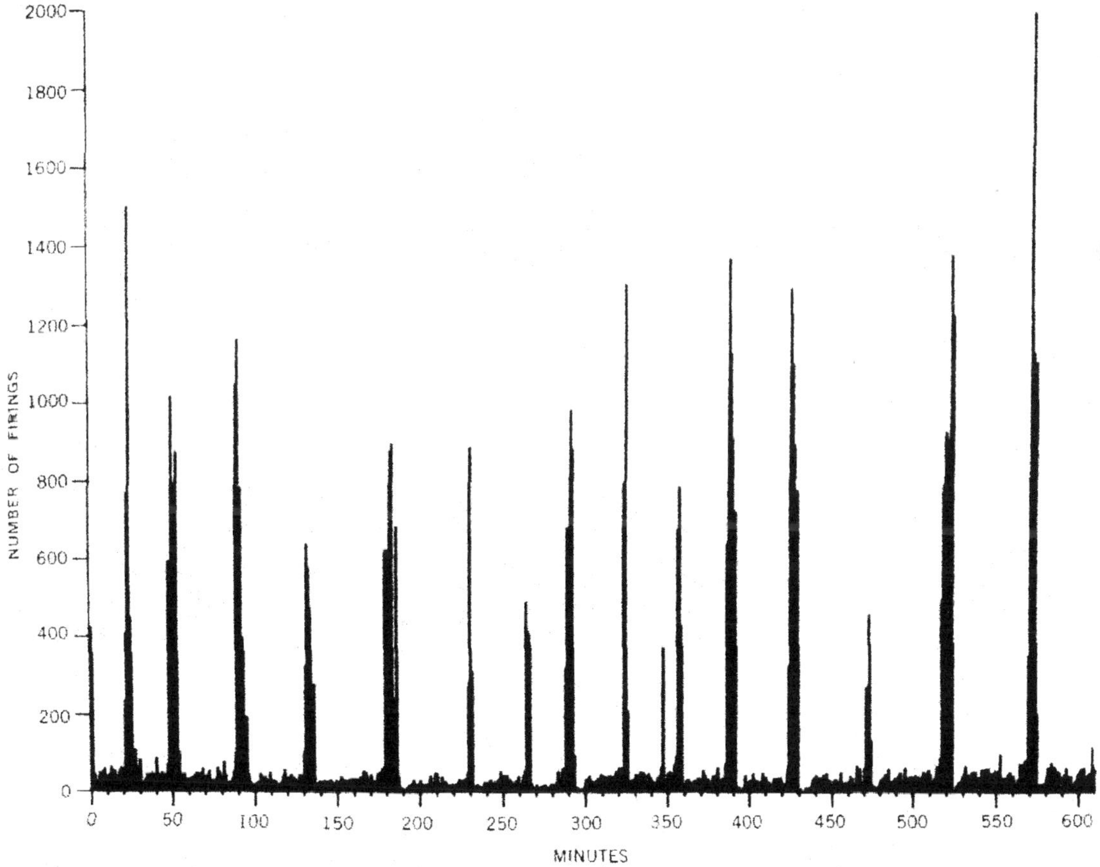

Figure 6. Discharge Activity of a Giant Cell Neuron Recorded over Multiple Sleep-Waking Cycles

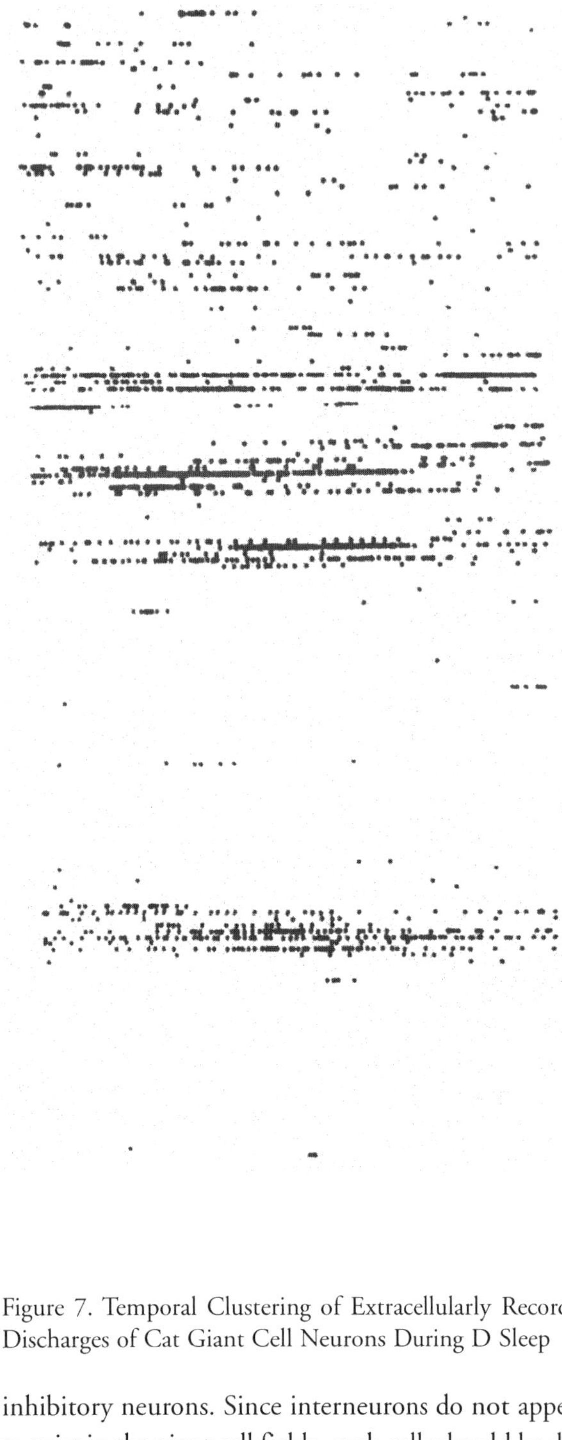

Figure 7. Temporal Clustering of Extracellularly Recorded Discharges of Cat Giant Cell Neurons During D Sleep

inhibitory neurons. Since interneurons do not appear to exist in the giant cell fields, such cells should be discrete from but proximal to the giant cell. To be effective, projections should be abundant and should have inhibitory transmitter action upon the giant cells. Reciprocal rate changes during the sleep cycle are to be expected if such cells exist. We have discovered just such changes in a small number of unidentified cells in the region of the posterior locus coeruleus and the nucleus subcoeruleus (32). Not only is discharge concentration of these elements quantitatively inverse to those of the giant cells in the phases of the cycle, but their decelerating rate curve is the approximate mirror image of that of the giant cells at desynchronized sleep onset as seen in part C. We called such cells "D-off" cells to contrast their activity curves with those of the giant cells, prototypes of the "D-on" species of neurons. We do not know if the "D-off" cells are catecholaminergic but their location and discharge properties make this possible.

McGinty and associates (33) have found similar reciprocal rate changes in the dorsal raphe nucleus (DRN) neurons and we have recently confirmed this finding. The low regular rates of discharge by these cells in waking suggest a level-setting or pacemaker function. Their location and discharge properties are the same as those cells thought to be serotonergic on the basis of pharmacological experiments (34). Since both the LC and DRN are adjacent to and project to giant cells, and since giant cells receive abundant serotonergic and catecholaminergic endings, we thought that the mutual interconnections of these D-on and D-off cells could form a substrate for reciprocal interaction which regulated sleep cycle oscillation (30).

A MODEL FOR A BRAIN STEM SLEEP CYCLE OSCILLATOR

Restricting attention to within-sleep changes, we constructed a physiological model that bears a striking resemblance to the a priori schema derived from Cajal (see figure 8, top portion). Most of the connections have been demonstrated but many of the synaptic assumptions are as yet unproven physiologically. In addition to being explanatory, the model suggests experiments, particularly those employing pharmacological methods, the results of which will lead to its future modification. Since the LC, DRN, and giant cell groups are chemically differentiated, we deduced that their action and interaction may involve specific neurotransmitters.

In preliminary tests of the model, we have found that microinjection of the cholinomimetic substance carbachol into the giant cell zone not only gives more potent desynchronized sleep phase enhancement than injections into the adjacent tegmental fields but simultaneously activates giant cells. The results also indicate that an opposite effect is obtained at locus

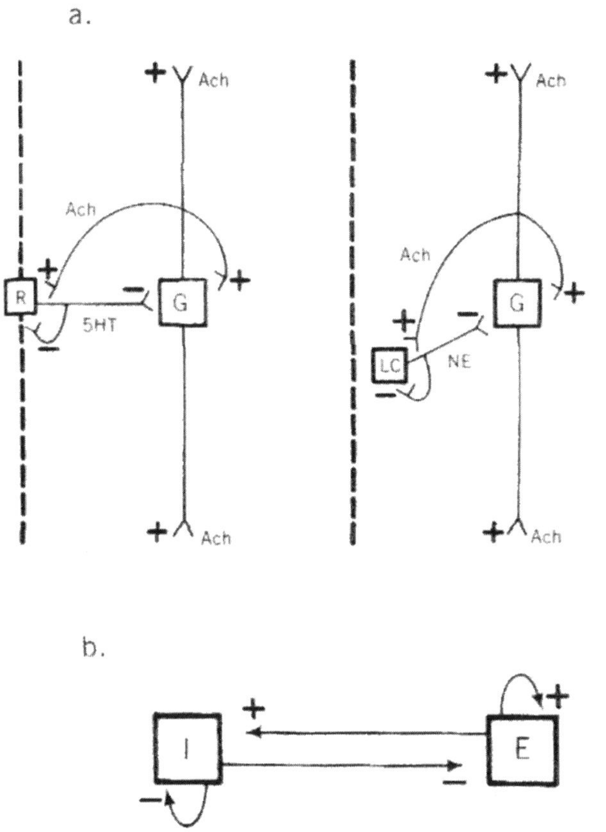

Figure 8. Reciprocal Interaction Model of Generator Process

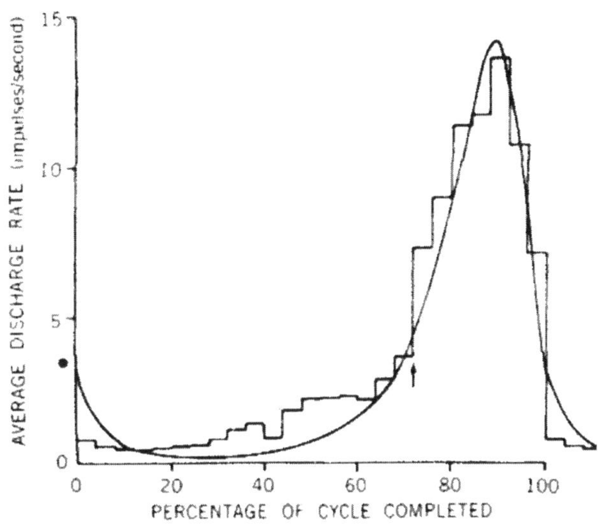

Figure 9. Time Course of Giant Cell Activity over the Sleep Cycle

coeruleus sites (as if an inhibitory cell group were being activated). We have not yet tested this last hypothesis directly, but the LC cells do resume firing before the end of D sleep. We assume that as FTG excitation declines and LC inhibition grows, the cycle ends. In the decerebrate cat, physostigmine-induced D episodes are associated with activation of neurons in the giant cell and suppression of firing by cells in the LC and DRN (35).

The physiological model can be reduced to a simple unit susceptible to mathematical analysis (see figure 8, bottom portion). Cell group E (giant cell) and cell group I (raphe and/or LC) are assumed to be mutually interconnected; cell group E is excitatory to itself and to group I, which inhibits itself and group E. Growth of activity in one group occurs at the expense of growth in the other, and vice versa. As such the cell groups are analogous to two populations, prey and predator, whose interaction can be described by a set of non-linear differential equations, the Lotka-Volterra equations (30). As shown in figure 9, the time course of activity of cell group E closely resembles that predicted by these equations. It is now possible to plot the activity curves of cell group I and compare the actual data with the curves predicted by the model. The phase lag between the reciprocal cycles remains to be explained and the previously noted fact that cycle length is proportional to brain size suggests that a distance factor may be at work. The distance between the two cell fields could be such a factor through its determination of protein transport time. Assuming an average LC-FTG internuclear distance of 2.5 mm and a fast protein transport time of 96 mm/day, a period length of about 35 minutes is predicted for the cat. This figure is within limits normal for that species. Another possible substrate for the long, size-dependent time constant of the cycle is the recently discovered class of long-duration postsynaptic transmitter actions (36) that may be mediated by second messengers such as cyclic AMP (37). Since the cyclic nucleotides activate protein kinases, the metabolic activity of the neuron, including the synthesis of neurotransmitters can be linked to and entrained by membrane events.

An important point is that the mathematical model parallels, but is not identical to, the physiological model. This means that even if the specific assumptions about physiological interaction are incorrect, the mathematical model may be viable and useful in another system—for example, the coupling of the circadian and ultradian oscillators (14) or, at another level of analysis, in a colecular system. This is particularly important to keep in mind since it is also at the

Figure 10
Two Models of the Dream Process*

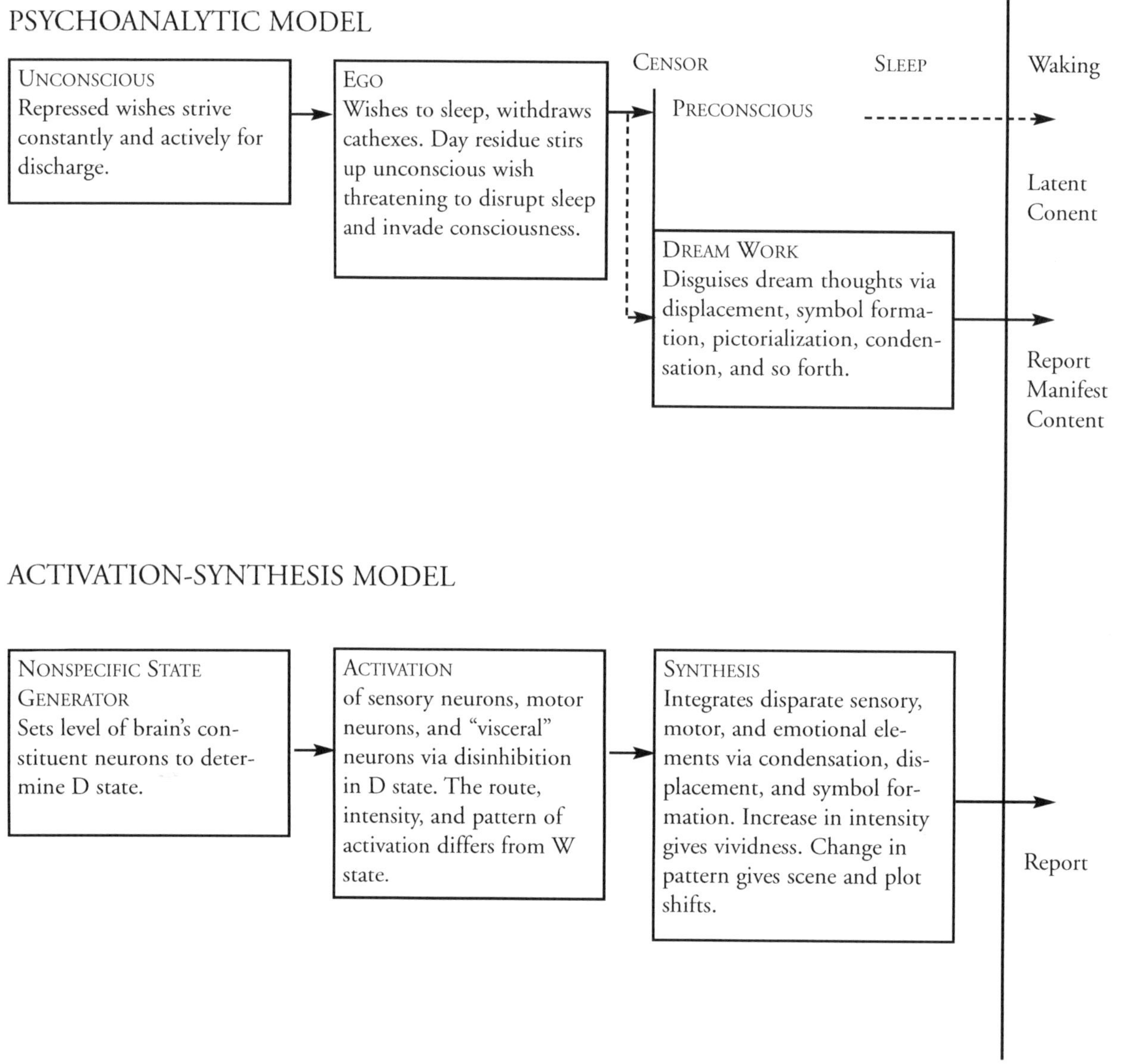

molecular level that time constant elements necessary to explain the long periodicity of the sleep-dream cycle may be found.

PSYCHOLOGICAL IMPLICATIONS OF THE CELLULAR NEUROPHYSIOLOGY OF DREAM SLEEP GENERATION

Hallucinoid dreaming is regarded as the psychological concomitant of D sleep. Brain activity in the D state has been analyzed to account for activation of the forebrain occlusion of sensory input, blockade of motor output at the spinal cord level, and the generation of information within the system. The evidence that the pontine brain stem contains a clock-trigger mechanism that contributes to activation of the forebrain, occlusion of sensory input, and the generation of internal information has been reviewed. The periodicity of the triggering mechanism is hypothesized to be a function of reciprocal interaction of reciprocally connected, chemically coded cell groups in the pontine brain stem.

The psychological implications of this model, which we call the activation-synthesis hypothesis of the dream process (schematically represented in figure 10), contrast sharply with many tenets of the dream theory provided by psychoanalysis (also represented in figure 10) in the following ways:

1. *The primary motivating force for dreaming* is not psychological but physiological since the time of occurrence and duration of dreaming sleep are quite constant, suggesting a preprogrammed, neurally determined genesis. In fact, the neural mechanisms involved can now be precisely specified. This conclusion does not, of course, mean that dreams are not also psychological events; nor does it imply that they are without psychological meaning or function. But it does imply that the process is much more basic than the psychodynamically determined, evanescent, "guardian of sleep" process that Freud had imagined it to be; and it casts serious doubt upon the exclusively psychological significance attached to both the occurrence and quality of dreams.

2. *Specific stimuli for the dream imagery* appear to arise intracerebrally but from the pontine brain stem and not in cognitive areas of the cerebrum. These stimuli, whose generation appears to depend upon a largely random or reflex process, may provide spatially specific information which can be used in constructing dream imagery; but the unusual intensity, intermittency, and velocity of the eye movements may also contribute to features of the dream experience which are formally bizarre and have been interpreted as defensive by psychoanalysis. Thus such features as scene shifts, time compression, personal condensations, splitting, and symbol formation may be directly isomorphic with the state of the nervous system during dreaming sleep. In other words, the forebrain may be making the best of a bad job in producing even partially coherent dream imagery from the relatively noisy signals sent up to it from the brain stem.

   The dream process is thus seen as having its origin in sensorimotor systems, with little or no primary ideational, volitional, or emotional content. This concept is markedly different from that of the "dream thoughts" or wishes seen by Freud as the primary stimulus for the dream. The sensorimotor stimuli are viewed as possibly providing a frame into which ideational, volitional, or emotional content may be projected to form the integrated dream image, but this frame is itself conflict free. Thus both the major energetic drive for the dream process and the specific stimulus of the dream content are genotypically deter- mined and therefore conflict free in the specifically psychodynamic sense of the term.

3. *The elaboration of the brainstem stimulus* by the perceptual, conceptual, and emotional structures of the forebrain is viewed as primarily a synthetic constructive process, rather than a distorting one as Freud presumed. Best fits to the relative inchoate and incomplete data provided by the primary stimuli are called up from memory, the access to which is facilitated during dreaming sleep. The brain, in the dreaming sleep state, is thus likened to a computer searching its addresses for key words. Rather than indicating a need for disguise, this fitting of phenotypic experiential data to genotypic stimuli is seen as the major basis of the "bizarre" formal qualities of dream mentation. There is, therefore, no need to postulate either a censor or an information degrading process working at the censor's behest. The dream content elaborated by the forebrain may include conflictually charged memories, but even this aspect of dream construction is seen as synthetic and transparent rather than degradative and opaque.

4. *With respect to the forgetting of dreams*, the normally poor recall is seen principally to reflect a state-dependent amnesia, since a carefully effected state change, to waking, may produce abundant recall even of highly charged dream material. There is thus no need to invoke repression to account for the forgetting of dreams. This hypothesis is appealingly economical, and in the light of the reciprocal interaction hypothesis dream amnesia can now be modeled in a testable way as the result of a different balance between cholinergic and aminergenic neuronal activity and the resulting effects on second messengers and macromolecules (5). Among its other surprising gifts to psychophysiology, dreaming sleep may thus also provide a biological model for the study of memory, and a functional role for dreaming sleep in promoting some aspect of the learning process is suggested.

SUMMARY AND CONCLUSIONS

Assuming that isomorphism, or identity of form, must characterize the simultaneous physiological and psychological events during dreaming, we have reviewed the general and cellular neurophysiology of dreaming sleep in search of new ways of accounting for some of the formal aspects of dream psychology. We have noted that the occurrence of dreaming depends upon the periodic activation of the forebrain during sleep. We have hypothesized that the activated forebrain synthesizes the dreams by fitting experiential data to information endogenously and automatically generated by reticular, vestibular, and oculomotor neurons in the pontine brain stem. A specific physiological and mathematical model of the pontine generator, based upon single cell recording studies in cats, is described: the model posits reciprocal interaction between inhibitory aminergic (level-setting) and excitatory cholinergic (generator) neurons.

Some of the "bizarre" formal features of the dream may directly reflect the properties of the brain stem neuronal generator mechanism. The physiological features of the generator mechanisms and their corresponding psychological implications include the following: the automaticity and periodicity of activation indicate a metabolically determined, conflict-free energetics of the dream process; the random but specific nature of the generator signals could provide abnormally sequenced and shaped, but spatiotemporally specific, frames for dream imagery and the clustering of runs of generator signals might constitute time-marks for dream subplots and scene changes. Further, the activation by generator neurons of diffuse postsynaptic forebrain elements in multiple parallel channels might account for the disparate sensory, motor, and emotional elements that contribute to the "bizarreness" of dreams; the suppression of motor output and sensory input simultaneous with central activation of both sensory and motor patterns could assure the maintenance of sleep in the face of massive central excitation of the brain; and the change in the ratio of neurotransmitters affecting forebrain neurons might account for dream amnesia and indicate a state-dependent alteration of neural plasticity, with implications for the learning process.

REFERENCES

1. Freud S: The interpretation of dreams (1900), in The Complete Psychological Works, standard ed, vols 4 and 5. Translated and edited by Strachey J. London, Hogarth Press. 1966
2. McCarley RW: Hobson JA: The neurobiological origins of psychoanalytic dream theory. Am J Psychiatry 134:1211-1221, 1977
3. McCarley RW: Mind-body isomorphism and the study of dreams, in Advances in Sleep Research. vol 6. Edited by Fishbein W. New York, Spectrum (in press)
4. Dement W, Kleitman N: The relation of eye movements during sleep to dream activity; an objective method for the study of dreaming. J Exp Psychol 53:89-97, 1957
5. Hobson JA: The reciprocal interaction model of sleep cycle control: implication for PGO wave generation and dream amnesia, in Sleep and Memory. Edited by Drucker-Colin R, McGaugh J. New York, Academic Press, 1977, pp 159-183
6. Pompeiano O: The neurophysiological mechanisms of the postural and motor events during desynchronized sleep. Res Publ Assoc Res Nerv Ment Dis 45:351-423, 1967
7. Jouvet M, Delorme F: Locus coeruleus et sommeil paradoxol. Soc Biol 159:895, 1965
8. Volkman F: Vision during voluntary saccadic eye movements. J Opt Soc Am 52:571-578, 1962
9. Bizzi E: Discharge pattern of single geniculate neurons during the rapid eye movements of sleep. J Neurophysiol 29:1087-1095, 1966
10. Evarts EV: Activity of individual cerebral neurons during sleep and arousal. Res Publ Assoc Res Nerv Ment Dis 45:319-337, 1967
11. Hobson JA, Goldfrank F, Snyder F: Sleep and respiration. J Psychiatr Res 3:79-90, 1965
12. Roffwarg HP, Dement WC, Muzio JN, et al: Dream imagery: relationship to rapid eye movements of sleep. Arch Gen Psychiatry 7:235-258, 1962
13. Pompeiano O: Sensory inhibition during motor activity in sleep, in Neurophysiological Basis of Normal and Abnormal Motor Activities. Edited by Yahr MD, Purpura DP. New York, Raven Press, 1967, pp. 323-375

14. Hobson JA: The sleep-dream cycle, a neurobiological rhythm, in Pathobiology Annual. Edited by Ioachim H. New York, Appleton-Century Crofts, 1975, pp 369-403

15. Zepelin H, Rechtschaffen A: Mammalian sleep, longevity and energy metabolism. Brain Behav Evol 10:425-470, 1974

16. Dement W: The occurrence of low-voltage fast electroencephalogram patterns during behavioral sleep in the cat. Electroencephalogr Clin Neurophysiol 10:291-296, 1958

17. Jouvet M: Recherches sur les structures nerveuses et les mecanismes responsables des differentes phases du sommeil physiologique. Arch Ital Biol 100:125-206, 1962

18. Pompeiano O, Morrison AR: Vestibular influences during sleep. I. Abolition of the rapid eye movements of desynchronized sleep following vestibular lesions. Arch Ital Biol 103:569-595, 1965

19. Magherini PC, Pompeiano O, Thoden U: Cholinergic mechanisms related to REM sleep. I. Rhythmic activity of the vestibulo-oculomotor system induced by an anticholinesterase in the decerebrate cat. Arch Ital Biol 110:234-259, 1972

20. Frederickson CH, Hobson JA: electrical stimulation of the brain stem and subsequent sleep. Arch Ital Biol 108:564-576, 1970

21. Amatruda TT, Black DA, McKenna TM, et al: Sleep cycle control and cholinergic mechanisms: differential effects of carbachol at pontine brain stem sites. Brain Res 98:501-515, 1975

22. Sitaram N, Wyatt RJ, Dawson S, et al: REM sleep induction by physostigmine infusion during sleep. Science 191:1281-1283, 1976

23. Cajal R: Histologie du System Nerveux, vol 1. Madrid, Consejo Superior de Investigaciones Cientificas, 1952

24. Brodal A: The Reticular Formation of the Brain Stem. Anatomical Aspects and Functional Correlations. Edinburgh, Oliver and Boyd, 1957

25. Scheibel ME, Scheibel AB: Anatomical basis of attention mechanisms in vertebrate brains, in The Neurosciences: A Study Program. Edited by Quarton GC, Melnechuk T, Schmitt FO. New York, Rockefeller University Press, 1967, pp 577-602

26. Dahlstrom A. Fuxe K: Evidence for the existence of monoamine-containing neurons in the central nervous system. I. Demonstration of monoamines in the cell bodies of brain stem neurons. Acta Physiol Scand 62:1-55, 1964

27. Hobson JA, McCarley RW, Pivik RT, et al: Selective firing by cat pontine brain stem neurons in desynchronized sleep. J Neurophysiol 37:497-511, 1974

28. Hobson JA, McCarley RW, Freedman R, el al: Time course of discharge rate changes by cat pontine brain stem neurons during the sleep cycle. J Neurophysiol 37:1297-1309, 1974

29. Pivik RT, McCarley RW, Hobson JA: Eye movement-associated discharge in brain stem neurons during desynchronized sleep. Brain Res 121:59-76, 1977

30. McCarley RW, Hobson JA: Neuronal excitability modulation over the sleep cycle: a structural and mathematical model. Science 189:58-60, 1975

31. McCarley RW, Hobson JA: Discharge patterns of cat pontine brain stem neurons during desynchronized sleep. J Neurophysiol 38:751-766, 1975

32. Hobson JA., McCarley RW, Wyzinksi PW: Sleep cycle oscillation: reciprocal discharge by two brainstem neuronal groups. Science 189:55-58, 1975

33. McGinty DJ, Harper RM, Fairbanks MK: 5 HT-containing neurons: unit activity in behaving cats, in Serotonin and Behavior. Edited by Barchas J, Usdin E. New York, Academic Press, 1973, pp 267-279

34. Aghajanian GK, Foote WE, and Sheard MH: Action of psychogenic drugs on single midbrain raphe neurons. J Pharmacol Exp Ther 171:178-187, 1970

35. Pompeiano O, Hoshino K: Central control of posture: reciprocal discharge by two pontine neuronal groups leading to suppression of decerbrate rigidity. Brain Res 116:131-138, 1976

36. Libel B: Generation of slow inhibitory and excitatory postsynaptic potentials. FED Proc 29:1945-1955,1970

37. Bloom FE: Role of cyclic nucleotides in central synaptic function. Rev Physiol Biochem Pharmacol 74:1-103, 1975.

12 The Effects of Choice and Enhanced Personal Responsibility for the Aged: A Field Experiment in an Institutional Setting

Ellen J. Langer, Graduate Center, City University of New York

Judith Rodin, Yale University

Requests for reprints should be sent to Ellen Langer, Social Personality Program, Graduate Center, City University of New York, 33 West 42nd Street, New York, New York, 10036, or to Judith Rodin, Department of Psychology, Yale University, New Haven, Connecticut, 06520.

The authors would like to express sincere thanks to Thomas Tolisano and the members of his staff at the Arden House in Hamden, Connecticut, for their thoughtful assistance in conducting this research.

A field experiment was conducted to assess the effects of enhanced personal responsibility and choice on a group of nursing home residents. It was expected that the debilitated condition of many of the aged residing in institutional settings is, at least in part, a result of living in a virtually decision-free environment and consequently is potentially reversible. Residents who were in the experimental group were given a communication emphasizing their responsibility for themselves, whereas the communication given to a second group stressed the staff's responsibility for them. In addition, to bolster the communication, the former group was given the freedom to make choices and the responsibility of caring for a plant rather than having decisions made and the plant taken care of for them by the staff, as was the case for the latter group. Questionnaire ratings and behavioral measures showed a significant improvement for the experimental group over the comparison group on alertness, active participation, and a general sense of well-being.

The transition from adulthood to old age is often perceived as a process of loss, physiologically and psychologically (Birren, 1958; Gould, 1972). However, it is as yet unclear how much of this change is biologically determined and how much is a function of the environment. The ability to sustain a sense of personal control in old age may be greatly influenced by societal factors, and this in turn may affect one's physical well-being.

Typically the life situation does change in old age. There is some loss of roles, norms, and reference groups, events that negatively influence one's perceived competence and feeling of responsibility (Bengston, 1973). Perception of these changes in addition to actual physical decrements may enhance a sense of aging and lower self-esteem (Lehr & Puschner, Note 1). In response to internal developmental changes, the aging individual may come to see himself in a position of lessened mastery relative to the rest of the world, as a passive object manipulated by the environment (Neugarten & Gutman, 1958). Questioning whether these factors can be counteracted, some studies have suggested that more successful aging—measured by decreased mortality, morbidity, and psychological disability—occurs when an individual feels a sense of usefulness and purpose (Bengston, 1973; Butler, 1967; Leaf, 1973; Lieberman, 1965).

The notion of competence is indeed central to much of human behavior. Adler (1930) has described the need to control one's personal environment as "an intrinsic necessity of life itself" (p. 398). deCharms (1968) has stated that "man's primary motivation propensity is to be effective in producing changes in his environment. Man strives to be a causal agent, to be the primary locus of, causation for, or the origin of, his behavior; he strives for personal causation" (p. 269).

Several laboratory studies have demonstrated that reduced control over aversive outcomes increases physiological distress and anxiety (Geer, Davison, & Gatchel, 1970; Pervin, 1963) and even a nonveridical perception of control over an impending event reduces the aversiveness of that event (Bowers, 1968; Glass & Singer, 1972; Kanfer & Seidner, 1973). Langer, Janis, and Wolfer (1975) found that by inducing the perception of control over stress in hospital patients by means of a communication that emphasized potential cognitive control, subjects requested fewer pain relievers and sedatives and were seen by nurses as evidencing less anxiety.

Choice is also a crucial variable in enhancing an induced sense of control. Stotland and Blumenthal (1964) studied the effects of choice on anxiety reduction. They told subjects that they were going to take a number of important ability tests. Half of the subjects were allowed to choose the order in which they wanted to take the tests, and half were told that the order was fixed. All subjects were informed that the order of the tests would have no bearing on their scores. They found that subjects not given the choice were more anxious, as measured by palmar sweating. In another study of the effects of choice, Corah and Boffa (1970) told their subjects that there were two conditions in the experiment, each of which would be signaled by a different light. In one condition they were given the choice of whether or not to press a button to escape from an aversive noise, and in the other one they were not given the option of escaping. They found that the choice instructions decreased the aversiveness of the threatening stimulus, apparently by increasing perceived control. Although using a very different paradigm, Langer (1975) also demonstrated the importance of choice. In that study it was found that the exercise of choice in a chance situation, where choice was objectively inconsequential, nevertheless had psychological consequences manifested in increased confidence and risk taking.

Lefcourt (1973) best summed up the essence of this research in a brief review article dealing with the perception of control in man and animals when he concluded that "the sense of control, the illusion that one can exercise personal choice, has a definite and a positive role in sustaining life" (p. 424). It is not surprising, then, that these important psychological factors should be linked to health and survival. In a series of retrospective studies, Schmale and his associates (Adamson & Schmale, 1965; Schmale 1958; Schmale & Iker, 1966) found that ulcerative colitis, leukemia, cervical cancer, and heart disease were linked with a feeling of helplessness and loss of hope experienced by the patient prior to the onset of the disease. Seligman and his co-workers have systematically investigated the learning of helplessness and related it to the clinical syndrome of depression (see Seligman, 1975). Even death is apparently related to control-relevant variables. McMahon and Rhudick (1964) found a relationship between depression or hopelessness and death. The most graphic description of this association comes from Bettelheim (1943), who in his analysis of the "Muselmanner," the walking corpses in the concentration camps, described them as:

> Prisoners who came to believe the repeated statements of the guards—that there was no hope for them, that they would never leave the camp except as a corpse—who came to feel that their environment was one over which they could exercise no influence whatsoever...Once his own life and the environment were viewed as totally beyond his ability to influence them, the only logical conclusion was to pay no attention to them whatsoever. Only then, all conscious awareness of stimuli coming from the outside was blocked out, and with it all response to anything but inner stimuli.

Death swiftly followed and, according to Bettelheim,

> [survival] depended on one's ability to arrange to preserve some areas of independent action, to keep control of some important aspects of one's life despite an environment that seemed overwhelming and total.

Bettelheim's description reminds us of Richter's (1957) rats, who also "gave up hope" of controlling their environment and subsequently died.

The implications of these studies for research in the area of aging are clear. Objective helplessness as well as feelings of helplessness and hopelessness—both enhanced by the environment and by intrinsic changes that occur with increasing old age—may contribute to psychological withdrawal, physical disease, and death. In contrast, objective control and feelings of mastery may very well contribute to physical health and personal efficacy.

In a study conceived to explore the effects of dissonance Ferrare (1962; cited in Seligman, 1975; Zimbardo & Ruch, 1975) presented data concerning the effects of the ability of geriatric patients to control their place of residence. Of 17 subjects who answered that they did not have any other alternative but to move to a specific old age home, 8 died after 4 weeks of residence and 16 after 10 weeks of residence. By comparison, among the residents who died during the initial period, only one person had answered that she had the freedom to choose other alternatives. All of these deaths were classified as unexpected because "not even insignificant disturbances had actually given warning of the impending disaster."

As Zimbardo (Zimbardo & Ruch, 1975) suggested, the implications of Ferrare's data are striking and merit further study of old age home settings. There is already evidence that perceived personal control in one's residential environment is important for younger and institutional populations. Rodin (in press), using children as subjects, demonstrated that diminished feelings of control produced by chronic crowding at home led to fewer attempts to control self-reinforcement in the laboratory and to greater likelihood of giving up in the face of failure.

The present study attempted to assess directly the effects of enhanced personal responsibility and choice in a group of nursing home patients. In addition to examining previous results from the control-helplessness literature in a field setting, the present study extended the domain of this conception by considering new response variables. Specifically, if increased control has generalized beneficial effects, then physical and mental alertness, activity, general level of satisfaction, and sociability should all be affected. Also, the manipulation of the independent variables, assigning greater responsibility and decision freedom for relevant behavior, allowed subjects real choices that were not directed toward a single behavior or stimulus condition. This manipulation tested the ability of the subjects to generalize from specific choices enumerated for them to other aspects of their lives, and thus tested the generalizability of feelings of control over certain elements of the situation to more broadly based, behavior and attitudes.

METHOD

Subjects

The study was conducted in a nursing home, which was rated by the state of Connecticut as being among the finest care units and offering quality medical, recreational, and residential facilities. The home was large and modern in design, appearing cheerful and comfortable as well as clean and efficient. Of the four floors in the home, two were selected for study because of similarity in the residents' physical and psychological health and prior socioeconomic status, as determined from evaluations made by the home's director, head nurses, and social worker. Residents were assigned to a particular floor and room simply on the basis of availability, and on the average, residents on the two floors had been at the home about the same length of time. Rather than randomly assigning subjects to experimental treatment, a different floor was randomly selected for each treatment. Since there was not a great deal of communication between floors, this procedure was followed in order to decrease the likelihood that the treatment effects would be contaminated. There were 8 males and 39 females in the responsibility-induced condition (all fourth-floor residents) and 9 males and 35 females in the comparison group (all second-floor residents). Residents who were either completely bedridden or judged by the nursing home staff to be completely noncommunicative (11 on the experimental floor and 9 on the comparison floor) were omitted from the sample. Also omitted was one woman on each floor, one 40 years old and the other 26 years old, due to their age. Thus, 91 ambulatory adults, ranging in age from 65 to 90, served as subjects.

Procedure

To introduce the experimental treatment, the nursing home administrator, an outgoing and friendly 33-year-old male who interacts with the residents daily, called a meeting in the lounge of each floor. He delivered one of the following two communications at that time:

> [Responsibility-induced group] I brought you together today to give you some information about Arden Home. I was surprised to learn that many of you don't know about the things that are available to you and more important, that many of you don't realize the influence you have over your own lives here. Take a minute to think of the decisions you can and should be making.
>
> For example, you have the responsibility of caring for yourselves, of deciding whether or not you want to make this a home you can be proud of and happy in. You should be deciding how you want your rooms to be arranged—whether you want it to be as it is or whether you want the staff to help you rearrange the furniture. You should be deciding how you want to spend your time, for example, whether you want to be visiting your friends who live on this floor or on other floors, whether you want to visit in your room or your friend's room, in the lounge, the dining room, etc., or whether you want to be watching television, listening to the radio, writing reading, or planning social events. In other words, it's your life and you can make of it whatever you want.
>
> This brings me to another point. If you are unsatisfied with anything here, you have the influence to change it. It's your responsibility to make your complaints known, to tell us what you would like to change, to tell us what you would like. These are just a few of the things you could and should be deciding and thinking about now and from time to time everyday. You made these decisions before you came here and you can and should be making them now.
>
> We're thinking of instituting some way for airing complaints, suggestions, etc. Let [nurse's name] know if you think this is a good idea and how you think we should go about it. In any case let her know what your complaints or suggestions are.
>
> Also, I wanted to take this opportunity to give you each a present from the Arden Home. [A box of small plants was passed around, and patients were given two decisions to make: first, whether or not they wanted a plant at all, and second, to choose which one they wanted. All residents did select a plant.] The plants are yours to keep and take care of as you'd like.
>
> One last thing, I wanted to tell you that we're showing a movie next week on Thursday and Friday. You should decide which night you'd like to go, if you choose to see it at all.
>
> [Comparison group] I brought you together today to give you some information about the Arden House. I was surprised to learn that many of you don't know about the things that are available to you; that many of you don't realize all you're allowed to do here. Take a minute to think of all the options that we've provided for you in order for your life to be fuller and more interesting. For example, you're permitted to visit people on the other floors and to use the lounge on this floor for visiting as well as the dining room or your own rooms. We want your rooms to be as nice as they can be, and we've tried to make them that way for you. We want you to be happy here. We feel that it's our responsibility to make this a home you can be proud of and happy in, and we want to do all we can to help you.
>
> This brings me to another point. If you have any complaints or suggestions about anything, let [nurse's name] know what they are. Let us know how we can best help you. You should feel that you have free access to anyone on the staff, and we will do the best we can to provide individualized attention and time for you.
>
> Also, I wanted to take this opportunity to give you each a present from the Arden House. [The nurse walked around with a box of plants and each resident was handed one.] The plants are yours to keep. The nurses will water and care for them for you.
>
> One last thing, I wanted to tell you that we're showing a movie next week on Thursday and Friday. We'll let you know later which day you're scheduled to see it.

The major difference between the two communications was that one one floor, the emphasis was on the residents' responsibility for themselves, whereas on the other floor, the communication stressed the staff's responsibility for them. In addition, several other differences bolstered this treatment: Residents in the responsibility-induced group were asked to give their opinion of the means by which complaints were handled rather than just being told that any complaints would be handled by staff members; they were given the opportunity to select their own plant and to care for it themselves, rather than being given a plant to be taken care of by someone else; and they were given their choice of a movie night, rather than being assigned a particular night, as was typically the case in the old age home. However, there was no difference in the amount of attention paid to the two groups.

Dependent Variables

Questionnaires. Two types of questionnaires were designed to assess the effects of induced responsibility. Each was administered 1 week prior to and 3 weeks after the communication. The first was administered directly to the residents by a female research assistant who was unaware of the experimental hypotheses or of the specific experimental treatment. The questions dealt with how much control they felt over general events in their lives and how happy and active they felt. Questions were responded to along 8-point scales ranging from 0 (none) to 8 (total). After completing each interview, the research assistant rated the resident on an 8-point scale for alterness.

The second questionnaire was responded to by the nurses, who staffed the experimental and comparison floors and who were unaware of the experimental treatments. Nurses on two different shifts completed the questionnaires in order to obtain two ratings for each subject. There were nine 10-point scales that asked for ratings of how happy, alert, dependent, sociable, and active the residents were as well as questions about their eating and sleeping habits. There were also questions evaluating the proportion of weekly time the patient spent engaged in a variety of activities. These included reading, watching television, visiting other patients, visiting outside guests, watching the staff, talking to the staff, sitting alone doing nothing, and others.

Behavioral measures. Since perceived personal control is enhanced by a sense of choice over relevant behaviors, the option to choose which night the experimental group wished to see the movie was expected to have measurable effects on active participation. Attendance records were kept by the occupational therapist, who was unaware that an experiment was being conducted.

Another measure of involvement was obtained by holding a competition in which all participants had to guess the number of jelly beans in a large jar. Each patient wishing to enter the contest simply wrote his or her name and estimate on a piece of paper and deposited it in a box that was next to the jar.[1]

Finally, an unobtrusive measure of activity was taken. The tenth night after the experimental treatment, the right wheels of the wheelchairs belonging to a randomly selected subsample of each patient group were covered with 2 inches (.05 m) of white adhesive tape. The following night, the tape was removed from the chairs and placed on index cards for later evaluation of amount of activity, as indicated by the amount of discoloration.

RESULTS

Questionnaires. Before examining whether or not the experimental treatment was effective, the pretest ratings made by the subjects, the nurses, and the interviewer were compared for both groups. None of the differences approached significance which indicates comparability between groups prior to the start of the investigation.

The means for responses to the various questionnaires are summarized in Table 1. Statistical tests compared the posttest minus pretest scores of the experimental and comparison groups.

In response to direct questions about how happy they currently were, residents in the responsibility-induced group reported significantly greater increases in happiness after the experimental treatment than did the comparison group, $t(43) = 1.96$, $p < 0.5$.[2] Although the comparison group heard a communication that had specifically stressed the home's commitment to making them happy, only 25% of them reported feeling happier by the time of the second interview, whereas 48% of the experimental group did so.

TABLE 1

MEAN SCORES FOR SELF-REPORT, INTERVIEWER RATINGS, AND NURSES' RATINGS FOR EXPERIMENTAL AND COMPARISON GROUPS

Questionnaire Responses	Responsibility induced (n = 24)			Comparison (n = 28)			Comparison of change scores (p <)
	Pre	Post	Change: Post—Pre	Pre	Post	Change: Post—Pre	
Self-report							
Happy	5.16	5.44	.28	4.90	4.78	-.12	.05
Active	4.07	4.27	.20	3.90	2.62	-1.28	.01
Perceived Control							
Have	3.26	3.42	.16	3.62	4.03	.41	–
Want	3.85	3.80	-.05	4.40	4.57	.17	–
Interviewer Rating							
Alertness	5.02	5.31	.29	5.75	5.38	-.37	.025
Nurses' Ratings							
General Improvement	41.67	45.64	3.97	42.69	40.32	-2.39	.005
Time Spent							
Visiting Patients	13.03	19.81	6.78	7.94	4.65	-3.30	.005
Visiting Others	11.50	13.73	2.14	12.38	8.21	-4.16	.05
Talking to Staff	8.21	16.43	8.21	9.11	10.71	1.61	.01
Watching Staff	6.78	4.64	-2.14	6.96	11.60	4.64	.05

The responsibility-induced group reported themselves to be significantly more active on the second interview than the comparison group, $t(43) = 2.67, p < .01$. The interviewer's ratings of altertness also showed significantly greater increase for the experimental group, $t(43) = 2.40, p < .025$. However, the questions that were relevant to perceived control showed no significant changes for the experimental group. Since over 20% of the patients indicated that they were unable to understand what we meant by control, these questions were obviously not adequate to discriminate between groups.

The second questionnaire measured nurses' ratings of each patient. The correlation between the two nurses' ratings of the same patient was .68 and .61 ($ps < .005$) on the comparison and responsibility-induced floors, respectively.[3] For each patient, a score was calculated by averaging the two nurses' ratings for each question, summing across questions, and subtracting the total pretreatment score from the total posttreatment score.[4] This yielded a positive average total change score of 3.97 for the responsibility-induced group as compared with an average negative total change of -2.37 for the comparison group. The difference between these means is highly significant, $t(50) = 5.18, p < .005$. If one looks at the percentage of people who were judged improved rather than at the amount of judged improvement, the same pattern emerges: 93% of the experimental group (all but one subject) were considered improved, whereas only 21% (six subjects) of the comparison group showed this positive change ($x^2 = 19.23, p <.005$).

The nurses' evaluation of the proportion of time subjects spent engaged in various interactive and noninteractive activities was analyzed by comparing the average change scores (post-precommunication) for all of the nurses for both groups of subjects on each activity. Several significant differences were found.

The experimental group showed increases in the proportion of time spent visiting with other patients (for the experimental group, $\bar{X} = 12.86$ vs. -6.61 for the comparison group), $t(50) = 3.83$, $p < .005$; visiting people from outside of the nursing home (for the experimental group, $\bar{X} = 4.28$ *vs.* -7.61 for the comparison group, $t(50) = 2.30$, $p < .05$; and talking to the staff (for the experimental group, $\bar{X} = 8.21$ *vs.* 1.61 for the comparison group), $t(50) = 2.98$, $p < .05$.[5] In addition, they spent less time passively watching the staff (for the experimental group, $\bar{X} = -4.28$ *vs.* 9.68 for the comparison group), $t(50) = 2.60$, $p < .05$. Thus, it appears that the treatment increased active, interpersonal activity but not passive activity such as watching television or reading.

Behavioral measures. As in the case of the questionnaires, the behavioral measures showed a pattern of differences between groups that was generally consistent with the predicted effects of increased responsibility. The movie attendance was significantly higher in the responsibility-induced group than in the control group after the experiment treatment ($z = 1.71$, $p < .05$, *one-tailed*), although a similar attendance check taken one month before the communications revealed no group differences.[6]

In the jelly-bean-guessing contest, 10 subjects (21%) in the responsibility-induced group and only 1 subject (2%) from the comparison group participated ($X^2 = 7.72$, $p < .01$). Finally, very little dirt was found on the tape taken from any of the patients' wheelchairs, and there was no significant difference between the two groups.

DISCUSSION

It appears that inducing a greater sense of personal responsibility in people who may have virtually relinquished decision making, either by choice or necessity, produces improvement. In the present investigation, patients in the comparison group were given a communication stressing the staff's desire to make them happy and were otherwise treated in the sympathetic manner characteristic of this high-quality nursing home. Despite the care provided for these people, 71% were rated as having become more debilitated over a period of time as short as 3 weeks. In contrast with this group, 93% of the people who were encouraged to make decisions for themselves, given decisions to make, and given responsibility for something outside of themselves, actually showed overall improvement. Based on their own judgments and by the judgments of the nurses with whom they interacted on a daily basis, they became more active and felt happier. Perhaps more important was the judged improvement in their mental alertness and increased behavioral involvement in many different kinds of activities.

The behavioral measures showed greater active participation and involvement for the experimental group. Whether this directly resulted from an increase in perceived choice and decision-making responsibility or from the increase in general activity and happiness occurring after the treatment cannot be assessed from the present results. It should also be clearly noted that although there were significant differences in active involvement, the overall level of participation in the activities that comprised the behavioral measures was low. Perhaps a much more powerful treatment would be one that is individually administered and repeated on several occasions. That so weak a manipulation had any effect suggests how important increased control is for these people, for whom decision making is virtually nonexistent.

The practical implications of this experimental demonstration are straightforward. Mechanisms can and should be established for changing situational factors that reduce real or perceived responsibility in the elderly. Furthermore, this study adds to the body of literature (Bengston, 1973; Butler, 1967; Leaf, 1973; Lieberman, 1965) suggesting that senility and diminished alertness are not an almost inevitable result of aging. In fact, it suggests that some of the negative consequences of aging may be retarded, reversed, or possibly prevented by returning to the aged the right to make decisions and a feeling of competence.

REFERENCE NOTE

Lehr, K., & Pushner, I. *Studies in the awareness of aging.* Paper presented at the 6th International Congress on Gerontology, Copenhagen, 1963.

REFERENCES

Adamson, J., & Schmale, A. Object loss, giving up, and the onset of psychiatric disease. *Psychosomatic Medicine*, 1965, *27*, 557-576.

Adler, A. Individual psychology. In C. Murchinson (Ed.), *Psychologies of 1930*. Worcester, Mass.: Clark University Press, 1930.

Bengston, V. L. Self determination: A social and psychological perspective on helping the aged. *Geriatrics*, 1973.

Bettelheim, B. Individual and mass behavior in extreme situations. *Journal of Abnormal and Social Psychology*, 1943, *38*, 417-452.

Birren, J. Aging and psychological adjustment. *Review of Educational Research*, 1958, *28*, 475-490.

Bowers, K. Pain, anxiety, and perceived control. *Journal of Consulting and Clinical Psychology*, 1968, *32*, 596-602.

Butler, R. Aspects of survival and adaptation in human aging. *American Journal of Psychiatry*, 1967, *123*, 1233-1243.

Corah, N., & Boffa, J. Perceived control, self-observation, and response to aversive stimulation. *Journal of Personality and Social Psychology*, 1970, *16*, 1-4.

deCharms, R. *Personal causation*. New York: Academic Press, 1968.

Geer, J., Davison, G., & Gatchel, R. Reduction of stress in humans through nonverdical perceived control of aversive stimulation. *Journal of Personality and Social Psychology*, 1970, *16*, 731-738.

Glass, D., & Singer, J. *Urban stress*. New York: Academic Press, 1972.

Gould, R. The phases of adult life: A study in developmental psychology. *American Journal of Psychiatry*, 1972, *129*, 521-531.

Kanfer, R., & Seidner, M. Self-Control: Factors enhancing tolerance of noxious stimulation. *Journal of Personality and Social Psychology*, 1975, *32*, 311-328.

Langer, E. J., & Abelson, R. P. The semantics of asking a favor: How to succeed in getting help without really dying. *Journal of Personality and Social Psychology*, 1972, *24*, 26-32.

Langer E. J., Janis, I. L., & Wolfer, J. A. Reduction of psychological stress in surgical patients. *Journal of Experimental Social Psychology*, 1975, *11*, 155-165.

Leaf, A. Threescore and forty. *Hospital Practice*, 1973, *34*, 70-71.

Lefcourt, H. The function of the illusion of control and freedom. *American Psychologist*, 1973, *28*, 417-425.

Lieberman, M. Psychological correlates of impending death: Some preliminary observations. *Journal of Gerontology*, 1965, *20*, 181-190.

McMahon, A., & Rhudick, P. Reminiscing, adaptational significance in the aged. *Archives of General Psychiatry*, 1964, *10*, 292-298.

Neugarten, B., & Gutman, D. Age-sex roles and personality in middle age: A thematic apperception study. *Psychological Monographs*, 1958, *72*(17, Whole No. 470).

Pervin, L. The need to predict and control under conditions of threat. *Journal of Personality*, 1963, *31*, 570-585.

Richter, C. On the phenomenon of sudden death in animals and man. *Psychosomatic Medicine*, 1957, *19*, 191-198.

Rodin, J. Crowding, perceived choice, and response to controllable and uncontrollable outcomes. *Journal of Experimental Social Psychology*, in press.

Schmale, A. Relationships of separation and depression to disease. I.: A report on a hospitalized medical population. *Psychosomatic Medicine*, 1958, *20*, 259-277.

Schmale, A., & Iker, H. The psychological setting of uterine cervical cancer. *Annals of the New York Academy of Sciences*, 1966, *125*, 807-813.

Seligman, M. E. P. *Helplessness.* San Francisco: Freeman, 1975.

Stotland, E., & Blumenthal, A. The reduction of anxiety as a result of the expectation of making a choice. *Canadian Review of Psychology,* 1964, *18*, 139-145.

Zimbardo, P. G., & Ruch, F. L. *Psychology and life* (9th ed.). Glenview, Ill.: Scott, Foresman, 1975.

(Received July 5, 1975)

FOOTNOTES

[1.] We also intended to measure the number of complaints that patients voiced. Since one often does not complain after becoming psychologically helpless, complaints in this context were expected to be a positive indication of perceived personal control. This measure was discarded however, since the nurses failed to keep a systematic written record.

[2.] All of the statistics for the self-report data and the interviewers' ratings are based on 45 subjects (25 in the responsibility-induced group and 20 in the comparison group), since these were the only subjects available at the time of the interview.

[3.] There was also significant agreement between the interviewer's and nurses' ratings of alertness $(r = .65)$.

[4.] Since one nurse on the day shift and one nurse on the night shift gave the ratings, responses to the questions regarding sleeping and eating habits were not included in the total score. Also, in order to reduce rater bias, patients for whom there were ratings by a nurse on only one shift were excluded from this calculation. This left 24 residents from the experimental group and 28 from the comparison group.

[5.] This statistic is based only on the responses of the nurse on duty in the evening.

[6.] Frequencies were transformed into arc sines and analyzed using the method that is essentially the same as that described by Langer and Abelson (1972).

13 The Reality of Repressed Memories

Elizabeth F. Loftus

American Psychologist, 1993, 48, 518-537. Copyright 1993 American Psychological Association

ABSTRACT

Repression is one of the most haunting concepts in psychology. Something shocking happens, and the mind pushes it into some inaccessible corner of the unconscious. Later, the memory may emerge into consciousness. Repression is one of the foundation stones on which the structure of psychoanalysis rests. Recently there has been a rise in reported memories of childhood sexual abuse that were allegedly repressed for many years. With recent changes in legislation, people with recently unearthed memories are suing alleged perpetrators for events that happened 20, 30, even 40 or more years earlier. These new developments give rise to a number of questions: (a) How common is it for memories of child abuse to be repressed? (b) How are jurors and judges likely to react to these repressed memory claims? (c) When the memories surface, what are they like? and (d) How authentic are the memories?

In 1990, a landmark case went to trial in Redwood City, California. The defendant, George Franklin, Sr., 51 years old, stood trial for a murder that had occurred more than 20 years earlier. The victim, 8-year-old (Susan Kay Nason, was murdered on September 22, 1969). Franklin's daughter, Eileen, only 8 years old herself at the time of the murder, provided the major evidence against her father. What was unusual about the case is that Eileen's memory of witnessing the murder had been repressed for more than 20 years.

Eileen's memory did not come back all at once. She claimed that her first flashback came one afternoon in January 1989 when she was playing with her two-year-old son, Aaron, and her five-year-old daughter, Jessica. At one moment, Jessica looked up and asked her mother a question like "Isn't that right, Mommy?" A memory of Susan Nason suddenly came back. Eileen recalled the look of betrayal in Susie's eyes just before the murder. Later, more fragments would return, until Eileen had a rich and detailed memory. She remembered her father sexually assaulting Susie in the back of a van. She remembered that Susie was struggling as she said "No don't" and "Stop." She remembered her father saying "Now Susie," and she even mimicked his precise intonation. Next, her memory took the three of them outside the van, where she saw her father with his hands raised above his head with a rock in them. She remembered screaming. She remembered walking back to where Susie lay, covered with blood, the silver ring on her finger smashed.

Eileen's memory report was believed by her therapist, by several members of her family, and by the San Mateo County district attorney's office, which chose to prosecute her father. It was also believed by the jury, which convicted George Franklin, Sr., of murder. The jury began its deliberations on November 29, 1990, and returned a verdict the next day. Impressed by Eileen's detailed and confident memory, they found her father guilty of murder in the first degree.

Eileen's detailed and confident memory impressed a number of people. But is her memory authentic? Did she really witness the murder of her best friend 20 years earlier? The idea of repression of early traumatic memories is a concept that many psychotherapists readily accept (Bruhn, 1990). In fact, it has been said that repression is the foundation on which psychoanalysis rests (Bower, 1990). According to the theory, something happens that is so shocking that the mind grabs hold of the memory and pushes it underground, into some inaccessible corner of the unconscious. There it sleeps for years, or even decades, or even forever–isolated from the rest of mental life. Then, one day, it may rise up and emerge into consciousness. Numerous clinical examples fitting this model can be readily found. Many of these examples involve not memory of murder but rather memory of other sorts of childhood trauma, such as sexual abuse, that allegedly has been repressed for decades until recovered in therapy. Rieker and Carmen (1986) described a woman who entered psychotherapy for sexual dysfunction and recovered memories of incest committed by her father. Schuker (1979) described a woman who entered psychotherapy for chronic insomnia, low self-esteem, and other problems and recovered memories of her father sexually assaulting her. M. Williams (1987) described a man who entered therapy for depression and sleep disturbances and recovered memories of a servant molesting him. These anecdotal reports constitute the clinical evidence that clients do indeed manage later to remember some earlier inaccessible painful experience (Erdelyi, 1985). The reports constitute evidence for the core ideas inherent in the theory of repression. Several respected scholars once made the point that, from a clinical standpoint, "the evidence for repression is overwhelming and obvious".

On the other hand, the clinical anecdotes and the loose theory used to explain them remain unconvincing to some psychotherapists and to many laboratory researchers. One psychiatrist who has seen more than 200 severely dissociative patients explicity referred to such anecdotes as "empirical observations lacking in scientific underpinnings" (Ganaway, 1992, p. 203). One researcher described them as "impressionistic case studies" and claimed that they could not be counted as "anything more than unconfirmed clinical speculations" (Holmes, 1990, p. 97). After reviewing 60 years of research and finding no controlled laboratory support for the concept of repression, Holmes suggested, only half jokingly, that any use of the concept be preceded by a warning: "Warning. The concept of repression has not been validated with experimental research and its use may be hazardous to the accurate interpretation of clinical behavior" (p. 97).

Even if Holmes (1990) was right that there is virtually no scientific evidence to demonstrate the authenticity of repressed memories that return, Eileen's memory could still be authentic. Even if Holmes is proved wrong and there does develop solid scientific evidence to support the authenticity of some repressed memories that return, that would not prove that Eileen's memory is authentic. If Eileen's memory is not authentic, where else might all those details come from? Media reports from 20 years before–December 1969, when the body was found–were filled with some of these same details. The facts that the murdered girl's skull was fractured on the right side and that a silver Indian ring was found on the body were reported prominently on the front page of the *San Francisco Chronicle* ("Susan Nason Body Found," 1969). The fact that she apparently held her hand up to protect herself, inferred from the crushed ring, was also well-known (e.g., *San Jose Mercury*, "Nason Girl Fought," 1969). Most of the details that fill the rich network of her memory, however, are unfalsifiable or uncheckable–such as her memory for the door of the van that her father got out of after he raped Susie. One additional feature of Eileen's memory, worth noting, is that it changed across various tellings. For example, when she gave a statement to the police in November 1989, she told the police that her father was driving her and her sister Janice to school when they first saw Susie and that he made Janice get out of the van when Susie got in. However, months later at the preliminary hearing, she did not report Janice being in the van. In the statement to the police, the trip happened on the way to school in the morning or on the way back from lunch. During the preliminary hearing, after she presumably was reminded that Susie had not been missing until after school was out, she said it was in the late afternoon because the sun was low. Eileen's memory changed over the tellings, and there were alternative possible sources for details that made the memory seem so rich. This proves that at least some portions of these distant memories are wrong, although other parts could, in theory, still be authentic.

When George Franklin, Jr., was convicted on the basis of little more that the return of a repressed memory, *Newsweek* magazine called it an "incredible" story ("Forgetting to Remember," 1991). It was apparently the first time that an American citizen had been tried and convicted of murder on the basis of a freshly unearthed repressed memory.

MORE REPRESSED MEMORIES

Soon after the Franklin case, a string of others involving newly emerged distant memories appeared in the media. People accused by the holders of repressed memories wrote letters asking for help. Lawyers found themselves being asked to represent parties in legal cases involving repressed memories.

Popular Articles

Long-repressed memories that return after decades, often while a person is in therapy, have become highly publicized through popular articles. In 1991, actress Roseanne Barr Arnold's story was on the cover of *People* magazine. Memories of her mother abusing her from the time she was an infant until she was 6 or 7 years old had returned in therapy ("A Star Cries Incest," 1991; Darnton, 1991). Barr Arnold's was not the first such case to capture the cover of *People* magazine that year. Just three months earlier, *People* had also reported a story about former Miss America Marilyn Van Derbur, who had repressed any knowledge of sexual violation by her father until she was 24 years old and told the world about it after her father died ("The Darkest Secret," 1991; Darnton, 1991). Highly publicized cases involving memories that recently sprang into consciousness were told repeatedly in numerous popular articles in such publications as the *Washington Post* (Oldenberg, 1991), the *Los Angeles Times* (Ritter, 1991), *Seventeen* (Dormen, 1991), *Glamour* (Edmiston, 1990), *Newsweek* (Kantrowitz, 1991), and *Time* (Toufexis, 1991).

Letters

Scores of spontaneously written letters from strangers also describe the emergence of memories. I have received letters written by people who had been accused of abuse by their children. A 75-year-old physician from Florida wrote, desperate to understand why his 49-year-old daughter was suddenly claiming that he had abused her during her early childhood and teen years. A woman from Canada wrote about the nightmare of being "falsely accused of sexual abuse by our 30-year-old daughter." A woman from Michigan wrote about her 38-year-old daughter who, "after a year of counseling now accuses us of abuse...very much like Roseanne Barr and the former Miss America, Marilyn Van Derbur." A couple from Texas wrote to tell about their youngest son, who had accused them of abusing him long ago. One letter from a mother in California well expresses the pain:

> One week before my husband died after an 8-month battle against lung cancer, our youngest daughter (age 38) confronted me with the accusation that he had molested her and I had not protected her. We know who her "therapist" was: a strange young woman... In the weeks, months that followed, the nature of the charges altered, eventually involving the accusation that my husband and I had molested our grandson, for whom we had sometimes cared while our daughter worked at her painting. This has broken my heart; it is so utterly untrue. This daughter has broken off all relationship with her four siblings. She came greatly under the influence of a book, *The Courage to Heal* [by Bass & Davis, 1988].

The letters articulately convey the living nightmares and broken hearts experienced by those accused by their adult children who suddenly remembered past abuse (see also Doe, 1991). The parents vehemently deny the abuse. Who is right and who is wrong? Is the adult child misremembering, or perhaps lying? Are the parents misremembering when they deny abuse, or are they deliberately lying?

Legal Cases

Another development after the Franklin conviction was that lawyers started calling psychologists to obtain assistance with a puzzling new type of legal case. For example, one case involved a 27-year-old San Diego woman (KL) who began to have recollections of molestation by her father (DL), that were repressed but then were later brought out through "counseling and therapeutic intervention" (*Lofft v. Lofft,* 1989). The daughter claimed that her father had routinely and continuously molested and sexually abused her, performing "lewd and lascivious acts, including but not limited to touching and fondling the genital areas, fornication and oral copulation." Her earliest memories were of the father fondling her in the master bedroom when she was three years old. Most of her memories appeared to date back to between the ages of three and eight. She sued her father for damages for emotional and physical distress, medical expenses, and lost earnings. She claimed that because of the trauma of the experience, she had no recollection or knowledge of the sexual abuse until her repression was lifted, shortly before she filed suit.

A few years ago, plaintiffs like KL who claimed to be survivors of childhood sexual abuse would have been barred from suing by statutes of limitations. Statutes of limitations, which force plaintiffs to initiate claims promptly, exist for good reason: They protect people from having to defend themselves against stale claims. They exist in recognition that with the passage of time, memories fade and evidence becomes more difficult to obtain. Succinctly and articulately put, the primary purpose of statutes of limitation is to prevent "surprises through the revival of claims that have been allowed to slumber until evidence has been lost, memories have faded, and witnesses have disappeared" (*Telegraphers v. Railway Express Agency*, 1944, pp. 348-349). When much time has passed, defendants find it hard to mount an effective defense. Although a statute of limitations on child sexual abuse might be suspended until a victim reaches the age of majority or a few years beyond, it previously would not typically have been extended to the age of 27, for example, when KL first recalled her abuse.

In 1989, things changed for plaintiffs in the state of Washington. Legislation went into effect that permitted people to sue for recovery of damages for injury suffered as a result of childhood sexual abuse at any time within three years of the time they *remembered* the abuse (Washington, 1989; see also *Petersen* v. *Bruen*, 1990). The legislature invoked a novel application of the *delayed discovery doctrine*, which essentially says that the statute of limitations does not begin to run until the plaintiff has discovered the facts that are essential to the cause of action. Traditionally, the delayed discovery doctrine has been used in the area of medical malpractice. For example, a patient who discovered during a physical examination that his abdominal discomfort was caused by a surgical instrument left after an appendectomy performed 20 years earlier could sue because he could not have discovered the facts essential to his harm until he had the examination. Analogizing to the surgical instrument that was hidden from the patient until an exam made its presence known, so the memory for abuse was hidden away until it too is discovered and the plaintiff possesses the facts that are essential to the cause of action.

Within three years of enactment of the Washington statute, 18 other states enacted similar legislation allowing for the tolling of the statue of limitations. [1] Many other states introduced bills in the 1991—1992 legislative sessions that would achieve the same result, or they have begun studying similar legislation. As a consequence, repressed memories now form the basis for a growing number of civil law suits. As one writer put it, "Such wholesale forgetting–or more precisely, the eventual remembering–is forcing society to grapple in unaccustomed ways with the old problem of child molestation" (Davis, 1991). Increasing numbers of women, and also some men, are coming out of therapy with freshly retrieved memories of abuse. They sue for damages rather than file criminal complaints, because criminal charges are often too difficult to prove (Davis, 1991). In a few states (e.g., Wyoming), they can also bring criminal charges, and moves are afoot to change laws in more states to permit criminal prosecutions to go forward. As a consequence, juries are now hearing cases in which plaintiffs are suing their parents, relatives, neighbors, teachers, church members, and others for acts of childhood sexual abuse that allegedly occurred 10, 20, 30, even 40 years earlier. Juries and judges are learning about repression of memory and about newly emerged memories of molestation not only in the United States but also in Canada, Great Britain, and other parts of the world. [2]

Many interesting questions leap to mind about repressed memories. Chief among them are, How common are claims of repressed memory? How do people in general and jurors in particular react to claims of recently unburied repressed memories? What are the memories like? How authentic are they?

HOW COMMON ARE CLAIMS OF REPRESSED MEMORY?

There is little doubt that actual childhood sexual abuse is tragically common. Even those who claim that the statistics are exaggerated still agree that child abuse constitutes a serious social problem (Kutchinsky, 1992). I do not question the commonness of childhood sexual abuse itself but ask here about how the abuse is recalled in the minds of adults. Specifically, how common is it to repress memories of childhood sexual abuse? Claims about the commonness of repressed memories are freely made: It is typical to read estimates such as "most incest survivors have limited recall about their abuse" or "half of all incest survivors do not remember that the abuse occurred" (Blume, 1990). One psychotherapist with 18 years of experience has claimed that "millions of people have blocked out frightening episodes of abuse, years of their life, or their entire childhood" (Fredrickson, 1992, p. 15). Later, she reported that "sexual abuse is particularly susceptible to memory repression" (p. 23).

Beliefs about the commonness of repressed memories are expressed not only by those in the therapeutic community but also by legal scholars who have used these beliefs to argue for changes in legislation. For example, Lamm (1991) argued in favor of legislation that would ease access to the courts for victims of childhood sexual abuse. She applauded legislation, such as that enacted in California in 1991, that allows victims, no matter how old they are, to sue within three years after discovering their injuries or eight years after reaching majority, whichever date occurs later. As part of her argument that victims should have more time to file claims against their abusers, she expressed a view that "total repression of memories of abuse is common" (p. 2198).

Despite the confidence with which these assertions are made, there are few studies that provide evidence of the extent to which repression occurs. One study (Briere & Conte, in press) sampled 450 adult clinical clients who had reported sexual abuse histories. Therapists approached their individual clients or group clients with this question: "During the period of time between when the first forced sexual experience happened and your 18th birthday was there ever a time when you could not remember the forced sexual experience?" The main result obtained in this largely female (93%) largely White (90%) sample was that 59% said yes. A yes response was more likely in cases involving violent abuse (physical injury, multiple perpetrators, and fears of death if abuse was disclosed) than nonviolent abuse. Reported amnesia was more likely with early molestation onset, longer abuse, and greater current symptomatology. The authors concluded that amnesia for abuse was a common phenomenon (see also Briere, 1992).

Briere and Conte's (in press) result has been taken by others as evidence for the widespread extent of repression. For example, Summit (1992) interpreted the 59% yes rate as evidence that this proportion of people "went through periods of amnesia when they were not aware of their prior abuse" (p. 22). He used the finding to support the commonness of childhood dissociation.

One problem with Briere and Conte's (in press) estimate is that it obviously depends on how the respondent interprets the eliciting question. A yes response to the question could be interpreted in a variety of ways other than "I repressed my memory for abuse." For example, it could mean "Sometimes I found it too unpleasant to remember, so I tried not to"; or "There were times when I could not remember without feeling terrible"; or "There were times I could not bring myself to remember the abuse because I would rather not think about it." Although no question is free of the possibility of multiple interpretations, the great potential for idiosyncratic interpretation by respondents to the particular wording used by Briere and Conte warrants a further examination of the issue with a different eliciting question.

A further problem with Briere and Conte's (in press) study is that the respondents were all in therapy. If some of their clinicians were under the belief that repression of memory is common, they may have communicated this belief to their clients. Clients could readily infer that, if repression of memory is so common, it is likely to have happened to them, thus the answer to the question is probably yes. This would, of course, inflate the estimates of the prevalence of repression.

Other studies have given much lower estimates for the existence of repression. Herman and Schatzow (1987) gathered data from 53 women in therapy groups for incest survivors in the Boston area. Of the 53 cases, 15 (28%) reported severe memory deficits (including women who could recall very little from childhood and women who showed a recently unearthed repressed memory). Severe memory problems were most likely in cases of abuse that began early in childhood and ended before adolescence. Cases of violent or sadistic abuse were most likely to be associated with "massive repression as a defense" (p. 5). [3]

An even lower estimate was obtained in a study of 100 women in outpatient treatment for substance abuse in a New York City hospital (Loftus, Polonsky, & Fullilove, 1993). More than one-half of the women in this sample reported memories of childhod sexual abuse. The vast majority of them remembered the abuse their whole lives. Only 18% claimed that they forgot the abuse for a period of time and later regained the memory. Whether the women remembered the abuse their whole lives or forgot it for a period was completely unrelated to the violence of the abuse.

Of course, the data obtained from the New York sample may include an underestimation factor because there could have been many more women in the sample who were sexually abused, repressed the memory, and had not yet regained it. In support of this hypothesis, one could point to the research of L. M. Williams (1992), who interviewed 100 women, mostly African American, known to have been abused 17 years earlier in their lives. Of these, 38% were amnestic for the abuse or chose not to report it. Perhaps there were women in the New York sample who denied sexual abuse but who were still repressing it. Possibly there are women who were actually abused but do not remember it; however, it is misleading to assume that simple failure to remember means that repression has occurred. If an event happened so early in life, before the offset of childhood amnesia, then a woman would not be expected to remember it as an adult, whether it was abuse or something else. This would not imply the mechanism of repression. Moreover, ordinary forgetting of all sorts of events is a fact of life but is not thought to involve some special repression mechanism. For example, studies have shown that people routinely fail to remember significant life events even a year after they have occurred. One study consisted of interviews with 590 persons known to have been in injury-producing motor vehicle accidents during the previous year. Approximately 14% did not remember the accident a year later. Another study consisted of interviews with 1,500 people who had been discharged from a hospital within the previous year. More than one-fourth did not remember the hospitalization a year later (U.S. government studies, cited in Loftus, 1982).

How common are repressed memories of childhood abuse? There is no absolute answer available. There are few satisfying ways to discover the answer, because we are in the odd position of asking people about a memory for forgetting a memory. For the moment, figures range from 18% to 59%. The range is disturbingly great, suggesting that serious scholarly exploration is warranted to learn how to interpret claims about the commonness of repression and what abuse characteristics the repression might be related to.

JURORS' REACTIONS TO REPRESSED MEMORY CASES

How do people in general and jurors in particular react to repressed memory cases? Are memories that were once previously repressed as credible as memories that were never repressed? Understanding laypeople's reactions and credibility judgments is important not only for theoretical reasons but for practical ones as well. Theoretically speaking, laypeople's implicit or intuitive theories about repressed memories guide society's thinking on this topic.[4] Such implicit theories can also illuminate how therapists' theories of repression are formed; in part they derive from a therapist's own implicit theories. On a more practical level, understanding implicit theories of repression is important. Plaintiffs' lawyers who are deciding whether to file repressed memory cases are eager to know their likelihood of a successful outcome. Defense lawyers also care, because such subjective probabilities affect their decisions about whether to proceed to trial or to settle a case early. Perhaps most importantly, the plaintiffs should care. Plaintiffs bring lawsuits for myriad reasons. Some therapists encourage their clients to sue as "hope for emotional justice" (Forward & Buck, 1988). One therapist who had treated more than 1,500 incest victims argued that the lawsuit, although grueling, is "a very important step towards devictimization," "a further source of validation," and that "the personal satisfaction can be significant" (Forward & Buck, p. 159). If the lawsuit is good for a plaintiff's mental health, what happens to mental health if a jury does not find the notion of repressed memories tenable and the plaintiff, consequently, does not prevail?

Actual Cases

I start by examining actual cases that have gone to trial in recent years, with a wide range of outcomes. Some trials ended in defense verdicts (e.g., *Lofft v. Lofft,* 1989, in San Diego; *Collier v. Collier,* 1991, in Santa Clara County). Others ended in plaintiff verdicts. For example, a 39-year-old woman sued her father in Los Angeles, and the jury awarded $500,000 (McMillan, 1992). A 33-year-old woman sued her uncle in Akron, Ohio, and the jury awarded $5.15 million ($150,000 in compensatory damages and $5 million in punitive damages; Fields, 1992). Because the laws are new and most cases have settled, there are too few actual trials from which to gather data about reactions to repressed memory claims. Until more cases are tried to verdict, it may be necessary to rely on simulated jury research to gather information on this issue.

Simulations

Several juror simulation studies have explored how people are likely to react to repressed memory cases (Loftus, Weingardt, & Hoffman, 1992). In these studies, mock jurors learned about a legal case that arose out of allegations of sexual assault. Subjects considered the case of a daughter (Roberta) and her father (Jim), a case modeled loosely after an actual case tried in the state of Washington in 1991. Roberta, they learned, accused her father of raping her on several occasions when she was approximately 10 years old. She claimed she repressed all memory for these incidents. At about age 20, Roberta's memory returned while she was in therapy. She filed charges against her father a year after her memory came back. Roberta and her therapist blamed her current problems of depression, anxiety, and sexual dysfunction on the sexual abuse that happened when she was 10. Jim denied the allegations, claiming that Roberta was influenced by her therapist's suggestive questioning and that she was looking for someone or something to blame for her troubles.

How did people react to Roberta's claim? Did their reactions differ from reactions to a case that was identical except for the repression of memory? A different set of subjects reacted to a modified scenario involving a different woman (Nancy) whose memory was not repressed. Nancy's factual situation was identical to Roberta's except, subjects were told, Nancy never told anyone until age 20, when she went into therapy and told her therapist. Who is believed more, Roberta or Nancy? Several consistent findings emerged from these studies. First, people tended to be slightly more skeptical about Roberta's case (the repressed memory) than they were about Nancy's case (the nonrepressed memory). Both male and female subjects reacted this way, with males overall being more skeptical.

When subjects disbelieved the claims, they were more likely to think that the false claims were due to an honest mistake than a deliberate lie. One small difference emerged–repressed and nonrepressed memory cases appear to bring slightly different thoughts to mind. When subjects considered Nancy's case, thoughts of lying were slightly more likely to be evoked than when they considered Roberta's case. One of the clearest results was that, in general, the majority of subjects believed that the claims of both Roberta and Nancy were true and accurate.

WHAT ARE THE MEMORIES LIKE?

The quality of the memories that filter back vary tremendously. They are sometimes detailed and vivid and sometimes very vague. Sometimes they pertain to events that allegedly happened in early childhood and sometimes in adolescence. Sometimes they pertain to events that allegedly happened 5 years ago and sometimes 40 years ago. Sometimes they include fondling, sometimes rape, and sometimes ritualism of an unimaginable sort.

Highly detailed memories have been reported even for events that allegedly happened more than 25 years earlier and during the first year of life. One father-daughter case recently tried in Santa Clara County, California, illustrates this pattern (*Collier v. Collier,* 1991). The daughter, DC, a college graduate who worked as a technical writer, claimed that her father sexually abused her from the time she was six months old until she was 18. She repressed the memories until the age of approximately 26, when she was in individual and group therapy.

Other cases involve richly detailed allegations of a more bizarre, ritualistic type, as in a case reported by Rogers (1992a). The plaintiff, Bonnie, in her late 40s at the time of trial, accused her parents of physically, sexually, and emotionally abusing her from birth to approximately age 25. A sister, Patti, in her mid-30s at the time of trial, said she was abused from infancy to age 15. The allegations involved torture by drugs, electric shock, rape, sodomy, forced oral sex, and ritualistic killing of babies born to or aborted by the daughters. The events were first recalled when the plaintiffs went into therapy in the late 1980s.

In short, reports of memories after years of repression are as varied as they can be. One important way that they differ is in terms of the age at which the events being remembered allegedly happened. In many instances, repressed memory claims refer to events that occurred when the child was one year old or less. This observation invites an examination of the literature on childhood amnesia. It is well known that humans experience a poverty of recollections of their first several years in life. Freud (1905/1953) identified the phenomenon in some of his earliest writings: "What I have in mind is the peculiar amnesia which...hides the earliest beginnings of the childhood up to their sixth or eighth year" (p. 174). Contemporary cognitive psychologists place the offset of childhood amnesia at a somewhat earlier age: "past the age of ten, or thereabouts, most of us find it impossible to recall anything that happened before the age of four or five" (Morton, 1990, p. 3). Most empirical studies of childhood amnesia suggest that people's earliest recollection does not date back before the age of about three or four (Kihlstrom & Harackiewicz, 1982; Howe & Courage, 1993; Pillemer & White, 1989). One study showed that few subjects who were younger than three recalled any information about where they were when they heard about the assassination of President Kennedy, although most subjects who were more than eight at the time had some recall (Winograd & Killinger, 1983).

Although one recent study suggests that some people might have a memory for a hospitalization or the birth of a sibling that occurred at age two (Usher & Neisser, in press), these data do not completely rule out the possibility that the memories are not true memories but remembrances of things told by others (Loftus, in press). Still, the literature on childhood amnesia ought to figure in some way into our thinking about recollections of child molestation that supposedly occurred in infancy.

ARE THE MEMORIES AUTHENTIC?

Therapists Beliefs about Authenticity

Many therapists believe in the authenticity of the recovered memories that they hear from their clients. Two empirical studies reveal this high degree of faith. Bottoms, Shaver, and Goodman (1991) conducted a large-scale survey of clinicians who had come across, in their practice, ritualistic and religion-related abuse cases. Satanic ritualistic abuse (SRA) cases involve allegations of highly bizarre and heinous criminal ritual abuse in the context of an alleged vast, covert network of highly organized, transgenerational satanic cults (Braun & Sachs, 1988; Ganaway, 1989, 1991). Clients with SRA memories have reported vividly detailed memories of cannibalistic revels and such experiences as being used by cults during adolescence as serial baby breeders to provide untraceable infants for ritual sacrifices (Ganaway, 1989; Rogers, 1992b). If therapists believe these types of claims, it seems likely that they would be even more likely to believe the less aggravated claims involving ordinary childhood sexual abuse. Bottoms, et al.'s (1991) analysis revealed that 30% of responding clinicians had seen at least one case of child sexual abuse. A detailed analysis of 200 clinicians' experiences revealed that a substantial number of cases involved amnesic periods (44% of adult survivor cases). Overall, 93% of clinicians believed the alleged harm was actually done and that the ritualistic aspects were actually experienced by the clients. The conclusion was, in the investigators' own words, "The clinical psychologists in our sample believe their clients' claims" (p. 10).

A different approach to the issue of therapist belief was taken by Loftus and Herzog (1991). This study involved in-depth interviews with 16 clinicians who had seen at least one repressed memory case. In this small, nonrandom sample, 13 (81%) said they invariably believed their clients. One therapist said, "if a woman said it happened, it happened." Another said, "I have no reason not to believe them." The most common basis for belief was symptomatology (low self-esteem, sexual dysfunction, self-destructive behavior), or body memories (voice frozen at young age, rash on body matching inflicted injury). More than two-thirds of the clinicians reacted emotionally to any use of the term *authentic*, feeling that determining what is authentic and what is not authentic is not the job of a therapist. The conclusion from this small study was that therapists believe their clients and often use symptomatology as evidence.

These and other data suggest that therapists believe in their clients' memories. They point to symptomatology as their evidence. They are impressed with the emotional pain that accompanies the expression of the memories. Dawes (1992) has argued that this "epidemic" of belief is based in large part on authority and social consensus (p. 214).

Are the Memories Accurate?

There are those with extreme positions who would like to deny the authenticity of all repressed memories and those who would accept them all as true. As Van Benschoten (1990) has pointed out, these extreme positions will exacerbate our problems: "Denial fosters overdetermination, and overdetermination invites denial" (p. 25).

If we assume, then, that some of the memories might be authentic and some might not be, we can then raise this question: If a memory is recovered that is not authentic, where would it come from? Ganaway (1989) proposed several hypotheses to explain SRA memories, and these same ideas are relevant to memories of a repressed past. If not authentic, the memories could be due to fantasy, illusion, or hallucination-mediated screen memories, internally derived as a defense mechanism. Further paraphrasing Ganaway, the SRA memories combine a mixture of borrowed ideas, characters, myths, and accounts from exogenous sources with idiosyncratic internal beliefs. Once activated, the manufactured memories are indistinguishable from factual memories. Inauthentic memories could also be externally derived as a result of unintentional implantation of suggestion by a therapist or other perceived authority figure with whom the client desires a special relationship, interest, or approval.

The Memories Are Authentic

There is no doubt that childhood sexual abuse is tragically common (Daro, 1988). Surveys reveal a large range in the estimated rates (10%—50%), but as Freyd (1991) has argued, even the most conservative of them are high enough to support the enormity of child abuse. A sizeable number of people who enter therapy were abused as children and have always remembered their abuse. Even when they have severe emotional problems, they can provide rich recollections of abuse, often with many unique, peripheral details (Rogers, 1992a). Occasionally the abuse is corroborated, sometimes with very cogent corroboration, such as pornographic photographs. If confirmed abuse is prevalent, many instances of repressed memory abuse cases also could be authentic. Unfortunately, in the repressed memory cases, particularly when memories do not return for 20 or 30 years, there is little in the way of documented corroboration. This, of course, does not mean that they are false.

Claims of corroborated repressed memories occasionally appear in the published literature. For example, Mack (1980) reported on a 1955 case involving a 27-year-old borderline man who, during therapy, recovered memories of witnessing his mother attempting to kill herself by hanging. The man's father later confirmed that the mother had attempted suicide several times and that the son had witnessed one attempt when he was 3 years old. The father's confirmation apparently led to a relief of symptoms in the son. It is hard to know what to make of examples such as these. Did the son really remember back to age 3, or did he hear discussions of his mother's suicide attempts later in life? The memories could be real, that is, genuine instances of repressed memories that accurately returned much later. If true, this would only prove that some memory reports are authentic but obviously not that all reports are authentic. Analogously, examples of repressed memories that were later retracted, later proved to be false, or later proved to be the result of suggestion would only prove that some memory reports are not authentic but obviously not that all such reports are illusory.

Some who question the authenticity of the memories of abuse do so in part because of the intensity and sincerity of the accused persons who deny the abuse. Many of the thousands of people who have been accused flatly deny the allegations, and the cry of "witch hunt" is often heard (Baker, 1992, p. 48; Gardner, 1991). *Witch hunt* is, of course, a term that has been loosely used by virtually anyone faced by a pack of accusers (Watson, 1992). Analogies have been drawn between the current allegations and the witch craze of the 16th and 17th centuries, when an estimated half million people were convicted of witch-craft and burned to death in Europe alone (Harris, 1974; Trott, 1991b). Although the denials during the witch craze are now seen as authentic in the light of hindsight, the current denials of those accused of sexual abuse are not proof that the allegations are false. Research with known rapists, pedophiles, and incest offenders has illustrated that they often exhibit a *cognitive distortion* – a tendency to justify, minimize, or rationalize their behavior (Gudjonsson, 1992). Because accused persons are motivated to verbally and even mentally deny an abusive past, simple denials cannot constitute cogent evidence that the victim's memories are not authentic.

The Memories Are Not Authentic

To say that memory might be false does not mean that the person is deliberately lying. Although lying is always possible, even psychotherapists who question the authenticity of reports have been impressed with the honesty and intensity of the terror, rage, guilt, depression, and overall behavioral dysfunction accompanying the awareness of abuse (Ganaway, 1989, p. 211).

There are at least two ways that false memories could come about. Honestly believed, but false, memories could come about, according to Ganaway (1989), because of internal or external sources. The internal drive to manufacture an abuse memory may come about as a way to provide a screen for perhaps more prosaic but, ironically, less tolerable, painful experiences of childhood. Creating a fantasy of abuse with its relatively clear-cut distinction between good and evil may provide the needed logical explanation for confusing experiences and feelings. The core material for the false memories can be borrowed from the accounts of others who are either known personally or encountered in literature, movies, and television.[5]

SOURCES OF DETAILS THAT COULD AFFECT MEMORY

There are at least two important sources that could potentially feed into the construction of false memories. These include popular writings and therapists' suggestions.

Popular Writings

All roads on the search for popular writings inevitably lead to one, *The Courage to Heal* (Bass & Davis, 1988), often referred to as the "bible" of the incest book industry. *The Courage to Heal* advertises itself as a guide for women survivors of child sexual abuse. Although the book is undoubtedly a great comfort to the sexual abuse survivors who have been living with their private and painful memories, one cannot help but wonder about its effects on those who have no such memories. Readers who are wondering whether they might be victims of child sexual abuse are provided with a list of possible activities ranging from the relatively bening (e.g., being held in a way that made them uncomfortable) to the unequivocally abusive (e.g., being raped or otherwise penetrated). Readers are then told "If you are unable to remember any specific instances like the ones mentioned above but still have a feeling that something abusive happened to you, it probably did" (p. 21). On the next page, the reader is told

> You may think you don't have memories, but often as you begin to talk about what you do remember, there emerges a constellation of feelings, reactions and recollections that add up to substantial information. To say, "I was abused," you don't need the kind of recall that would stand up in a court of law. Often the knowledge that you were abused starts with a tiny feeling, an intuition... Assume your feelings are valid. So far, no one we've talked to thought she might have been abused, and then later discovered that she hadn't been. The progression always goes the other way, from suspicion to confirmation. If you think you were abused and your life shows the symptoms, then you were. (p. 22)

What symptoms? The authors list low self-esteem, suicidal or self-destructive thoughts, depression, and sexual dysfunction, among others. [6]

Others have worried about the role played by *The Courage to Heal.* A recent survey of several hundred families accused by derepressed memories revealed that the book was implicated "in almost all cases" (Wakefield & Underwager, 1992, p. 486). Complaints about the book range from its repeated suggestion that abuse probably happened even if one has no memories of it and that demands for corroboration are not reasonable, to its overt encouragement of "revenge, anger, fantasies of murder or castration, and deathbed confrontations" (Wakefield & Underwager, 1992, p. 485). In all fairness, however, it should be mentioned that the book is long (495 pages), and sentences taken out of context may distort their intended meaning. Nonetheless, readers without any abuse memories of their own cannot escape the message that there is a strong likelihood that abuse occurred even in the absence of such memories.

The recent incest book industry has published not only stories of abuse but also suggestions to readers that they were likely abused even if there are no memories, that repressed memories of abuse undoubtedly underlie one's troubles, or that benefits derive from uncovering repressed memories and believing them. [7] One popular book about incest is the paperback by E. Sue Blume (1990), the book jacket of which itemizes one of the author's chief credentials as the "Creator of the Incest Survivors' Aftereffects Checklist." [8] Blume, a private practice therapist, tells readers that she has "found that most incest survivors have limited recall about their abuse" (p. 81). She goes on to say that "Indeed, so few incest survivors in my experience have identified themselves as abused in the beginning of therapy that I have concluded that perhaps half of all incest survivors do not remember that the abuse occurred" (p. 81).

Some of the volumes provide exercises to help readers lift the repression. Farmer (1989), for example, tells readers to try one particular exercise "whether or not you have any conscious recollection of the abuse you suffered" (p. 91). The reader is to sit down, relax, and mentally return to childhood. The next step is to choose a particular memory, whether fuzzy or clear, and "bring that memory to your full attention" (p. 91). Details about what to do with the memory are provided, along with an example from the life of "Danielle," who thought about how verbally abusive her father had been, and "Hazel," who remembered anger at her mother's treating her like a rag doll. This exercise allegedly helped to "lift the lid of repression" and unbury the "Hurting Child."

Do these examples lift the lid of repression? Perhaps. But another equally viable hypothesis is that the examples influence the creation of memories or, at the very least, direct the search through memory that the reader will ultimately take. [9]

Therapists' Suggestions

Blume's (1990) observation that so many individuals enter therapy without memories of abuse but acquire memories during therapy naturally makes one wonder about what might be happening in therapy. According to Ganaway (1989), honestly believed but false memories could come about in another way, through unintentional suggestion from therapists. Ganaway noted a growing trend toward the facile acceptance and expressed validation of uncorroborated trauma memories, perhaps in part due to sensitization from years of accusations that the memories are purely fantasy. Herman (1992, p. 180) made a similar point: Whereas an earlier generation of therapists might have been discounting or minimizing their patients' traumatic experiences, the recent rediscovery of psychological trauma has led to errors of the opposite kind. Some contemporary therapists have been known to tell patients, merely on the basis of a suggestive history or symptom profile, that they definitely had a traumatic experience. Even if there is no memory, but merely some vague symptoms, certain therapists will inform a patient after a single session that he or she was very likely the victim of a satanic cult. Once the "diagnosis" is made, the therapist urges the patient to pursue the recalcitrant memories. Although some therapists recommend against persistent, intrusive probing to uncover early traumatic memories (e.g., Bruhn, 1990), others enthusiastically engage in these therapeutic strategies. Evidence for this claim comes in a variety of forms: (a) therapist accounts of what is appropriate to do with clients, (b) client accounts of what happened during therapy, (c) sworn statements of clients and therapists during litigation, and (d) taped interviews of therapy sessions.

Therapist accounts.

One therapist, who has treated more than 1,500 incest victims, openly discussed her method of approaching clients (Forward & Buck, 1988). "You know, in my experience, a lot of people who are struggling with many of the same problems you are, have often had some kind of really painful things happen to them as kids–maybe they were beaten or molested. And I wonder if anything like that ever happened to you?" (p. 161). Other clinicians claim to know of therapists who say "Your symptoms sound like you've been abused when you were a child. What can you tell me about that?" (Trott, 1991a, p. 18); or worse, "You sound to me like the sort of person who must have been sexually abused. Tell me what that bastard did to you" (Davis, 1991, p. 82).

At least one clinician advocated "It is crucial...that clinicians ask about sexual abuse during every intake" (Frawley, 1990). The rationale for this prescription is that a clinician who asks conveys to the client that the client will be believed and that the clinician will join with the client in working through the memories and emotions linked with childhood sexual abuse. Asking about sexual abuse along with a list of other past life events makes sense given the high instance of actual abuse, but the concern is how the issue is raised and what therapists do when clients initially deny an abusive past.

Evidence exists that some therapists do not take no for an answer. One therapist (who otherwise seemed sensitive to problems of memory tampering) still recommended "When the client does not remember what happened to her, the therapist's encouragement to 'guess' or 'tell a story' will help the survivor regain access to the lost material" (Olio, 1989, p. 6). She went on to provide the example of a client who suspected sexual abuse but had no memories. The client had become extremely anxious at a social gathering in the presence of a three-year-old girl. She had no idea why she was upset except that she wanted the little girl to keep her dress down. When encouraged in therapy to tell a story about what was going to happen to the little girl, the client ultimately related with tears and trembling one of the first memories of her own abuse. She used the story to "bypass her cognitive inhibitions and express the content of the memory" (p. 6). Later she "integrated the awareness that she was indeed the little girl in the story" (p. 6). One cannot help but wonder about these mental fantasy exercises in light of known research showing that the simple act of imagination makes an event subjectively more likely (e.g., Sherman, Cialdini, Schwartzman, & Reynolds, 1985).

Even if the therapist does not encourage the client to guess or tell a story, stories sometimes get told in the form of client dreams. If discussions of incest go on during the day, and day residue gets into the dreams at night, it would not be surprising to see that dreams of incest might result. Poston and Lison (1990) described a woman with "repressed memories" of incest who reported a dream about watching a little girl ice skate on a frozen river. In her dream, the woman tried desperately to warn the child that monsters and snakes were making their way through the ice to devour her. Although frightened, the woman was powerless and could not warn the innocent child. A few days later, the client began remembering incest from her childhood. Knowing she had "a trusted relationship with a therapist and a survivor's group that would understand and accept her" (p. 197), the memories began to flow.

Examples of therapists interpreting dreams as signs of memory of abuse can be found throughout the literature. One clinician described with pride how she communicated to her male patient the basis for her suspicions that he had been abused: "On many occasions, I explained that these dreams had preserved experiences and impressions of an indelible nature" (M. Williams, 1987, p. 152).

Frederickson (1992), who has worked with many incest survivors, has also described in detail her methods of getting patients to remember. She recommended that the therapist guide the patient "to expand on or explore images that have broken through to the conscious mind, allowing related images of the abuse to surface. The process lets the survivor complete the picture of what happened, using a current image or flash as a jumping-off point" (p. 97). She also suggested that the therapist help the patient expand on the images and sensations evoked by dreams "to shed light on or recover our repressed memories" (p. 98). She extolled the virtues of hypnosis to "retrieve buried memories" (p. 98) and recommended that patients "jot down suspected memories of abuse you would like to explore. Include your own felt sense of how you think you were abused" (p. 102).

Even if clinicians are not the first to bring up sexual abuse, they will often reinforce what begins as a mere suspicion. One client developed the idea that she might have been sexually abused, tried hypnosis to help her recover memories, and obsessed for years. Only after her therapist stated that she believed sexual assault was "indeed possible" and cited nightmares, phobia of men, and other symptoms as evidence did the client come up with some specific memories (Schuker, 1979, p. 569).

Before leaving the examples of therapist accounts of what goes on in therapy, it is important to add a word of caution. Sherrill Mulhern, a psychiatric anthropologist, has documented the alarming discrepancies that often exist between therapists' accounts of what they have done in therapy and what is revealed in video- or audiotapes of those same sessions (Mulhern, 1991).

If memories are uncovered–whether after repeated probing, after telling stories, after dreams, or seemingly spontaneously–or even if the memories remain buried, therapists often send their clients to support groups. In one study of clients who had, in the course of therapy, verbalized their victimization through ritualistic abuse, the majority reported that they had participated in these types of groups (Shaffer & Cozolino, 1992). One group, Survivors of Incest Anonymous (SIA), publishes extensive reading materials intended to aid the recovery of incest survivors. (SIA merged with Sexual Abuse Anonymous in 1987.) The criteria for admission make it clear that entry is fine for those with no memories of sexual abuse: "Do you have blocks of your childhood you can't remember? Do you have a sense that 'something happened'?" (SIA, 1985). These and other questions (e.g., Do you have problems with self-confidence and self esteem? Do you feel easily intimidated by authority figures?) are among the set of 20 questions that help a potential survivor decide whether SIA can be of assistance. SIA emphasizes that it is OK not to remember at first, because "Many survivors have 'repressed' actual abuse memories in order to survive." However, the goal is to remember: "Participating in SIA helps us to remember what happened to us so we can stop being controlled by incest" (SIA, 1990, p. 1).

Although support groups are undoubtedly invaluable for genuine survivors of sexual abuse, as they are for other survivors of extreme situations, such as combat and political persecution (Herman, 1992, p. 215), concerns about the incest survivor groups have been expressed. Do these groups foster the development of constructed memories? An investigative journalist attending a four-day workshop watched the construction of memory at work (Nathan, 1992). With members recounting graphic details of SRA abuse, how long will they listen to the person who can only say "I think I was abused, but I don't have any memories." Others have worried in the literature that such groups may induce proto-extension – that is, they actually encourage a troubled person to remember details from other survivor stories as having happened to them as well (Ellis, 1992).

Client accounts.

Another source for suggestions in therapy can be found in client accounts of what happened to them. Recently, clients have been reporting that a therapist has suggested that childhood abuse was the cause of their current distress. However, these clients have no memories of such abuse. One woman from Oregon entered therapy to deal with depression and anxiety, and within a few months her therapist suggested that the cause could be childhood sexual abuse. She wrote asking for help in remembering:

> Since that time, he has become more and more certain of his diagnosis... I have no direct memories of this abuse.... The question I can't get past is how something so terrible could have happened to me without me remembering anything. For the past two years I have done little else but try to remember. I've tried self-hypnosis and light trance work with my therapist. And I even travelled to childhood homes...in an attempt to trigger memories.

One client revealed the suggestive nature of his therapist's questioning on ABC's *Primetime Live* (ABC News, 1992). Attorney Greg Zimmerman went to a psychotherapist in Boulder, Colorado, to deal with his father's suicide. He told ABC, "I would try to talk to her about the things that were very painful in my life and she kept saying that there was something else" (p. 1). Zimmerman grew more and more depressed as the mystery of that "something else" would not unravel, and then, during a therapy session, his therapist stunned him with her diagnosis: "I don't know how to tell you this, but you display the same kinds of characteristics as some of my patients who are victims of Satanic ritualistic abuse" (p. 1). Zimmerman had said nothing whatsoever to her to provoke this diagnosis, apparently her standard.

It is easy to find published accounts that describe the emergence of memories in therapy and the techniques that therapists have used to uncover those memories (e.g., Bass & Thornton, 1991). One account, written under the pseudonym of Jill Morgan, told of a series of positively horrifying memories of abuse by her father. He raped her when she was 4 years old, again at age 9, once again at age 13, for seven straight days and nights at age 15, and for the final time at age 18. For the next several years, all misery was withheld from conscious memory, and then, at age 29, she was helped to remember in therapy: "Through hypnosis and age regression, a skilled therapist gave me back my memory" (p. 111). The involvement of hypnosis and age regression prompts the natural inquiry into whether these techniques produce authentic memories. Unfortunately, the evidence is discouraging: There is an extensive literature seriously questioning the reliability of hypnotically enhanced memory in general (Smith, 1983), and hypnotic age regression in particular (Nash, 1987). Hypnotic attempts to improve memory increase the confidence in what is recalled more than the accuracy (Bowers, 1992). Even more worrisome is the impossibility of reversing the process; the hypnotically induced memory becomes the person's reality (Orne, 1979). With hypnotic regression, men and women have been known to recall being abducted by aliens aboard exotic spacecraft and other forgotten events (Gordon, 1991).

A more detailed client account is that of Betsy Petersen (1991), as described in an autobiographical account, *Dancing With Daddy*. Petersen, a Harvard graduate and accomplished writer, revealed in her first book that she repressed memory of sexual abuse by her father until she was 45 years old. She now remembers sexual abuse from the time she was 3½ until she was 18. Betsy entered therapy (with "Kris") for problems relating to her children, and almost a year after starting therapy she started worrying, "I'm afraid my father did something to me." She tried hard to recall, putting "together a scenario of what might have happened" (p. 65). When she told her therapist about this, she said "I don't know if I made it up or if it's real." Kris replied, "It feels like a story to you, because when something like that happens, everybody acts like it didn't." Betsy: "You mean it might really have happened?" Kris told her there was a good chance it had happened. Kris told her, in Betsy's words, "It was consistent with what I remembered about my father and my relationship with him, and with the dreams I had been having, and with the difficulties I had being close to my children, and also, she said, with the feelings I had during and after sex with my husband" (p. 65). Betsy worked hard to retrieve incest memories: "I had no memory of what my father had done to me, so I tried to reconstruct it. I put all my skill–as a reporter, novelist, scholar–to work making that reconstruction as accurate and vivid as possible. I used the memories I had to get to the memories I didn't have" (p. 66).[10] If accurate, this account tells us something about one therapist's approach. The therapist convinces the patient with no memories that abuse is likely, and the patient obligingly uses reconstructive strategies to generate memories that would support that conviction. These techniques can be found in numerous autobiographical accounts (see also Smith & Pazder, 1980).

In addition to the first-person accounts, more formal studies of incest survivors provide clues to what might be happening in therapy. One study (Shaffer & Cozolino, 1992) of 20 adults who uncovered ritualistic abuse memories stemming from childhood revealed that the majority sought psychotherapy because of symptoms (e.g., depression and anxiety). The primary focus of their therapy was "the uncovering of memories" (p. 189). The majority participated in 12-step programs (e.g., Incest Survivors Anonymous) as "necessary adjuncts to their psychotherapy" (p. 190). These groups provided substitute families for the clients who had severed ties with their families of origin. Other similar studies of ritualistic abuse rememberers have revealed that most of the victims have no memory of the abuse before therapy (e.g., Driscoll & Wright, 1991) but that techniques such as hypnosis (Driscoll & Wright, 1991) or dreams and artwork (e.g., Young, Sachs, Braun, & Watkins, 1991) were used by therapists to unlock those recalcitrant memories.

Litigation accounts.

Information gathered during litigation is another source of knowledge about the emergence of memories in therapy. Take the case of Patti Barton against her father, John Peters, a successful businessman. [11] Depositions taken in the case of *Barton v. Peters* (1990) reveal that Patti Barton began therapy with a Dr. CD, a doctor of divinity, in July 1986. Dr. CD's notes indicate that, during the 32nd session of therapy, Patti expressed "fear her father has sexually tampered with her" (Deposition of CD, April 21, 1991, *Barton v. Peters,* 1990, p. 39). This was the first time that anything like that had come up in any of the sessions. Shortly thereafter, Patti related a dream that a man was after her. [12] Dr. CD apparently then used the technique of visualization wherein Patti would try to visualize her past. He got her to remember eye surgery at the age of 7 months. As for the abuse, one of the earliest acts of abuse he managed to dredge up with this method occurred when Patti was 15 months old. "I visualized that my father stuck his tongue in my mouth".

After he stuck his tongue in my mouth–Well, it seemed to last for hours and hours even though I know it didn't. But it was awful to me and an event that seemed to last for hours. I started crying, and I crawled over to the wall. And I started banging my head on the wall. And my mother came into the room, and she picked me up. And I tried to tell her in baby talk what had happened. I said "Ma, ma, ma, ma," and I said, "Da, Da, Da, Da" and I said, "Me-e-e-." And that's all that I can remember. (Deposition of PB, May 1991, *Barton v. Peters,* 1990, p. 193.)

Later, Patti would remember that her father touched her in her crotch and put his penis in her mouth when she was three years old, and that she stroked his penis over and over at age four. Rape would come later. Patti's father eventually agreed to give his daughter the deed to a piece of land he owned, but he continued to deny the charges. Her brother, a Baptist minister in Alaska, claimed that Satan's wicked spirits planted untruths in Patti's head (Laker, 1992). Did it take 30-some sessions for the therapist to uncover actual memories of abuse, or 30-some sessions for false memories of abuse to begin to be visualized and constructed?

Taped interviews.

Often, confidentiality considerations prevent access to interactions between therapists and clients. However, when cases get into litigation, special interviewing is frequently done, and occasionally it is recorded. Recordings were done in a case implicating a man named Paul Ingram from Olympia, Washington (Watters, 1991). Ingram was arrested for child abuse in 1988, amid expressions of shock from his community. At the time he was chair of the county Republican committee and was chief civil deputy in the sheriff's office. He had worked in law enforcement for more than a decade.

The Ingram case began at a time when waves of rumor and media hype over satanic ritualistic abuse were rampant. At first Ingram denied everything, and detectives told him he was in denial. With the help of a psychologist who exerted enormous pressure over endless hours of interrogation, Ingram's memories of abusing his daughter began to appear. Then the psychologist, with the help of a detective, "interviewed" Ingram's son. In that interview, the son reported on his dreams, and the therapist and detective convinced him that the dreams were real. [13]

In another case, a father (Mr. K) hired a private investigator after his 26-year-old daughter reported a recently uncovered repressed memory and accused him of incest. The investigator, acting under cover, went to see the daughter's therapist complaining that she had nightmares and had trouble sleeping. On the third visit, the therapist told undercover agent that she was an incest survivor. According to the investigator's report (Monesi, 1992), the therapist said this to her pseudopatient: "She then told me that she was certain I was experiencing body memory from a trauma, earlier in life, that I could not remember. I could not remember because my brain had blocked the memory that was too painful to deal with." When the patient said she didn't remember any trauma, the therapist told her "that is the case and many people at far later times in their lives go through this when the memory starts to surface." The therapist told her that many people go through this experience, such as "Viet Nam Vets, Earthquake Survivors and Incest Survivors." When the patient said that she had never been in Vietnam or in an earthquake, the therapist nodded her head and said "Yes, I know." The therapist then said she should read *Courage to Heal,* a book she recommends to all abuse survivors. After that there was the *Courage to Heal Work-book,* which tells survivors how to cope with the fears and memories. She pulled *Secret Survivors* by E. S. Blume (1990) from the shelf, opened the cover, and read the list of symptoms of incest survivors. With two-thirds of the symptoms, she would look at the pseudopatient and shake her head yes as if this was confirmation of her diagnosis. She recommended incest survivor groups. In the fourth session, the diagnosis of probable incest victim was confirmed on the basis of the "classic symptoms" of body memory and sleep disorders. When the patient insisted that she had no memory of such events, the therapist assured her this was often the case.

Why Would Therapists Suggest Things to Their Patients?

The core of treatment, it is widely believed, is to help clients reclaim their "traumatic past" (Rieker & Carmen, 1986, p. 369). Therapists routinely dig deliberately into the ugly underbelly of mental life. They dig for memories purposefully because they believe that in order to get well, to become survivors rather than victims, their clients must overcome the protective denial that was used to tolerate the abuse during childhood (Sgroi, 1989, p. 112). Memory blocks can be protective in many ways, but they come at a cost; they cut off the survivors from a significant part of their past histories and leave them without good explanations for their negative self-image, low self-esteem, and other mental problems. These memories must be brought into consciousness, not as an end in itself but only insofar as it helps the survivors acknowledge reality and overcome denial processes that are now dysfunctional (p. 115).

Another reason therapists may be unwittingly suggesting ideas to their clients is that they have fallen prey to a bias that affects all of us, known as the "confirmatory bias" (Baron, Beattie, & Hershey, 1988). People in general, therapists included, have a tendency to search for evidence that confirms their hunches rather than search for evidence that disconfirms. It is not easy to discard long-held or cherished beliefs, in part because we are eager to verify those beliefs and are not inclined to seek evidence that might disprove them.

The notion that the beliefs that individuals hold can create their own social reality is the essence of the self-fulfilling prophecy (Snyder, 1984). How does "reality" get constructed? One way this can happen is through interview strategies. Interviewers are known to choose questions that inquire about behaviors and experiences thought to be characteristic, rather than those thought to be uncharacteristic, of some particular classification. If therapists ask questions that tend to elicit behaviors and experiences thought to be characteristic of someone who had been a victim of childhood trauma, might they too be creating this social reality?

Whatever the good intentions of therapists, the documented examples of rampant suggestion should force us to at least ponder whether some therapists might be suggesting illusory memories to their clients rather than unlocking authentic distant memories. Or, paraphrasing Gardner (1992), what is considered to be present in the client's unconscious mind might actually be present solely in the therapist's conscious mind (p. 689). Ganaway (1989) worried that, once seeded by the therapist, false memories could develop that replace previously unsatisfactory internal explanations for intolerable but more prosaic childhood trauma.

Creation of False Memories

The hypothesis that false memories could be created invites an inquiry into the important question of what is known about false memories. Since the mid-1970s at least, investigations have been done into the creation of false memories through exposure to misinformation. Now, nearly two decades later, there are hundreds of studies to support a high degree of memory distortion. People have recalled nonexistent broken glass and tape recorders, a cleanshaven man as having a mustache, straight hair as curly, and even something as large and conspicuous as a barn in a bucolic scene that contained no buildings at all (Loftus & Ketcham, 1991). This growing body of research shows that new, postevent information often becomes incorporated into memory, supplementing and altering a person's recollection. The new information invades us, like a Trojan horse, precisely because we do not detect its influence. Understanding how we can become tricked by revised data about our past is central to understanding the hypothesis that suggestions from popular writings and therapy sessions can affect autobiographical recall.

One frequently heard comment about the research on memory distortion is that all changes induced by misinformation are about trivial details (Darnton, 1991; Franklin & Wright, 1991). There is no evidence, the critics allege, that one can tinker with memories of real traumatic events or that one can inject into the human mind whole events that never happened.

CAN REAL TRAUMATIC MEMORIES BE CHANGED?

There are some who argue that traumatic events leave some sort of indelible fixation in the mind (e.g., "traumatic events create lasting visual images...burned-in visual impressions," Terr, 1988, p. 103; "memory imprints are indelible, they do not erase–a therapy that tries to alter them will be uneconomical," Kantor, 1980, p. 163). These assertions fail to recognize known examples and evidence that memory is malleable even for life's most traumatic experiences. If Eileen Franklin's memory of witnessing her father murder her eight-year-old best friend is a real memory, then it too is a memory replete with changes over different tellings. However, there are clearer examples–anecdotal reports in which definite evidence exists that the traumatic event itself was actually experienced and yet the memory radically changed.

In the category of documented anecdotes there is the example of one of the worst public and personal tragedies in the history of baseball (Anderson, 1990; described in Loftus & Kaufman, 1992). Baseball aficionados may recall that Jack Hamilton, then a pitcher with the California Angels, crushed the outfielder, Tony Conigliaro, in the face with a first-pitch fastball. Although Hamilton thought he remembered this horrible event perfectly, he misremembered it as occurring during a day game, when it was actually at night, and misremembered it in other critical ways. Another example will be appreciated by history buffs, particularly those with an interest in the second World War. American Brigadier General Elliot Thorpe recalled the day after the bombing of Pearl Harbor one way in a memoir and completely differently in an oral history taken on his retirement. Both accounts, in fact, were riddled with errors (Weintraub, 1991).

Evidence of a less anecdotal, more experimental nature supports the imperfections of personally experienced traumatic memories. For example, one study examined people's recollections of how they heard the news of the 1986 explosion of the space shuttle *Challenger* (Harsch & Neisser, 1989; Neisser & Harsch, 1992). Subjects were questioned on the morning after the explosion and again nearly three years later. Most described their memories as vivid, but none of them were entirely correct, and more than one-third were wildly inaccurate. One subject, for example, was on the telephone having a business discussion when her best friend interrupted the call with the news. Later she would remember that she heard the news in class and at first thought it was a joke, and that she later walked into a TV lounge and saw the news, and then reacted to the disaster.

Another study (Abhold, 1992) demonstrated the malleability of memory for a serious life-and-death situation. The subjects had attended an important high school football game at which a player on the field went into cardiac arrest. Paramedics tried to resuscitate the player and apparently failed. The audience reactions ranged from complete silence, to sobbing, to screaming. (Ultimately, fortunately, the player was revived at the hospital.) Six years later, many of these people were interviewed. Errors of recollection were common. Moreover, when exposed to misleading information about this life-and-death event, many individuals absorbed the misinformation into their recollections. For example, more than one-fourth of the subjects were persuaded that they had seen blood on the player's jersey after receiving a false suggestion to this effect.

These anecdotes and experimental examples suggest that even details of genuinely experienced traumatic events are, as Christianson (1992) put it, "by no means, completely accurate" (p. 207).

Can One Inject a Complete Memory for Something That Never Happened?

It is one thing to discover that memory for an actual traumatic event is changed over time but quite another to show that one can inject a whole event into someone's mind for something that never happened. There are numerous anecdotes and experimental studies that show it is indeed possible to lead people to construct entire events.

Piaget's memory.

Whole memories can be implanted into a person's real-life autobiography, as is best shown by Piaget's classic childhood memory of an attempted kidnapping (Piaget, 1962; described in Loftus & Ketcham, 1991, p. 19). The false memories were with him for at least a decade. The memory was of an attempted kidnapping that occurred when he was an infant. He found out it was false when his nanny confessed years later that she had made up the entire story and felt guilty about keeping the watch she had received as a reward. In explaining this false memory, Piaget assumed, "I, therefore, must have heard, as a child, the account of this story, which my parents believed, and projected into the past in the form of a visual memory."

Loud noises at night.

Although widely disseminated and impressive at first glance, Piaget's false memory is still but a single anecdote and subject to other interpretations. Was this really a memory, or an interesting story? Could it be that the assault actually happened and the nurse, for some inexplicable reason, lied later? For these reasons it would be nice to find stronger evidence that a false memory for a complete event was genuinely implanted.

An apparently genuine 19th-century memory implantation was reported by Laurence and Perry (1983): Bernheim, during hypnosis, suggested to a female subject that she had awakened four times during the previous night to go to the toilet and had fallen on her nose on the fourth occasion. After hypnosis, the woman insisted that the suggested events had actually occurred, despite the hypnotist's insistence that she had dreamed them. Impressed by Bernheim's success, and by explorations by Orne (1979), Laurence and Perry asked 27 highly hypnotizable individuals during hypnosis to choose a night from the previous week and to describe their activities during the half hour before going to sleep. The subjects were then instructed to relive that night, and a suggestion was implanted that they had heard some loud noises and had awakened. Almost one-half (13) of the 27 subjects accepted the suggestion and stated *after* hypnosis that the suggested event had actually taken place. Of the 13, 6 were unequivocal in their certainty. The remainder came to the conclusion on the basis of reconstruction. Even when told that the hypnotist had actually suggested the noises, these subjects still maintained that the noises had occurred. One said "I'm pretty certain I heard them. As a matter of fact, I'm pretty damned certain. I'm positive I heard these noises" (Laurence & Perry, 1983, p. 524).

The paradigm of inducing pseudomemories of being awakened by loud noises has now been used extensively by other researchers who readily replicate the basic findings. Moreover, the pseudomemories are not limited to hypnotic conditions. Simply inducing subjects to imagine and describe the loud noises resulted in later "memories" for noises that had never occurred (Weekes, Lynn, Green, & Brentar, 1992).

Other false memories.

Other evidence shows that people can be tricked into believing that they experienced an event even in the absence of specific hypnotic suggestions. For example, numerous studies have shown that people misremember that they voted in a particular election when they actually had not (Abelson, Loftus, & Greenwald, 1992). One interpretation of these findings is that people fill in the gaps in their memory with socially desirable constructions, thus creating for themselves a false memory of voting.

In other studies, people have been led to believe that they witnessed assaultive behavior when in fact they did not (e.g., Haugaard, Reppucci, Laurd, & Nauful, 1991). In this study, children aged four to seven years were led to believe that they saw a man hit a girl, when he had not, after hearing the girl lie about the assault. Not only did they misrecall the nonexistent hitting, but they added their own details: Of 41 false claims, 39 children said it happened near a pond, 1 said it was at the girl's house, and 1 could not specify exactly where the girl was when the man hit her.

Violent false memories

People can hold completely false memories for something far more traumatic than awakening at night, voting in a particular election, or a simulation involving a man and a girl. Pynoos and Nader (1989) studied children's recollections of a sniper attack at an elementary school playground. Some of the children who were interviewed were not at the school during the shooting, including some who were already on the way home or were on vacation. Yet, even the nonwitnesses had memories:

One girl initially said that she was at the school gate nearest the sniper when the shooting began. In truth she was not only out of the line of fire, she was half a block away. A boy who had been away on vacation said that he had been on his way to the school, had seen someone lying on the ground, had heard the shots, and then turned back. In actuality, a police barricade prevented anyone from approaching the block around the school (p. 238).

The memories apparently were created by exposure to the stories of those who truly experienced the trauma.

Memories of being lost.

A question arises as to whether one could experimentally implant memories for nonexistent events that, if they had occurred, would have been traumatic. Given the need to protect human subjects, devising a means of accomplishing this was not an easy task. Loftus and Coan (in press), however, developed a paradigm for instilling a specific childhood memory for being lost on a particular occasion at the age of five. They chose getting lost because it is clearly a great fear of both parents and children. Their initial observations show how subjects can be readily induced to believe this kind of false memory. The technique involved a subject and a trusted family member who played a variation of "Remember the time that....?" To appreciate the methodology, consider the implanted memory of 14-year-old Chris. Chris was convinced by his older brother, Jim, that he had been lost in a shopping mall when he was 5 years old. Jim told Chris this story as if it were the truth: "It was 1981 or 1982. I remember that Chris was 5. We had gone shopping at the University City shopping mall in Spokane. After some panic, we found Chris being led down the mall by a tall, oldish man (I think he was wearing a flannel shirt). Chris was crying and holding the man's hand. The man explained that he had found Chris walking around crying his eyes out just a few mements before and was trying to help him find his parents."

Just two days later, Chris recalled his feelings about being lost: "That day I was so scared that I would never see my family again. I knew that I was in trouble." On the third day, he recalled a conversation with his mother: "I remember mom telling me never to do that again." On the fourth day: "I also remember that old man's flannel shirt." On the fifth day, he started remembering the mall itself: "I sort of remember the stores." In his last recollection, he could even remember a conversation with the man who found him: "I remember the man asking me if I was lost."

It would be natural to wonder whether perhaps Chris had really gotten lost that day. Maybe it happened, but his brother forgot. But Chris's mother was subjected to the same procedure and was never able to remember the false event. After five days of trying, she said "I feel very badly about it, but I just cannot remember anything like this ever happening."

A couple of weeks later, Chris described his false memory and he greatly expanded on it.

> I was with you guys for a second and I think I went over to look at the toy store, the Kay-bee toy and uh, we got lost and I was looking around and I thought, "Uh-oh. I'm in trouble now." You know. And then I...I thought I was never going to see my family again. I was really scared you know. And then this old man, I think he was wearing a blue flannel, came up to me...he was kind of old. He was kind of bald on top...he had like a ring of gray hair...and he had glasses.

Thus, in two short weeks, Chris now could even remember the balding head and the glasses worn by the man who rescued him. He characterized his memory as reasonably clear and vivid.

Finally, Chris was debriefed. He was told that one of the memories presented to him earlier had been false. When asked to guess, he guessed one of the genuine memories. When told that it was the getting-lost memory, he said, "Really? I thought I remembered being lost...and looking around for you guys. I do remember that. And then crying. And mom coming up and saying 'Where were you? Don't you...Don't you ever do that again.'"

A false memory of abuse.

The lost-in-a-shopping-mall example shows that memory of an entire mildly traumatic event can be created. It is still natural to wonder whether one could go even further and implant a memory of abuse. Ethically, of course, it would not be possible, but anecdotally, as it happens, it was done. It is one of the most dramatic cases of false memory of abuse ever to be documented–the case of Paul Ingram from Olympia, Washington (Ofshe, 1992; Watters, 1991). As described above, Ingram, was arrested for child abuse in 1988 at the time he was chair of the county Republican committee. At first Ingram denied everything, and detectives told him he was in denial. After five months of interrogation, suggestions from a psychologist, and continuing pressure from detectives and advisors, Ingram began to confess to rapes, assaults, child sexual abuse, and participation in a Satan-worshiping cult alleged to have murdered 25 babies (Ofshe, 1992). To elicit specific memories, the psychologist or detectives would suggest some act of abuse (e.g., that on one occasion, Ingram and several other men raped his daughter). Ingram would at first not remember these fragments, but after a concerted effort on his part, he would later come up with a detailed memory.

Richard Ofshe, a social psychologist hired by the prosecution to interview Ingram and his family members, decided to test Ingram's credibility. Ofshe had made up a completely fabricated scenario. He told Ingram that two of his children (a daughter and a son) had reported that Ingram had forced them to have sex in front of him. As with the earlier suggestions, Ingram at first could not remember this. But Ofshe urged Ingram to try to think about the scene and try to see it happening, just as the interrogators had done to him earlier. Ingram began to get some visual images. Ingram then followed Ofshe's instructions to "pray on" the scene and try to remember more over the next few hours. Several hours later, Ingram had developed detailed memories and wrote a three-page statement confessing in graphic detail to the scene that Ofshe had invented (Ofshe, 1992; Watters, 1991). Ofshe (1989, 1992) noted that this was not the first time that a vulnerable individual had been made to believe that he had committed a crime for which he originally had no memory and which evidence proved he could not have committed. What is crucial about the Ingram case is that some of the same methods that are used in repressed memory cases were used with Ingram. These include the use of protracted imagining of events and authority figures establishing the authenticity of these events.

These examples provide further insights into the malleable nature of memory. They suggest that memories for personally experienced traumatic events can be altered by new experiences. Moreover, they reveal that entire events that never happened can be injected into memory. The false memories range from the relatively trivial (e.g., remembering voting) to the bizarre (e.g., remembering forcing one's daughter and son to have sex). These false memories, with more or less detail, of course do not prove that repressed memories of abuse that return are false. They do demonstrate a mechanism by which false memories can be created by a small suggestion from a trusted family member, by hearing someone lie, by suggestion from a psychologist, or by incorporation of the experiences of others into one's own autobiography. Of course, the fact that false memories can be planted tells nothing about whether a given memory of child sexual abuse is false or not; nor does it tell how one might distinguish the real cases from the false ones. These findings on the malleability of memory do, however, raise questions about the wisdom of certain recommendations being promoted in self-help workbooks, in handbooks for therapists, and by some therapists themselves. The false memories created in the examples above were accomplished with techniques that are not all that different from what some therapists regularly do–suggesting that the client was probably abused because of some vague symptoms, labeling a client's ambiguous recollections as evidence of abuse, and encouraging mental exercises that involve fantasy merging with reality.

FINAL REMARKS

The 1990s brought a blossoming of reports of awakenings of previously repressed memories of childhood abuse. One reason for the increase may be the widespread statistics on sex abuse percentages that are published almost daily: "By 1980...the government tallied almost 43,000 cases of child sex abuse annually" (Nathan, 1991, p. 154); "One in five women are 'incest victims,"' (p. 155); "6.8 million women nationwide would say they had been raped once, 4.7 million more than once" (Johnston, 1992, p. A9); "In 1972, 610,000 [child abuse cases] were reported nationally, and by 1985 the number had exceeded 1.7 million" (Baker, 1992, p. 37). "If it happens so often, did it happen to me?" is a question many women and some men are asking themselves now more than ever before. The appearance of abuse statistics is one battle in the war waged against an earlier tendency on the part of society to disbelieve the abuse reports of women and children a tendency that we should all deplore. The repressed memory cases are another outlet for women's rage over sexual violence. Although women's anger is certainly justified in many cases, and may be justified in some repressed memory cases too, it is time to stop and ask whether the net of rage has been cast too widely, creating a new collective nightmare.

Repressed memories of abuse often return in therapy, sometimes after suggestive probing. Today, popular writings have been so fully absorbed by the culture that these too can serve as a source of suggestion that can greatly influence what happens in therapy and outside of it (Guze, 1992). The result is memories that are often detailed and confidently held. Despite lack of corroboration, some of these recollections could be authentic. Others might not be.

Several implications of these observations follow. First, we need a renewed effort at research on the problem of repressed memories. This should encompass, in part, a reexamination of some of the widely cherished beliefs of psychotherapists. Is it true that repression of extremely traumatic experiences is common? Do these experiences invade us despite the fact that "all the good juice of consciousness has drained out" (Dennett, 1991, p. 325). It is common to see analogies drawn between Vietnam War veterans and the incest survivors (e.g., Herman, 1992; Rieker & Carmen, 1986). Do they share in common the use of "massive repression" (Wolf & Alpert, 1991, p. 314) as a mechanism for coping? If so, how do we explain findings obtained with children who witness parental murder and other atrocities? In one study (Malmquist, 1986), not a single child aged 5 to 10 years who had witnessed the murder of a parent repressed the memory. Rather, they were continually flooded with pangs of emotion about the murder and preoccupation with it.

Is it true that repressed material, like radioactive waste, "lies there in leaky canisters, never losing potency, eternally dangerous" (Hornstein, 1992, p. 260) and constantly threatens to erupt into consciousness? Psychotherapists have assumed for years that repressed memories are powerful influences because they are not accessible to consciousness (Bowers, 1992). Is there evidence for this assumption? Is it necessarily true that all people who display symptoms of severe mental distress have had some early childhood trauma (probably abuse) that is responsible for the distress? With cutting-edge research now showing that mental distress involves neuronal and hormonal systems of a much wider scope than previously realized (Chrousos & Gold, 1992; Gershon & Rieder, 1992), should not other potential causes be at least considered?

Questions must also be examined about the well-intentioned treatment strategies of some clinicians. Is it possible that the therapist's interpretation is the cause of the patient's disorder rather than the effect of the disorder, to paraphrase Guze (1992, p. 78)? Is it necessarily true that people who cannot remember an abusive childhood are repressing the memory? Is it necessarily true that people who dream about or visualize abuse are actually getting in touch with true memories? Good scientific research needs to be done to support these assumptions, or they should be challenged. Challenging these core assumptions will not be an easy thing to do, anymore than it was for psychologists of the 1930s to challenge the radical subjectivity of psychoanalysis (Hornstein, 1992), or for psychologists of the 1980s to challenge the reliability of the clinical judgments made by psychologists and psychiatrists (Faust & Ziskin, 1988; Fowler & Matarazzo, 1988). [14] Nonetheless, when we move from the privacy of the therapy session, in which the client's reality may be the only reality that is important, into the courtroom, in which there can be but a single reality, then we as citizens in a democratic society are entitled to more solid evidence.

Until we have better empirical answers, therapists might consider whether it is wise to "suggest" that childhood trauma happened, to probe relentlessly for recalcitrant memories, and then to uncritically accept them as fact. Uncritical acceptance of uncorroborated trauma memories by therapists, social agencies, and law enforcement personnel has been used to promote public accusations by alleged abuse survivors. If the memories are fabricated, this will of course lead to irreparable damage to the reputations of potentially innocent people, according to Ganaway (1989), who discussed the problem in the context of SRA memories.

Uncritical acceptance of uncorroborated trauma memories poses other potentially dangerous problems for society. According to Ganaway (1991), reinforcing the validity of unverifiable memories in the therapeutic setting may lead to diversionary paths in the patient's therapy away from actual childhood trauma. This could lead to interminable therapy and a total draining of the patient's financial resources as the therapist and patient collaborate in a mutual deception to pursue a bottomless pit of memories. Worse, the patient's initial wonderings supported by therapist affirmations could then become fixed beliefs, precipitating suicidal thoughts and behaviors based on the new belief system, because the patient would no longer challenge the veracity of the new memories. Like Betsy Ross sewing the first American flag, the abuse becomes a myth that was never true but always will be (E. Frishholz, personal communication, May 1992). Patients who are reinforced into a new belief system could develop newer, larger problems. If actual childhood sexual abuse is associated with numerous negative long-term effects (e.g., severe sexual dysfunction; Ambrosoe-Bienkowski, Stahly, & Wideman, 1991), what might be the consequence of implanted childhood sexual abuse? If the memories are ultimately shown to be false, therapists may then become the targets of future ethics violations and lawsuits. They will be charged with a grave form of mind abuse–charges that have already been initiated in several states.

What should therapists do instead? As a first step, it is worth recognizing that we do not yet have the tools for reliably distinguishing the signal of true repressed memories from the noise of false ones. Until we gain these tools, it seems prudent to consider some combination of Herman's (1992) advice about probing for traumatic memories and Ganaway's (1991) advice about SRA memories. Zealous conviction is a dangerous substitute for an open mind. Psychotherapists, counselors, social service agencies, and law enforcement personnel would be wise to be careful how they probe for horrors on the other side of some presumed amnesic barrier. They need to be circumspect regarding uncorroborated repressed memories that return. Techniques that are less potentially dangerous would involve clarification, compassion, and gentle confrontation along with a demonstration of empathy for the painful struggles these patients must endure as they come to terms with their personal truths.

There is one last tragic risk of suggestive probing and uncritical acceptance of all allegations made by clients, no matter how dubious. These activities are bound to lead to an increased likelihood that society in general will disbelieve the genuine cases of childhood sexual abuse that truly deserve our sustained attention.

REFERENCES

ABC News. (1992, April 2). *Primetime Live* [Transcript]. (Washington, DC: American Broadcasting Corporation.)

Abelson, R. P., Loftus, E. F., & Greenwald, A. G. (1992). Attempts to improve the accuracy of self-reports of voting. (In J. M. Tanur (Ed.), *Questions about survey questions: Meaning, memory, expression, and social interactions in surveys* (pp. 138—153). New York: Russell Sage Foundation.)

Abhold, J. (1992). [Unpublished doctoral dissertation data.](University of Arkansas.)

Ambroso-Bienkowski, M., Stahly, G. B., & Wideman, K. (1991, August). *Relationship of sexual fantasy and sexual dysfunction to childhood molestation.* (Paper presented at the 99th Annual Convention of the American Psychological Association, San Francisco.)

Anderson, D. (1990, February 27). Handcuffed in history to Tony C. *New York Times,* p. B9.

Baker, R. A. (1992). *Hidden memories.* (Buffalo, NY: Prometheus Books.)

Baron, J., Beattie, J., & Hershey, J. D. (1988). Heuristics and biases in diagnostic reasoning: Congruence, information, and certainty. *Organizational Behavior and Human Decision Processes, 42*, 88-110.

Barton v. Peters. Case No 4FA-90-0157, Superior Court for the State of Alaska, 4th Judicial District.

Bass, E., & Davis, L. (1988). *The courage to heal.* (New York: Harper & Row.)

Bass, E., & Thornton, L. (1991). *I never told anyone: Writings by women survivors of child sexual abuse.* (New York: Harper Perennial.)

Blume, E. S. (1990). *Secret survivors: Uncovering incest and its aftereffects in women.* (New York: Ballantine.)

Bottoms, B. L., Shaver, P. R., & Goodman, G. S. (1991, August). *Profile of ritualistic and religion-related abuse allegation reported to clinical psychologists in the United States.* (Paper presented at the 99th Annual Convention of the American Psychological Association, San Francisco.)

Bower, G. H. (1990). Awareness, the unconscious, and repression: An experimental psychologist's perspective. (In J. Singer (Ed.), *Repression and dissociation: Implications for personality, theory, psychopathology, and health* (pp. 209-231). Chicago: University of Chicago Press.)

Bowers, K. S. (1992, November 2). *Preconscious processes: How do we distinguish mental representations that correspond to perceived events from those that reflect imaginal processes?* (Paper presented at National Institute of Mental Health workshop "Basic behavioral and psychological research: Building a bridge," Rockville, MD.)

Bradshaw, J. (1990). *Homecoming.* (New York: Bantam Books.)

Bradshaw, J. (1992). Discovering what we want. *Lear's, 5*, 49.

Braun, B. G., & Sachs, R. G. (1988, October). *Recognition of possible cult involvement in MPD patients.* (Paper presented at the Fifth International Conference on Multiple Personality/Dissociative States, Chicago.)

Briere, J. (1992). Studying delayed memories of childhood sexual abuse. *The Advisor (Publication of the American Professional Society on the Abuse of Children), 5*, 17-18.

Briere, J., & Conte, J. (in press). Self-reported amnesia for abuse in adults molested as children. (Journal of Traumatic Stress.)

Bruhn, A. R. (1990). *Earliest childhood memories: Vol.1. Theory and application to clinical practice.* (New York: Praeger.)

Cannon, L. (1991). *President Reagan: The role of a lifetime.* (New York: Simon & Shuster.)

Christianson, S. A. (1992). Do flashbulb memories differ from other types of emotional memories? (In E. Winograd & U. Neisser (Eds.), *Affect and accuracy in recall: studies of "flashbulb" memories* (pp. 191—211). (New York: Cambridge University Press.)

Chrousos, G. P., & Gold, P. W. (1992). The concept of stress and stress system disorders: Overview of physical and behavioral homeostasis. *JAMA: Journal of the American Medical Association, 267*, 1244-1252.

Collier D. v. Collier, J. Deposition of plaintiff, Case No. 711752, Superior Court, County of Santa Clara, California.

Culhane, D. (1991, August 4). *Sins of the father [Peterson, B. Review of Dancing with Daddy] New York Times Book Review,* p. 18.

The darkest secret *People,* pp. 88-94.

Daro, D. (1988). *Confronting child abuse.* (New York: Free Press.)

Darnton, N. (1991, October 7). The pain of the last taboo. *Newsweek,* pp. 70-72.

Davis, L. (1991). Murdered memory. *In Health, 5*, 79-84.

Dawes, R. M. (1992). Why believe that for which there is no good evidence? *Issues in Child Abuse Accusations, 4*, 214-218.

Dennett, D. C. (1991). *Consciousness explained.* (Boston: Little, Brown.)

Doe, J. (1991). How could this happen? Coping with a false accusation of incest and rape. *Issues in Child Abuse Accusations, 3*, 154-165.

Dormen, L. (1991, April). A secret life. *Seventeen,* pp. 164-167.

Driscoll, L. N., & Wright, C. (1991). Survivors of childhood ritual abuse: Multi-generational satanic cult involvement. *Treating Abuse Today, 1*, 5-13.

Edmiston, S. (1990, November). Daddy's girl. (*Glamour,* pp. 228-231, 280-285.)

Ellis, B. (1992). Satanic ritual abuse and legend ostension. *Journal of Psychology and Theology, 20*, 274-277.

Erdelyi, M. H. (1985). *Psychoanalysis: Freud's cognitive psychology.* (New York: Freeman.)

Erdelyi, M. H., & Goldberg, B. (1979). Let's not sweep repression under the rug: Toward a cognitive psychology of repression. (In J. F. Kihlstrom & F. J. Evans (Eds.), *Functional disorders of memory* (pp. 355-402). Hillsdale, NJ: Erlbaum.)

Farmer, S. (1989). *Adult children of abusive parents.* (New York: Ballantine.)

Faust, D., & Ziskin, J. (1988). The expert witness in psychology and psychiatry. *Science, 241*, 31-35.

Fields, R. (1992, August 4). Hood must pay in sex-abuse case. *Beacon Journal [Akron, OH],* p. C5.

Forgetting to remember. *Newsweek,* p. 58.

Forward, S., & Buck, C. (1988). *Betrayal of innocence: Incest and its devastation.* (New York: Penguin Books.)

Fowler, R. D., & Matarazzo, J. D. (1988). Psychologists and psychiatrists as expert witnesses. *Science, 241*, 1143-1144.

Franklin, E., & Wright, W. (1991). *Sins of the father.* (New York: Crown.)

Frawley, M. G. (1990). From secrecy to self-disclosure: Healing the scars of incest. (In G. Stricker & M. Fisher (Eds.), *Self-disclosure in the therapeutic relationship* (pp. 247-259). New York: Plenum Press.)

Fredrickson, R. (1992). *Repressed memories: A journey to recovery from sexual abuse.* (New York: Simon & Schuster.)

Freud, S. (1953). Three essays on the theory of sexuality. (In J. Strachey (Ed.), *The standard edition of the complete psychological works of Sigmund Freud* (Vol. 7, pp. 135-243). London: Hogarth Press. Original work published 1905.)

Freyd, J. J. (1991, August 21). *Memory repression, dissociative states, and other cognitive control processes involved in adult sequelae of childhood trauma.* (Paper presented at the Second Annual Conference on Psychodynamics—Cognitive Science Interface, University of California, San Francisco.)

Ganaway, G. K. (1989). Historical versus narrative truth: Clarifying the role of exogenous trauma in the etiology of MPD and its variants. *Dissociation, 2*, 205-220.

Ganaway, G. K. (1991, August). *Alternative hypotheses regarding satanic ritual abuse memories.* (Paper presented at the 99th Annual Convention of the American Psychological Association, San Francisco.)

Ganaway, G. K. (1992). Some additional questions. *Journal of Psychology and Theology, 20*, 201-205.

Gardner, R. A. (1991). *Sex abuse hysteria.* (Cresskill, NJ: Creative Therapeutics.)

Gardner, R. A. (1992). *True and false accusations of child sex abuse.* (Cresskill, NJ: Creative Therapeutics.)

Gershon, E. S., & Rieder, R. O. (1992). Major disorders of mind and brain. *Scientific American, 267*, (3) 127-133.

Gordon, J. S. (1991). The UFO experience. *The Atlantic Monthly, 268*, 82-92.

Gudjonsson, G. (1992). *The psychology of interrogations, confessions and testimony.* (Chichester, England: Wiley.)

Guze, S. B. (1992). *Why is psychiatry a branch of medicine?* (New York: Oxford University Press.)

Harris, M. (1974). *Cows, pigs, wars, and witches: The riddles of culture.* (NY: Vintage Books.)

Harsch, N., & Neisser, U. (1989, November). *Substantial and irreversible errors in flashbulb memories of the Challenger explosion.* (Poster presented at the annual meeting of the Psychonomic Society, Atlanta, GA.)

Haugaard, J. J., Reppucci, N. D., Laurd, J., & Nauful, T. (1991). Children's definitions of the truth and their competency as witnesses in legal proceedings. *Law and Human Behavior, 15*, 253-272.

Herman, J. L. (1981). *Father—daughter incest.* (Cambridge, MA: Harvard University Press.)

Herman, J. L. (1992). *Trauma and recovery.* (New York: Basic Books.)

Herman, J. L., & Schatzow, E. (1987). Recovery and verification of memories of childhood sexual trauma. *Psychoanalytic Psychology, 4*, 1-14.

Holmes, D. (1990). The evidence for repression: An examination of sixty years of research. (In J. Singer (Ed.), *Repression and dissociation: Implications for personality, theory, psychopathology, and health* (pp. 85—102). Chicago: University of Chicago Press.)

Hornstein, G. A. (1992). The return of the repressed. *American Psychologist, 47*, 254-263.

Howe, M. L., & Courage, M. L. (1993). On resolving the enigma of infantile amnesia. *Psychological Bulletin, 113*, 305-326.

Johnston, D. (1992, April 24). Survey shows number of rapes far higher than official figures. *New York Times*, p. A9.

Kantor, D. (1980). Critical identity image. (In J. K. Pearce & L. J. Friedman (Eds.), *Family therapy: Combining psychodynamic and family systems approaches* (pp. 137-167) New York: Grune & Stratton.)

Kantrowitz, B. (1991, February 11). Forgetting to remember. *Newsweek*, p. 58.

Kihlstrom, J. F., & Harackiewicz, J. (1982). The earliest recollection: A new survey. *Journal of Personality, 50*, 134-148.

Kutchinsky, B. (1992). The child sexual abuse panic. *Nordisk Sexoligi, 10*, 30-42.

Laker, B. (1992, April 14). A nightmare of memories. *Seattle Post-Intelligencer*, p. C1.

Lamm, J. B. (1991). Easing access to the courts for incest victims: Toward an equitable application of the delayed discovery rule. *The Yale Law Journal, 100*, 2189-2208.

Laurence, J. R., & Perry, C. (1983). Hypnotically created memory among highly hypnotizable subjects. *Science, 222*, 523-524.

Lofft, K. v. Lofft, D. (1989). Complaint for Damages. (Case No. 617151, Superior Court of the State of California for County of San Diego.)

Loftus, E. F. (1982). Memory and its distortions. (In A. G. Kraut (Ed.), *G. Stanley Hall lectures* (pp. 119-154). Washington, DC: American Psychological Association.)

Loftus, E. F. (in press). Desperately seeking memories of the first few years of childhood. (*Journal of Experimental Psychology: General.*)

Loftus, E. F., & Coan, D. (in press). The construction of childhood memories. (In D. Peters (Ed.), *The child witness in context: Cognitive, social and legal perspectives.* (New York: Kluwer.)

Loftus, E. F., & Herzog, C. (1991). Unpublished data. (University of Washington.)

Loftus, E. F., & Kaufman, L. (1992). Why do traumatic experiences sometimes produce good memory (flashbulbs) and sometimes no memory (repression)? (In E. Winograd & U. Neisser (Eds.), *Affect and accuracy in recall: Studies of "flashbulb" memories* (pp. 212-223). New York: Cambridge University Press.)

Loftus, E. F., & Ketcham, K. (1991). *Witness for the defense.* (New York: St. Martin's Press.)

Loftus, E. F., Polonsky, S., & Fullilove, M. T. (1993). *Memories of childhood sexual abuse: Remembering and repressing.* (Unpublished manuscript, University of Washington and Columbia University School of Public Health.)

Loftus, E. F., Weingardt, K., & Hoffman, H. (1992). *Sleeping memories on trial: Reactions to memories that were previously repressed.* (Unpublished manuscript, University of Washington.)

Mack, J. E. (1980). Psychoanalysis and biography: Aspects of a developing affinity. *Journal of the American Psychoanalytic Association, 28*, 543-562.

Malmquist, C. P. (1986). Children who witness parental murder: Posttraumatic aspects. *Journal of the American Academy of Child Psychiatry, 25*, 320-325.

McMillan, P. (1992, April 28). Woman, 39, wins $500,000 in incest case. *Los Angeles Times*, p. B3.

Medin, D. L., & Ross, B. H. (1992). *Cognitive psychology.* (Ft. Worth, TX: Harcourt Brace Jovanovich.)

Monesi, L. (1992). [Reports of a private investigator, Falcon International Inc. Columbus, Ohio.]

Morton, J. (1990). The development of even memory. *The Psychologist, 1*, 3-10.

Mulhern, S. (1991). Satanism and psychotherapy: A rumor in search of an inquisition. (In J. T. Richardson, J. Best, & D. Bromley (Eds.), *The satanism scare* (pp. 145-172). New York: Aldine de Gruyter.)

Napier, C. W. (1990). Civil incest suits: Getting beyond the statute of limitations. *Washington University Law Quarterly, 68*, 995-1020.

Nash, M. (1987). What, if anything, is regressed about hypnotic age regression? A review of the empirical literature. *Psychological Bulletin, 102*, 42-52.

Nason girl fought. *San Jose Mercury.*

Nathan, D. (1991). *Women and other aliens.* (El Paso, TX: Cinco Puntos Press.)

Nathan, D. (1992, October). Cry incest. (*Playboy*, pp. 84-88, 162-164.)

Neisser, U., & Harsch, N. (1992). Phantom flashbulbs: False recollections of hearing the news about *Challenger.* (In E. Winograd & U. Neisser (Eds.), *Affect and accuracy in recall: Studies of "flashblub" memories* (pp. 9-31). New York: Cambridge University Press.)

Ofshe, R. (1989). Coerced confessions: The logic of seemingly irrational action. *Cultic Studies Journal, 6*, 1-15.

Ofshe, R. J. (1992). Inadvertent hypnosis during interrogation: False confession due to dissociative state, misidentified multiple personality and the satanic cult hypothesis. *International Journal of Clinical and Experimental Hypnosis, 40*, 125-156.

Oldenberg, D. (1991, June 20). Dark memories: Adults confront their childhood abuse. *Washington Post,* p. D1.

Olio, K. A. (1989). Memory retrieval in the treatment of adult survivors of sexual abuse. *Transactional Analysis Journal, 19*, 93-94.

Orne, M. T. (1979). The use and misuse of hypnosis in court. *International Journal of Clinical and Experimental Hypnosis, 27*, 311-341.

Petersen, B. (1991). *Dancing with daddy: A childhood lost and a life regained.* (New York: Bantam.)

Petersen v. Bruen, (1990). 792 P.2d 18 (Nev. 1990).

Piaget, J. (1962). *Plays, dreams and imitation in childhood.* (New York: Norton.)

Pillemer, D. B., & White, S. H. (1989). Childhood events recalled by children and adults. (In *Advances in child development and behavior* (Vol. 21). San Diego, CA: Academic Press.)

Poston, C., & Lison, K. (1990). *Reclaiming our lives: Hope for adult survivors of incest.* (New York: Bantam.)

Pynoos, R. S., & Nader, K. (1989). Children's memory and proximity to violence. *Journal of the American Academy of Child and Adolescent Psychiatry, 28*, 236-241.

Rieker, P. P., & Carmen, E. H. (1986). The victim-to-patient process: The disconfirmation and transformation of abuse. *American Journal of Orthopsychiatry, 56*, 360-370.

Ritter, M. (1991, June 30). Sudden recall of forgotten crimes is a puzzler for juries, experts say. *Los Angeles Times,* p. A10.

Rogers, M. L. (1992a, March). A case of alleged satanic ritualistic abuse. (Paper presented at the meeting of the American Psychology—Law Society, San Diego.)

Rogers, M. L. (1992b). A call for discernment–natural and spiritual: Introductory editorial to a special issue on SRA. *Journal of Psychology and Theology, 20*, 175-186.

Schuker, E. (1979). Psychodynamics and treatment of sexual assault victims. *Journal of the American Academy of Psychoanalysis, 7*, 553-573.

Sgroi, S. M. (1989). Stages of recovery for adult survivors of child sex abuse. (In S. M. Sgroi (Ed.), *Vulnerable populations: Sexual abuse treatment for children, adult survivors, offenders and persons with mental retardation* (Vol. 2, p. 112). Lexington, MA: Lexington Books.)

Shaffer, R. E., & Cozolino, L. J. (1992). Adults who report childhood ritualistic abuse. *Journal of Psychology and Theology, 20*, 188-193.

Sherman, S. J., Cialdini, R. B., Schwartzman, D. F., & Reynolds, K. D. (1985). Imagining can heighten or lower the perceived likelihood of contracting a disease. *Personality and Social Psychology Bulletin, 11*, 118-127.

Smith, M. (1983). Hypnotic memory enhancement of witnesses: Does it work *Psychological Bulletin, 94*, 387-407.

Smith, M., & Pazder, L. (1980). *Michelle remembers.* (New York: Congdon & Lattes.)

Snyder, M. (1984). When belief creates reality? (In L. Berkowitz (Ed.), *Advances in experimental social psychology* (Vol. 18, pp. 247-305). San Diego, CA: Academic Press.)

Snyder, M., & Swann, W. (1978). Hypothesis-testing processes in social interaction. *Journal of Personality and Social Psychology, 11*, 1202-1212.

"A star cries incest." *People,* pp. 84-88.

Sternberg, R. (1992). *Five-part theory of giftedness.* (Paper presented at the Conference on Developmental Approaches to Identifying Exceptional Ability, Lawrence, KS.)

Stubbings v. Webb and Another, (1991). 3 Weekly Law Reports 383. (Cited in Reports and Developments (1992). *Expert Evidence: The International Digest of Human Behavior, Science, and Law, 1*, 26.)

Summit, R. (1992). Misplaced attention to delayed memory. *The Advisor (published by the American Professional Society on the Abuse of Children), 5*, 21-25.

Survivors of Incest Anonymous. (1985). *Is Survivors of Incest Anonymous for you?* (Baltimore, MD: Author.)

Survivors of Incest Anonymous. (1990). *Questions and answers.* (Distributed at Thursday night San Francisco SIA meeting, October 17.)

Susan Nason body found in a dump. *San Francisco Chronicle,* p. 1.

Telegraphers v. Railway Express Agency. (1994). 321 U.S. 342, 348-349.

Terr, L. (1988). What happens to early memories of trauma? A study of 20 children under age five at the time of documented traumatic events. *Journal of the American Academy of Child and Adolescent Psychiatry, 27*, 96-104.

Trevor-Roper, H. R. (1967). *Religion, the Reformation, and social change.* (London: Macmillan.)

Trott, J. (1991a). The grade five syndrome. *Cornerstone, 20*, 16-18.

Trott, J. (1991b). Satanic panic. *Cornerstone, 20*, 9-12.

Toufexis, A. (1991, October 28). When can memories be trusted? *Time,* pp. 86-88.

Usher, J. A., & Neisser, U. (in press). Childhood amnesia and the beginnings of memory for four early life events. (*Journal of Experimental Psychology: General.*)

Van Benschoten, S. C. (1990). Multiple personality disorder and satanic ritual abuse: The issue of credibility. *Dissociation, 3*, 22-30.

Wakefield, H., & Underwager, R. (1992). Recovered memories of alleged sexual abuse: Lawsuits against parents. *Behavioral Sciences and the Law, 10*, 483-507.

Washington., (1989). Rev. Code Ann. (Sec. 4.16.340 (1989 Supp.)

Watson, B. (1992). Salem's dark hour: Did the devil make them do it? *Smithsonian, 23*, 117-131.

Watters, E. (1991). The devil in Mr. Ingram. *Mother Jones, July-August*, 65-68.

Watters, E. (1993). Doors of memory. (*Mother Jones,* January-February, pp. 24-29, 76-77.)

Weekes, J. R., Lynn, S. J., Green, J. P., & Brentar, J. T. (1992). Pseudomemory in hypnotized and task-motivated subjects. *Journal of Abnormal Psychology, 101*, 356-360.

Weintraub, S. (1991, December 4). Three myths about Pearl Harbor. *New York Times,* p. A27.

Williams, L. M. (1992). Adult memories of childhood abuse: Preliminary findings from a longitudinal study. *The Advisor, 5*, 19-20.

Williams, M. (1987). Reconstruction of an early seduction and its aftereffects. *Journal of the American Psychonalytic Association, 15*, 145-163.

Winograd, E., & Killinger, W. A. (1983). Relating age at encoding in early childhood to adult recall: Development of flashbulb memories. *Journal of Experimental Psychology: General, 112*, 413-422.

Wolf, E. K., & Alpert, J. L. (1991). Psychoanalysis and child sexual abuse: A review of the post-freudian literature. *Psychoanalytic Psychology, 8*, 305-327.

Young, W. C., Sachs, R. G., Braun, B. G., & Watkins, R. T. (1991). Patients reporting ritual abuse in childhood: A clinical syndrome report of 37 cases. *International Journal of Child Abuse and Neglect, 15*, 181-189.

FOOTNOTES

[1.] Alaska, California, Colorado, Connecticut, Florida, Idaho, Illinois, Iowa, Maine, Minnesota, Missouri, Montana, Nevada, New Hampshire (revising an earlier law), Oregon, South Dakota, Vermont, and Virginia (see, for example, Napier, 1990).

[2.] In *Stubbings v. Webb and Another,* 1991, in which a British plaintiff claimed she was raped by her adoptive father and brother while she was a child. She sued 12 years after entering adulthood. The court permitted her suit, even though she knew she had been raped, arguing that she might not have associated the mental impairment that she was experiencing with the past rapes until she gained that knowledge as an adult.

[3.] One curiosity about this report is that the chief investigator published a landmark book on incest six years before this study (Herman, 1981). In the earlier book, the word *repression* did not even appear in the index. The 40 incest victims interviewed in depth appeared to have persisting, intrusive memories.

[4.] Many cognitive psychologists have argued that implicit theories about any topic (e.g., giftedness) guide a given society's thinking on that topic (e.g., Sternberg, 1992). More generally, intuitive theories are considered constructing working models of the world that people use in the service of understanding their world (Medin & Ross, 1992).

[5.] For those who think it is unlikely that one would ever borrow episodes from movies and popular literature and misremember them as actual events, one only has to examine Lou Cannon's (1991) biography of former President Reagan. A curious journalist who tried to verify Reagan's most famous mismemory of heroism found two that were suspiciously similar–one in the movie *A Wing and a Prayer,* and the other in a *Reader's Digest* story.

[6.] Since the publication of *Courage to Heal,* a number of cases have emerged in which women were led to believe they were abused, and later realized their memories were false (Watters, 1993). Lynn Gondolf is a case in point. During more than a year of therapy she discovered repressed memories of her father raping her. After she stopped therapy, she realized that her therapist had "coerced her and the other members of her group into imagining memories of abuse" (Watters, 1993, p. 26).

[7.] Consider a brief sampling: From Poston and Lison (1990), "Women usually do not make an immediate incest connection. They may not recall for years that the incest occurred: memories have an uncanny way of coming only when the survivor can deal with them" (p. 193); and "Many women do not remember the incest; how are they then to connect adult problems with childhood pain?" (p. 196). From Farmer (1989): "You may have even repressed the memories of the abuse. The more severe the abuse, the more likely you were to repress any conscious recollection of it" (p. 52).

[8.] This book proudly displays an endorsement by Gloria Steinem: "This book, like the truth it helps uncover, can set millions free."

[9.] Popular writings might also be the source of some questionable lay beliefs about early memories. Bradshaw (1990, 1992), a leading figure in the field of recovery and dysfunctional families, invited readers to consult his "index of suspicion": Do you have trouble knowing what you want? Are you afraid to try new experiences? If someone gives you a suggestion, do you feel you ought to follow it? According to Bradshaw, if you answered even one of these questions "yes," then you "can count on some damage having been done to you...between the 9th and 18th months of your life" (1992, p. 49). How many Bradshaw aficionados have struggled through their memories trying to find that childhood trauma?

[10.] *Dancing with Daddy* was reviewed in the *New York Times* by Culhane (1991). The reviewer called the book "as much a story about our desperate search for one-dimensional solutions to multidimensional problems as it is a story about incest and its consequences" (p. 18).

[11.] The laws in Washington and other states were changed in part due to the efforts of Kelly Barton and Patti Barton of Seattle. Patti's allegations were described in Seattle newspapers, in *Newsweek* magazine (Darnton, 1991), and on the *Sally Jesse Raphael* show. According to the *Newsweek* account, Patti remembered the alleged abuse when she was in her 30s–too late to sue under the old Washington law. So, with the help of a lawyer, she lobbied to extend the statute of limitations to allow victims to bring suit for up to three years after their memory returns. Patti's father, who denied all charges, moved to Alaska, whereupon Patti turned her efforts on the Alaska legislature and introduced the same legislation there.

[12.] In the dream, there was "a fellow who was out to hurt and perhaps rape her. In the dream she could not get rid of him. In her primal, she fought him with words until I nudged her on the shoulder with a batacka (a padded bat), and what I did was, I nudged her on the shoulder and she was there.... She came unglued at that. She took the batacka, grabbed it, and began striking out. She worked and worked until she got rid of him at the door. She opened the door of the room and kicked him out and locked the door. The man looked like her manic-depressive brother but had mannerisms like Kelly (her husband)" (p. 43).

[13.] Here is one segment:

Son: "I would have dreams of uh little people...short people coming and walking on me...walking on my bed."

Psychologist: "What you saw was real."

Son: "Well, this is a different dream...everytime a train came by, a whistle would blow and...witch would come in my window... I would wake up, but I couldn't move. It was like the blankets were tucked under and...I couldn't move my arms."

Psychologist: "You were being restrained?"

Son: "Right and there was somebody on top of me."

Psychologist: "[Son's name] these things happened to you.... It's real. It's not an hallucination."

Before long, the dreams became the reality: The son soon remembered witches holding him down and joining his father in abuse.

[14.] British historian, Hugh Trevor-Roper (1967) pointed out that the skeptics during the 16th century witchcraft craze did not make much dent in the frequency of bonfires and burnings until they figured out that they had to challenge the core belief–that is, the belief in Satan.

14 A Theory of Human Motivation

A. H. Maslow (1943)

Originally Published in *Psychological Review*, 50, 370-396 • Posted August 2000

[P. 370] I. INTRODUCTION

In a previous paper (13) various propositions were presented which would have to be included in any theory of human motivation that could lay claim to being definitive. These conclusions may be briefly summarized as follows:

1. The integrated wholeness of the organism must be one of the foundation stones of motivation theory.

2. The hunger drive (or any other physiological drive) was rejected as a centering point or model for a definitive theory of motivation. Any drive that is somatically based and localizable was shown to be atypical rather than typical in human motivation.

3. Such a theory should stress and center itself upon ultimate or basic goals rather than partial or superficial ones, upon ends rather than means to these ends. Such a stress would imply a more central place for unconscious than for conscious motivations.

4. There are usually available various cultural paths to the same goal. Therefore conscious, specific, local-cultural desires are not as fundamental in motivation theory as the more basic, unconscious goals.

5. Any motivated behavior, either preparatory or consummatory, must be understood to be a channel through which many basic needs may be simultaneously expressed or satisfied. Typically an act has more than one motivation.

6. Practically all organismic states are to be understood as motivated and as motivating.

7. Human needs arrange themselves in hierarchies of pre-potency. That is to say, the appearance of one need usually rests on the prior satisfaction of another, more pre-potent need. Man is a perpetually wanting animal. Also no need or drive can be treated as if it were isolated or discrete; every drive is related to the state of satisfaction or dissatisfaction of other drives.

8. Lists of drives will get us nowhere for various theoretical and practical reasons. Furthermore any classification of motivations [p. 371] must deal with the problem of levels of specificity or generalization of the motives to be classified.

9. Classifications of motivations must be based upon goals rather than upon instigating drives or motivated behavior.

10. Motivation theory should be human-centered rather than animal-centered.

11. The situation or the field in which the organism reacts must be taken into account but the field alone can rarely serve as an exclusive explanation for behavior. Furthermore the field itself must be interpreted in terms of the organism. Field theory cannot be a substitute for motivation theory.

12. Not only the integration of the organism must be taken into account, but also the possibility of isolated, specific, partial or segmental reactions. It has since become necessary to add to these another affirmation.

13. Motivation theory is not synonymous with behavior theory. The motivations are only one class of determinants of behavior. While behavior is almost always motivated, it is also almost always biologically, culturally and situationally determined as well.

The present paper is an attempt to formulate a positive theory of motivation which will satisfy these theoretical demands and at the same time conform to the known facts, clinical and observational as well as experimental. It derives most directly, however, from clinical experience. This theory is, I think, in the functionalist tradition of James and Dewey, and is fused with the holism of Wertheimer (19), Goldstein (6), and Gestalt Psychology, and with the dynamicism of Freud (4) and Adler (1). This fusion or synthesis may arbitrarily be called a 'general-dynamic' theory.

It is far easier to perceive and to criticize the aspects in motivation theory than to remedy them. Mostly this is because of the very serious lack of sound data in this area. I conceive this lack of sound facts to be due primarily to the absence of a valid theory of motivation. The present theory then must be considered to be a suggested program or framework for future research and must stand or fall, not so much on facts available or evidence presented, as upon researches to be done, researches suggested perhaps, by the questions raised in this paper.[p. 372]

II. THE BASIC NEEDS

The 'physiological' needs. — The needs that are usually taken as the starting point for motivation theory are the so-called physiological drives. Two recent lines of research make it necessary to revise our customary notions about these needs, first, the development of the concept of homeostasis, and second, the finding that appetites (preferential choices among foods) are a fairly efficient indication of actual needs or lacks in the body.

Homeostasis refers to the body's automatic efforts to maintain a constant, normal state of the blood stream. Cannon (2) has described this process for (1) the water content of the blood, (2) salt content, (3) sugar content, (4) protein content, (5) fat content, (6) calcium content, (7) oxygen content, (8) constant hydrogen-ion level (acid-base balance) and (9) constant temperature of the blood. Obviously this list can be extended to include other minerals, the hormones, vitamins, etc.

Young in a recent article (21) has summarized the work on appetite in its relation to body needs. If the body lacks some chemical, the individual will tend to develop a specific appetite or partial hunger for that food element.

Thus it seems impossible as well as useless to make any list of fundamental physiological needs for they can come to almost any number one might wish, depending on the degree of specificity of description. We can not identify all physiological needs as homeostatic. That sexual desire, sleepiness, sheer activity and maternal behavior in animals, are homeostatic, has not yet been demonstrated. Furthermore, this list would not include the various sensory pleasures (tastes, smells, tickling, stroking) which are probably physiological and which may become the goals of motivated behavior.

In a previous paper (13) it has been pointed out that these physiological drives or needs are to be considered unusual rather than typical because they are isolable, and because they are localizable somatically. That is to say, they are relatively independent of each other, of other motivations [p. 373] and of the organism as a whole, and secondly, in many cases, it is possible to demonstrate a localized, underlying somatic base for the drive. This is true less generally than has been thought (exceptions are fatigue, sleepiness, maternal responses) but it is still true in the classic instances of hunger, sex, and thirst.

It should be pointed out again that any of the physiological needs and the consummatory behavior involved with them serve as channels for all sorts of other needs as well. That is to say, the person who thinks he is hungry may actually be seeking more for comfort, or dependence, than for vitamins or proteins. Conversely, it is possible to satisfy the hunger need in part by other activities such as drinking water or smoking cigarettes. In other words, relatively isolable as these physiological needs are, they are not completely so.

Undoubtedly these physiological needs are the most pre-potent of all needs. What this means specifically is that in the human being who is missing everything in life in an extreme fashion, it is most likely that the major motivation would be the physiological needs rather than any others. A person who is lacking food, safety, love, and esteem would most probably hunger for food more strongly than for anything else.

If all the needs are unsatisfied, and the organism is then dominated by the physiological needs, all other needs may become simply non-existent or be pushed into the background. It is then fair to characterize the whole organism by saying simply that it is hungry, for consciousness is almost completely preempted by hunger. All capacities are put into the service of hunger-satisfaction, and the organization of these capacities is almost entirely determined by the one purpose of satisfying hunger. The receptors and effectors, the intelligence, memory, habits, all may now be defined simply as hunger-gratifying tools. Capacities that are not useful for this purpose lie dormant, or are pushed into the background. The urge to write poetry, the desire to acquire an automobile, the interest in American history, the desire for a new pair of shoes are, in the extreme case, forgotten or become of secondary importance [p.374]. For the man who is extremely and dangerously hungry, no other interests exist but food. He dreams food, he remembers food, he thinks about food, he emotes only about food, he perceives only food and he wants only food. The more subtle determinants that ordinarily fuse with the physiological drives in organizing even feeding, drinking or sexual behavior, may now be so completely overwhelmed as to allow us to speak at this time (but only at this time) of pure hunger drive and behavior, with the one unqualified aim of relief.

Another peculiar characteristic of the human organism when it is dominated by a certain need is that the whole philosophy of the future tends also to change. For our chronically and extremely hungry man, Utopia can be defined very simply as a place where there is plenty of food. He tends to think that, if only he is guaranteed food for the rest of his life, he will be perfectly happy and will never want anything more. Life itself tends to be defined in terms of eating. Anything else will be defined as unimportant. Freedom, love, community feeling, respect, philosophy, may all be waved aside as fripperies which are useless since they fail to fill the stomach. Such a man may fairly be said to live by bread alone.

It cannot possibly be denied that such things are true but their *generality* can be denied. Emergency conditions are, almost by definition, rare in the normally functioning peaceful society. That this truism can be forgotten is due mainly to two reasons. First, rats have few motivations other than physiological ones, and since so much of the research upon motivation has been made with these animals, it is easy to carry the rat-picture over to the human being. Secondly, it is too often not realized that culture itself is an adaptive tool, one of whose main functions is to make the physiological emergencies come less and less often. In most of the known societies, chronic extreme hunger of the emergency type is rare, rather than common. In any case, this is still true in the United States. The average American citizen is experiencing appetite rather than hunger when he says "I am hungry [p. 375]." He is apt to experience sheer life-and-death hunger only by accident and then only a few times through his entire life.

Obviously a good way to obscure the "higher" motivations, and to get a lopsided view of human capacities and human nature, is to make the organism extremely and chronically hungry or thirsty. Anyone who attempts to make an emergency picture into a typical one, and who will measure all of man's goals and desires by his behavior during extreme physiological deprivation is certainly being blind to many things. It is quite true that man lives by bread alone — when there is no bread. But what happens to man's desires when there is plenty of bread and when his belly is chronically filled?

At once other (and "higher") needs emerge and these, rather than physiological hungers, dominate the organism. And when these in turn are satisfied, again new (and still "higher") needs emerge and so on. This is what we mean by saying that the basic human needs are organized into a hierarchy of relative prepotency.

One main implication of this phrasing is that gratification becomes as important a concept as deprivation in motivation theory, for it releases the organism from the domination of a relatively more physiological need, permitting thereby the emergence of other more social goals. The physiological needs, along with their partial goals, when chronically gratified cease to exist as active determinants or organizers of behavior. They now exist only in a potential fashion in the sense that they may emerge again to dominate the organism if they are thwarted. But a want that is satisfied is no longer a want. The organism is dominated and its behavior organized only by unsatisfied needs. If hunger is satisfied, it becomes unimportant in the current dynamics of the individual.

This statement is somewhat qualified by a hypothesis to be discussed more fully later, namely that it is precisely those individuals in whom a certain need has always been satisfied who are best equipped to tolerate deprivation of that need in the future, and that furthermore, those who have been deprived in the past will react differently to current satisfactions than the one who has never been deprived [p. 376].

The safety needs. — If the physiological needs are relatively well gratified, there then emerges a new set of needs, which we may categorize roughly as the safety needs. All that has been said of the physiological needs is equally true, although in lesser degree, of these desires. The organism may equally well be wholly dominated by them. They may serve as the almost exclusive organizers of behavior, recruiting all the capacities of the organism in their service, and we may then fairly describe the whole organism as a safety-seeking mechanism. Again we may say of the receptors, the effectors, of the intellect and the other capacities that they are primarily safety-seeking tools. Again, as in the hungry man, we find that the dominating goal is a strong determinant not only of his current world-outlook and philosophy but also of his philosophy of the future. Practically everything looks less important than safety, (even sometimes the physiological needs which being satisfied, are now underestimated). A man, in this state, if it is extreme enough and chronic enough, may be characterized as living almost for safety alone.

Although in this paper we are interested primarily in the needs of the adult, we can approach an understanding of his safety needs perhaps more efficiently by observation of infants and children, in whom these needs are much more simple and obvious. One reason for the clearer appearance of the threat or danger reaction in infants, is that they do not inhibit this reaction at all, whereas adults in our society have been taught to inhibit it at all costs. Thus even when adults do feel their safety to be threatened we may not be able to see this on the surface. Infants will react in a total fashion and as if they were endangered, if they are disturbed or dropped suddenly, startled by loud noises, flashing light, or other unusual sensory stimulation, by rough handling, by general loss of support in the mother's arms, or by inadequate support.[1][p. 377]

In infants we can also see a much more direct reaction to bodily illnesses of various kinds. Sometimes these illnesses seem to be immediately and *per se* threatening and seem to make the child feel unsafe. For instance, vomiting, colic or other sharp pains seem to make the child look at the whole world in a different way. At such a moment of pain, it may be postulated that, for the child, the appearance of the whole world suddenly changes from sunniness to darkness, so to speak, and becomes a place in which anything at all might happen, in which previously stable things have suddenly become unstable. Thus a child who because of some bad food is taken ill may, for a day or two, develop fear, nightmares, and a need for protection and reassurance never seen in him before his illness.

Another indication of the child's need for safety is his preference for some kind of undisrupted routine or rhythm. He seems to want a predictable, orderly world. For instance, injustice, unfairness, or inconsistency in the parents seems to make a child feel anxious and unsafe. This attitude may be not so much because of the injustice *per se* or any particular pains involved, but rather because this treatment threatens to make the world look unreliable, or unsafe, or unpredictable. Young children seem to thrive better under a system which has at least a skeletal outline of rigidity, in which there is a schedule of a kind, some sort of routine, something that can be counted upon, not only for the present but also far into the future. Perhaps one could express this more accurately by saying that the child needs an organized world rather than an unorganized or unstructured one.

The central role of the parents and the normal family setup are indisputable. Quarreling, physical assault, separation, divorce or death within the family may be particularly terrifying. Also parental outbursts of rage or threats of punishment directed to the child, calling him names, speaking to him harshly, shaking him, handling him roughly, or actual physical punishment sometimes elicit such total panic and terror in the child that we must assume more is involved than the physical pain alone [p. 378]. While it is true that in some children this terror may represent also a fear of loss of parental love, it can also occur in completely rejected children, who seem to cling to the hating parents more for sheer safety and protection than because of hope of love.

Confronting the average child with new, unfamiliar, strange, unmanageable stimuli or situations will too frequently elicit the danger or terror reaction, as for example, getting lost or even being separated from the parents for a short time, being confronted with new faces, new situations or new tasks, the sight of strange, unfamiliar or uncontrollable objects, illness or death. Particularly at such times, the child's frantic clinging to his parents is eloquent testimony to their role as protectors (quite apart from their roles as food-givers and love-givers).

From these and similar observations, we may generalize and say that the average child in our society generally prefers a safe, orderly, predictable, organized world, which he can count on, and in which unexpected, unmanageable or other dangerous things do not happen, and in which, in any case, he has all-powerful parents who protect and shield him from harm.

That these reactions may so easily be observed in children is in a way a proof of the fact that children in our society feel too unsafe (or, in a word, are badly brought up). Children who are reared in an unthreatening, loving family do not ordinarily react as we have described above (17). In such children the danger reactions are apt to come mostly to objects or situations that adults too would consider dangerous.[2]

The healthy, normal, fortunate adult in our culture is largely satisfied in his safety needs. The peaceful, smoothly [p. 379] running, "good" society ordinarily makes its members feel safe enough from wild animals, extremes of temperature, criminals, assault and murder, tyranny, etc. Therefore, in a very real sense, he no longer has any safety needs as active motivators. Just as a sated man no longer feels hungry, a safe man no longer feels endangered. If we wish to see these needs directly and clearly we must turn to neurotic or near-neurotic individuals, and to the economic and social underdogs. In between these extremes, we can perceive the expressions of safety needs only in such phenomena as, for instance, the common preference for a job with tenure and protection, the desire for a savings account, and for insurance of various kinds (medical, dental, unemployment, disability, old age).

Other broader aspects of the attempt to seek safety and stability in the world are seen in the very common preference for familiar rather than unfamiliar things, or for the known rather than the unknown. The tendency to have some religion or world-philosophy that organizes the universe and the men in it into some sort of satisfactorily coherent, meaningful whole is also in part motivated by safety-seeking. Here too we may list science and philosophy in general as partially motivated by the safety needs (we shall see later that there are also other motivations to scientific, philosophical or religious endeavor).

Otherwise the need for safety is seen as an active and dominant mobilizer of the organism's resources only in emergencies, *e.g.*, war, disease, natural catastrophes, crime waves, societal disorganization, neurosis, brain injury, chronically bad situation.

Some neurotic adults in our society are, in many ways, like the unsafe child in their desire for safety, although in the former it takes on a somewhat special appearance. Their reaction is often to unknown, psychological dangers in a world that is perceived to be hostile, overwhelming and threatening. Such a person behaves as if a great catastrophe were almost always impending, i.e., he is usually responding as if to an emergency. His safety needs often find specific [p. 380] expression in a search for a protector, or a stronger person on whom he may depend, or perhaps, a Fuehrer.

The neurotic individual may be described in a slightly different way with some usefulness as a grown-up person who retains his childish attitudes toward the world. That is to say, a neurotic adult may be said to behave 'as if' he were actually afraid of a spanking, or of his mother's disapproval, or of being abandoned by his parents, or having his food taken away from him. It is as if his childish attitudes of fear and threat reaction to a dangerous world had gone underground, and untouched by the growing up and learning processes, were now ready to be called out by any stimulus that would make a child feel endangered and threatened.[3]

The neurosis in which the search for safety takes its dearest form is in the compulsive-obsessive neurosis. Compulsive-obsessives try frantically to order and stabilize the world so that no unmanageable, unexpected or unfamiliar dangers will ever appear (14); They hedge themselves about with all sorts of ceremonials, rules and formulas so that every possible contingency may be provided for and so that no new contingencies may appear. They are much like the brain injured cases, described by Goldstein (6), who manage to maintain their equilibrium by avoiding everything unfamiliar and strange and by ordering their restricted world in such a neat, disciplined, orderly fashion that everything in the world can be counted upon. They try to arrange the world so that anything unexpected (dangers) cannot possibly occur. If, through no fault of their own, something unexpected does occur, they go into a panic reaction as if this unexpected occurrence constituted a grave danger. What we can see only as a none-too-strong preference in the healthy person, e.g., preference for the familiar, becomes a life-and-death necessity in abnormal cases.

The love needs. — If both the physiological and the safety needs are fairly well gratified, then there will emerge the love and affection and belongingness needs, and the whole cycle [p. 381] already described will repeat itself with this new center. Now the person will feel keenly, as never before, the absence of friends, or a sweetheart, or a wife, or children. He will hunger for affectionate relations with people in general, namely, for a place in his group, and he will strive with great intensity to achieve this goal. He will want to attain such a place more than anything else in the world and may even forget that once, when he was hungry, he sneered at love.

In our society the thwarting of these needs is the most commonly found core in cases of maladjustment and more severe psychopathology. Love and affection, as well as their possible expression in sexuality, are generally looked upon with ambivalence and are customarily hedged about with many restrictions and inhibitions. Practically all theorists of psychopathology have stressed thwarting of the love needs as basic in the picture of maladjustment. Many clinical studies have therefore been made of this need and we know more about it perhaps than any of the other needs except the physiological ones (14).

One thing that must be stressed at this point is that love is not synonymous with sex. Sex may be studied as a purely physiological need. Ordinarily sexual behavior is multi-determined, that is to say, determined not only by sexual but also by other needs, chief among which are the love and affection needs. Also not to be overlooked is the fact that the love needs involve both giving *and* receiving love.[4]

The esteem needs. — All people in our society (with a few pathological exceptions) have a need or desire for a stable, firmly based, (usually) high evaluation of themselves, for self-respect, or self-esteem, and for the esteem of others. By firmly based self-esteem, we mean that which is soundly based upon real capacity, achievement and respect from others. These needs may be classified into two subsidiary sets. These are, first, the desire for strength, for achievement, for adequacy, for confidence in the face of the world, and for independence and freedom.[5] Secondly, we have what we may call the desire for reputation or prestige (defining it as respect or esteem from other people), recognition, attention, importance or appreciation [p. 382].[6] These needs have been relatively stressed by Alfred Adler and his followers, and have been relatively neglected by Freud and the psychoanalysts. More and more today however there is appearing widespread appreciation of their central importance.

Satisfaction of the self-esteem need leads to feelings of self-confidence, worth, strength, capability and adequacy of being useful and necessary in the world. But thwarting of these needs produces feelings of inferiority, of weakness and of helplessness. These feelings in turn give rise to either basic discouragement or else compensatory or neurotic trends. An appreciation of the necessity of basic self-confidence and an understanding of how helpless people are without it, can be easily gained from a study of severe traumatic neurosis (8).[7]

The need for self-actualization. — Even if all these needs are satisfied, we may still often (if not always) expect that a new discontent and restlessness will soon develop, unless the individual is doing what he is fitted for. A musician must make music, an artist must paint, a poet must write, if he is to be ultimately happy. What a man *can* be, he *must* be. This need we may call self-actualization.

This term, first coined by Kurt Goldstein, is being used in this paper in a much more specific and limited fashion. It refers to the desire for self-fulfillment, namely, to the tendency for him to become actualized in what he is potentially. This tendency might be phrased as the desire to become more and more what one is, to become everything that one is capable of becoming.[p. 383]

The specific form that these needs will take will of course vary greatly from person to person. In one individual it may take the form of the desire to be an ideal mother, in another it may be expressed athletically, and in still another it may be expressed in painting pictures or in inventions. It is not necessarily a creative urge although in people who have any capacities for creation it will take this form.

The clear emergence of these needs rests upon prior satisfaction of the physiological, safety, love and esteem needs. We shall call people who are satisfied in these needs, basically satisfied people, and it is from these that we may expect the fullest (and healthiest) creativeness.[8] Since, in our society, basically satisfied people are the exception, we do not know much about self-actualization, either experimentally or clinically. It remains a challenging problem for research.

The preconditions for the basic need satisfactions. — There are certain conditions which are immediate prerequisites for the basic need satisfactions. Danger to these is reacted to almost as if it were a direct danger to the basic needs themselves. Such conditions as freedom to speak, freedom to do what one wishes so long as no harm is done to others, freedom to express one's self, freedom to investigate and seek for information, freedom to defend one's self, justice, fairness, honesty, orderliness in the group are examples of such preconditions for basic need satisfactions. Thwarting in these freedoms will be reacted to with a threat or emergency response. These conditions are not ends in themselves but they are *almost* so since they are so closely related to the basic needs, which are apparently the only ends in themselves. These conditions are defended because without them the basic satisfactions are quite impossible, or at least, very severely endangered.[p. 384]

If we remember that the cognitive capacities (perceptual, intellectual, learning) are a set of adjustive tools, which have, among other functions, that of satisfaction of our basic needs, then it is clear that any danger to them, any deprivation or blocking of their free use, must also be indirectly threatening to the basic needs themselves. Such a statement is a partial solution of the general problems of curiosity, the search for knowledge, truth and wisdom, and the ever-persistent urge to solve the cosmic mysteries.

We must therefore introduce another hypothesis and speak of degrees of closeness to the basic needs, for we have already pointed out that *any* conscious desires (partial goals) are more or less important as they are more or less close to the basic needs. The same statement may be made for various behavior acts. An act is psychologically important if it contributes directly to satisfaction of basic needs. The less directly it so contributes, or the weaker this contribution is, the less important this act must be conceived to be from the point of view of dynamic psychology. A similar statement may be made for the various defense or coping mechanisms. Some are very directly related to the protection or attainment of the basic needs, others are only weakly and distantly related. Indeed if we wished, we could speak of more basic and less basic defense mechanisms, and then affirm that danger to the more basic defenses is more threatening than danger to less basic defenses (always remembering that this is so only because of their relationship to the basic needs).

The desires to know and to understand. — So far, we have mentioned the cognitive needs only in passing. Acquiring knowledge and systematizing the universe have been considered as, in part, techniques for the achievement of basic safety in the world, or, for the intelligent man, expressions of self-actualization. Also freedom of inquiry and expression have been discussed as preconditions of satisfactions of the basic needs. True though these formulations may be, they do not constitute definitive answers to the question as to the motivation role of curiosity, learning, philosophizing, experimenting, etc. They are, at best, no more than partial answers.[p. 385]

This question is especially difficult because we know so little about the facts. Curiosity, exploration, desire for the facts, desire to know may certainly be observed easily enough. The fact that they often are pursued even at great cost to the individual's safety is an earnest of the partial character of our previous discussion. In addition, the writer must admit that, though he has sufficient clinical evidence to postulate the desire to know as a very strong drive in intelligent people, no data are available for unintelligent people. It may then be largely a function of relatively high intelligence. Rather tentatively, then, and largely in the hope of stimulating discussion and research, we shall postulate a basic desire to know, to be aware of reality, to get the facts, to satisfy curiosity, or as Wertheimer phrases it, to see rather than to be blind.

This postulation, however, is not enough. Even after we know, we are impelled to know more and more minutely and microscopically on the one hand, and on the other, more and more extensively in the direction of a world philosophy, religion, etc. The facts that we acquire, if they are isolated or atomistic, inevitably get theorized about, and either analyzed or organized or both. This process has been phrased by some as the search for 'meaning.' We shall then postulate a desire to understand, to systematize, to organize, to analyze, to look for relations and meanings.

Once these desires are accepted for discussion, we see that they too form themselves into a small hierarchy in which the desire to know is prepotent over the desire to understand. All the characteristics of a hierarchy of prepotency that we have described above, seem to hold for this one as well.

We must guard ourselves against the too easy tendency to separate these desires from the basic needs we have discussed above, i.e., to make a sharp dichotomy between "cognitive" and "conative" needs. The desire to know and to understand are themselves conative, i.e., have a striving character, and are as much personality needs as the "basic needs" we have already discussed (19).[p. 386]

III. FURTHER CHARACTERISTICS OF THE BASIC NEEDS

The degree of fixity of the hierarchy of basic needs. — We have spoken so far as if this hierarchy were a fixed order but actually it is not nearly as rigid as we may have implied. It is true that most of the people with whom we have worked have seemed to have these basic needs in about the order that has been indicated. However, there have been a number of exceptions.

(1) There are some people in whom, for instance, self-esteem seems to be more important than love. This most common reversal in the hierarchy is usually due to the development of the notion that the person who is most likely to be loved is a strong or powerful person, one who inspires respect or fear, and who is self confident or aggressive. Therefore such people who lack love and seek it, may try hard to put on a front of aggressive, confident behavior. But essentially they seek high self-esteem and its behavior expressions more as a means-to-an-end than for its own sake; they seek self-assertion for the sake of love rather than for self-esteem itself.

(2) There are other, apparently innately creative people in whom the drive to creativeness seems to be more important than any other counter-determinant. Their creativeness might appear not as self-actualization released by basic satisfaction, but in spite of a lack of basic satisfaction.

(3) In certain people the level of aspiration may be permanently deadened or lowered. That is to say, the less pre-potent goals may simply be lost, and may disappear forever, so that the person who has experienced life at a very low level, i.e., chronic unemployment, may continue to be satisfied for the rest of his life if only he can get enough food.

(4) The so-called "psychopathic personality" is another example of permanent loss of the love needs. These are people who, according to the best data available (9), have been starved for love in the earliest months of their lives and have simply lost forever the desire and the ability to give and to receive affection (as animals lose sucking or pecking reflexes that are not exercised soon enough after birth).[p. 387]

(5) Another cause of reversal of the hierarchy is that when a need has been satisfied for a long time, this need may be underevaluated. People who have never experienced chronic hunger are apt to underestimate its effects and to look upon food as a rather unimportant thing. If they are dominated by a higher need, this higher need will seem to be the most important of all. It then becomes possible, and indeed does actually happen, that they may, for the sake of this higher

need, put themselves into the position of being deprived in a more basic need. We may expect that after a long-time deprivation of the more basic need there will be a tendency to reevaluate both needs so that the more pre-potent need will actually become consciously prepotent for the individual who may have given it up very lightly. Thus, a man who has given up his job rather than lose his self-respect, and who then starves for six months or so, may be willing to take his job back even at the price of losing his self-respect.

(6) Another partial explanation of *apparent* reversals is seen in the fact that we have been talking about the hierarchy of prepotency in terms of consciously felt wants or desires rather than of behavior. Looking at behavior itself may give us the wrong impression. What we have claimed is that the person will want the more basic of two needs when deprived of both. There is no necessary implication here that he will act upon his desires. Let us say again that there are many determinants of behavior other than the needs and desires.

(7) Perhaps more important than all these exceptions are the ones that involve ideals, high social standards, high values and the like. With such values people become martyrs; they give up everything for the sake of a particular ideal, or value. These people may be understood, at least in part, by reference to one basic concept (or hypothesis) which may be called "increased frustration-tolerance through early gratification". People who have been satisfied in their basic needs throughout their lives, particularly in their earlier years, seem to develop exceptional power to withstand present or future thwarting of these needs simply because they have strong, healthy character structure as a result of basic satisfaction [p. 388]. They are the "strong" people who can easily weather disagreement or opposition, who can swim against the stream of public opinion and who can stand up for the truth at great personal cost. It is just the ones who have loved and been well loved, and who have had many deep friendships who can hold out against hatred, rejection or persecution.

I say all this in spite of the fact that there is a certain amount of sheer habituation which is also involved in any full discussion of frustration tolerance. For instance, it is likely that those persons who have been accustomed to relative starvation for a long time, are partially enabled thereby to withstand food deprivation. What sort of balance must be made between these two tendencies, of habituation on the one hand, and of past satisfaction breeding present frustration tolerance on the other hand, remains to be worked out by further research. Meanwhile we may assume that they are both operative, side by side, since they do not contradict each other. In respect to this phenomenon of increased frustration tolerance, it seems probable that the most important gratifications come in the first two years of life. That is to say, people who have been made secure and strong in the earliest years, tend to remain secure and strong thereafter in the face of whatever threatens.

Degree of relative satisfaction. — So far, our theoretical discussion may have given the impression that these five sets of needs are somehow in step-wise, all-or-none relationships to each other. We have spoken in such terms as the following: "If one need is satisfied, then another emerges." This statement might give the false impression that a need must be satisfied 100 per cent before the next need emerges. In actual fact, most members of our society who are normal, are partially satisfied in all their basic needs and partially unsatisfied in all their basic needs at the same time. A more realistic description of the hierarchy would be in terms of decreasing percentages of satisfaction as we go up the hierarchy of prepotency. For instance, if I may assign arbitrary figures for the sake of illustration, it is as if the average citizen [p. 389] is satisfied perhaps 85 per cent in his physiological needs, 70 per cent in his safety needs, 50 per cent in his love needs, 40 per cent in his self-esteem needs, and 10 per cent in his self-actualization needs.

As for the concept of emergence of a new need after satisfaction of the prepotent need, this emergence is not a sudden, saltatory phenomenon but rather a gradual emergence by slow degrees from nothingness. For instance, if prepotent need A is satisfied only 10 per cent: then need B may not be visible at all. However, as this need A becomes satisfied 25 per cent, need B may emerge 5 per cent, as need A becomes satisfied 75 per cent, need B may emerge go per cent, and so on.

Unconscious character of needs. — These needs are neither necessarily conscious nor unconscious. On the whole, however, in the average person, they are more often unconscious rather than conscious. It is not necessary at this point to overhaul the tremendous mass of evidence which indicates the crucial importance of unconscious motivation. It would by now be expected, on *a priori* grounds alone, that unconscious motivations would on the whole be rather more important than the conscious motivations. What we have called the basic needs are very often largely unconscious although they may, with suitable techniques, and with sophisticated people become conscious.

Cultural specificity and generality of needs. — This classification of basic needs makes some attempt to take account of the relative unity behind the superficial differences in specific desires from one culture to another. Certainly in any particular culture an individual's conscious motivational content will usually be extremely different from the conscious motivational content of an individual in another society. However, it is the common experience of anthropologists that people, even in different societies, are much more alike than we would think from our first contact with them, and that as we know them better we seem to find more and more of this commonness. We then recognize the most startling differences to be superficial rather than basic, e.g., differences in style of hair-dress, clothes, tastes in food, etc. Our classification of basic [p. 390] needs is in part an attempt to account for this unity behind the apparent diversity from culture to culture. No claim is made that it is ultimate or universal for all cultures. The claim is made only that it is relatively *more* ultimate, more universal, more basic, than the superficial conscious desires from culture to culture, and makes a somewhat closer approach to common-human characteristics. Basic needs are *more* common-human than superficial desires or behaviors.

Multiple motivations of behavior. — These needs must be understood not to be *exclusive* or single determiners of certain kinds of behavior. An example may be found in any behavior that seems to be physiologically motivated, such as eating, or sexual play or the like. The clinical psychologists have long since found that any behavior may be a channel through which flow various determinants. Or to say it in another way, most behavior is multi-motivated. Within the sphere of motivational determinants any behavior tends to be determined by several or *all* of the basic needs simultaneously rather than by only one of them. The latter would be more an exception than the former. Eating may be partially for the sake of filling the stomach, and partially for the sake of comfort and amelioration of other needs. One may make love not only for pure sexual release, but also to convince one's self of one's masculinity, or to make a conquest, to feel powerful, or to win more basic affection. As an illustration, I may point out that it would be possible (theoretically if not practically) to analyze a single act of an individual and see in it the expression of his physiological needs, his safety needs, his love needs, his esteem needs and self-actualization. This contrasts sharply with the more naive brand of trait psychology in which one trait or one motive accounts for a certain kind of act, i.e., an aggressive act is traced solely to a trait of aggressiveness.

Multiple determinants of behavior. — Not all behavior is determined by the basic needs. We might even say that not all behavior is motivated. There are many determinants of behavior other than motives.[9] For instance, one other important class of determinants is the so-called 'field' determinants [p. 391]. Theoretically, at least, behavior may be determined completely by the field, or even by specific isolated external stimuli, as in association of ideas, or certain conditioned reflexes. If in response to the stimulus word "table" I immediately perceive a memory image of a table, this response certainly has nothing to do with my basic needs.

Secondly, we may call attention again to the concept of "degree of closeness to the basic needs" or "degree of motivation." Some behavior is highly motivated, other behavior is only weakly motivated. Some is not motivated at all (but all behavior is determined).

Another important point [10] is that there is a basic difference between expressive behavior and coping behavior (functional striving, purposive goal seeking). An expressive behavior does not try to do anything; it is simply a reflection of the personality. A stupid man behaves stupidly, not because he wants to, or tries to, or is motivated to, but simply because he is what he is. The same is true when I speak in a bass voice rather than tenor or soprano. The random movements of a healthy child, the smile on the face of a happy man even when he is alone, the springiness of the healthy man's walk, and the erectness of his carriage are other examples of expressive, non-functional behavior. Also the *style* in which a man carries out almost all his behavior, motivated as well as unmotivated, is often expressive.

We may then ask, is *all* behavior expressive or reflective of the character structure? The answer is 'No.' Rote, habitual, automatized, or conventional behavior may or may not be expressive. The same is true for most "stimulus-bound" behaviors. It is finally necessary to stress that expressiveness of behavior, and goal-directedness of behavior are not mutually exclusive categories. Average behavior is usually both.

Goals as centering principle in motivation theory. — It will be observed that the basic principle in our classification has [p. 392] been neither the instigation nor the motivated behavior but rather the functions, effects, purposes, or goals of the behavior. It has been proven sufficiently by various people that this is the most suitable point for centering in any motivation theory.[11]

Animal- and human-centering. — This theory starts with the human being rather than any lower and presumably "simpler" animal. Too many of the findings that have been made in animals have been proven to be true for animals but not for the human being. There is no reason whatsoever why we should start with animals in order to study human motivation. The logic or rather illogic behind this general fallacy of "pseudo-simplicity" has been exposed often enough by philosophers and logicians as well as by scientists in each of the various fields. It is no more necessary to study animals before one can study man than it is to study mathematics before one can study geology or psychology or biology.

We may also reject the old, naive, behaviorism which assumed that it was somehow necessary, or at least more "scientific" to judge human beings by animal standards. One consequence of this belief was that the whole notion of purpose and goal was excluded from motivational psychology simply because one could not ask a white rat about his purposes. Tolman (18) has long since proven in animal studies themselves that this exclusion was not necessary.

Motivation and the theory of psychopathogenesis. — The conscious motivational content of everyday life has, according to the foregoing, been conceived to be relatively important or unimportant accordingly as it is more or less closely related to the basic goals. A desire for an ice cream cone might actually be an indirect expression of a desire for love. If it is, then this desire for the ice cream cone becomes extremely important motivation. If however the ice cream is simply something to cool the mouth with, or a casual appetitive reaction, then the desire is relatively unimportant. Everyday conscious desires are to be regarded as symptoms, as *surface indicators of more basic needs* [p. 393]. If we were to take these superficial desires at their face value we would find ourselves in a state of complete confusion which could never be resolved, since we would be dealing seriously with symptoms rather than with what lay behind the symptoms.

Thwarting of unimportant desires produces no psychopathological results; thwarting of a basically important need does produce such results. Any theory of psychopathogenesis must then be based on a sound theory of motivation. A conflict or a frustration is not necessarily pathogenic. It becomes so only when it threatens or thwarts the basic needs, or partial needs that are closely related to the basic needs (10).

The role of gratified needs. — It has been pointed out above several times that our needs usually emerge only when more prepotent needs have been gratified. Thus gratification has an important role in motivation theory. Apart from this, however, needs cease to play an active determining or organizing role as soon as they are gratified.

What this means is that, e.g., a basically satisfied person no longer has the needs for esteem, love, safety, etc. The only sense in which he might be said to have them is in the almost metaphysical sense that a sated man has hunger, or a filled bottle has emptiness. If we are interested in what *actually* motivates us, and not in what has, will, or might motivate us, then a satisfied need is not a motivator. It must be considered for all practical purposes simply not to exist, to have disappeared. This point should be emphasized because it has been either overlooked or contradicted in every theory of motivation I know.[12] The perfectly healthy, normal, fortunate man has no sex needs or hunger needs, or needs for safety, or for love, or for prestige, or self-esteem, except in stray moments of quickly passing threats. If we were to say otherwise, we should also have to aver that every man had all the pathological reflexes, e.g., Babinski, etc., because if his nervous system were damaged, these would appear.

It is such considerations as these that suggest the bold [p. 394] postulation that a man who is thwarted in any of his basic needs may fairly be envisaged simply as a sick man. This is a fair parallel to our designation as "sick" of the man who lacks vitamins or minerals. Who is to say that a lack of love is less important than a lack of vitamins? Since we know the pathogenic effects of love starvation, who is to say that we are invoking value-questions in an unscientific or illegitimate way, any more than the physician does who diagnoses and treats pellagra or scurvy? If I were permitted this usage, I should then say simply that a healthy man is primarily motivated by his needs to develop and actualize his fullest potentialities and capacities. If a man has any other basic needs in any active, chronic sense, then he is simply an unhealthy man. He is as surely sick as if he had suddenly developed a strong salt-hunger or calcium hunger.[13]

If this statement seems unusual or paradoxical the reader may be assured that this is only one among many such paradoxes that will appear as we revise our ways of looking at man's deeper motivations. When we ask what man wants of life, we deal with his very essence.

IV. SUMMARY

(1) There are at least five sets of goals, which we may call basic needs. These are briefly physiological, safety, love, esteem, and self-actualization. In addition, we are motivated by the desire to achieve or maintain the various conditions upon which these basic satisfactions rest and by certain more intellectual desires.

(2) These basic goals are related to each other, being arranged in a hierarchy of prepotency. This means that the most prepotent goal will monopolize consciousness and will tend of itself to organize the recruitment of the various capacities of the organism. The less prepotent needs are minimized, even forgotten or denied [p. 395]. But when a need is fairly well satisfied, the next prepotent ("higher") need emerges, in turn to dominate the conscious life and to serve as the center of organization of behavior, since gratified needs are not active motivators.

Thus man is a perpetually wanting animal. Ordinarily the satisfaction of these wants is not altogether mutually exclusive, but only tends to be. The average member of our society is most often partially satisfied and partially unsatisfied in all of his wants. The hierarchy principle is usually empirically observed in terms of increasing percentages of non-satisfaction as we go up the hierarchy. Reversals of the average order of the hierarchy are sometimes observed. Also it has been observed that an individual may permanently lose the higher wants in the hierarchy under special conditions. There are not only ordinarily multiple motivations for usual behavior, but in addition many determinants other than motives.

(3) Any thwarting or possibility of thwarting of these basic human goals, or danger to the defenses which protect them, or to the conditions upon which they rest, is considered to be a psychological threat. With a few exceptions, all psychopathology may be partially traced to such threats. A basically thwarted man may actually be defined as a "sick" man, if we wish.

(4) It is such basic threats which bring about the general emergency reactions.

(5) Certain other basic problems have not been dealt with because of limitations of space. Among these are (*a*) the problem of values in any definitive motivation theory, (*b*) the relation between appetites, desires, needs and what is "good" for the organism, (*c*) the etiology of the basic needs and their possible derivation in early childhood, (*d*) redefinition of motivational concepts, i.e., drive, desire, wish, need, goal, (*e*) implication of our theory for hedonistic theory, (*f*) the nature of the uncompleted act, of success and failure, and of aspiration-level, (*g*) the role of association, habit and conditioning, (*h*) relation to the theory of inter-personal relations [p. 396], (*i*) implications for psychotherapy, (*j*) implication for theory of society, (*k*) the theory of selfishness, (*l*) the relation between needs and cultural patterns, (*m*) the relation between this theory and Alport's theory of functional autonomy. These as well as certain other less important questions must be considered as motivation theory attempts to become definitive.

NOTES

[1] As the child grows up, sheer knowledge and familiarity as well as better motor development make these "dangers" less and less dangerous and more and more manageable. Throughout life it may be said that one of the main conative functions of education is this neutralizing of apparent dangers through knowledge, e.g., I am not afraid of thunder because I know something about it.

[2] A "test battery" for safety might be confronting the child with a small exploding firecracker, or with a bewhiskered face; having the mother leave the room, putting him upon a high ladder, a hypodermic injection, having a mouse crawl up to him, etc. Of course I cannot seriously recommend the deliberate use of such "tests" for they might very well harm the child being tested. But these and similar situations come up by the score in the child's ordinary day-to-day living and may be observed. There is no reason why those stimuli should not be used with, for example, young chimpanzees.

[3] Not all neurotic individuals feel unsafe. Neurosis may have at its core a thwarting of the affection and esteem needs in a person who is generally safe.

[4] For further details see (12) and (16, Chap. 5).

[5] Whether or not this particular desire is universal we do not know. The crucial question, especially important today, is "Will men who are enslaved and dominated inevitably feel dissatisfied and rebellious?" We may assume on the basis of commonly known clinical data that a man who has known true freedom (not paid for by giving up safety and security but rather built on the basis of adequate safety and security) will not willingly or easily allow his freedom to be taken away from him. But we do not know that this is true for the person born into slavery. The events of the next decade should give us our answer. See discussion of this problem in (5).

[6] Perhaps the desire for prestige and respect from others is subsidiary to the desire for self-esteem or confidence in oneself. Observation of children seems to indicate that this is so, but clinical data give no clear support for such a conclusion.

[7] For more extensive discussion of normal self-esteem, as well as for reports of various researches, see (11).

[8] Clearly creative behavior, like painting, is like any other behavior in having multiple determinants. It may be seen in "innately creative" people whether they are satisfied or not, happy or unhappy, hungry or sated. Also it is clear that creative activity may be compensatory, ameliorative or purely economic. It is my impression (as yet unconfirmed) that it is possible to distinguish the artistic and intellectual products of basically satisfied people from those of basically unsatisfied people by inspection alone. In any case, here too we must distinguish, in a dynamic fashion, the overt behavior itself from its various motivations or purposes.

[9] I am aware that many psychologists md psychoanalysts use the term "motivated" and "determined" synonymously, e.g., Freud. But I consider this an obfuscating usage. Sharp distinctions are necessary for clarity of thought, and precision in experimentation.

[10] To be discussed fully in a subsequent publication.

[11] The interested reader is referred to the very excellent discussion of this point in Murray's *Explorations in Personality* (15).

[12] Note that acceptance of this theory necessitates basic revision of the Freudian theory

[13] If we were to use the word "sick" in this way, we should then also have to face squarely the relations of man to his society. One clear implication of our definition would be that (1) since a man is to be called sick who is basically thwarted, and (2) since such basic thwarting is made possible ultimately only by forces outside the individual, then (3) sickness in the individual must come ultimately from sickness in the society. The "good" or healthy society would then be defined as one that permitted man's highest purposes to emerge by satisfying all his prepotent basic needs.

REFERENCES

1. Adler, A. *Social interest.* London: Faber & Faber, 1938.
2. Cannon, W. B. *Wisdom of the body.* New York: Norton, 1932.
3. Freud, A. *The ego and the mechanisms of defense.* London: Hogarth, 1937.
4. Freud, S. *New introductory lectures on psycho-analysis.* New York: Norton, 1933.
5. Fromm, E. *Escape from freedom.* New York: Farrar and Rinehart, 1941.
6. Goldstein, K. *The organism.* New York: American Book Co., 1939.
7. Horney, K. *The neurotic personality of our time.* New York: Norton, 1937.
8. Kardiner, A. *The traumatic neuroses of war.* New York: Hoeber, 1941.
9. Levy, D. M. Primary affect hunger. *Amer. J. Psychiat.*, 1937, 94, 643-652.
10. Maslow, A. H. Conflict, frustration, and the theory of threat. *J. abnorm. (soc.) Psychol.*, 1943, 38, 81-86.
11. ————. Dominance, personality and social behavior in women. *J. soc. Psychol.*, 1939, 10, 3-39.
12. ————. The dynamics of psychological security-insecurity. *Character & Pers.*, 1942, 10, 331-344.
13. ————. A preface to motivation theory. *Psychosomatic Med.*, 1943, 5, 85-92.
14. ————. & Mittlemann, B. *Principles of abnormal psychology.* New York: Harper & Bros., 1941.
15. Murray, H. A., *et al. Explorations in Personality.* New York: Oxford University Press, 1938.
16. Plant, J. *Personality and the cultural pattern.* New York: Commonwealth Fund, 1937.
17. Shirley, M. Children's adjustments to a strange situation. *J. abrnorm. (soc.) Psychol.*, 1942, 37, 201-217.
18. Tolman, E. C. *Purposive behavior in animals and men.* New York: Century, 1932.

15 Behavioral Study of Obedience[1]

Stanley Milgram[2], Yale University

This article describes a procedure for the study of destructive obedience in the laboratory. It consists of ordering a naive S to administer increasingly more severe punishment to a victim in the context of a learning experiment. Punishment is administered by means of a shock generator with 30 graded switches ranging from Slight Shock to Danger: Severe Shock. The victim is confederate of the E. The primary dependent variable is the maximum shock the S is willing to administer before he refuses to continue further. 26 Ss obeyed the experimental commands fully, and administered the highest shock on the generator. 14 Ss broke off the experiment at some point after the victim protested and refused to provide further answers. The procedure created extreme levels of nervous tension in some Ss. Profuse sweating, trembling, and stuttering were typical expressions of this emotional disturbance. One unexpected sign of tension—yet to be explained—was the regular occurrence of nervous laughter, which in some Ss developed into uncontrollable seizures. The variety of interesting behavioral dynamics observed in the experiment, the reality of the situation for the S, and the possibility of parametric variation within the framework of the procedure, point to the fruitfulness of further study.

Obedience is as basic an element in the structure of social life as one can point to. Some system of authority is a requirement of all communal living, and it is only the man dwelling in isolation who is not forced to respond, through defiance or submission, to the commands of others. Obedience, as a determinant of behavior, is of particular relevance to our time. It has been reliably established that from 1933-45 millions of innocent persons were systematically slaughtered on command. Gas chambers were built, death camps were guarded, daily quotas of corpses were produced with the same efficiency as the manufacture of appliances. These inhumane policies may have originated in the mind of a single person, but they could only be carried out on a massive scale if a very large number of persons obeyed orders.

Obedience is the psychological mechanism that links individual action to political purpose. It is the dispositional cement that binds men to systems of authority. Facts of recent history and observation in daily life suggest that for many persons obedience may be a deeply ingrained behavior tendency, indeed, a prepotent impulse overriding training in ethics, sympathy, and moral conduct. C. P. Snow (1961) points to its importance when he writes:

> When you think of the long and gloomy history of man, you will find more hideous crimes have been committed in the name of obedience than have ever been committed in the name of rebellion. If you doubt that, read William Shirer's "Rise and Fall of the Third Reich." The German Officer Corps were brought up in the most rigorous code of obedience . . . in the name of obedience they were party to, and assisted in, the most wicked large scale actions in the history of the world [p.24].

While the particular form of obedience dealt with in the present study has its antecedents in these episodes, it must not be thought all obedience entails acts of aggression against others. Obedience serves numerous productive functions. Indeed, the very life of society is predicated on its existence. Obedience may be ennobling and educative and refer to acts of charity and kindness, as well as to destruction.

General Procedure

A procedure was devised which seems useful as a tool for studying obedience (Milgram, 1961). It consists of ordering a naive subject to administer electric shock to a victim. A simulated shock generator is used, with 30 clearly marked voltage levels that range from 15 to 450 volts. The instrument bears verbal designations that range from Slight Shock to Danger: Severe Shock. The responses of the victim, who is a trained confederate of the experimenter, are standardized. The orders to administer shocks are given to the naive subject in the context of a "learning experiment" ostensibly set up to study the effects of punishment on memory. As the experiment proceeds the naive subject is commanded to administer increasingly more intense shocks to the victim, even to the point of reaching the level marked Danger: Severe Shock. Internal resistances become stronger, and at a certain point the subject refuses to go on with the experiment. Behavior prior to this rupture is considered "obedience," in that the subject complies with the commands of the experimenter. The point of rupture is the act of disobedience. A quantitative value is assigned to the subject's performance based on the maximum intensity shock he is willing to administer before he refuses to participate further. Thus for any particular subject and for any particular experimental condition the degree of obedience may be specified with a numerical value. The crux of the study is to systematically vary the factors believed to alter the degree of obedience to the experimental commands.

The technique allows important variables to be manipulated at several points in the experiment. One may vary aspects of the source of command, content and form of command, instrumentalities for its execution, target object, general social setting, etc. The problem, therefore, is not one of designing increasingly more numerous experimental conditions, but of selecting those that best illuminate the *process* of obedience from the socio-psychological standpoint.

Related Studies

The inquiry bears an important relation to philosophic analyses of obedience and authority (Arendt, 1958; Friedrich, 1958; Weber, 1947), an early experimental study of obedience by Frank (1944), studies in "authoritarianism" (Adorno, Frenkel-Brunswik, Levinson, & Sanford, 1950; Rokeach, 1961), and a recent series of analytic and empirical studies in social power (Cartwright, 1959). It owes much to the long concern with suggestion in social psychology, both in normal forms (e.g., Binet, 1900) and in clinical manifestations (Charcot, 1881). But it derives, in the first instance, from direct observation of a social fact; the individual who is commanded by a legitimate authority ordinarily obeys. Obedience comes easily and often. It is a ubiquitous and indispensable feature of social life.

METHOD

Subjects

The subjects were 40 males between the ages of 20 and 50, drawn from New Haven and the surrounding communities. Subjects were obtained by a newspaper advertisement and direct mail solicitation. Those who responded to the appeal believed they were to participate in a study of memory and learning at Yale University. A wide range of occupations is represented in the sample. Typical subjects were postal clerks, high school teachers, salesmen, engineers, and laborers. Subjects ranged in educational level from one who had not finished elementary school, to those who had doctorate and other professional degrees. They were paid $4.50 for their participation in the experiment. However, subjects were told that payment was simply for coming to the laboratory, and that the money was theirs no matter what happened after they arrived. Table 1 shows the proportion of age and occupational types assigned to the experimental condition.

Personnel and Locale

The experiment was conducted on the grounds of Yale University in the elegant interaction laboratory. (This detail is relevant to the perceived legitimacy of the experiment. In further variations, the experiment was dissociated from the university, with consequences for performance.) The role of experimenter was played by a 31-year-old high school teacher of biology. His manner was impassive, and his appearance somewhat stern

TABLE 1
DISTRIBUTION OF AGE AND OCCUPATIONAL TYPES IN THE EXPERIEMENT

Occupations	20-29 years *n*	30-39 years *n*	40-50 years *n*	Percentage of total (Occupations)
Workers, skilled and unskilled	4	5	6	37.5
Sales, business, and white-collar	3	6	7	40.0
Professional	1	5	3	22.5
Percentage of total (Age)	20	40	40	

Note—Total $N = 40$

throughout the experiment. He was dressed in a gray technician's coat. The victim was played by a 47-year-old accountant, trained for the role; he was of Irish American stock, whom most observers found mild-mannered and likable.

Procedure

One naive subject and one victim (an accomplice) performed in each experiment. A pretext had to be devised that would justify the administration of electric shock by the naive subject. This was effectively accomplished by the cover story. After a general introduction on the presumed relation between punishment and learning, subjects were told:

> But actually, we know *very little* about the effect of punishment on learning, because almost no truly scientific studies have been made of it in human beings.
>
> For instance, we don't know how *much* punishment is best for learning—and we don't know how much difference it makes as to who is giving the punishment, whether an adult learns best from a younger or an older person than himself—or many things of that sort.
>
> So in this study we are bringing together a number of adults of different occupations and ages. And we're asking some of them to be teachers and some of them to be learners.
>
> We want to find out just what effect different people have on each other as teachers and learners, and also what effect *punishment* will have on learning in this situation.
>
> Therefore, I'm going to ask one of you to be the teacher here tonight and the other one to be the learner.
>
> Does either of you have a preference?

Subjects then drew slips of paper from a hat to determine who would be the teacher and who would be the learner in the experiment. The drawing was rigged so that the naive subject was always the teacher and the accomplice always the learner. (Both slips contained the word "Teacher.") Immediately after the drawing, the teacher and learner were taken to an adjacent room and the learner was strapped into an "electric chair" apparatus.

The experimenter explained that the straps were to prevent excessive movement while the learner was being shocked. The effect was to make it impossible for him to escape from the situation. An electrode was attached to the learner's wrist, and electrode paste was applied "to avoid blisters and burns." Subjects were told that the electrode was attached to the shock generator in the adjoining room. In order to improve credibility the experimenter declared, in response to a question by the learner: "Although the shocks can be extremely painful, they cause no permanent tissue damage."

Learning task. The lesson administered by the subject was a paired-associate learning task. The subject read a series of word pairs to the learner, and then read the first word of the pair along with four terms. The learner was to indicate which of the four terms had originally been paired with the first word. He communicated his answer by pressing one of four switches in front of him, which in turn lit up one of four numbered quadrants in an answer-box located atop the shock generator.

Shock generator. The instrument panel consists of 30 lever switches set in a horizontal line. Each switch is clearly labeled with a voltage designation that ranges from 15 to 450 volts. There is a 15-volt increment from one switch to the next going from left to right. In addition, the following verbal designations are clearly indicated for groups of four switches going from left to right: Slight Shock, Moderate Shock, Strong Shock, Very Strong Shock, Intense Shock, Extreme Intensity Shock, Danger: Severe Shock. (Two switches after this last designation are simply marked XXX.)

Upon depressing a switch: a pilot light corresponding to each switch is illuminated in bright red; an electric buzzing is heard; an electric blue light, labeled "voltage energizer," flashes; the dial on the voltage meter swings to the right; various relay clicks are sounded.

The upper left-hand corner of the generator is labeled Shock Generator, Type ZLB, Dyson Instrument Company, Waltham, Mass. Output 15 Volts–450 Volts.

Details of the instrument were carefully handled to insure an appearance of authenticity. The panel was engraved by precision industrial engravers, and all components were of high quality. No subject in the experiment suspected that the instrument was merely a simulated shock generator.[3]

Sample shock. Each naive subject is given a sample shock on the shock generator, prior to beginning his run as teacher. This shock is always 45 volts, and is applied by pressing the third switch of the generator. The shock is applied to the wrist of the naive subject, and has its source in a 45-volt battery wired into the generator. This further convinces the subject of the authenticity of the generator.

Shock instructions. The subject is told to administer a shock to the learner each time he gives a wrong response. Moreover—and this is the key command—the subject is instructed to "move one level higher on the shock generator each time the learner flashes a wrong answer." He is also instructed to announce the voltage level before administering a shock. This serves to continually remind subjects of the increasing intensity of shocks administered to the learner.

Preliminary and regular run. Pretests revealed that the procedure of reading words and administering shocks requires some practice before it can be handled smoothly. Therefore, immediately preceding the regular run, the teacher is given a preliminary series of 10 words to read to the learner. There are 3 neutral words in the practice series (i.e., words that the learner answers correctly), so that shocks are administered for 7 of the words, with the maximum shock at 105 volts (moderate shock). Almost all subjects master the procedure by the time the preliminary run is over.

Subjects are then presented with a second list, and are told that the procedure is the same as for the first list; the experimenter adds, however:

> When you get to the bottom of the list, repeat it over again, and continue giving shocks, until the learner has learned all the pairs correctly.

The experimenter instructs the subject to,

> start from 15 volts and increase the shock level one step each time the learner gives a wrong answer.

Feedback from the victim. In all conditions the learner gives a predetermined set of responses to the word pair test, based on a schedule of approximately three wrong answers to one correct answer. In the present experimental condition no vocal response or other sign of protest is heard from the learner until Shock Level 300 is reached. When the 300-volt shock is administered, the learner pounds on the wall of the room in which he is bound to the electric chair. The pounding can be heard by the subject. From this point on, the learner's answers no longer appear on the four-way panel.

At this juncture, subjects ordinarily turn to the experimenter for guidance. The experimenter instructs the subject to treat the absence of a response as a wrong answer, and to shock the subject according to the usual schedule. He advises the subjects to allow 5-10 seconds before considering no response as a wrong answer, and to increase the shock level one step each time the learner fails to respond correctly. The learner's pounding is repeated after the 315-volt shock is administered; afterwards he is not heard from, nor do his answers reappear on the four-way signal box.

Experimenter feedback. At various points in the experiment the subject may turn to the experimenter for advice on whether he should continue to administer shocks. Or he may indicate that he does not wish to go on. It was important to standardize the experimenter's responses to these inquiries and reactions.

If the subject indicated his unwillingness to go on, the experimenter responded with a sequence of "prods," using as many as necessary to bring the subject into line.

> Prod 1: Please continue. *or* Please go on.
>
> Prod 2: The experiment requires that you continue.
>
> Prod 3: It is absolutely essential that you continue.
>
> Prod 4: You have no other choice, you *must* go on.

The prods were always made in sequence: Only if Prod 1 had been unsuccessful, could Prod 2 be used. If the subject refused to obey the experimenter after Prod 4, the experiment was terminated. The experimenter's tone of voice was at all times firm, but not impolite. The sequence was begun anew on each occasion that the subject balked or showed reluctance to follow orders.

Special prods. If the subject asked if the learner was liable to suffer permanent physical injury, the experimenter said:

> Although the shocks may be painful, there is no permanent tissue damage, so please go on. [Followed by Prods 2, 3, and 4 if necessary.]

If the subject said that the learner did not want to go on, the experimenter replied:

> Whether the learner likes it or not, you must go on until he has learned all the word pairs correctly. So please go on. [Followed by Prods 2, 3, and 4 if necessary.]

Dependent Measures

The primary dependent measure for any subject is the maximum shock he administers before he refuses to go any further. In principle this may vary from 0 (for a subject who refuses to administer even the first shock) to 30 (for a subject who administers the highest shock on the generator). A subject who breaks off the experiment at any point prior to administering the thirtieth shock level is termed a *defiant* subject. One who complies with experimental commands fully, and proceeds to administer all shock levels commanded, is termed an *obedient* subject.

Further records. With few exceptions, experimental sessions were recorded on magnetic tape. Occasional photographs were taken through one-way mirrors. Notes were kept on any unusual behavior occurring during the course of the experiments. On occasion, additional observers were directed to write objective descriptions of the subjects' behavior. The latency and duration of shocks were measured by accurate timing devices.

Interview and dehoax. Following the experiment, subjects were interviewed; open-ended questions, projective measures, and attitude scales were employed. After the interview, procedures were undertaken to assure that the subject would leave the laboratory in a state of well being. A friendly reconciliation was arranged between the subject and the victim, and an effort was made to reduce any tensions that arose as a result of the experiment.

Preliminary Notions

Before giving an account of the experimental results, it is instructive to consider how persons predict others will perform when commanded to administer powerful shocks to another person. Fourteen Yale seniors, all psychology majors, were provided with a detailed description of the experimental situation. They were asked to reflect carefully on it, and to predict the behavior of 100 hypothetical subjects. More specifically, they were instructed to plot the distribution of obedience of "100 Americans of diverse occupations, and ranging in age from 20 to 50 years," who were placed in the experimental situation.

There was considerable agreement among the respondents on the expected behavior of hypothetical subjects. All respondents predicted that only an insignificant minority would go through to the end of the shock series. (The estimates ranged from 0 to 3%; i.e., the most "pessimistic" member of the class predicted that of 100 persons, 3 would continue through to the most potent shock available on the shock generator—450 volts.) The class mean was 1.2%. The question was also posed informally to colleagues of the author, and the most general feeling was that few if any subjects would go beyond the designation Very Strong Shock.

Result of Experiment I

Subjects accept situation. With few exceptions subjects were convinced of the reality of the experimental situation, that they were administering shocks to another person, and the most potent shocks were extremely painful. In the post-experimental interview subjects were asked: "How painful to the learner were the last few shocks that you administered to him?" Subjects were instructed to indicate their answers on a printed 14-point scale ranging from "Not at all painful" to "Extremely painful." The modal response was 14 (Extremely painful) with the mean at 13.42.

Signs of extreme tension. Many subjects showed signs of nervousness in the experimental situation, and especially upon administering the more powerful shocks. In a large number of cases the degree of tension reached extremes that are rarely seen in sociopsychological laboratory studies. Subjects were observed to sweat, tremble, stutter, bite their lips, groan, and dig their fingernails into their flesh. These were characteristic rather than exceptional responses to the experiment.

One sign of tension was the regular occurrence of nervous laughing fits. Fourteen of the 40 subjects showed definite signs of nervous laughter and smiling. The laughter seemed entirely out of place, even bizarre. Full-blown, uncontrollable seizures were observed for 3 subjects. On one occasion we observed a seizure so violently convulsive that it was necessary to call a halt to the experiment. The subject, a 46-year-old encyclopedia salesman, was seriously embarrassed by his untoward and uncontrollable behavior. In the post-experimental interviews subjects took pains to point out that they were not sadistic types, and that the laughter did not mean they enjoyed shocking the victim.

Distribution of scores. It had been conjectured that persons would not, in general, agree to administer shocks beyond the level designated as Very Strong Shock. The distribution of maximum shocks for this experiment is shown in Table 2. The obtained distribution of scores deviates radically from the prediction.

Upon command of the experimenter, each of the 40 subjects went beyond the expected breakoff point. No subject stopped prior to administering Shock Level 20. (At this level —300 volts—the victim kicks on the wall and no longer provides answers to the teacher's multiple-choice questions.)

Of the 40 subjects, 5 refused to obey the experimental commands beyond the 300-volt level. Four more subjects administered one further shock, and then refused to go on. Two broke off at the 330-volt level, and 1 each at 345, 360, and 375 volts. Thus a total of 14 subjects defied the experimenter. It is instructive to reprint their remarks at the point of defiance, as transcribed from the tape recordings:

> [0124] I think he's trying to communicate, he's knocking. . . . Well it's not fair to shock the guy . . . these are terrific volts. I don't think this is very humane. . . . Oh, I can't go on with this; no, this isn't right. It's a hell of an experiment. The guy is suffering in there. No, I don't want to go on. This is crazy. [Subject refused to administer more shocks.]

> [0123] He's banging in there. I'm gonna chicken out. I'd like to continue, but I can't do that to a man. . . . I'm sorry I can't do that to a man. I'll hurt his heart. You take your check. . . . No, really, I couldn't do it.

These subjects were frequently in a highly agitated and even angered state. Sometimes, verbal protest was at a minimum, and the subject simply got up from his chair in front of the shock generator, and indicated that he wished to leave the laboratory. Of the 40 subjects, 26 obeyed the orders of the experimenter to the end, proceeding to punish the victim until they reached the most potent shock available on the shock generator. At that point, the experimenter called a halt to the session. (The maximum shock is labeled 450 volts, and is two steps beyond the designation: Danger: Severe Shock.) Although obedient subjects continued to administer shocks, they often did so under extreme stress. Some expressed reluctance to administer shocks beyond the 300-volt level, and displayed fears similar to those who defied the experimenter; yet they obeyed.

After the maximum shocks had been delivered, and the experimenter called a halt to the proceedings, many obedient subjects heaved sighs of relief, mopped their brows, rubbed their fingers over their eyes, or nervously fumbled cigarettes. Some shook their heads, apparently in regret. Some subjects had remained calm throughout the experiment, and displayed only minimal signs of tension from beginning to end.

DISCUSSION

The experiment yielded two findings that were surprising. The first finding concerns the sheer strength of obedient tendencies manifested in this situation. Subjects have learned from childhood that it is a fundamental breach of moral conduct to hurt another person against his will. Yet, 26 subjects abandon this tenet in following the instructions of an authority who has no special powers to enforce his commands. To disobey would bring no material loss to the subject; no punishment would ensue. It is clear from the remarks and outward behavior

TABLE 2
Distribution of Breakoff Points

Verbal designation and voltage indication	Number of subjects for whom this was maximum shock
Slight Shock	
15	0
30	0
45	0
60	0
Moderate Shock	
75	0
90	0
105	0
120	0
Strong Shock	
135	0
150	0
165	0
180	0
Very Strong Shock	
195	0
210	0
225	0
240	0
Intense Shock	
255	0
270	0
285	0
300	5
Extremely Intense Shock	
315	4
330	2
345	1
360	1
Danger: Severe Shock	
375	1
390	0
405	0
420	0
XXX	
435	0
450	26

of many participants that in punishing the victim they are often acting against their own values. Subjects often expressed deep disapproval of shocking a man in the face of his objections, and others denounced it as stupid and senseless. Yet the majority complied with the experimental commands. This outcome was surprising from two perspectives: first, from the standpoint of predictions made in the questionnaire described earlier. (Here, however, it is possible that the remoteness of the respondents from the actual situation, and the difficulty of conveying to them the concrete details of the experiment, could account for the serious underestimation of obedience.)

But the results were also unexpected to persons who observed the experiment in progress, through one-way mirrors. Observers often uttered expressions of disbelief upon seeing a subject administer more powerful shocks to the victim. These persons had a full acquaintance with the details of the situation, and yet systematically underestimated the amount of obedience that subjects would display.

The second unanticipated effect was the extraordinary tension generated by the procedures. One might suppose that a subject would simply break off or continue as his conscience dictated. Yet, this is very far from what happened. There were striking reactions of tension and emotional strain. One observer related:

> I observed a mature and initially poised businessman enter the laboratory smiling and confident. Within 20 minutes he was reduced to a twitching, stuttering wreck, who was rapidly approaching a point of nervous collapse. He constantly pulled on his earlobe, and twisted his hands. At one point he pushed his fist into his forehead and muttered: "Oh God, let's stop it." And yet he continued to respond to every word of the experimenter, and obeyed to the end.

Any understanding of the phenomenon of obedience must rest on an analysis of the particular conditions in which it occurs. The following features of the experiment go some distance in explaining the high amount of obedience observed in the situation.

1. The experiment is sponsored by and takes place on the grounds of an institution of unimpeachable reputation, Yale University. It may be reasonably presumed that the personnel are competent and reputable. The importance of this background authority is now being studied by conducting a series of experiments outside of New Haven, and without any visible ties to the university.

2. The experiment is, on the face of it, to attain a worthy purpose—advancement of knowledge about learning and memory. Obedience occurs not as an end in itself, but as an instrumental element in a situation that the subject construes as significant, and meaningful. He may not be able to see its full significance, but he may properly assume that the experimenter does.

3. The subject perceives that the victim has voluntarily submitted to the authority system of the experimenter. He is not (at first) an unwilling captive impressed for involuntary service. He has taken the trouble to come to the laboratory presumably to aid the experimental research. That he later becomes an involuntary subject does not alter the fact that, initially, he consented to participate without qualification. Thus he has in some dgeree incurred an obligation toward the experimenter.

4. The subject, too, has entered the experiment voluntarily, and perceives himself under obligation to aid the experimenter. He has made a commitment, and to disrupt the experiment is a repudiation of this initial promise of aid.

5. Certain features of the procedure strengthen the subject's sense of obligation to the experimenter. For one, he has been paid for coming to the laboratory. In part this is canceled out by the experimenter's statement that:

   Of course, as in all experiments, the money is yours simply for coming to the laboratory. From this point on, no matter what happens, the money is yours.[4]

6. From the subject's standpoint, the fact that he is the teacher and the other man the learner is purely a chance consequence (it is determined by drawing lots) and he, the subject, ran the same risk as the other man in being assigned the role of learner. Since the assignment of positions in the experiment was achieved by fair means, the learner is deprived of any basis of complaint

on this count. (A similar situation obtains in Army units, in which—in the absence of volunteers—a particularly dangerous mission may be assigned by drawing lots, and the unlucky soldier is expected to bear his misfortune with sportsmanship.)

7. There is, at best, ambiguity with regard to the prerogatives of a psychologist and the corresponding rights of his subject. There is a vagueness of expectation concerning what a psychologist may require of his subject, and when he is overstepping acceptable limits. Moreover, the experiment occurs in a closed setting, and thus provides no opportunity for the subject to remove these ambiguities by discussion with others. There are few standards that seem directly applicable to the situation, which is a novel one for most subjects.

8. The subjects are assured that the shocks administered to the subject are "painful but not dangerous." Thus they assume that the discomfort caused the victim is momentary, while the scientific gains resulting from the experiment are enduring.

9. Through Shock Level 20 the victim continues to provide answers on the signal box. The subject may construe this as a sign that the victim is still willing to "play the game." It is only after Shock Level 20 that the victim repudiates the rules completely, refusing to answer further. These features help to explain the high amount of obedience obtained in this experiment. Many of the arguments raised need not remain matters of speculation, but can be reduced to testable propostions to be confirmed or disproved by further experiments[5]

The following features of the experiment concern the nature of the conflict which the subject faces.

10. The subject is placed in a position in which he must respond to the competing demands of two persons: the experimenter and the victim. The conflict must be resolved by meeting the demands of one or the other; satisfaction of the victim and the experimenter are mutually exclusive. Moreover, the resolution must take the form of a highly visible action, that of continuing to shock the victim or breaking off the experiment. Thus the subject is forced into a public conflict that does not permit any completely satisfactory solution.

11. While the demands of the experimenter carry the weight of scientific authority, the demands of the victim spring from his personal experience of pain and suffering. The two claims need not be regarded as equally pressing and legitimate. The experimenter seeks an abstract scientific datum; the victim cries out for relief from physical suffering caused by the subject's actions.

12. The experiment gives the subject little time for reflection. The conflict comes on rapidly. It is only minutes after the subject has been seated before the shock generator that the victim begins his protests. Moreover, the subject perceives that he has gone through but two-thirds of the shock levels at the time the subject's first protests are heard. Thus he understands that the conflict will have a persistent aspect to it, and may well become more intense as increasingly more powerful shocks are required. The rapidity with which the conflict descends on the subject, and his realization that it is predictably recurrent may well be sources of tension to him.

13. At a more general level, the conflict stems from the opposition of two deeply ingrained behavior dispositions: first, the disposition not to harm other people, and second, the tendency to obey those whom we perceive to be legitimate authorities.

REFERENCES

Adorno T., Frenkel-Brunswik, Else, Levinson, D. J., & Sandford, R. N. *The authoritarian personality.* New York: Harper, 1950.

Arendt H. What was authority? In C. J. Friedrich (Ed.), *Authority.* Cambridge: Harvard Univer. Press, 1958. Pp. 81-112.

Binet, A. *La suggestibilité.* Paris: Schleicher, 1900.

Buss, A. H. *The psychology of aggression.* New York: Wiley, 1961.

Cartwright S. (Ed.) *Studies in social power.* Ann Arbor: University of Michigan Institute for Social Research, 1959.

Charcotr, J. M. *Oeuvres complétes.* Paris: Bureaus du Medical, 1881.

Frank, J. D. Experimental studies of personal pressure and resistance. *J. gen. Psychol.,* 1944, 30, 23-64.

Friedrich, C. J. (Ed.) *Authority.* Cambridge: Harvard Univer. Press, 1958.

Milgram, S. Dynamics of obedience. Washington: National Science Foundation, 25 January 1961. (Mimeo)

Milgram, S. Some conditions of obedience and a disobedience to authority. *Hum. Relat.*, 1964, in press.

Rockeach, M. Authority, authoritarianism, and conformity. In I. A. Berg & B. M. Bass (Eds.), *Conformity and deviation.* New York: Harper, 1961. Pp. 230-257.

Snow, C. P. Either-or. *Progressive,* 1961 (Feb.), 24.

Weber, M. *The theory of social and economic organization.* Oxford: Oxford Univer. Press, 1947.

(Received July 27, 1962)

FOOTNOTES

[1.] This research was supported by a grant (NSF G-17916) from the National Science Foundation. Exploratory studies conducted in 1960 were supported by a grant from the Higgins Fund at Yale University. The research assistance of Alan C. Elms and Jon Wayland is gratefully acknowledged.

[2.] Now at Harvard University.

[3.] A related technique, making use of a shock generator, was reported by Buss (1961) for the study of aggression in the laboratory. Despite the considerable similarity of technical detail in the experimental procedures, both investigators proceeded in ignorance of the other's work. Milgram provided plans and photographs of his shock generator, experimental procedure, and first results in a report to the National Science Foundation in January 1961. This report received only limited circulation. Buss reported his procedure 6 months later, but to a wider audience. Subsequently, technical information and reports were exchanged. The present article was first received in the Editor's office on December 27, 1961; it was resubmitted with deletions on July 27, 1962.

[4.] Forty-three subjects, undergraduates at Yale University, were run in the experiment without payment. The results are very similar to those obtained with paid subjects.

[5.] A series of recently completed experiments employing the obedience paradigm is reported in Milgram (1964).

16 The Stages of the Intellectual Development of the Child*

Jean Piaget, D.Sc.

A consideration of the stages of the development of intelligence should be preceded by asking the question, What is intelligence? Unfortunately, we find ourselves confronted by a great number of definitions. For Claparède, intelligence is an adaptation to new situations. When a situation is new, when there are no reflexes, when there are no habits to rely on, then the subject is obliged to search for something new. That is to say, Claparède defines intelligence as groping, as feeling one's way, trial-and-error behavior. We find this trial-and-error behavior in all levels of intelligence, even at the superior level, in the form of hypothesis testing. As far as I am concerned, this definition is too vague, because trial and error occurs in the formation of habits, and also in the earliest established reflexes: when a newborn baby learns to suck.

Karl Bühler defines intelligence as an act of immediate comprehension; that is to say, an insight. Bühler's definition is also very precise, but it seems to me too narrow. I know that when a mathematician solves a problem, he ends by having an insight, but up to that moment he feels, or gropes for, his way; and to say that the trial-and-error behavior is not intelligent and that intelligence starts only when he finds the solution to the problem, seems a very narrow definition. I would, therefore, propose to define intelligence not by a static criterion, as in previous definitions, but by the direction that intelligence follows in its evolution, and then I would define intelligence as a form of equilibration, or forms of equilibration, toward which all cognitive functions lead.

But I must first define equilibration. Equilibration in my vocabulary is not an exact and automatic balance, as it would be in Gestalt theory; I define equilibration principally as a compensation for an external disturbance.

When there is an external disturbance, the subject succeeds in compensating for this by an activity. The maximum equilibration is thus the maximum of the activity, and not a state of rest. It is a mobile equilibration, and not an immobile one. So equilibration is defined as compensation; compensation is the annulling of a transformation by an inverse transformation. The compensation which intervenes in equilibration implies the fundamental idea of reversibility, and this reversibility is precisely what characterizes the operations of the intelligence. An operation is an internalized action, but it is also a reversible action. But an operation is never isolated; it is always subordinated to other operations; it is part of a more inclusive structure. Consequently, we define intelligence in terms of operations, coordination of operations.

Take, for example, an operation like addition: Addition is a material action, the action of reuniting. On the other hand, it is a reversible action, because addition may be compensated by subtraction. Yet addition leads to a structure of a whole. In the case of numbers, it will be the structure that the mathematicians call a "group." In the case of addition of classes which intervene in the logical structure it will be a more simple structure that we will call a grouping, and so on.

Consequently, the study of the stages of intelligence is first a study of the formation of operational structures. I shall define every stage by a structure of a whole, with the possibility of its integration into succeeding stages, just as it was prepared by preceding stages. Thus, I shall distinguish four great stages, or four great periods, in the development of intelligence: first, the sensori-motor period before the appearance of language; second, the period from about two to seven years of age, the preoperational period which precedes real operations; third, the period from seven to 12 years of age, a period of concrete operations (which refers to concrete objects); and finally after 12 years of age, the period of formal operations, or positional operations.

SENSORI-MOTOR STAGE

Before language develops, there is behavior that we can call intelligent. For example, when a baby of 12 months or more wants an object which is too far from him, but which rests on a carpet or blanket, and he pulls it to get to the object, this behavior is an act of intelligence. The child uses an intermediary, a means to get to his goal. Also, getting to an object by means of pulling a string when the object is tied to the string, or when the child uses a stick to get the object, are acts of intelligence. They demonstrate in the sensori-motor period a certain number of stages, which go from simple reflexes, from the formation of the first habits, up to the coordination of means and goals.

Remarkable in this sensori-motor stage of intelligence is that there are already structures. Sensori-motor intelligence rests mainly on actions, on movements and perceptions without language, but these actions are coordinated in a relatively stable way. They are coordinated under what we may call schemata of action. These schemata can be generalized in actions and are applicable to new situations, For example, pulling a carpet to bring an object within reach constitutes a schema which can be generalized to other situations when another object rests on a support. In other words, a schema supposes an incorporation of new situations into the previous schemata, a sort of continuous assimilation of new objects or new situations to the actions already schematized. For example, I presented to one of my children an object completely new to him-a box of cigarettes, which is not a usual toy for a baby. The child took the object, looked at it, put it in his mouth, shook it, then took it with one hand and hit it with the other hand, then rubbed it on the edge of the crib, then shook it again, and gave the impression of trying to see if there were noise. This behavior is a way of exploring the object, of trying to understand it by assimilating it to schemata already known. The child behaves in this situation as he will later in Binet's famous vocabulary test, when he defines by usage, saying, for instance, that a spoon is for eating, and so on.

But in the presence of a new object, even without knowing how to talk, the child knows how to assimilate, to incorporate this new object into each of his already developed schemata which function as practical concepts. Here is a structuring of intelligence. Most important in this structuring is the base, the point of departure of all subsequent operational constructions. At the sensori-motor level, the child constructs the schema of the permanent object.

The knowledge of the permanent object starts at this point. The child is not convinced at the beginning that when an object disappears from view, he can find it again. One can verify by tests that object permanence is not yet developed at this stage. But there is there the beginning of a subsequent fundamental idea which starts being constructed at the sensori-motor level. This is also true of the construction of the ideas of space, of time, of causality. What is being done at the sensori-motor level concerning all the foregoing ideas will constitute the substructure of the subsequent, fully achieved ideas of permanent objects, of space, of time, of causality.

In the formation of these substructures at the sensori-motor level, it is very interesting to note the beginning of a *reversibility*, not in thought, since there is not yet representation in thought, but in action itself. For example, the formation of the conception of space at the sensori-motor stage leads to an amazing decentration if one compares the conception of space at the first weeks of the development with that at one and one-half to two years of age. In the beginning there is not one space which contains all the objects, including the child's body itself; there is a multitude of spaces which are not coordinated: there are the buccal space, the tactilokinesthetic space, the visual and auditory spaces; each is separate and each is centered essentially on the body of the subject and on actions. After a few months, however, after a kind of Copernican evolution, there is a total reversal, a decentration such that space becomes homogenous, a one-and-only space that envelops the others. Then space becomes a container that envelops all objects, including the body itself; and after that, space is mainly coordinated in a structure, a coordination of positions and displacements, and these constitute what the geometricians call a "group"; that is to say, precisely a reversible system. One may move from A to B, and may come back from B to A; there is the possibility of returning, of reversibility. There is also the possibility of making detours and combinations which give a clue to what the subsequent operations will be when thought will supersede the action itself.

PRE-OPERATIONAL STAGE

From one and one-half to two years of age, a fundamental transformation in the evolution of intelligence takes place in the appearance of symbolic functions. Every action of intelligence consists in manipulating significations (or meanings) and whenever (or wherever) there is significations, there are on the one hand the "significants" and on the other the "significates." This is true in the sensori-motor level, but the only significants that intervene there are perceptual signs or signals (as in conditioning) which are undifferentiated in regard to the significate; for example, a perceptual cue, like distance, which will be a cue for the size of the distant object, or the apparent size of an object, which will be the cue for the distance of the object. There, perhaps, both indices are different aspects of the same reality, but they are not yet differentiated significants. At the age of one and one-half to two years a new class of significants arises, and these significants are differentiated in regard to their significates. These differentiations can be called symbolic function. The appearance of symbols in a children's game is an example of the appearance of new significants. At the sensori-motor level the games are nothing but exercises; now they become symbolic play, a play of fiction; these games consist in representing something by means of something else. Another example is the beginning of delayed imitation, an imitation that takes place not in the presence of the original object but in its absence, and which consequently constitutes a kind of symbolization or mental image.

At the same time that symbols appear, the child acquires language; that is to say, there is the acquisition of another phase of differentiated significants, verbal signals, or collective signals. This symbolic function then brings great flexibility into the field of intelligence. Intelligence up to this point refers to the immediate space which surrounds the child and to the present perceptual situation; thanks to language, and to the symbolic functions, it becomes possible to invoke objects which are not present perceptually, to reconstruct the past, or to make projects, plans for the future, to think of objects not present but very distant in space—in short, to span spatio-temporal distances much greater than before.

But this new stage, the stage of representation of thought which is superimposed on the sensori-motor stage, is not a simple extension of what was referred to at the previous level. Before being able to prolong, one must in fact reconstruct, because behavior in words is a different thing from representing something in thought. When a child knows how to move around in his house or garden by following the different successive cues around him, it does not mean that he is capable of representing or reproducing the total configuration of his house or his garden. To be able to represent, to reproduce something, one must be capable of reconstructing this group of displacements, but at a new level, that of the representation of the thought.

I recently made an amusing test with Nel Szeminska. We took children of four to five years of age who went to school by themselves and came back home by themselves, and asked them if they could trace the way to school and back for us, not in design, which would be too difficult, but like a construction game, with concrete objects. We found that they were not capable of representation; there was a kind of motor-memory, but it was not yet a representation of a whole-the group of displacements had not yet been reconstructed on the plan of the representation of thought. In other words, the operations were not yet formed. There are representations which are internalized actions, but actions still centered on the body itself, on the activity itself. These representations do not allow the objective combinations, the decentrated combinations that the operations would. The actions are centered on the body. I used to call this egocentrism; but it is better thought of as lack of reversibility of action.

At this level, the most certain sign of the absence of operations which appear at the next stage is the absence of the knowledge of conservation. In fact, an operation refers to the transformation of reality. The transformation is not of the whole, however; something constant is always untransformed. If you pour a liquid from one glass to another there is transformation; the liquid changes form, but its liquid property stays constant. So at the pre-operational level, it is significant from the point of view of the operations of intelligence that the child has not yet a knowledge of conservation. For example, in the case of liquid, when the child pours it from one bottle to the other, he thinks that the quantity of the liquid has changed. When the level of the liquid changes, the child thinks the quantity has changed—there is more or less in the second glass than in the first. And if you ask the child where the larger quantity came from, he does not answer this question. What is important for the child is that perceptually it is not the same thing any more. We find this absence of conservation in all object properties, in the length, surface, quantity, and weight of things.

This absence of conservation indicates essentially that at this stage the child reasons from the configuration. Confronted with a transformation, he does not reason from the transformation itself; he starts from the initial configuration, then sees the final configuration, compares the two but forgets the transformation, because he does not know how to reason about it. At this stage the child is still reasoning on the basis of what he sees because there is no conservation. He is able to master this problem only when the operations are formed and these operations, which we have already sensed at the sensori-motor level, are not formed until around seven to eight years of age. At that age the elementary problems of conservation are solved, because the child reasons on the basis of the transformation per se, and this requires a manipulation of the operation. The ability to pass from one stage to the other and be able to come back to the point of departure, to manipulate the reversible operations, which appears around seven to eight years of age, is limited when compared with the operations of the superior level only in the sense that they are concrete. That is to say, the child can manipulate the operations only when he manipulates the object concretely.

STAGES OF CONCRETE OPERATIONS

The first operations of the manipulation of objects, the concrete operations, deal with logical classes and with logical relations, or the number. But these operations do not deal yet with propositions, or hypotheses, which do not appear until the last stage.

Let me exemplify these concrete operations: the simplest operation is concerned with classifying objects according to their similarity and their difference. This is accomplished by including the subclasses within larger and more general classes, a process that implies inclusion. This classification, which seems very simple at first, is not acquired until around seven to eight years of age. Before that, at the pre-operational level, we do not find logical inclusion. For example, if you show a child at the pre-operational level a bouquet of flowers of which one half is daisies and the other half other flowers and you ask him if in this bouquet there are more flowers or more daisies, you are confronted with this answer, which seems extraordinary until it is analyzed: The child cannot tell you whether there are more flowers than daisies; either he reasons on the basis of the whole or of the part. He cannot understand that the part is complementary to the rest, and he says there are more daisies than flowers, or as many daisies as flowers, without understanding this inclusion of the subclass, the daisies, in the class of flowers. It is only around seven to eight years of age that a child is capable of solving a problem of inclusion.

Another system of operation that appears around seven to eight years of age is the operation of serializing; that is, to arrange objects according to their size, or their progressive weight. It is also a structure of the whole, like the classification which rests on concrete operations, since it consists of manipulating concrete objects. At this level there is also the construction of numbers, which is, too, a synthesis of classification and seriation. In numbers, as in classes, we have inclusion, and also a serial order, as in serializing. These elementary operations constitute structures of wholes. There is no class without classification; there is no symmetric relation without serialization; there is not a number independent of the series of numbers. But the structures of these wholes are simple structures, groupings in the case of classes and relations, which are already groups in the case of numbers, but very elementary structures compared to subsequent structures.

STAGE OF FORMAL OPERATIONS

The last stage of development of intelligence is the stage of formal or propositional operations. At about eleven to twelve years of age we see great progress; the child becomes capable of reasoning not only on the basis of objects, but also on the basis of hypotheses, or of propositions.

An example which neatly shows the difference between reasoning on the basis of propositions and reasoning on the basis of concrete objects comes from Burt's tests. Burt asked children of different ages to compare the colors of the hair of three girls: Edith is fairer than Susan, Edith is darker than Lilly; who is the darkest of the three? In this question there is seriation, not of concrete objects, but of verbal statements which supposes a more complicated mental manipulation. This problem is rarely solved before the age of 12.

Here a new class of operations appears which is superimposed on the operations of logical class and number, and these operations are the propositional operations. Here, compared to the previous stage, are fundamental changes. It is not simply that these operations refer to language, and then to operations with concrete objects, but that these operations have much richer structures.

The first novelty is a combinative structure; like mathematical structures, it is a structure of a system which is superimposed on the structure of simple classifications or seriations which are not themselves systems, because they do not involve a combinative system. A combinative system permits the grouping in flexible combinations of each element of the system with any other element of that system. The logic of propositions supposes such a combinative system. If children of different ages are shown a number of colored disks and asked to combine each color with each other two by two, or three by three, we find these combinative operations are not accessible to the child at the stage of concrete operations. The child is capable of some combination, but not of all the possible combinations. After the age of 12, the child can find a method to make all the possible combinations. At the same time he acquires both the logic of mathematics and the logic of propositions, which also supposes a method of combining.

A second novelty in the operations of propositions is the appearance of a structure which constitutes a group of four transformations. Hitherto there were two reversibilities: reversibility by inversion, which consists of annulling, or canceling; and reversibility which we call reciprocity, leading not to cancellation, but to another combination. Reciprocity is what we find in the field of a relation. If A equals B, by reciprocity B equals A. If A is smaller than B, by reciprocity B is larger than A. At the level of propositional operations a new system envelops these two forms of reversibility. Here the structure combines inversion and reversibility in one single but larger and more complicated structure. It allows the acquisition of a series of fundamental operational schemata for the development of intelligence, which schemata are not possible before the constitution of this structure.

It is around the age of 12 that the child, for example, starts to understand in mathematics the knowledge of proportions, and becomes capable of reasoning by using two systems of reference at the same time. For example, if you advance the position of a board and a car moving in opposite directions, in order to understand the movement of the board in relation to the movement of the car and to other movement, you need a system of four transformations. The same is true in regard to proportions, to problems in mathematics or physics, or to other logical problems.

The four principal stages of the development of intelligence of the child progress from one stage to the other by the construction of new operational structures, and these structures constitute the fundamental instrument of the intelligence of the adult.

FOOTNOTE

[*] The three lectures by Doctor Piaget contained in this issue of the Bulletin were presented as a series to the Menninger School of Psychiatry March 6, 13 and 22, 1961.

17 On Being Sane in Insane Places

D. L. Rosenhan

The author is professor of psychology and law at Stanford University, Stanford, California, 94305. Portions of these data were presented to colloquiums of the psychology departments at the University of California at Berkeley and at Santa Barbara; University of Arizona, Tucson: and Harvard University, Cambridge, Massachusetts.

If sanity and insanity exist, how shall we know them?

The question is neither capricious nor itself insane. How much we may be personally convinced that we can tell the normal from the abnormal, the evidence is simply not compelling. It is commonplace, for example, to read about murder trials wherein eminent psychiatrists for the defense are contradicted by equally eminent psychiatrists for the prosecution on the matter of a defendant's sanity. More generally, there are a great deal of conflicting data on the reliability, utility, and meaning of such terms as "sanity," "insanity," "mental illness," and "schizophrenia" (1). Finally, as early as 1934, Benedict suggested that normality and abnormality are not universal (2). What is viewed as normal in one culture may be seen as quite aberrant in another. Thus, notions of normality and abnormality may not be quite as accurate as people believe they are.

To raise questions regarding normality and abnormality is in no way to question the fact that some behaviors are deviant or odd. Murder is deviant. So, too, are hallucinations. Nor does raising such questions deny the existence of the personal anguish that is often associated with "mental illness." Anxiety and depression exist. Psychological suffering exists. But normality and abnormality, sanity and insanity, and the diagnoses that flow from them may be less substantive than many believe them to be.

At its heart, the question of whether the sane can be distinguished from the insane (and whether degrees of insanity can be distinguished from each other) is a simple matter: do the salient characteristics that lead to diagnoses reside in the patients themselves or in the environments and contexts in which observers find them? From Bleuler, through Kretchmer, through the formulators of the recently revised *Diagnostic and Statistical Manual* of the American Psychiatric Association, the belief has been strong that patients present symptoms, that those symptoms can be categorized, and, implicitly, that the sane are distinguishable from the insane. More recently, however, this belief has been questioned. Based in part on theoretical and anthropological considerations, but also on philosophical, legal, and therapeutic ones, the view has grown that psychological categorization of mental illness is useless at best and downright harmful, misleading, and pejorative at worst. Psychiatric diagnoses, in this view, are in the minds of the observers and are not valid summaries of characteristics displayed by the observed (3-5).

Gains can be made in deciding which of these is more nearly accurate by getting normal people (that is, people who do not have, and have never suffered, symptoms of serious psychiatric disorders) admitted to psychiatric hospitals and then determining whether they were discovered to be sane and, if so, how. If the sanity of such pseudopatients were always detected, there would be prima facie evidence that a sane individual can be distinguished from the insane context in which he is found. Normality (and presumably abnormality) is distinct enough that it can be recognized whenever it occurs, for it is carried within the person. If, on the other hand, the sanity of the pseudopatients were never discovered, serious difficulties would arise for those who support traditional modes of psychiatric diagnosis. Given that the hospital staff was not incompetent, that the pseudopatient had been behaving as sanely as he had been outside of the hospital, and that it had never been previously suggested that he belonged in a psychiatric hospital, such an unlikely outcome would support the view that psychiatric diagnosis betrays little about the patient but much about the environment in which an observer finds him.

This article describes such an experiment. Eight sane people gained secret admission to 12 different hospitals (6). Their diagnostic experiences constitute the data of the first part of this article; the remainder is devoted to a description of their experiences in psychiatric institutions. Too few psychiatrists and psychologists, even those who have worked in such hospitals, know what the experience is like. They rarely talk about it with former patients, perhaps because they distrust information coming from the previously insane. Those who have worked in psychiatric hospitals are likely to have adapted so thoroughly to the settings that they are insensitive to the impact of that experience. And while there have been occasional reports of researchers who submitted themselves to psychiatric hospitalization (7), these researchers have commonly remained in the hospitals for short periods of time, often with the knowledge of the hospital staff. It is difficult to know the extent to which they were treated like patients or like research colleagues. Nevertheless, their reports about the inside of the psychiatric hospital have been valuable. This article extends those efforts.

PSEUDOPATIENTS AND THEIR SETTINGS

The eight pseudopatients were a varied group. One was a psychology graduate student in his 20's. The remaining seven were older and "established." Among them were three psychologists, a pediatrician, a psychiatrist, a painter, and a housewife. Three pseudopatients were women, five were men. All of them employed pseudonyms, lest their alleged diagnoses embarrass them later. Those who were in mental health professions alleged another occupation in order to avoid the special attentions that might be accorded by staff, as a matter of courtesy or caution, to ailing colleagues (8). With the exception of myself (I was the first pseudopatient and my presence was known to the hospital administrator and chief psychologist and, so far as I can tell, to them alone), the presence of pseudopatients and the nature of the research program was not known to the hospital staffs (9).

The settings were similarly varied. In order to generalize the findings, admission into a variety of hospitals was sought. The 12 hospitals in the sample were located in five different states on the East and West coasts. Some were old and shabby, some were quite new. Some were research-oriented, others not. Some had good staff-patient ratios, others were quite understaffed. Only one was a strictly private hospital. All of the others were supported by state or federal funds or, in one instance, by university funds.

After calling the hospital for an appointment, the pseudopatient arrived at the admissions office complaining that he had been hearing voices. Asked what the voices said, he replied that they were often unclear, but as far as he could tell they said "empty," "hollow," and "thud." The voices were unfamiliar and were of the same sex as the pseudopatient. The choice of these symptoms was occasioned by their apparent similarity to existential symptoms. Such symptoms are alleged to arise from painful concerns about the perceived meaninglessness of one's life. It is as if the hallucinating person were saying, "My life is empty and hollow." The choice of these symptoms was also determined by the *absence* of a single report of existential psychoses in the literature.

Beyond alleging the symptoms and falsifying name, vocation, and employment, no further alterations of person, history, or circumstances were made. The significant events of the pseudopatient's life history were presented as they had actually occurred. Relationships with parents and siblings, with spouse and children, with people at work and in school, consistent with the aforementioned exceptions, were described as they were or had been. Frustrations and upsets were described along with joys and satisfactions. These facts are important to remember. If anything, they strongly biased the subsequent results in favor of detecting sanity, since none of their histories or current behaviors were seriously pathological in any way.

Immediately upon admission to the psychiatric ward, the pseudopatient ceased simulating *any* symptoms of abnormality. In some cases, there was a brief period of mild nervousness and anxiety, since none of the pseudopatients really believed that they would be admitted so easily. Indeed, their shared fear was that they would be immediately exposed as frauds and greatly embarrassed. Moreover, many of them had never visited a psychiatric ward; even those who had, nevertheless had some genuine fears about what might happen to them. Their nervousness, then, was quite appropriate to the novelty of the hospital setting, and it abated rapidly.

Apart from that short-lived nervousness, the pseudopatient behaved on the ward as he "normally" behaved. The pseudopatient spoke to patients and staff as he might ordinarily. Because there is uncommonly little to do on a psychiatric ward, he attempted to engage others in conversation. When asked by staff how he was feeling, he indicated that he was fine, that he no longer experienced symptoms. He responded to instructions from attendants, to calls for medication (which was not swallowed), and to dining-hall instructions. Beyond such activities as were available to him on the admissions ward, he spent his time writing down his observations about the ward, its patients, and the staff. Initially these notes were written "secretly," but as it soon became clear that no one much cared, they were subsequently written on standard tablets of paper in such public places as the dayroom. No secret was made of these activities.

The pseudopatient, very much as a true psychiatric patient, entered a hospital with no foreknowledge of when he would be discharged. Each was told that he would have to get out by his own devices, essentially by convincing the staff that he was sane. The psychological stresses associated with hospitalization were considerable, and all but one of the pseudopatients desired to be discharged almost immediately after being admitted. They were, therefore, motivated not only to behave sanely, but to be paragons of cooperation. That their behavior was in no way disruptive is confirmed by nursing reports, which have been obtained on most of the patients. These reports uniformly indicate that the patients were "friendly," "cooperative," and "exhibited no abnormal indications."

THE NORMAL ARE NOT DETECTABLY SANE

Despite their public "show" of sanity, the pseudopatients were never detected. Admitted, except in one case, with a diagnosis of schizophrenia (10), each was discharged with a diagnosis of schizophrenia "in remission." The label "in remission" should in no way be dismissed as a formality, for at no time during any hospitalization had any question been raised about any pseudopatient's simulation. Nor are there any indications in the hospital records that the pseudopatient's status was suspect. Rather, the evidence is strong that, once labeled schizophrenic, the pseudopatient was stuck with that label. If the pseudopatient was to be discharged, he must naturally be "in remission"; but he was not sane, nor, in the institution's view, had he ever been sane.

The uniform failure to recognize sanity cannot be attributed to the quality of the hospitals, for, although there were considerable variations among them, several are considered excellent. Nor can it be alleged that there was simply not enough time to observe the pseudopatients. Length of hospitalization ranged from 7 to 52 days, with an average of 19 days. The pseudopatients were not, in fact, carefully observed, but this failure clearly speaks more to traditions within psychiatric hospitals than to lack of opportunity.

Finally, it cannot be said that the failure to recognize the pseudopatients' sanity was due to the fact that they were not behaving sanely. While there was clearly some tension present in all of them, their daily visitors could detect no serious behavioral consequences—nor, indeed, could other patients. It was quite common for the patients to "detect" the pseudopatients' sanity. During the first three hospitalizations, when accurate counts were kept, 35 of a total of 118 patients on the admissions ward voiced their suspicions, some vigorously. "You're not crazy. You're a journalist, or a professor [referring to the continual note-taking]. You're checking up on the hospital." While most of the patients were reassured by the pseudopatient's insistence that he had been sick before he came in but was fine now, some continued to believe that the pseudopatient was sane throughout his hospitalization (11). The fact that the patients often recognized normality when staff did not raises important questions.

Failure to detect sanity during the course of hospitalization may be due to the fact that physicians operate with a strong bias toward what statisticians call the type 2 error (5). This is to say that physicians are more inclined to call a healthy person sick (a false positive, type 2) than a sick person healthy (a false negative, type 1). The reasons for this are not hard to find: it is clearly more dangerous to misdiagnose illness than health. Better to err on the side of caution, to suspect illness even among the healthy. But what holds for medicine does not hold equally well for psychiatry. Medical illnesses, while unfortunate, are not commonly pejorative. Psychiatric diagnoses, on the contrary, carry with them personal, legal, and social stigma (12). It was therefore important to see whether the tendency toward diagnosing the sane insane could be reversed. The following experiment was arranged at a research and teaching hospital whose staff had heard these findings but doubted that such an error could occur in their hospital. The staff was informed that at some time during the following 3 months, one or more pseudopatients would attempt to be admitted into the psychiatric hospital. Each staff member was asked to rate each patient who presented himself at admissions or on the ward according to the likelihood that the patient was a pseudopatient. A 10-point scale was used, with a 1 and 2 reflecting high confidence that the patient was a pseudopatient.

Judgments were obtained on 193 patients who were admitted for psychiatric treatment. All staff who had had sustained contact with or primary responsibility for the patient—attendants, nurses, psychiatrists, physicians, and psychologists—were asked to make judgments. Forty-one patients were alleged, with high confidence, to be pseudopatients by at least one member of the staff. Twenty-three were considered suspect by at least one psychiatrist. Nineteen were suspected by one psychiatrist *and* one other staff member, Actually, no genuine pseudopatient (at least from my group) presented himself during this period.

The experiment is instructive. It indicates that the tendency to designate sane people as insane can be reversed when the stakes (in this case, prestige and diagnostic acumen) are high. But what can be said of the 19 people who were suspected of being "sane" by one psychiatrist and another staff member? Were these people truly "sane," or was it rather the case that in the course of avoiding the type 2 error the staff tended to make more errors of the first sort—calling the crazy "sane"? There is no way of knowing. But one thing is certain: any diagnostic process that lends itself so readily to massive errors of this sort cannot be a very reliable one.

THE STICKINESS OF PSYCHODIAGNOSTIC LABELS

Beyond the tendency to call the healthy sick—a tendency that accounts better for diagnostic behavior on admission than it does for such behavior after a lengthy period of exposure—the data speak to the massive role of labeling in psychiatric assessment. Having once been labeled schizophrenic, there is nothing the pseudopatient can do to overcome the tag. The tag profoundly colors others' perceptions of him and his behavior.

From one viewpoint, these data are hardly surprising, for it has long been known that elements are given meaning by the context in which they occur. Gestalt psychology made this point vigorously and Asch (13) demonstrated that there are "central" personality traits (such as "warm" versus "cold") which are so powerful that they markedly color the meaning of other information in forming an impression of a given personality (14). "Insane," "schizophrenic," "manic-depressive," and "crazy" are probably among the most powerful of such central traits. Once a person is designated abnormal, all of his other behaviors and characteristics are colored by that label. Indeed, that label is so powerful that many of the pseudopatients' normal behaviors were overlooked entirely or profoundly misinterpreted. Some examples may clarify this issue.

Earlier I indicated that there were no changes in the pseudopatient's personal history and current status beyond those of name, employment, and, where necessary, vocation. Otherwise, a veridical description of personal history and circumstances was offered. Those circumstances were not psychotic. How were they made consonant with the diagnosis of psychosis? Or were those diagnoses modified in such a way as to bring them into accord with the circumstances of the pseudopatient's life, as described by him?

As far as I can determine, diagnoses were in no way affected by the relative health of the circumstances of a pseudopatient's life. Rather, the reverse occurred: the perception of his circumstances was shaped entirely by the diagnosis. A clear example of such translation is found in the case of a pseudopatient who had had a close relationship with his mother but was rather remote from his father during his early childhood. During adolescence and beyond, however, his father became a close friend, while his relationship with his mother cooled. His present relationship with his wife was characteristically close and warm. Apart from occasional angry exchanges, friction was minimal. The children had rarely been spanked. Surely there is nothing especially pathological about such a history. Indeed, many readers may see a similar pattern in their own experiences, with no markedly deleterious consequences. Observe, however, how such a history was translated in the psychopathological context, this from the case summary prepared after the patient was discharged.

> This white 39-year-old male . . . manifests a long history of considerable ambivalence in close relationships, which begins in early childhood. A warm relationship with his mother cools during his adolescence. A distant relationship to his father is described as becoming very intense. Affective stability is absent. His attempts to control emotionality with his wife and children are punctuated by angry outbursts and, in the case of the children, spankings. And while he says that he has several good friends, one senses considerable ambivalence embedded in those relationships also. . . .

The facts of the case were unintentionally distorted by the staff to achieve consistency with a popular theory of the dynamics of a schizophrenic reaction (15). Nothing of an ambivalent nature had been described in relations with parents, spouse, or friends. To the extent that ambivalence could be inferred, it was probably not greater than is found in all human relationships. It is true the pseudopatient's relationships with his parents changed over time, but in the ordinary context that would hardly be remarkable—indeed, it might very well be expected. Clearly, the meaning ascribed to his verbalizations (that is, ambivalence, affective instability) was determined by the diagnosis: schizophrenia. An entirely different meaning would have been ascribed if it were known that the man was "normal."

All pseudopatients took extensive notes publicly. Under ordinary circumstances, such behavior would have raised questions in the minds of observers, as, in fact, it did among patients. Indeed, it seemed so certain that the notes would elicit suspicion that elaborate precautions were taken to remove them from the ward each day. But the precautions proved needless. The closest any staff member came to questioning these notes occurred when one pseudopatient asked his physician what kind of medication he was receiving and began to write down the response. "You needn't write it," he was told gently. "If you have trouble remembering, just ask me again."

If no questions were asked of the pseudopatients, how was their writing interpreted? Nursing records for three patients indicate that the writing was seen as an aspect of their pathological behavior. "Patient engages in writing behavior" was the daily nursing comment on one of the pseudopatients who was never questioned about his writing. Given that the patient is in the hospital, he must be psychologically disturbed. And given that he is disturbed, continuous writing must be a behavioral manifestation of that disturbance, perhaps a subset of the compulsive behaviors that are sometimes correlated with schizophrenia.

One tacit characteristic of psychiatric diagnosis is that it locates the sources of aberration within the individual and only rarely within the complex of stimuli that surrounds him. Consequently, behaviors that are stimulated by the environment are commonly misattributed to the patient's disorder. For example, one kindly nurse found a pseudopatient pacing the long hospital corridors. "Nervous, Mr. X?" she asked. "No, bored," he said.

The notes kept by pseudopatients are full of patient behaviors that were misinterpreted by well-intentioned staff. Often enough, a patient would go "berserk" because he had, wittingly or unwittingly, been mistreated by, say, an attendant. A nurse coming upon the scene would rarely inquire even cursorily into the environmental stimuli of the patient's behavior. Rather, she assumed that his upset derived from his pathology, not from his present interactions with other staff members. Occasionally, the staff might assume that the patient's family (especially when they had recently visited) or other patients had stimulated the outburst. But never were the staff found to assume that one of themselves or the structure of the hospital had anything to do with a patient's behavior. One psychiatrist pointed to a group of patients who were sitting outside the cafeteria entrance half an hour before lunchtime. To a group of young residents he indicated that such behavior was characteristic of the oral-acquisitive nature of the syndrome. It seemed not to occur to him that there were very few things to anticipate in a psychiatric hospital besides eating.

A psychiatric label has a life and an influence of its own. Once the impression has been formed that the patient is schizophrenic, the expectation is that he will continue to be schizophrenic. When a sufficient amount of time has passed, during which the patient has done nothing bizarre, he is considered to be in remission and available for discharge. But the label endures beyond discharge, with the unconfirmed expectation that he will behave as a schizophrenic again. Such labels, conferred by mental health professionals, are as influential on the patient as they are on his relatives and friends, and it should not surprise anyone that the diagnosis acts on all of them as a self-fulfilling prophecy. Eventually, the patient himself accepts the diagnosis, with all of its surplus meanings and expectations, and behaves accordingly (5).

The inferences to be made from these matters are quite simple. Much as Zigler and Phillips have demonstrated that there is enormous overlap in the symptoms presented by patients who have been variously diagnosed (16), so there is enormous overlap in the behaviors of the sane and the insane. The sane are not "sane" all of the time. We lose our tempers "for no good reason." We are occasionally depressed or anxious, again for no good reason. And we may find it difficult to get along with one or another person—again for no reason that we can specify. Similarly, the insane are not always insane. Indeed, it was the impression of the pseudopatients while living with them that they were sane for long periods of time—that the bizarre behaviors upon which their diagnoses were allegedly predicated constituted only a small fraction of their total behavior. If it makes no sense to label ourselves permanently depressed on the basis of an occasional depression, then it takes better evidence than is presently available to label all patients insane or schizophrenic on the basis of bizarre behaviors or cognitions. It seems more useful, as Mischel (17) has pointed out, to limit our discussions to *behaviors,* the stimuli that provoke them, and their correlates.

It is not known why powerful impressions of personality traits, such as "crazy" or "insane," arise. Conceivably, when the origins of and stimuli that give rise to a behavior are remote or unknown, or when the behavior strikes us as immutable, trait labels regarding the *behaver* arise. When, on the other hand, the origins and stimuli are known and available, discourse is limited to the behavior itself. Thus, I may hallucinate because I am sleeping, or I may hallucinate because I have ingested a peculiar drug. These are termed sleep-induced hallucinations, or dreams, and drug-induced hallucinations, respectively. But when the stimuli to my hallucinations are unknown, that is called craziness, or schizophrenia—as if that inference were somehow as illuminating as the others.

THE EXPERIENCE OF PSYCHIATRIC HOSPITALIZATION

The term "mental illness" is of recent origin. It was coined by people who were humane in their inclinations and who wanted very much to raise the station of (and the public's sympathies toward) the psychologically disturbed from that of witches and "crazies" to one that was akin to the physically ill. And they were at least partially successful, for the treatment of the mentally ill *has* improved considerably over the years. But while treatment has improved, it is doubtful that people really regard the mentally ill in the same way that they view the physically ill. A broken leg is something one recovers from, but mental illness allegedly endures forever (18). A broken leg does not threaten the observer, but a crazy schizophrenic? There is by now a host of evidence that attitudes toward the mentally ill are characterized by fear, hostility, aloofness, suspicion, and dread (19). The mentally ill are society's lepers.

That such attitudes infect the general population is perhaps not surprising, only upsetting. But that they affect the professionals—attendants, nurses, physicians, psychologists, and social workers—who treat and deal with the mentally ill is more disconcerting, both because such attitudes are self-evidently pernicious and because they are unwitting. Most mental health professionals would insist that they are sympathetic toward the mentally ill, that they are neither avoidant nor hostile. But it is more likely that an exquisite ambivalence characterizes their relations with psychiatric patients, such that their avowed impulses are only part of their entire attitude. Negative attitudes are there too and can easily be detected. Such attitudes should not surprise us. They are the natural offspring of the labels patients wear and the places in which they are found.

Consider the structure of the typical psychiatric hospital. Staff and patients are strictly segregated. Staff have their own living space, including their dining facilities, bathrooms, and assembly places. The glassed quarters that contain the professional staff, which the pseudopatients came to call "the cage," sit out on every dayroom. The staff emerge primarily for caretaking purposes—to give medication, to conduct a therapy or group meeting, to instruct or reprimand a patient. Otherwise, staff keep to themselves, almost as if the disorder that afflicts their charges is somehow catching.

So much is patient-staff segregation the rule that, for four public hospitals in which an attempt was made to measure the degree to which staff and patients mingle, it was necessary to use "time out of the staff cage" as the operational measure. While it was not the case that all time spent out of the cage was spent mingling with patients (attendants, for example, would occasionally emerge to watch television in the dayroom), it was the only way in which one could gather reliable data on time for measuring.

The average amount of time spent by attendants outside of the cage was 11.3 percent (range, 3 to 52 percent). This figure does not represent only time spent mingling with patients, but also includes time spent on such chores as folding laundry, supervising patients while they shave, directing ward cleanup, and sending patients to off-ward activities. It was the relatively rare attendant who spent time talking with patients or playing games with them. It proved impossible to obtain a "percent mingling time" for nurses, since the amount of time they spent out of the cage was too brief. Rather, we counted instances of emergence from the cage. On the average, daytime nurses emerged from the cage 11.5 times per shift, including instances when they left the ward entirely (range, 4 to 39 times). Late afternoon and night nurses were even less available, emerging on the average 9.4 times per shift (range, 4 to 41 times). Data on early morning nurses, who arrived usually after midnight and departed at 8 a.m., are not available because patients were asleep during most of this period.

Physicians, especially psychiatrists, were even less available. They were rarely seen on the wards. Quite commonly, they would be seen only when they arrived and departed, with the remaining time being spent in their offices or in the cage. On the average, physicians emerged on the ward 6.7 times per day (range, 1 to 17 times). It proved difficult to make an accurate estimate in this regard, since physicians often maintained hours that allowed them to come and go at different times.

The hierarchical organization of the psychiatric hospital has been commented on before (20), but the latent meaning of that kind of organization is worth noting again. Those with the most power have least to do with patients, and those with the least power are most involved with them. Recall, however, that the acquisition of role-appropriate behaviors occurs mainly through the observation of others, with the most powerful having the most influence. Consequently, it is understandable that attendants not only spend more time with patients than do any other members of the staff—that is required by their station in the hierarchy—but also, insofar as they learn from their superiors' behavior, spend as little time with patients as they can. Attendants are seen mainly in the cage, which is where the models, the action, and the power are.

I turn now to a different set of studies, these dealing with staff response to patient-initiated contact. It has long been known that the amount of time a person spends with you can be an index of your significance to him. If he initiates and maintains eye contact, there is reason to believe that he is considering your requests and needs. If he pauses to chat or actually stops and talks, there is added reason to infer that he is individuating you. In four hospitals, the pseudopatient approached the staff member with a request which took the following form: "Pardon me, Mr. [or Dr. or Mrs.] X, could you tell me when I will be eligible for grounds privileges? " (or " . . . when I will be presented at the staff meeting?" or "... When I am likely to be discharged?"). While the content of the question varied according to the appropriateness of the target and the pseudopatient's (apparent) current needs the form was always a courteous and relevant request for information. Care was taken never to approach a particular member of the staff more than once a day, lest the staff member become suspicious or irritated. In examining these data, remember that the behavior of the pseudopatients was neither bizarre nor disruptive. One could indeed engage in good conversation with them.

The data for these experiments are shown in Table 1, separately for physicians (column 1) and for nurses and attendants (column 2). Minor differences between these four institutions were overwhelmed by the degree to which staff avoided continuing contacts that patients had initiated. By far, their most common response consisted of either a brief response to the question, offered while they were "on the move" and with head averted, or no response at all. The encounter frequently took the following bizarre form: (pseudopatient) "Pardon me, Dr. X. Could you tell me when I am eligible for grounds privileges?" (physician) "Good morning, Dave. How are you today?" (Moves off without waiting for a response.)

It is instructive to compare these data with data recently obtained at Stanford University. It has been alleged that large and eminent universities are characterized by faculty who are so busy that they have no time for students. For this comparison, a young lady approached individual faculty members who seemed to be walking purposefully to some meeting or teaching engagement and asked them the following six questions.

1) "Pardon me, could you direct me to Encina Hall?" (at the medical school: ". . . to the Clinical Research Center?").
2) "Do you know where Fish Annex is?" (there is no Fish Annex at Stanford).
3) "Do you teach here?"
4) "How does one apply for admission to the college?" (at the medical school: ". . . to the medical school?").
5) "Is it difficult to get in?"
6) "Is there financial aid?"

Without exception, as can be seen in Table 1 (column 3), all of the questions were answered. No matter how rushed they were, all respondents not only maintained eye contact, but stopped to talk. Indeed, many of the respondents went out of their way to direct or take the questioner to the office she was seeking, to try to

TABLE 1. SELF-INITIATED CONTACT BY PSEUDOPATIENTS WITH PSYCHIATRISTS AND NURSES AND ATTENDANTS, COMPARED TO CONTACT WITH OTHER GROUPS.

Contact	Psychiatric hospitals		Universitiy campus (nonmedical)	University medical center Physicians		
	(1) Psychiatrists	(2) Nurses and attendants	(3) Faculty	(4) "Looking for a psychiatrist"	(5) "Looking for an internist"	(6) No additional comment
Responses						
Moves on, head averted (%)	71	88	0	0	0	0
Makes eye contact (%)	23	10	0	11	0	0
Pauses and chats (%)	2	2	0	11	0	10
Stops and talks (%)	4	0.5	100	78	100	90
Mean number of questions answered (out of 6)	*	*	6	3.8	4.8	4.5
Respondents (No.)	13	47	14	18	15	10
Attempts (No.)	185	1283	14	18	15	10

* Not applicable.

locate "Fish Annex," or to discuss with her the possibilities of being admitted to the university.

Similar data, also shown in Table 1 (columns 4, 5, and 6), were obtained in the hospital. Here too, the young lady came prepared with six questions. After the first question, however, she remarked to 18 of her respondents (column 4), "I'm looking for a psychiatrist," and to 15 others (column 5), "I'm looking for an internist." Ten other respondents received no inserted comment (column 6). The general degree of cooperative responses is considerably higher for these university groups than it was for pseudopatients in psychiatric hospitals. Even so, differences are apparent within the medical school setting. Once having indicated that she was looking for a psychiatrist, the degree of cooperation elicited was less than when she sought an internist.

POWERLESSNESS AND DEPERSONALIZATION

Eye contact and verbal contact reflect concern and individuation; their absence, avoidance and depersonalization. The data I have presented do not do justice to the rich daily encounters that grew up around matters of depersonalization and avoidance. I have records of patients who were beaten by staff for the sin of having initiated verbal contact. During my own experience, for example, one patient was beaten in the presence of other patients for having approached an attendant and told him, "I like you." Occasionally, punishment meted out to patients for misdemeanors seemed so excessive that it could not be justified by the most radical interpretations of psychiatric canon. Nevertheless, they appeared to go unquestioned. Tempers were often short. A patient who had not heard a call for medication would be roundly excoriated, and the morning attendants would often wake patients with, "Come on, you m——-f——-s, out of bed!"

Neither anecdotal nor "hard" data can convey the overwhelming sense of powerlessness which invades the individual as he is continually exposed to the depersonalization of the psychiatric hospital. It hardly matters *which* psychiatric hospital—the excellent public ones and the very plush private hospital were better than the rural and shabby ones in this regard, but, again, the features that psychiatric hospitals had in common overwhelmed by far their apparent differences.

Powerlessness was evident everywhere. The patient is deprived of many of his legal rights by dint of his psychiatric commitment (21). He is shorn of credibility by virtue of his psychiatric label. His freedom of movement is restricted. He cannot initiate contact with the staff, but may only respond to such overtures as they make. Personal privacy is minimal. Patient quarters and possessions can be entered and examined by any staff member, for whatever reason. His personal history and anguish is available to any staff member (often including the "grey lady" and "candy striper" volunteer) who chooses to read his folder, regardless of their therapeutic relationship to him. His personal hygiene and waste evacuation are often monitored. The water closets may have no doors.

At times, depersonalization reached such proportions that pseudopatients had the sense that they were invisible, or at least unworthy of account. Upon being admitted, I and other pseudopatients took the initial physical examinations in a semipublic room, where staff members went about their own business as if we were not there.

On the ward, attendants delivered verbal and occasionally serious physical abuse to patients in the presence of other observing patients, some of whom (the pseudopatients) were writing it all down. Abusive behavior, on the other hand, terminated quite abruptly when other staff members were known to be coming. Staff are credible witnesses. Patients are not.

A nurse unbuttoned her uniform to adjust her brassiere in the presence of an entire ward of viewing men. One did not have the sense that she was being seductive. Rather, she didn't notice us. A group of staff persons might point to a patient in the dayroom and discuss him animatedly, as if he were not there.

One illuminating instance of depersonalization and invisibility occurred with regard to medications. All told, the pseudopatients were administered nearly 2100 pills, including Elavil, Stelazine, Compazine, and Thorazine, to name but a few. (That such a variety of medications should have been administered to patients presenting identical symptoms is itself worthy of note.) Only two were swallowed. The rest were either pocketed or deposited in the toilet. The pseudopatients were not alone in this. Although I have no precise records on how many patients rejected their medications, the pseudopatients frequently found the medications of other patients in the toilet before they deposited their own. As long as they were cooperative, their behavior and the pseudopatients' own in this matter, as in other important matters, went unnoticed throughout.

Reactions to such depersonalization among pseudopatients were intense. Although they had come to the hospital as participant observers and were fully aware that they did not "belong," they nevertheless found themselves caught up in and fighting the process of depersonalization. Some examples: a graduate student in psychology asked his wife to bring his textbooks to the hospital so he could "catch up on his homework"—this despite the elaborate precautions taken to conceal his professional association. The same student, who had trained for quite some time to get into the hospital, and who had looked forward to the experience, "remembered" some drag races that he had wanted to see on the weekend and insisted that he be discharged by that time. Another pseudopatient attempted a romance with a nurse. Subsequently, he informed the staff that he was applying for admission to graduate school in psychology and was very likely to be admitted, since a graduate professor was one of his regular hospital visitors. The same person began to engage in psychotherapy with other patients—all of this as a way of becoming a person in an impersonal environment.

THE SOURCES OF DEPERSONALIZATION

What are the origins of depersonalization? I have already mentioned two. First are attitudes held by all of us toward the mentally ill—including those who treat them—attitudes characterized by fear, distrust, and horrible expectations on the one hand, and benevolent intentions on the other. Our ambivalence leads, in this instance as in others, to avoidance.

Second, and not entirely separate, the hierarchical structure of the psychiatric hospital facilitates depersonalization. Those who are at the top have least to do with patients, and their behavior inspires the rest of the staff. Average daily contact with psychiatrists, psychologists, residents, and physicians combined ranged from 3.9 to 25.1 minutes, with an overall mean of 6.8 (six pseudopatients over a total of 129 days of hospitalization). Included in this average are time spent in the admissions interview, ward meetings in the presence of a senior staff member, group and individual therapy contacts, case presentation conferences, and discharge meetings. Clearly, patients do not spend much time in interpersonal contact with doctoral staff. And doctoral staff serve as models for nurses and attendants.

There are probably other sources. Psychiatric installations are presently in serious financial straits. Staff shortages are pervasive, staff time at a premium. Something has to give, and that something is patient contact. Yet, while financial stresses are realities, too much can be made of them. I have the impression that the psychological forces that result in depersonalization are much stronger than the fiscal ones and that the addition of more staff would not correspondingly improve patient care in this regard. The incidence of staff meetings and the enormous amount of recordkeeping on patients, for example, have not been substantially reduced as has patient contact. Priorities exist, even during hard times. Patient contact is not a significant priority in the traditional psychiatric hospital, and fiscal pressures do not account for this. Avoidance and depersonalization may.

Heavy reliance upon psychotropic medication tacitly contributes to depersonalization by convincing staff that treatment is indeed being conducted and that further patient contact may not be necessary. Even here, however, caution needs to be exercised in understanding the role of psychotropic drugs. If patients were powerful rather than powerless, if they were viewed as interesting individuals rather than diagnostic entities, if they were socially significant rather than social lepers, if their anguish truly and wholly compelled our sympathies and concerns, would we not *seek* contact with them, despite the availability of medications? Perhaps for the pleasure of it all?

THE CONSEQUENCES OF LABELING AND DEPERSONALIZATION

Whenever the ratio of what is known to what needs to be known approaches zero, we tend to invent "knowledge" and assume that we understand more than we actually do. We seem unable to acknowledge that we simply don't know. The needs for diagnosis and remediation of behavioral and emotional problems are enormous. But rather than acknowledge that we are just embarking on understanding, we continue to label patients "schizophrenic," "manic-depressive," and "insane," as if in those words we had captured the essence of understanding. The facts of the matter are that we have known for a long time that diagnoses are often not useful or reliable, but we have nevertheless continued to use them. We now know that we cannot distinguish insanity from sanity. It is depressing to consider how that information will be used.

Not merely depressing, but frightening. How many people, one wonders, are sane but not recognized as such in our psychiatric institutions? How many have been needlessly stripped of their privileges of citizenship, from the right to vote and drive to that of handling their own accounts? How many have feigned insanity in order to avoid the criminal consequences of their behavior, and, conversely, how many would rather stand trial than live interminably in a psychiatric hospital—but are thought to be mentally ill? How many have been stigmatized by well-intentioned, but nevertheless erroneous, diagnoses? On the last point, recall again that a "type 2 error" in psychiatric diagnosis does not have the same consequences it does in medical diagnosis. A diagnosis of cancer that has been found to be in error is cause for celebration. But psychiatric diagnoses are rarely found to be in error. The label sticks, a mark of inadequacy forever.

Finally, how many patients might be "sane" outside the psychiatric hospital but seem insane in it—not because craziness resides in them, as it were, but because they are responding to a bizarre setting, one that may be unique to institutions which harbor nether people? Goffman (4) calls the process of socialization to such institutions "mortification"—an apt metaphor that includes the processes of depersonalization that have been described here. And while it is impossible to know whether the pseudopatients' responses to these processes are characteristic of all inmates—they were, after all, not real patients—it is difficult to believe that these processes of socialization to a psychiatric hospital provide useful attitudes or habits of response for living in the "real world."

SUMMARY AND CONCLUSIONS

It is clear that we cannot distinguish the sane from the insane in psychiatric hospitals. The hospital itself imposes a special environment in which the meanings of behavior can easily be misunderstood. The consequences to patients hospitalized in such an environment—the powerlessness, depersonalization, segregation, mortification, and self-labeling—seem undoubtedly counter-therapeutic.

I do not, even now, understand this problem well enough to perceive solutions. But two matters seem to have some promise. The first concerns the proliferation of community mental health facilities, of crisis intervention centers, of the human potential movement, and of behavior therapies that, for all of their own problems, tend to avoid psychiatric labels, to focus on specific problems and behaviors, and to retain the individual in a relatively nonpejorative environment. Clearly, to the extent that we refrain from sending the distressed to insane places, our impressions of them are less likely to be distorted. (The risk of distorted perceptions, it seems to me, is always present, since we are much more sensitive to an individual's behaviors and verbalizations than we are to the subtle contextual stimuli that often promote them. At issue here is a matter of magnitude. And, as I have shown, the magnitude of distortion is exceedingly high in the extreme context that is a psychiatric hospital.)

The second matter that might prove promising speaks to the need to increase the sensitivity of mental health workers and researchers to the *Catch 22* position of psychiatric patients. Simply reading materials in this area will be of help to some such workers and researchers. For others, directly experiencing the impact of psychiatric hospitalization will be of enormous use. Clearly, further research into the social psychology of such total institutions will both facilitate treatment and deepen understanding.

I and the other pseudopatients in the psychiatric setting had distinctly negative reactions. We do not pretend to describe the subjective experiences of true patients. Theirs may be different from ours, particularly with the passage of time and the necessary process of adaptation to one's environment. But we can and do speak to the relatively more objective indices of treatment within the hospital. It could be a mistake, and a very unfortunate one, to consider that what happened to us derived from malice or stupidity on the part of the staff. Quite the contrary, our overwhelming impression of them was of people who really cared, who were committed and who were uncommonly intelligent. Where they failed, as they sometimes did painfully, it would be more accurate to attribute those failures to the environment in which they, too, found themselves than to personal callousness. Their perceptions and behavior were controlled by the situation, rather than being motivated by a malicious disposition. In a more benign environment, one that was less attached to global diagnosis, their behaviors and judgments might have been more benign and effective.

REFERENCES AND NOTES

1. P. Ash, *J. Abnorm. Soc. Psychol.* 44, 272 (1949); A. T. Beck, *Amer. J. Psychiat.* 119, 210 (1962); A. T. Boisen, *Psychiatry* 2, 233 (1938); N. Kreitman, *J. Ment. Sci.* 107, 876 (1961); N. Kreitman, P. Sainsbury, J. Morrisey, J. Towers., J. Scrivener, *ibid.*, p. 887; H. O. Schmitt and C. P. Fonda, *J. Abnorm. Soc. Psychol.* 52, 262 (1956); W. Seeman, *J. Nerv. Ment. Dis.* 118, 541 (1953). For an analysis of these artifacts and summaries of the disputes, see J. Zubin, *Annu. Rev. Psychol.* 18, 373 (1967); L. Phillips and J. G. Draguns, *ibid.* 22, 447 (1971).

2. R. Benedict, *J. Gen. Psychol.* 10, 59 (1934).

3. See in this regard H. Becker, *Outsiders: Studies in the Sociology of Deviance* (Free Press, New York, 1963); B. M. Braginsky, D. D. Braginsky, K. Ring, *Methods of Madness: The Mental Hospital as a Last Resort* (Holt, Rinehart & Winston, New York, 1969); G. M. Crocetti and P. V. Lemkau, *Amer. Sociol. Rev.* 30, 577 (1965); E. Goffman, *Behavior in Public Places* (Free Press, New York, 1964); R. D. Laing, *The Divided Self: A Study of Sanity and Madness* (Quadrangle, Chicago, 1960); D. L. Phillips, *Amer. Sociol. Rev.* 28, 963 (1963); T. R. Sarbin, *Psychol. Today* 6, 18 (1972); E. Schur, *Amer. J. Sociol.* 75, 309 (1969); T. Szasz, *Law, Liberty and Psychiatry* (Macmillan, New York, 1963); *The Myth of Mental Illness: Foundations of a Theory of Mental Illness* (Hoeber-Harper, New York, 1963). For a critique of some of these views, see W. R. Gove, *Amer. Sociol. Rev.* 35, 873 (1970).

4. E. Goffman, *Asylums* (Doubleday, Garden City, N.Y., 1961).

5. T. J. Scheff, *Being Mentally Ill: A Sociological Theory* (Aldine, Chicago, 1966).

6. Data from a ninth pseudopatient are not incorporated in this report because, although his sanity went undetected, he falsified aspects of his personal history, including his marital status and parental relationships. His experimental behaviors therefore were not identical to those of the other pseudopatients.

7. A. Barry, *Bellevue Is a State of Mind* (Harcourt Brace Jovanovich, New York, 1971); I. Belknap, *Human Problems of a State Mental Hospital* (McGraw-Hill, New York, 1956); W. Caudill, F. C. Redlich, H. R. Gilmore, E. B. Brody, *Amer. J. Orthopsychiat*, 22, 314 (1952); A. R. Goldman, R. H. Bohr, T. A. Steinberg, *Prof. Psychol.* 1, 427 (1970); unauthored, *Roche Report* 1 (No. 13), 8 (1971).

8. Beyond the personal difficulties that the pseudopatient is likely to experience in the hospital, there are legal and social ones that, combined, require considerable attention before entry. For example, once admitted to a psychiatric institution, it is difficult, if not impossible, to be discharged on short notice, state law to the contrary notwithstanding. I was not sensitive to these difficulties at the outset of the project, nor to the personal and situational emergencies that can arise, but later a writ of habeas corpus was prepared for each of the entering pseudopatients and an attorney was kept "on call" during every hospitalization. I am grateful to John Kaplan and Robert Bartels for legal advice and assistance in these matters.

9. However distasteful such concealment is, it was a necessary first step to examining these questions. Without concealment, there would have been no way to know how valid these experiences were; nor was there any way of knowing whether whatever detections occurred were a tribute to the diagnostic acumen of the staff or to the hospital's rumor network. Obviously, since my concerns are general ones that cut across individual hospitals and staffs, I have

respected their anonymity and have eliminated clues that might lead to their identification.

10. Interestingly, of the 12 admissions, 11 were diagnosed as schizophrenic and one, with the identical symptomatology, as manic-depressive psychosis. This diagnosis has a more favorable prognosis, and it was given by the only private hospital in our sample. On the relations between social class and psychiatric diagnosis, see A. deB. Hollingshead and F. C. Redlich, *Social Class and Mental Illness: A Community Study* (Wiley, New York, 1958).

11. It is possible, of course, that patients have quite broad latitudes in diagnosis and therefore are inclined to call many people sane, even those whose behavior is patently aberrant. However, although we have no hard data on this matter, it was our distinct impression that this was not the case. In many instances, patients not only singled us out for attention, but came to imitate our behaviors and styles.

12. J. Cumming and E. Cumming, *Community Ment. Health* 1, 135 (1965); A. Farina and K. Ring, *J. Abnorm. Psychol.* 70, 47 (1965); H. E. Freeman and O. G. Simmons, *The Mental Patient Comes Home* (Wiley: New York, 1963): W. J. Johannsen, *Ment. Hygiene* 53, 218 (1969); A. S. Linsky, *Soc. Psychiat.* 5, 166 (1970).

13. S. E. Asch, *J. Abnorm. Soc. Psychol.* 41, (1946); *Social Psychology* (Prentice-Hall, New York, 1952).

14. See also, I. N. Mensh and J. Wishner, *J. Personality* 16, 188 (1947); J. Wishner, *Psychol. Rev.* 67, 96 (1960); J. S. Bruner and R. Tagiuri, in *Handbook of Social Psychology*, G. Lindzey, Ed. (Addison-Wesley, Cambridge, Mass., 1954), vol. 2, pp. 634-654; J. S. Bruner, D. Shapiro, R. Tagiuri, in *Person Perception and Interpersonal Behavior*, R. Tagiuri and L. Petrullo, Eds. (Stanford Univ. Press, Stanford, Calif., 1958), pp. 277-288.

15. For an example of a similar self-fulfilling prophecy, in this instance dealing with the "central" trait of intelligence, see R. Rosenthal and L. Jacobson, *Pygmalion in the Classroom* (Holt, Rinehart & Winston, New York, 1968).

16. E. Zigler and L. Phillips, *J. Abnorm. Soc. Psychol.* 63, 69 (1961). See also R. K. Freudenberg and J. P. Robertson, *A.M.A. Arch. Neurol. Psychiatr.* 76, 14 (1956).

17. W. Mischel, *Personality and Assessment* (Wiley, New York, 1968).

18. The most recent and unfortunate instance of this tenet is that of Senator Thomas Eagleton.

19. T. R. Sarbin and J. C. Mancuso, *J. Clin. Consult. Psychol.* 35, 159 (1970); T. R. Sarbin, *ibid.* 31, 447 (1967); J. C. Nunnally, Jr., *Popular Conceptions of Mental Health* (Holt, Rinehart & Winston, New York, 1961).

20. A. H. Stanton and M. S. Schwartz, *The Mental Hospital: A Study of Institutional Participation in Psychiatric Illness and Treatment* (Basic, New York, 1954).

21. D. B. Wexler and S. E. Scoville, *Ariz. Law Rev.* 13, 1 (1971).

22. I thank W. Mischel, E. Orne, and M. S. Rosenhan for comments on an earlier draft of this manuscript.

18 Teachers' Expectancies: Determinants of Pupils' IQ Gains

Robert Rosenthal and Lenore Jacobson (1968)

Psychological research is sometimes difficult to correctly interpret, in part because people can unintentionally bring bias into the research setting. Without being aware of it, our expectations can alter our perception and behavior. The pioneering work of Robert Rosenthal and Lenore Jacobson helped psychologists become more aware of the potential for bias in research studies. Rosenthal (b. 1933) earned his Ph.D. in psychology in 1956 from the University of California, Los Angeles. In 1962 he began a career at Harvard University, where he stayed until he retired and accepted his current position as professor of psychology at University of California at Riverside. Jacobson was with the South San Francisco Unified School District at the time of their research. Rosenthal and Jacobson co-authored a book on expectancy effect entitled, Pygmalion in the Classroom: Teacher Expectations and Pupils' Intellectual Development (Holt, Rinehart & Winston, 1968).

This selection, from "Teacher's Expectancies: Determinants of Pupils' IQ Gains," was published in Psychological Reports in 1966. It demonstrated how teacher expectancy (in this study, expectancy that certain students would "intellectually bloom" during a school year) had a significant effect on student behavior (the randomly selected students increased their IQ scores). As you read this selection, think about your elementary school years. Did you do best in classes in which your teachers expected high performance? How does expectancy play a role in our everyday lives? How could we design research studies to minimize the effects of expectancy?

KEY CONCEPT:

Bias in psychological research

APA Citation: *Rosenthal, R., & Jacobson, L. (1968). Teachers' expectancies: Determinants of pupils' I.Q. gains. Psychological Reports, 19, 115-118.*

Experiments have shown that in behavioral research employing human or animal *Ss*, *E's* expectancy can be a significant determinant of *S's* response (Rosenthal, 1964, in press). In studies employing animals, for example, *Es* led to believe that their rat *Ss* has been bred for superior learning ability obtained performance superior to that obtained by *Es* led to believe that their rats had been bred for inferior learning ability (Rosenthal & Fode, 1963; Rosenthal & Lawson, 1964). The present study was designed to extend the generality of this finding from *Es* to teachers and from animal *Ss* to school children.

Flanagan (1960) has developed a nonverbal intelligence test (Tests of General Ability or TOGA) which is not explicitly dependent on such school-learned skills as reading, writing, and arithmetic. The test is composed of two types of items, "verbal" and "reasoning." The "verbal" items measure the child's level of information, vocabulary, and concepts. The "reasoning" items measure the child's concept formation ability by employing abstract line drawings. Flanagan's purpose in developing the TOGA was "to provide a relatively fair measure of intelligence for all individuals, even those who have had atypical opportunities to learn" (1960, p. 6).

Flanagan's test was administered to all children in an elementary school, disguised as a test designed to predict academic "blooming" or intellectual gain. Within each of the six grades in the school were three classrooms, one each of children performing at above average, average, and below average levels of scholastic achievement. In each of the 18 classes an average of 20% of the children were assigned to the experimental condition. The names of these children were given to each teacher who was told that their scores on the "test for intellectual blooming" indicated that they would show unusual intellectual gains during the academic year. Actually, the children had been assigned to the experimental condition by means of a table of random numbers. The experimental treatment for these children, then, consisted of nothing more than being identified to their teachers as children who would show unusual intellectual gains.

Eight months after the experimental conditions were instituted all children were retested with the same IQ test and a change score was computed for each child. Table 1 shows the mean gain in IQ points among experimental and control *Ss* in each of the six grades. For the school as a whole those children from whom the teachers had been led to expect greater intellectual gain showed a significantly greater gain in IQ score than did the control children ($p = .02$, one-tail). Inspection of Table 1 shows that the effects of teachers' expectancies were not uniform across the six grade levels. The lower the grade level, the greater was the effect ($rho = -.94$, $p = .02$, two-tail). It was in the first and second grades that the effects were most dramatic. The largest gain among the three first grade classrooms occurred for experimental *Ss* who gained 24.8 IQ points *in excess* of the gain (+16.2) shown by the controls. The largest gain among the three second grade classrooms was obtained by experimental *Ss* who gained 18.2 IQ points in excess of the gain (+4.3) shown by the controls.. . .

There are a number of possible explanations of the finding that teachers' expectancy effects operated primarily at the lower grade levels, including: (a) Younger children have less well-established reputations so that the creation of expectations about their performance would be more credible. (b) Younger children may be more susceptible to the unintended social influence exerted by the expectation of their teacher. (c) Younger children may be more recent arrivals in the school's neighborhood and may differ from the older children in characteristics other than age. (d) Teachers of lower grades may differ from teachers of higher grades on a variety of dimensions which are correlated

TABLE 1 Mean Gains in IQ

Grade	Controls		Experimentals		Diff.	*t*	p†
	M	σ	M	σ			
1	12.0	16.6	27.4	12.5	15.4	2.97	.002
2	7.0	10.0	16.5	18.6	9.5	2.28	.02
3	5.0	11.9	5.0	9.3	0.0		
4	2.2	13.4	5.6	11.0	3.4		
5	17.5	13.1	17.4	17.8	-0.1		
6	10.7	10.0	10.0	6.5	-0.7		
Weighted *M*	8.4*	13.5	12.2**	15.0	3.8	2.15	.02

* Mean number of children per grade = 42.5
** Mean number of children per grade = 10.8
†*p* one-tailed

with the effectiveness of the unintentional communication of expectancies.

The most important question which remains is that which asks how a teacher's expectation becomes translated into behavior in such a way as to elicit the expected pupil behavior. Prior research on the unintentional communication of expectancies in experimentally more carefully controlled interactions suggests that this question will not be easily unanswered (Rosenthal, in press). But, regardless of the mechanism involved, there are important substantive and methodological implications of these findings.. . . For now, one example, in question form, will do: How much of the improvement in intellectual performance attributed to the contemporary educational programs is due to the content and methods of the programs and how much is due to the favorable expectancies of the teachers and administrators involved? Experimental designs to answer such questions are available (Rosenthal, in press) and in view of the psychological, social and economic importance of these programs the use of such designs seems strongly indicated.

REFERENCES

Flanagan, J. C. *Tests of general ability: technical report.* Chicago, Ill.: Science Research Associates, 1960.

Rosenthal, R. The effect of the experimenter on the results of psychological research. In B. A. Maher (Ed.), *Progress in experimental personality research.* Vol. I. New York: Academic Press, 1964. Pp. 79-114.

Rosenthal, R. *Experimenter effects in behavioral research.* New York: Appleton-Century-Crofts, in press.

Rosenthal, R., & Fode, K. L. The effect of experimenter bias on the performance of the albino rat. *Behavioral Science,* 1963, 8, 183-189.

Rosenthal, R., & Lawson, R. A longitudinal study of the effects of experimenter bias on the operant learning of laboratory rats. *Journal of Psychiatric Research,* 1964, 2, 61-72.

19 Failure to Escape Traumatic Shock[1]

Martin E. P. Seligman[2] and Steven F. Maier[3],
University of Pennsylvania

Dogs which had 1st learned to panel press in a harness in order to escape shock subsequently showed normal acquisition of escape/avoidance behavior in a shuttle box. In contrast, yoked, inescapable shock in the harness produced profound interference with subsequent escape responding in the shuttle box. Initial experience with escape in the shuttle box led to enhanced panel pressing during inescapable shock in the harness and prevented interference with later responding in the shuttle box. Inescapable shock in the harness and failure to escape in the shuttle box produced interference with escape responding after a 7-day rest. These results were interpreted as supporting a learned "helplessness" explanation of interference with escape responding: Ss failed to escape shock in the shuttle box following inescapable shock in the harness because they had learned that shock termination was independent of responding.

Overmier and Seligman (1967) have shown that the prior exposure of dogs to inescapable shock in a Pavlovian harness reliably results in interference with subsequent escape/avoidance learning in a shuttle box. Typically, these dogs do not even escape from shock in the shuttle box. They initially show normal reactivity to shock, but after a few trials, they passively "accept" shock and fail to make escape movements. Moreover, if an escape or avoidance response does occur, it does not reliably predict future escapes or avoidances, as it does in normal dogs.

This pattern of effects is probably not the result of incompatible skeletal responses reinforced during the inescapable shocks, because it can be shown even when the inescapable shocks are delivered while the dogs are paralyzed by curare. This behavior is also probably not the result of adaptation to shock, because it occurs even when escape/avoidance shocks are intensified. However, the fact that interference does not occur if 48 hr. elapse between exposure to inescapable shock in the harness and escape/avoidance training, suggests that the phenomenon may be partially dependent upon some other temporary process.

Overmier and Seligman (1967) suggested that the degree of control over shock allowed to the animal in the harness may be an important determinant of this interference effect. According to this hypothesis, if shock is terminated independently of *S's* responses during its initial experience with shock, interference with subsequent escape/avoidance responding should occur. If, however, *S's* responses terminate shock during its initial experience with shock, normal escape/avoidance responding should subsequently occur. Experiment I investigates the effects of escapable as compared with inescapable shock on subsequent escape/avoidance responding.

EXPERIMENT I

Method

Subjects.—The *Ss* were 30 experimentally naive, mongrel dogs, 15-19 in. high at the shoulder, and weighing between 25 and 29 lb. They were maintained on ad lib food and water in individual cages. Three dogs were discarded from the Escape group, two because they failed to learn to escape shock in the harness (see procedure), and one because of a procedural error. Three dogs were discarded from the "Yoked" control group, two because they were too small at the neck to be adequately restrained in the harness; the third died during treatment. This left 24 *Ss*, eight in each group.

Apparatus.—The apparatus was the same as that described in Overmier and Seligman (1967). It consisted of two distinctively different units, one for escapable/inescapable shock sessions and the other for escape/avoidance training. The unit in which *Ss* were exposed to escapable/inescapable shock consisted of a rubberized, cloth hammock located inside a shielded, white, sound-attenuating cubicle. The hammock was constructed so that *Ss* legs hung down below its body through four holes. The *S's* legs were secured in this position, and *S* was strapped into the hammock. In addition, *S's* head was held in position by panels placed on either side and a yoke between the panels across *S's* neck. The *S* could press the panels with its head. For the Escape group pressing the panels terminated shock, while for the "Yoked" control group, panel presses did not effect the preprogrammed shock. The shock source for this unit consisted of 500 v. ac transformer and a parallel voltage divider, with the current applied through a fixed resistance of 20,000 ohms. The shock was applied to *S* through brass plate electrodes coated with commercial electrode paste and taped to the footpads of *S's* hind feet. The shock intensity was 6.0 ma. Shock presentations were controlled by automatic relay circuitry located outside the cubicle. Escape/avoidance training was conducted in a two-way shuttle box with two black compartments separated by an adjustable barrier (described in Solomon & Wynne, 1953). The barrier height was adjusted to *S's* shoulder height. Each shuttle-box compartment was illuminated by two 50-w. and one 7½-w. lamps. The CS consisted of turning off the four 50-w. lamps. The US, electric shock, was administered through the grid floor. A commutator shifted the polarity of the grid bars four times per second. The shock was 550 v. ac applied through a variable current limiting resistor in series with *S*. The shock was continually regulated by E at 4.5 ma. Whenever *S* crossed the barrier, photocell beams were interrupted, a response was automatically recorded, and the trial terminated. Latencies of barrier jumping were measured from CS onset to the nearest .01 sec. by an electric clock. Stimulus presentations and temporal contingencies were controlled by automatic relay circuitry in a nearby room.

White masking noise at approximately 70-db. SPL was presented in both units.

Procedure.—The Escape group received escape training in the harness. Sixty-four unsignaled 6.0 ma. shocks were presented at a mean interval of 90 sec. (range, 60-120 sec.). If the dog pressed either panel with its head during shock, shock terminated. If the dog failed to press a panel during shock, shock terminated automatically after 30 sec. Two dogs were discarded for failing to escape 18 of the last 20 shocks.[4]

Twenty-four hours later dogs in the Escape group were given 10 trials of escape/avoidance training in the shuttle box: *S* was placed in the shuttle box and given 5 min. to adapt before any treatment was begun. Presentation of the CS began each trial. The CS-US interval was 10 sec. If *S* jumped the barrier during this interval, the CS terminated and no shock was presented. Failure to jump the barrier during the CS-US interval led to shock which remained on until *S* did jump the barrier. If no response occurred within 60 sec. after CS onset, the trial was automatically terminated and a 60-sec. latency recorded. The average intertrial interval was 90 sec. with a range of 60-120 sec. If *S* failed to cross the barrier on all of the first five trials, it was removed, placed on the other side of the shuttle box, and training then continued. At the end of the tenth trial, *S* was removed from the shuttle box and returned to its home cage.

The Normal control group received only 10 escape/avoidance trials in the shuttle box as described above.

The "Yoked" control group received the same exposure to shock in the harness as did the Escape group, except that panel pressing did not terminate shock. The duration of shock on any given trial was determined by the mean duration of the corresponding trial in the Escape group. Thus each *S* in the "Yoked" control group received a series of shocks of decreasing duration totaling to 226 sec.

Twenty-four hours later, *Ss* in the "Yoked" control

group received 10 escape/avoidance trials in the shuttle box as described for the Escape group. Seven days later, those *Ss* in this group which showed the interference effect received 10 more trials in the shuttle box.

Results[5]

The Escape group learned to panel press to terminate shock in the harness. Each *S* in this group showed decreasing latencies of panel pressing over the course of the session (p = .008, sign test, Trials 1-8 vs. Trials 57-64). Individual records revealed that each *S* learned to escape shock by emitting a single, discrete panel press following shock onset. The *Ss* in the "Yoked" control group typically ceased panel pressing altogether after about 30 trials.

Table 1 presents the mean latency of shuttle box responding, the mean number of failures to escape shock, and the percentage of *Ss* which failed to escape nine or more of the 10 trials during escape/avoidance training in the shuttle box for each group. The "Yoked" control group showed marked interference with escape responding in the shuttle box. It differed significantly from the Escape group and from the Normal control group on mean latency and mean number of failures to escape (in both cases, $p < .05$, Duncan's multiple-range test). The Escape group and the Normal control group did not differ on these indexes.

Six *Ss* in the "Yoked" control group failed to escape shock on 9 or more of the 10 trials in the shuttle box. Seven days after the first shuttle-box treatment, these six *Ss* received 10 further trials in the shuttle box. Five of them continued to fail to escape shock on every trial.

Discussion

The degree of control over shock allowed a dog during its initial exposure to shock was a determinant of whether or not interference occurred with subsequent escape/avoidance learning. Dogs which learned to escape shock by panel pressing in the harness did not differ from untreated dogs in subsequent escape/avoidance learning in the shuttle box. Dogs for which shock termination was independent of responding in the harness showed interference with subsequent escape learning.

Because the Escape group differed from the "Yoked" control group during their initial exposure to shock only in their control over shock termination, we suggest that differential learning about their control over shock occurred in these two groups. This learning may have acted in the following way: (*a*) Shock initially elicited active responding in the harness in both groups. (*b*) *Ss* in the "Yoked" control group learned that shock termination was independent of their responding, i.e., that the conditional probability of shock termination in the presence of any given response did not differ from the conditional probability of shock termination in the

TABLE 1
INDEXES OF SHUTTLE BOX ESCAPE/AVOIDANCE RESPONDING: EXP. 1

Group	Mean Latency (in sec.)	% *Ss* Failing to Escape Shock on 9 or More of the 10 Trials	Mean No. Failures to Escape Shock*
Escape	27.00	0	2.63
Normal Control	25.93	12.5	2.25
"Yoked" Control	48.22	75	7.25

*Out of 10 trials.

absence of that response. (*c*) The incentive for the initiation of active responding in the presence of electric shock is the expectation that responding will increase the probability of shock termination. In the absence of such incentive, the probability that responding will be initiated decreases. (*d*) Shock in the shuttle box mediated the generalization of *b* to the new situation for the "Yoked" control group, thus decreasing the probability of escape response initiation in the shuttle box.

Escapable shock in the harness (Escape group) did not produce interference, because *Ss* learned that their responding was correlated with shock termination. The incentive for the maintenance of responding was thus present, and escape response initiation occurred normally in the shuttle box.

Learning that shock termination is independent of responding seems related to the concept of learned "helplessness" or "hopelessness" advanced by Richter (1957), Mowrer (1960, p. 197), Cofer and Appley (1964, p. 452), and to the concept of external control of reinforcement discussed by Lefcourt (1966).

In untreated *Ss* the occurrence of an escape or avoidance response is a reliable predictor of future escape and avoidance responding. Dogs in the "Yoked" control group and in the groups which showed the interference effect in Overmier and Seligman (1967) occasionally made an escape or avoidance response and then reverted to "passively" accepting shock. These dogs did not appear to benefit from the barrier-jumping-shock termination contingency. A possible interpretation of this finding is that the prior learning that shock termination was independent of responding inhibited the formation of the barrier-jumping—shock-termination association.

The *Ss* in the "Yoked" control group which showed the interference effect 24 hr. after inescapable shock in the harness again failed to escape from shock after a further 7-day interval. In contrast, Overmier and Seligman (1967) found that no interference occurred when 48 hr. elapsed between inescapable shock in the harness and shuttle-box training. This time course could result from a temporary state of emotional depletion (Brush, Myer, & Palmer, 1963), which was produced by experience with inescapable shock, and which could be prolonged by being conditioned to the cues of the shuttle box. Such a state might be related to the parasympathetic death which Richter's (1957) "hopeless" rats died. Further research is needed to clarify the relationship between the learning factor, which appears to cause the initial occurrence of the interference effect, and an emotional factor, which may be responsible for the time course of the effect.

The results of Exp. I provide a further disconfirmation of the adaptation explanation of the interference effect. If *Ss* in the "Yoked" control group had adapted to shock and, therefore, were not sufficiently motivated to respond in the shuttle box, *Ss* in the Escape group should also have adapted to shock. Further, the Escape and the "Yoked" control groups were equated for the possibility of adventitious punishment for active responding by shock onset in the harness. Thus it seems unlikely that the "Yoked" control group failed to escape in the shuttle box because it had been adventitiously punished for active responding in the harness.

EXPERIMENT II

Experiment I provided support for the hypothesis that *S* learned that shock termination was independent of its responding in the harness and that this learning inhibited subsequent escape responding in the shuttle box. Experiment II investigates whether prior experience with *escapable* shock in the shuttle box will mitigate the effects of inescapable shock in the harness on subsequent escape/avoidance behavior. Such prior experience might be expected *(a)* to inhibit *S's* learning in the harness that its responding is not correlated with shock termination and (*b*) to allow *S* to discriminate between the escapability of shock in the shuttle box and the inescapability of shock in the harness.

Method

Subjects.—The *Ss* were 30 experimentally naive, mongrel dogs, weight, height, and housing as above. Three dogs were discarded: two because of procedural errors and one because of illness. The remaining 27 dogs were randomly assigned to three groups of nine *Ss* each.

Apparatus.—The two units described for Exp. I were used.

Procedure.—The Preescape group received 3 days of treatment. On Day 1, each *S* received 10 escape/avoidance trials in the shuttle box as described in Exp. I. On Day 2, approximately 24 hr. after the shuttlebox treatment, each *S* in this group received an inescapable shock session in the harness. All inescapable shocks were unsignaled. The inescapable shock session consisted of 64, 5-sec. shocks, each of 6.0 ma. The average intershock interval was 90 sec. with a range of 60-120 sec. On Day 3, approximately 24 hr. after the inescapable shock, *S* was returned to the shuttle box and given 30 more escape/avoidance trials, as described for Day 1.

The No Pregroup received no experience in the shuttle box prior to receiving inescapable shock. On the first treatment day for this group, each *S* was placed in the harness and exposed to an inescapable shock session as described for the Preescape group, Day 2. Approximately 24 hr. later, *S* was placed in the shuttle box and given 40 trials of escape/avoidance training as described above. If *S* failed to respond on all of the first five trials, *S* was moved to the other side of the shuttle box. If *S* continued to fail to respond on all trials, it was put back on the original side after the twenty-fifth trial. Thus, if *S* failed to escape on every trial, it received a total of 2,000 sec. of shock.

The No Inescapable group was treated exactly as the Preescape group except that it received no shock in the harness. On Day 1, *S* received 10 escape/avoidance trials in the shuttle box. On Day 2, it was strapped in the harness for 90 min., but received no shock. On Day 3, it was returned to the shuttle box and given 30 more escape/avoidance trials.

Results

The No Pregroup showed significant interference with escape/avoidance responding in the shuttle box on Day 3. The Preescape and the No Inescapable groups did not show such interference. Figure 1 presents the mean median latency of jumping responses for the three groups (and a posterior control group, see below) over the four blocks of 10 trials. Analysis of variance on the three groups revealed that the effect of groups, $F(2, 24) = 3.55$, $p < .05$, and the effect of trial blocks, $F(3, 72) = 6.84$, $p < .01$, were significant. Duncan's multiple-range test indicated that the No Pregroup differed from the other two groups across all 40 trials both $p < .05$. The Preescape and the No Inescapable groups did not differ from each other. Similar results held for the mean of mean latencies. A small, transitory disruption of improvement in shuttle-box performance following inescapable shock in the harness occurred in the Preescape group relative to the No Inescapable group. Difference scores for latencies between consecutive blocks of trials measure improvement in performance. A comparison of the Preescape group with the No Inescapable group on the difference between the mean latency on Trials 1-10 and the mean latency on Trials 11-20 revealed that the No Inescapable group showed significantly more improvement than the Preescape group, Mann-Whitney *U* test, $U = 15$, $p < .05$. No significant differences were found on difference scores for any subsequent blocks of trials.

Figure 2 presents the mean number of failures to escape shock for the three groups across the four blocks of trials. Analysis of variance revealed a significant overall effect of blocks, $F(3, 72) = 5.94$, $p < .01$, and a significant Groups x Blocks interaction, $F(6, 72) = 17.82$, $p < .01$. Duncan's tests indicated that the No Pregroup showed significantly more failures to escape than the other two groups across the 40 trials, both $p < .05$. The Preescape and the No Inescapable groups did not differ.

Figure 3 presents the total number of avoidance responses for the groups across the blocks of trials. Only the blocks effect was significant in the overall analysis of variance, $F(3, 72) = 27.90$, $p < .01$. No other effects were significant.

Panel presses made in the harness during the inescapable shock session were counted. On either side of *S's* head were panels which *S* could press; pressing had no effect on the shock, but merely indicated attempts to respond and/or struggling in the harness. The Preescape group, having received 10 trials with *escapable* shock in the shuttle box the previous day, made more panel presses during the inescapable shock session than did the No Pregroup, the group for which the inescapable shock in the harness was the first experimental treatment, Mann-Whitney *U* test, $U = 9$, $p < .02$.

Posterior control group.—Subsequent to this experiment, a control group was run to determine if the *escapability* of shock in the shuttle box on Day 1 for the Preescape group was responsible for its enhanced panel pressing in the harness and lack of interference with responding in the shuttle box. Or would the mere occurrence of inescapable shock for a free-moving animal in the shuttle box have produced these

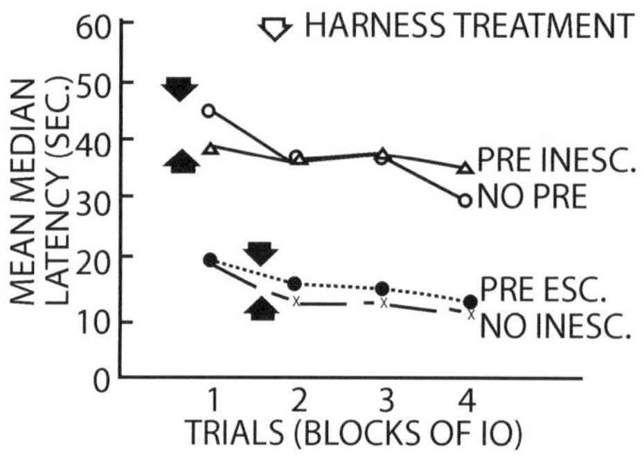

FIG. 1. Mean median latency of escape/avoidance responding. (The position of the arrow denotes whether the harness treatment occurred 24 hr. before the first or second block of trials.)

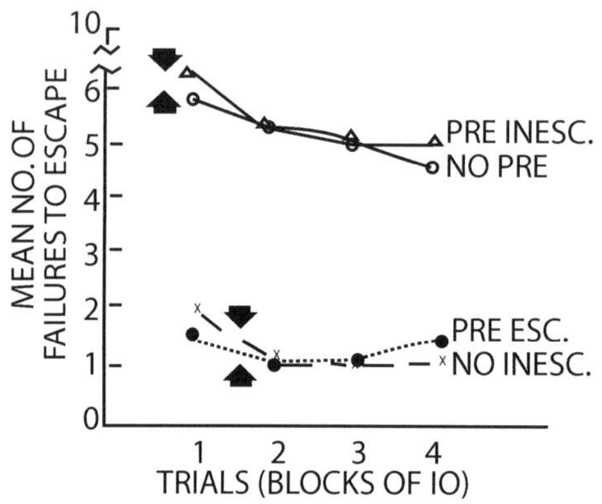

FIG. 2. Mean number of failures to escape shock. (The position of the arrow denotes whether the harness treatment occurred 24 hr. before the first or second block of trials.)

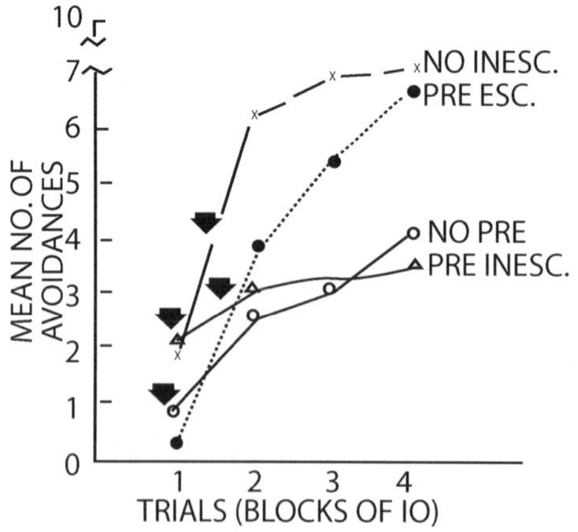

FIG. 3. Mean number of avoidances. (The position of the arrow denotes whether the harness treatment occurred 24 hr. before the first or second block of trials.)

results? Nine naive dogs received the following treatment: On Day 1, *Ss* were placed in shuttle box and given 10 trials as for the Preescape and the No Inescapable groups. Unlike these groups, however, *S's* barrier jumping did not (except adventitiously) terminate the shock and CS, because trial durations were programmed independently of *S's* behavior. The duration of each of the 10 trials for this Preinescapable group corresponded to the mean trial duration for the Preescape and the No Inescapable groups on that trial. On Day 2, *Ss* received 64 trials of inescapable shock in the harness. On Day 3, *Ss* received 40 escape/avoidance trials in the shuttle box.

Figures 1, 2, and 3 present the escape/avoidance performance of the Preinescapable group on Day 3. In general this group performed like the No Pregroup. This impression was borne out by statistical tests. The Preinescapable group showed significantly slower median latency of barrier jumping than the Preescape and the No Inescapable groups across all 40 trials, both $p < .05$, Duncan's test. The Preinescapable group did not differ from the No Pregroup. Similar results held for the other indexes.

Analysis of the panel press data showed that the Preinescapable group made significantly fewer panel presses in the harness than the Preescape group, Mann-Whitney U test, $U = 14$, $p < .05$. The Preinescapable group did not differ significantly from the No Pregroup, $U = 26$.

Discussion

Three main findings emerged from Exp. II : *(a) Ss* (Preescape), which first received escapable shock in the shuttle box, then inescapable shock in the harness, did not react passively to subsequent shock in the shuttle box, as did *Ss* which either first received inescapable shock in the shuttle box (Preinescapable) or no treatment prior to shock in the harness (No Pre). (*b*) The Preescape group, having received experience with escapable shock in the shuttle box, showed enhanced panel pressing when exposed to inescapable shock in the harness, relative to naive *Ss* given inescapable shock in the harness. Such enhanced panel pressing was specifically the result of the *escapability* of shock in the shuttle box: The Preinescapable group did not show enhanced panel pressing. (*c*) The interference effect persisted for 40 trials.

The *Ss* which have had prior experience with *escapable* shock in the shuttle box showed more energetic behavior in response to inescapable shock in the harness. This contrasts with the interference effect produced by *inescapable* shock in *Ss* which have had no prior experience with shock or in *Ss* which have had prior experience with inescapable shock. Thus, if an animal first learns that its responding produces shock termination and then faces a situation in which reinforcement is independent of its responding, it is more persistent in its attempts to escape shock than is a naive animal.

GENERAL DISCUSSION

We have proposed that *S* learned as a consequence of inescapable shock that its responding was independent of shock termination, and therefore the probability of response initiation during shock decreased. Alternative explanations might be offered: (*a*) Inactivity, somehow, reduces the aversiveness of shock. Thus S failed to escape shock in the shuttle box because it had been reinforced for inactivity in the harness. Since the interference effect occurred in *Ss* which had been curarized during inescapable shock, such an aversiveness-reducing mechanism would have to be located inward of the neuro-myal junction. *(b) S* failed to escape in the shuttle box because certain responses which facilitate barrier jumping were *extinquished* in the harness during inescapable shock. In conventional extinction procedures, some response is first explicitly reinforced by correlation with shock termination, and then that response is extinguished by removing shock altogether from the situation. Responding during extinction is conventionally not *un*correlated with shock termination; rather, responding is correlated with the total absence of shock. In our harness situation, no response was first explicitly reinforced, and shock was presented throughout the session. A broader concept of extinction, however, might be tenable. On this view, any procedure which decreases the probability of a response by eliminating the incentive to respond is an extinction procedure. If the independence of shock termination and responding eliminates the incentive to respond (as assumed), then our harness procedure could be thought of as an extinction procedure. Such an explanation seems only semantically different from the one we have advanced, since both entail that the probability of responding during shock has decreased because *S* learned that shock termination was independent of its responses.

Learning that one's own responding and reinforcement are independent might be expected to play a role in appetitive situations. If *S* received extensive pretraining with rewarding brain stimulation delivered independently of its operant responding, would the subsequent acquisition of a bar press to obtain this reward be retarded? Further, might learned "helplessness" transfer from aversive to appetitive situations or vice versa?

If dogs learn in one situation that their active responding is to no avail, and then transfer this training to another shock situation, the opposite type of transfer (avoidance learning sets) might be possible: If a dog first learned a barrier-hurdling response which avoided shock in the shuttle box, would that dog be facilitated in learning to panel press to avoid shock in the harness (to a different CS)? Our finding, that dogs which first successfully escape shock in the shuttle box later showed enhanced panel pressing in the harness, is consonant with this prediction.

Does learning about response-reinforcement contingencies have its analogs in classical conditioning? If *S* experienced two stimuli randomly interspersed with each other (adventitious pairings possible), would it be retarded in forming an association between the two stimuli once true pairing was begun? Conversely, pretraining in which one stimulus is correlated with a US might facilitate the acquisition of the CR to a new CS. Pavlov (1927, p. 75) remarked that the first establishment of a conditioned inhibitor took longer than any succeeding one.

In conclusion, learning theory has stressed that two operations, explicit contiguity between events (acquisition) and explicit noncontiguity (extinction), produce learning. A third operation that is proposed, independence between events, also produces learning, and such learning may have effects upon behavior that differ from the effects of explicit pairing and explicit nonpairing. Such learning may produce an S who does not attempt to escape electric shock; an S who, even if he does respond, may not benefit from instrumental contintengies.

REFERENCES

Brush F. R., Myer, J. S., & Palmer, M. E. Effects of kind of prior training and intersession interval upon subsequent avoidance learning. *J. comp. physiol. Psychol.*, 1963, 56, 539-545.

Cofer, C. N., & Appley, M. H. *Motivation: Theory and research.* New York: Wiley, 1964.

Lefcourt, H. M. Internal vs. external control of reinforcement: A review. *Psychol. Bull.*, 1966, 65, 206-221.

Mowrer, O. H., *Learning theory and behavior.* New York: Wiley, 1960.

Overmier, J. B., & Seligman, M. E. P. Effects of inescapable shock on subsequent escape and avoidance learning. *J. comp. physiol. Psychol.*, 1967, 63, 28-33.

Pavlov, I. P. *Conditional reflexes.* New York: Dover, 1927.

Richter, C. On the phenomenon of sudden death in animals and man. *Psychosom. Med.*, 1957, 19, 191-198.

Solomon, R. L., & Wynne, L. C. Traumatic avoidance learning: Acquisition in normal dogs. *Psychol. Monogr.*, 1953, 67 (4, Whole No. 354).

(Received June 1, 1966)

FOOTNOTES

[1.] This research was supported by grants to R. L. Solomon from the National Science Foundation (GB-2428) and the National Institute of Mental Health (MH-04202). The authors are grateful to R. L. Solomon, J. Aronfreed, J. Geer, H. Gleitman, F. Irwin, D. Williams, and J. Wishner for their advice in the conduct and reporting of these experiments. The authors also thank J. Bruce Overmier with whom Exp. I was begun.

[2.] National Science Foundation predoctoral fellow.

[3.] National Institute of Mental Health predoctoral fellow.

[4.] It might be argued that eliminating these two dogs would bias the data. Thus naive dogs which failed to learn the panel-press escape response in the harness might also be expected to be unable to learn shuttle box escape/avoidance. One of these dogs was run 48 hr. later in the shuttle box. It escaped and avoided normally. The other dog was too ill to be run in the shuttle box 48 hr. after it received shock in the harness.

[5.] All *p* values are based upon two-tailed tests.

20 Storage and Retrieval Processes in Long-Term Memory[1]

R. M. Shiffrin[2] and R. C. Atkinson, Stanford University

A theory of human memory is described in which a distinction is made between three memory stores: the sensory register, the short-term store, and the long-term store. Primary emphasis is given to the processes by which information is stored in and retrieved from the long-term store, a store which is considered to be a permanent repository for information. Forgetting and related phenomena are attributed to a failure of the retrieval process, in which the search through some memory area becomes less efficient as new information is placed in it. Storage and retrieval in the long-term store are conceived of as parallel processes, one mirroring the other, and each is divided into three stages for conceptual clarity. The memory trace is viewed as an ensemble of information stored in some memory location, the location of storage determined largely by the components of the ensemble itself. The ability of the system to cope with diverse phenomena is demonstrated by a consideration of a number of selected experimental paradigms.

Theories of human long-term memory have given primary emphasis either to the organization of that memory, in terms of the dimensions of storage and the associations between the stored information (e.g., Cofer, 1965; Deese, 1966; Mandler, 1968; Osgood, 1963), or to the characteristics of temporal decay from that memory as in the interference theories (e.g., Keppel, 1968; Melton, 1963; Postman, 1961; Underwood, 1957). The processes by which information is stored in, and retrieved from, long-term memory have been relatively neglected. An example of this type of process is the memory search during retrieval; during the search, a succession of memory codes is examined, each examination followed by a decision process in which the search is either terminated or continued, and in which information recovered is either accepted as that desired and output, or rejected. It is the intention of this paper to elaborate the memory input and output processes. As will be indicated later, our view of storage and retrieval eliminates the necessity for assuming decay of information from long-term memory. It will be assumed that long-term memory is permanent; decrements in performance over time are ascribed to an increasingly ineffective search of the stored information.

We begin by describing the overall conception of the memory system. The system follows that described in Atkinson and Shiffrin (1965, 1968a), and is similar to those proposed by Feigenbaum (1966) and Norman (1968). The major components of the system are diagrammed in Figure 1: the sensory register, the short-term store (STS) and the long-term store (LTS). The solid arrows in the diagram represent directions in which information is transferred from one part of the system to another. Note that transfer is not meant to imply the removal of information from one store and the placing of it in the next; rather, transfer is an operation in which information in one store is "copied" into the next without affecting its status in the original store. It should be emphasized that our hypotheses about the various memory stores do not require

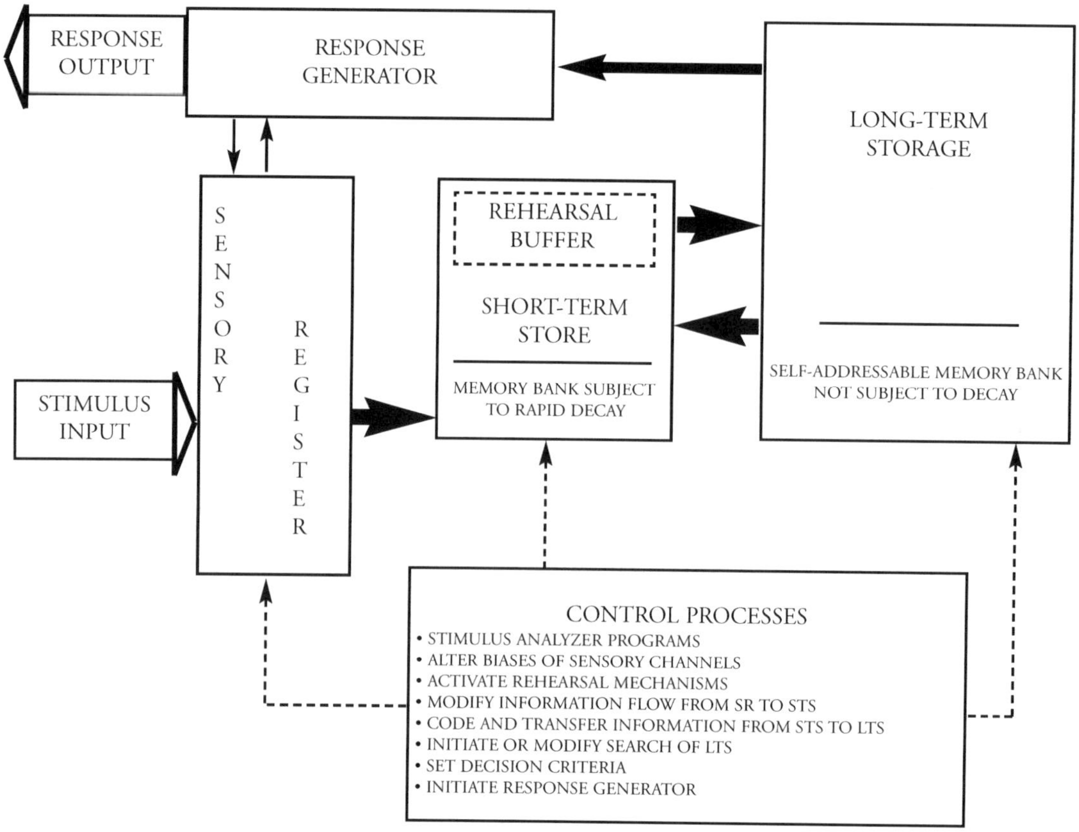

FIG. 1. A flow chart of the memory system. (Solid lines indicate paths of information transfer. Dashed lines indicate connections which permit comparison of information arrays residing in different parts of the system; they also indicate paths along which control signals may be sent which activate information transfer, rehearsal mechanisms, etc.)

any assumptions regarding the physiological locus of these stores; the system is equally consistent with the view that the stores are separate physiological structures as with the view that the short-term store is simply a temporary activation of information permanently stored in the long-term store. The control processes listed in Figure 1 are a sample of those which the subject *(S)* can call into play at his discretion, depending upon such factors as the task and the instructions. Control processes govern informational flow, rehearsal, memory search, output of responses, and so forth.

The sensory register is a very short-lived memory store which temporarily holds incoming sensory information while it is being initially processed and transferred to the short-term store. In the visual modality, for example, information will decay from the sensory register in a period of several hundred milliseconds (Sperling, 1960). Information in the short-term store, if not attended to by *S,* will decay and be lost in a period of about 30 seconds or less, but control processes such as rehearsal can maintain information in STS for as long as *S* desires (the buffer process in Figure 1 is one highly organized rehearsal scheme). While information resides in STS, portions of it are transferred to LTS. The long-term store is assumed to be a *permanent* repository of information; we realize that factors such as traumatic brain damage, lesions, and deterioration with extreme age must lead to memory loss, but such effects should be negligible in the types of experiments considered in this paper. Thus it is hypothesized that information, once stored in LTS, is never thereafter destroyed or eliminated. Nevertheless, the ability to retrieve information from LTS varies considerably with time and interfering material.

The short-term store serves a number of useful functions. On the one hand it decouples the memory system from the external environment and relieves the system from the responsibility of moment-to-moment attention to environmental changes. On the other hand, STS provides a working memory in which manipulations of information may take place on a temporary basis. Because STS is a memory store in which information can be maintained if desired, it is often used as the primary memory device in certain types of tasks; in these tasks the information presented for retention is maintained in STS until the moment of test and then emitted. Tasks in which STS is utilized for this purpose, and the mechanisms and control processes that may come into play, have been examined extensively in Atkinson and Shiffrin (1968a). In this report we are primarily interested in STS as a temporary store in which information is manipulated for the purposes of storage and retrieval from LTS, rather than as a store in which information is maintained until test. In the remainder of this paper, discussion is limited to that component of memory performance which involves LTS retrieval, and the components arising from STS and the sensory register will not be considered.

LONG-TERM STORE

In describing the structure of LTS, an analogy with computer memories is helpful. The usual computer memory is "location addressable"; if the system is given a certain location it will return with the contents of that location. When given the contents of a word (a "word" refers to a single computer memory location), such a system must be programmed to examine each location in turn in order to find the possible locations of these contents in the memory. It seems untenable that an exhaustive serial search is made of all of LTS whenever retrieval is desired. An alternative type of memory may be termed "content-addressable"; if the system is given the contents of a word it will return with the locations in memory containing those contents. One way in which such a memory may be constructed utilizes a parallel search through all memory locations; the system then returns with the locations of all matches. If this view is adopted, however, an additional process is needed to select the desired location from among the many returned by the parallel search. Thus, if we feed the system the word "red," it would not be useful for the system to return with all references or locations of "red"; there are simply too many and the original retrieval problem would not be significantly reduced in scale. There is, however, an alternative method for forming a content-addressable memory; in this method, the contents to be located themselves contain the information necessary to specify the storage location(s). This can occur if the information is originally stored in locations specified by some master plan dependent upon the contents of the information. Such a system will be termed "self-addressing." A self-addressing memory may be compared with a library shelving system which is based upon the contents of the books. For example, a book on "caulking methods used for 12th century Egyptian rivercraft" will be placed in a specific library location (in the Egyptian room, etc.). If a user desires this book, it may be located by following the same shelving plan used to store it in the first place. We propose that LTS is to a large degree just such a self-addressable memory. An ensemble of information presented to the memory system will define a number of memory areas in which that information is likely to be stored; the memory search will therefore have certain natural starting points. The system is assumed to be only partially self-addressing in that the degree to which the storage locations are specified will vary from one ensemble to the next and one moment to the next, in much the way as proposed in stimulus sampling theory (Estes, 1959). Thus it may be necessary to embark upon a memory search within the specified locations, a search which may proceed serially from one location to the next. This conception of LTS leads to a number of predictions. For example, a recognition test of memory will not proceed via exhaustive scanning of all stored codes, nor will a recognition test eliminate in all cases the necessity for an LTS search. If information is presented and *S* must indicate whether this information has been presented previously, then the likely storage location (s) is queried. To the degree that the information has highly salient characteristics which precisely identify the storage location, the extent of the LTS search will be reduced. Thus, for items with highly salient characteristics, *S* should be able to identify quickly and accurately whether the item was presented previously, and the identification might not require a memory search which interrogates more than a single storage location. The less well-specified the storage location, the greater the memory search needed to make an accurate recognition response. This view is in many respects similar to that proposed by Martin (1967), in which he suggests that certain stimuli tend to give rise to identical encoding responses from one instance to the next, that is, on both study and test trials. From the present viewpoint "identical encoding responses" is taken to be equivalent to identical storage locations.

Although it is assumed that information ensembles are sorted into LTS locations according to a master plan, it is beyond the scope of this paper to attempt to outline this organizational structure; other workers have been dealing with this problem (e.g., Handler, 1968; Pollio, 1966). Undoubtedly this organization is highly complex, but the form of the organization will not be crucial to our discussions of input and output mechanisms. There is one dimension of organization that must be mentioned here, however; this is the "temporal" dimension. We are assuming that this dimension is like the other organizational dimensions in that information may be stored along it, and that retrieval may be based upon it. In the remaining sections of this paper, the temporal dimension will often be singled out for special mention, not because it differs in substance from other organizational dimensions, but because it is virtually impossible to eliminate it as a systematic variable in most memory experiments.

The term "location" is used in relation to the organizational schema; an LTS location is defined by the place in the organizational structure occupied by an information ensemble. The location will be defined in terms of the modality of the information (e.g., visual versus auditory), the level of analysis, (e.g., spelling versus syntactic structure), and all other dimensions of organization that may be relevant. Two locations will be said to be "close" if the information in them tends to be retrieved together. In particular, we shall refer to a *code,* or an *image,* as an ensemble of information that is closely related and very likely to be retrieved together. We do not wish to imply that there is some unitary atom of storage called a code or an image. The information making up a code in one task may be considered to be several codes in a different task. For example, an entire sentence may be considered a code if we are comparing the meaning of that sentence with others; however, the same sentence might be considered to be made up of a series of codes if we are comparing it with sentences of the same meaning but different grammatical form. Nevertheless, for most tasks the concept of a code or image as representing a cohesive array of information in a single storage location proves useful. This view of the memory trace is consistent with the analysis given by Bower (1967). In his model, a trace, or image, is represented by a vector of attributes which serves to identify both the information contained in the trace and the location of the trace in LTS. The values of the attributes in the vector serve to indicate the position of the trace on the various organizational dimensions; for example, one of the positions in the vector might indicate whether the trace is auditory or visual. It should be apparent that this quantitative view is compatible with our description of an image or code, and also with the description of LTS as a self-addressable store.

STORAGE AND RETRIEVAL

Since LTS is self-addressing, storage and retrieval have many features in common, one process mirroring the other. Storage is assumed to consist of three primary mechanisms: *transfer, placement,* and *image-production.* The transfer mechanism includes those control processes by which *S* decides what to store, when to store, and how to store information in LTS. The placement mechanism determines the locations in which the ensemble of information under consideration will be stored. To a large degree, the components of the ensemble itself will determine the location of storage. That is, in the action of encoding the desired information for storage, S may supplement the information currently in STS with pertinent information retrieved from LTS; the resultant ensemble in STS determines the storage location. The image-production mechanism determines what proportion of the current ensemble of information in STS will be placed in the designated LTS location(s). The proportion stored should be a function of the duration of the period that the ensemble is maintained in STS. Retrieval, like storage, is assumed to consist of three primary mechanisms: *search, recovery,* and *response generation.* The search process is a recursive loop in which locations or images are successively selected for examination. As each image is examined, the recovery process determines how much information will be recovered from the image and placed in STS. The response generation process then examines the recovered information and decides whether to continue the search or terminate and emit a response. If the search does not terminate, the selection of the next location or image for examination may depend upon information already uncovered during the search.

Although storage and retrieval are treated separately in this paper, we do not wish to imply that these processes are separated in time, one following the other. Rather, long-term storage is continually occurring for the information residing in short-term store. In addition, retrieval is continually occurring during storage attempts by *S;* for example, *S* may try to store a paired-associate by searching LTS for prominent associations to the stimulus, associations which could then be used as mediators.

The remaining portions of this report will be directed toward a delineation of these input and output processes. It is beyond the scope of this paper to do more than briefly describe the major mechanisms of the theory. Nevertheless, an attempt will be made to indicate how these processes work, what evidence supports our assumptions, what predictions may be derived, and how the theory may be applied to a number of selected tasks.

Storage Processes

Transfer. The decisions involving what to store, when to store, and how to store information are under a high degree of control by *S,* and therefore can result in striking performance changes from one task to another. Although we shall be discussing experimental situations in which storage takes place largely during designated study periods, we should note that storage in general occurs whenever information is cycled through the short-term store; for example, in reflective thinking, in daydreaming, and in moment-to-moment consideration of the day's happenings.

The decision concerning when to store information is especially important in situations where a large amount of information is being input rapidly to STS. Such a situation taxes the capacity of the system and forces *S* to select a subset of the presented information for special attention and coding. There are a number of factors that determine the information so selected. Important or easily stored information is likely to be given preference. For example, Harley (1965) has shown in a mixed-list design that paired-associate items given high monetary payoffs are selectively attended in preference to items given low payoffs. Information selection will also be governed by the degree to which the incoming material is already known. For example, there is considerable evidence that *S*s tend to store more information on a given item if that item's presentation is followed by other items that are well-known as opposed to being followed by items that are not known (Atkinson, Brelsford, & Shiffrin, 1967; Thompson, 1967). Finally, note that the decision when to store may be determined by strategies associated with the list or task as a whole, rather than with the individual item. For example, in an experiment employing a paired-associate list with only the two responses A and B, *S* might decide to store only information about those stimuli paired with Response A, and always guess Response B if the answer is not known at test.

The decisions concerning how to store information will also affect performance: storage via visual images may be more effective than auditory storage (Schnorr & Atkinson, 1969); overt and covert rehearsal methods may result in very different effects (Brelsford & Atkinson, 1968); and mediating versus nonmediating instructions may give rise to considerable performance differences (Runquist & Farley, 1964). On a somewhat different level, *S* may engage in organizational storage strategies such that different items are stored in locations determined by some fixed organizational framework (Tulving, 1962).

What information is stored, given the presentation of a particular information ensemble, will also be highly dependent upon the control processes utilized by *S.* In some cases, as Underwood (1963) points out in making a distinction between the nominal and functional stimulus, not all the information contained in the presented item is necessary for correct responding (e.g., if the stimuli are all nonsense syllables differing only in the first letter, then only the first letters need be stored). In these cases only the relevant characteristics of the input need be stored. In most cases *S* will select relevant characteristics of the presented information and add to this additional coding information from LTS; for example, a paired-associate plus a mediator might be stored in many cases. One type of information which *S* often attempts to store is information indicating that a particular response (usually one just given in error) is not correct; Millward (1964) has examined evidence for this process in simple paired-associate tasks. This process of tagging responses as incorrect is particularly important in studies of negative transfer; the higher the probability that the first response assigned to a stimulus will be tagged as incorrect (when the response changes), the less will be the proactive interference effect observed in the data (Shiffrin, 1968).

The examples of transfer mechanisms given above are by no means exhaustive, but they serve to indicate the pervasiveness and importance of these processes. Relatively simple decisions to select one transfer scheme rather than another can and do lead to large performance effects. These facts emphasize the need for carefully establishing the transfer mechanisms used before extending analysis to other aspects of the data.

Placement. The location in which an image will be stored is determined by the contents of that image; *S* therefore controls the storage location by manipulating the information complex in STS. For any given ensemble of information, however, there is a certain amount of randomness in placement. For this reason, a search for an image may have to be undertaken at test even if the entire information ensemble originally present in STS during study is presented for consideration. Information to be remembered may be stored in images in more than one location; for example, a paired-associate may be encoded by the use of two entirely different mnemonics. This notion has been given quantitative form in "multiple-copy" models for the memory trace (Atkinson & Shiffrin, 1965).

The primary mechanism determining storage location is in all cases an organizational framework. The self-addressing characteristic of input information depends upon the prior, already established, LTS organization; each item is sent to locations that depend upon the preexisting organizational framework. However, in many cases (especially situations involving free-recall learning and paired-associate learning in which the same list of items is presented over a series of trials) it is an effective technique for *S* to form new organizational structures. In free-recall learning, for example, output on successive trials becomes increasingly organized and similar to output on the preceding trial (Gofer, 1965; Tulving, 1962); it may be inferred that a consistent new organization has been imposed upon a set of words which were disorganized at the start of learning. This point regarding growth of organization is especially important with regard to list-structured paired-associate tasks, that is, a task in which a list of paired-associates is presented over and over on successive trials (possibly in a new random order from trial to trial). In such a task, organizational effects between items will tend to occur over trials, and care must be taken in inferring that effects seen by averaging data over all items in the list will also apply to the individual items. For example, there is evidence indicating that interference effects found by averaging over items in a list do not apply to the individual items making up the list (DaPolito, 1966; Greeno, 1967). For this reason we shall often consider in the rest of this paper results from what is termed a "continuous" paired-associate task (Bjork, 1966; Brelsford, Shiffrin, & Atkinson, 1968; Rumelhart, 1967). This type of task employs a long series of presentations, each involving first a test and then a study on a paired-associate item. The character of the experiment is essentially homogeneous over time because new items are continually being introduced and old items deleted; a new item may appear at any point in the sequence, receive a fixed number of presentations distributed over a subset of trials, and then be dropped and replaced by yet another item. In this way the list-structure feature of the typical paired-associate experiment is eliminated, and it is extremely difficult for *S* to develop special schemes for interitem organization.

In most cases, *S*'s placement strategy involves choosing one of many preexisting organizational dimensions for storage. In these cases, an organizational clue contained in the experimental design may prove useful. In categorized free-recall, for example, *S* will be induced to store (and retrieve) in the given categories (Bousfield & Cohen, 1956; Cofer, 1965; Cohen, 1963). Thus the location in which the word *division* will be stored will be quite different if preceded by *multiplication, addition,* and *subtraction* than if preceded by *platoon, regiment,* and *battalion.*

In the interests of effective memory, the most important requirement of the placement process is that it results in a storage location which will later be searched during test. If organizational schemes are used for placement, the schemes themselves will have to be stored, recovered, and utilized in order for retrieval to be optimal.

Image-production. When an ensemble of information is present in STS, some portion of it will be stored in a designated location in LTS as a permanent image. The proportion of information that is stored will be a function of the duration of time that the ensemble stays in STS, or of the number of times that ensemble is cycled through STS. It would be most natural to look for evidence of this mechanism in experiments varying study time for particular items. However, improved performance with longer study times can be attributed to a higher chance of finding a good mnemonic. Better evidence is found in experiments in which *Ss* are induced to utilize rote rehearsal rather than coding, and in which longer periods of rote verbal rehearsal lead to improved performance (Brelsford & Atkinson, 1968; Hellyer, 1962).

To conclude the discussion of storage, we consider the content of the image: the range and form of the stored information. A single image may contain a wide variety of information, including characteristics of the item presented for study (its sound, meaning, color, size, shape, position, etc.) and characteristics added by *S* (such as codes, mnemonics, mediators, images, associations, etc.). In addition, an image usually will contain links to other images (other information which was in the short-term store at the same time); these links can be regarded as a set of directions to the locations of related images in LTS.

Retrieval Processes

The retrieval mechanism forms the crux of the present theory, since it enables a permanent long-term store to exhibit the characteristics of a failing memory. The basic mechanism by which memory loss occurs involves a partially random search through an increasingly large set of images in some local set of memory locations. This local area may be defined by one or more dimensions in the organizational structure of LTS; as the number of images in the local area increases, the search for the desired information will become increasingly ineffective. For example, consider two areas, one consisting of three images, the other consisting of 10 images, and both containing the desired code. A random search through the smaller set will result in successful retrieval in a shorter period of time than a search through the larger set.

The retrieval process begins with the presentation of an information complex which places constraints on the response desired and also provides a number of clues, or delimiting information, concerning that desired output (i.e., a stimulus). On the basis of this presented information, or as the result of an external search strategy, *S* is led to look in some local memory area and select (possibly randomly) an image for examination. The process by which information is recovered from this image is called *recovery.* The recovered information will be placed in the short-term store which may also contain other information such as the search strategy being employed, salient information recovered previously in the search, the LTS locations that have been examined already, and some of the links to other images that have been examined already, and some of the links to other images that have been noted in the search but not yet examined. The short-term store thus acts as a "window" upon LTS, allowing *S* to deal sequentially with a manageable amount of information. The current contents of STS are now examined and various decisions made concerning whether the desired response has been found, whether to emit it, whether to terminate the search unsuccessfully, or whether to continue the search. These decisions and the generation of the response are called the *response-generation* process. If a decision is made to continue the search, then a new location is selected either randomly, on the basis of information just recovered, or in accord with an overriding external search strategy. The process which continues cycling in this manner until termination is called the *search* process.

Search. Each cycle in the search recursion begins with a mechanism which locates the next image for examination. This mechanism may be separated into *directed* and *random* components. The directed component includes strategies controlled by *S* and depends upon the input information and the self-addressing nature of the system. As a result of the directed component, a number of locations in some area of memory are marked for examination. The locations and images so marked will be referred to as the *examination subset,* and the directed component of the search may be characterized by the probability that the sought-after code is in the examination subset.

The directed component of the search can be either under a high degree of *S* control or relatively automatic. For example, the control factor is high in a situation where *S* engages in a first-letter alphabetic search, or where *S* attempts to remember lunch of 2 days previously by reconstructing the events of that day. In cases like this, the search assumes many of the aspects of problem solving. At the other extreme is the almost completely automatic direction of search which occurs, say, in the attempted recognition of a word as having been presented earlier in the session. In such a case, the word itself serves to direct the search via the self-addressing feature of the system. In its most general form the search process can be viewed as a series of stages in which searches are made successively in different examination subsets. That is, after choosing codes randomly for a time from one subset, information recovered during the search may cause *S* to change the memory area currently being examined for one quite different. This type of search could occur, for example, in a categorized free-recall task, in which the various categories are searched successively (Cohen, 1963). In most applications, however, a restricted search model should be adequate, the restriction allowing only a single examination subset to be searched during any retrieval period. This model should be particularly applicable to tasks in which only a short response period is allowed.

The random component of the search specifies the selection of codes in the examination subset from one cycle of the search to the next. It is assumed that the likelihood of any particular code being selected at some point will depend upon the amount of information contained in it, as well as the total number of codes and their temporal ordering in the examination subset. It will be seen that the extent to which the search depends upon the temporal ordering of the items is an important variable which, among other things, determines interference effects.

The division of search into directed and random components leads to somewhat different memory models, depending upon which component is selected for elaboration. Feigenbaum (1966) and Hintzman (1968), for example, have elaborated upon the directed component in computer simulation models. In these formulations there is a mechanism termed a "discrimination net," which enables *S* to sort through the organizational structure of LTS to reach the local memory area where desired information is stored. On the other hand, there are models which emphasize the probabilistic search through an examination subset of items in some memory area (Atkinson & Shiffrin, 1965). It is upon this latter type of model that attention will be focused in this paper.

Recovery. Once an image has been located, it is appropriate to ask what information contained in the image will be entered into the short-term store. This process is called recovery. The amount of information recovered from an image is assumed to be probabilistic, depending upon the current noise level in the system and the amount of information in the image. In particular, the amount of information recovered should be an increasing function of the amount of information in the image.

Response generation. Having recovered information from LTS, *S* is faced with decisions as to whether to terminate the search and respond or to continue to search. These decisions must first of all depend upon the consistency of the recovered information with that indicated by the test information. Inconsistent information can be ruled out at once. If information consistent with the test stimulus is found, and a recognition response is desired, then the response will be given when temporal or contextual information is recovered indicating that the image was stored recently. In a paired-associate test, three types of information may be recovered: that associated with the stimulus, that associated with the response, or associative information linking the two. Recovery of stimulus or response information will serve to lead to recognition of either; if both are recovered in nearby locations in memory, then the response may be emitted. On the other hand, a response might be output following recovery of associative information linking the response to the stimulus. Since the ability to output a response depends upon the amount of response information recovered, the process may often be represented by a decision-theoretic model in which *S* is attempting to filter information through a noisy background (Bernbach, 1967; Kintsch, 1967; Wickelgren & Norman, 1966). In situations where a long time period exists for responding, a likely response may be recovered but not emitted; in these cases the search will be continued in the hope of finding a better response. An extended search of this kind leads naturally to predictions that *S* will be able to rank responses in the order of their probability of being correct, with responses ranked after the first being correct at an above-chance level (Binford & Gettys, 1965).

A decision can be made to terminate the search unsuccessfully if response time has run out, or if response time is expected to run out and *S* wishes to make a guess before it does, or if *S* decides that further search would not be useful. Termination schemes of the latter type are quite varied. One simple rule would terminate the search when all images in the examination subset have been interrogated unsuccessfully. Other schemes would end the search when some fixed time limit expired, or some fixed number of items examined. These schemes are described in more detail in Atkinson and Shiffrin (1965).

The extensive decision structure that has been outlined may make it seem unlikely that time is available during the search for examination of a very large number of images. This is indeed the point of view we adopt: in most cases it is assumed that only a few images will be examined in the search before termination. For example, in a continuous paired-associate task analyzed by Shiffrin (1968), the estimated number of codes examined prior to termination was from about one to five.

APPLICATIONS OF THE SYSTEM

Forgetting

Decrements in performance occur in the system as a result of the input of additional information to LTS. These decrements result from three related mechanisms. First is a mechanical effect; information sufficient to respond correctly at one point in time may prove inadequate after additional information has been added. For example, a paired-associate GAX-4 may be stored as G**-4, and this code will be sufficient for correct responding (if recovered) when GAX is tested. Suppose, however, that GEK-3 is now presented and stored as G**-3. When either of these stimuli is tested later, both codes may be retrieved from LTS and therefore *S* will have to guess whether the correct response is 3 or 4.

The second cause of forgetting arises from a breakdown in the directed component of the search mechanism. That is, correct retrieval requires that the same memory area be searched at test as was used for storage during study. This may not occur, however, if only a portion of the input information is used to direct storage during study, for a different portion might be utilized to locate the storage area during retrieval. This process could be viewed within the framework of stimulus sampling theory (Estes, 1959) if the stimulus elements are taken to represent dimensions of organization. For clarity, let us denote the image which encodes the correct response for the current test as a "*c* code," and denote the other codes as "*i* codes." Thus the *i* codes are irrelevant codes which should lead to intrusion errors, whereas the *c* code, if examined, should lead to a correct response. Then the directed component of search can be characterized by the probability that the *c* code is in the examination subset, called p_c. In experiments in which clues are available to denote the organizational dimensions to be searched, p_c may be close to 1.0. In other situations, such as continuous tasks with randomly chosen stimuli and responses, p_c will be lower and dependent upon such factors as the amount of information in the *c* code and its age (where "age" denotes the position of the code on the temporal dimension). Although the breakdown in the directed component can provide a reasonable degree of forgetting, we shall focus primarily upon the third mechanism of forgetting: the increasing size of the examination subset.

When searching the examination subset, there are a number of possible results. The *c* code may be examined and give rise to a correct response, one of the *i* codes may be examined and produce an intrusion response, or none of the codes may give rise to a response and the search terminates. If the search through the examination subset is at least partially random, then the following conclusions may be reached. When the size of the subset is increased (i.e., the number of *i* codes is increased), then the probability of giving an intrusion will increase, the average time until the *c* code is examined will increase, and the probability of giving a correct response will decrease. When we say that the order of search is *partially* random, we mean to imply that the order in which codes in the examination subset are selected for consideration may depend upon both the amount of information in the code and the age of the code. Clearly, as the amount of information in a code tends toward zero, or as the age of a code increases, the probability of examining that code early in the search should decrease.

In order to make the sequence of events in the search clear, an example of a search is presented in Figure 2 for a continuous paired-associate task. In this task, suppose that on successive trials stimulus-response pairs are presented; on each trial the stimulus is tested first and then the pair is studied. A new pair may be presented on any trial, and given several reinforcements and tests at varying intervals. The bottom row in the figure gives the trial number for a section of the task from Trials 51-70. The number of the stimulus-response pairs tested and studied is given in the second row. The third row shows which pairs have had codes stored in LTS, and the height of the bar indicates the amount of information in the code. The fourth row indicates those codes that are in the examination subset on Trial 70 when Stimulus 18 is presented for test. For example, the stimulus tested may have begun with a vowel, and the items in the examination subset could have stimulus components which also begin with a vowel. Note that in this example the code for Stimulus 18 was stored on Trial 52, and happens to be in the examination subset. The top row of the table gives the order of search through the subset; the first four codes were examined and rejected but the fifth code examined was the *c* code and enabled the search to end with a correct response. It may be seen how forgetting occurs if it is imagined that Item 18 had not been tested until Trial 90 or 100. In this event, more *i* codes would be present in the examination subset and the probability would be greater that an intrusion would occur, or that the search would terminate before the *c* code was examined.

Interference

Various interference phenomena are readily predicted by the system. Although in general the order of search through the examination subset will depend upon the age and amount of information in the codes, suppose for simplicity that the search order is entirely random. Then both nonspecific proactive and retroactive interference effects are predicted, and in a sense are predicted to be equal. That is, extra *i* codes in the examination subset added either temporally before or after the *c* code will cause the correct retrieval probability to drop; in the case of a random search the probability decrease will be the same whether caused by an *i* code preceding or following the *c* code. The drop occurs because the extra codes increase the amount of time required to find the *c* code. Therefore, if the size of the examination subset is increased, it is more likely that either response time will run out or an intrusion response will occur. Obviously the greater the degree to which the search is ordered temporally backwards from the most recent item, the less the proactive, and the greater the retroactive interference effect. Thus if codes are examined strictly in temporal order, the average amount of time until the *c* code is examined will be independent of the number of codes which are older than the *c* code and hence no proactive effect will be expected. One of the best places to examine nonspecific proactive and retroactive interference effects is in the study of free-verbal recall as a function of list length (Murdock, 1962). In this task a list of words is read to *S*, who attempts to recall as many of

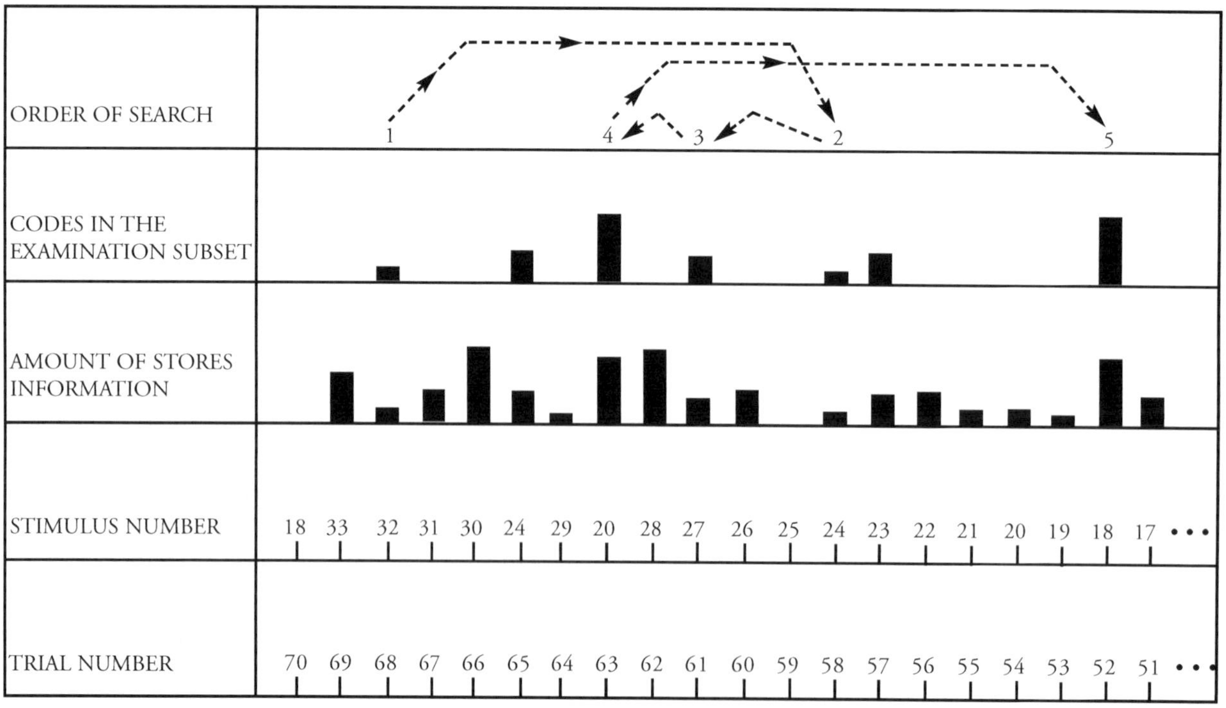

FIG. 2. A schematic representation of an LTS search in a continuous memory task.

them as possible following their presentation. The data are usually graphed as a serial-position curve which gives the probability of correct recall as a function of the presentation position (and hence as a function of the number of preceding and succeeding items in the list). As the list length is varied, the number of preceding and succeeding items is systematically varied and it is possible to apply the theory to the resultant data. The application of the theory is made particularly easy in this case because S is trying to recall all of the list, and hence the examination subset can be assumed to consist of all codes that have been stored. In fact, a model derived from the theory has been applied to free-verbal recall data as a function of list length and has proved remarkably successful (Atkinson & Shiffrin, 1965, 1968a). The model assumes that performance decreases with list length because more codes are missed in the memory search at longer list lengths. This model also predicts that some of the missed codes should be retrieved if a second recall test is given following the first. Just such an effect was found by Tulving (1967), and its magnitude is predicted accurately by the model. Three successive recall tests were given following a single list presentation and only 50% of the items recalled were recalled on all three tests, even though the actual number recalled remained constant over the three tests.

Item-specific interference is also readily predicted via the search mechanism. Item interference refers to that condition arising when a stimulus originally paired with one response is later paired with a second, different response. In this case two different codes with the same stimulus may be placed in LTS. Thus, the amount of proactive or retroactive interference will depend upon the number of times the wrong code is examined and accepted prior to the correct code. In particular, the degree of temporal ordering in the search will affect the relative amounts of proactive and retroactive effects. That is, the greater the degree that the search is ordered temporally backwards from the most recent item, the less proactive and the greater retroactive effect is predicted. The reasoning is similar to that in the previous paragraph for nonspecific effects. This rather simple view of interference is complicated by at least two factors. First, if *S* is aware that he will eventually be tested for both responses, he may link them in nearby codes, or in a single code, and thereby reduce interference effects (Dallet & D'Andrea, 1965). Second, when the first response is changed, *S* may tag the first code with the information that the response is now wrong. If the first code is later recovered during search, then this information will enable him to inhibit an intrusion and continue the search; an effect like this was found by Shiffrin (1968).

We might ask how this view of interference phenomena compares with traditional theories such as the various "two-factor" interference theories (Melton & Irwin, 1940; Postman, 1961; Underwood, 1957). In a number of respects, the present system differs sharply with the traditional views; for example, in the assumption of a permanent store. It might be expected in the present framework, where memory is permanent, that interference effects which appear under one form of test (say recall) would be reduced under less stringent tests (say recognition) whenever the less stringent test succeeds in making both the old and new codes available. Evidence of this sort has been found by McGovern (1964). Note that the present search system does not necessitate the introduction of such processes as proactive and retroactive inhibition and spontaneous recovery, each with associated changes over time. The effects accounted for by these processes are easy to handle within the search framework, at least in continuous tasks of the type presented in Figure 2. In list-structured tasks, however, there is room for considerable complication, in that learning of lists allows for organization and retrieval schemes based on the list as a whole. Thus, when the first-list responses to stimuli are all changed in a second list, the organizational strategy or the retrieval scheme, (in the present terms, the "directed" search component) may be the mechanism which is disturbed, and it may be this disturbance which is described by the traditional interference theories. Indeed, there is evidence from list-structured tasks that interference effects found over lists as a whole may *not* be related to individual stimulus-response assignments within those lists (DaPolito, 1966; Greeno, 1967). In any event, when quantitative models derived from the present theory have been applied to data (Atkinson & Shiffrin, 1968a; Shiffrin, 1968), the search scheme outlined here handled forgetting and interference effects in a parsimonious and accurate manner.

Intrusions

Another useful feature of the model is its natural prediction of intrusions, and of variations in intrusion rates over differing conditions. In a paired-associate task, an intrusion occurs when the response contained in an *i* code is recovered and emitted. Actually, the intrusion process has not yet been specified clearly, since both the probability of being in the examination subset and the probability of accepting the recovered response will be smaller for an *i* code than a *c* code containing an equal amount of information. It may be assumed that the likelihood of an *i* code being in the examination subset will be a function of its similarity to the test stimulus, since storage is carried out primarily on the basis of stimulus information. The probability of accepting an *i* code as being correct will similarly depend upon the generalization from the test stimulus to the stimulus information encoded in the *i* code. Given that the *i* code is examined and accepted, however, the probability that a response will be recovered and emitted should depend directly upon the response information encoded, just as for a *c* code. The above statements allow intrusion probabilities to be predicted for various conditions. In the situation of Figure 2, for example, an increase in intrusions will be predicted over the course of the session (since the number of *i* codes in the examination subset on tests during the course of the session will increase). This increase has been found in such a task, and a model based on the present theory predicts the increase accurately (Shiffrin, 1968).

Another phenomenon predicted by the theory is that of second-guessing, where second-guessing refers to the giving of a second response after *S* has been told that his first response is incorrect. A variety of assumptions can be made about this process, the simplest of which postulates that *S* continues his search of the examination subset from the point where the intrusion occurred. This assumption predicts that the level of second-guessing will be above chance, an effect found by Binford and Gettys (1965). If the search is temporally ordered to any degree, then strong predictions can be made concerning the second-guessing rate depending upon whether the response given in error was paired in the sequence with a stimulus occurring before or after the tested stimulus (assuming that the task utilizes a set of unique responses). In fact, examination of this effect is one method of determining the temporal characteristics of the search.

Latency of *Responses*

Another variable which may be predicted from the theory in a straightforward way is the latency of responses. The basic assumption requires latency to be a monotonic increasing function of the number of images examined before a response is emitted. Among the implications of this assumption are the following. Latencies of correct responses should increase with increases in the number of intervening items. This prediction holds whenever there is some temporal component to the search, or whenever the number of items preceding the tested item is large. If the reasonable assumption is made that codes containing more information are examined earlier in the search, then a decrease in correct response latency is expected as the number of reinforcements increase, since the item will gain stored information over reinforcements and therefore tend to be examined earlier in the search. This effect has been found by Rumelhart (1967) and Shiffrin (1968) in a continuous paired-associate task. In general, any manipulation designed to vary the number of codes examined, whether by instructions, by organization of the presented material, or by other means should affect the response latencies in a specifiable way.

Recognition and Recall

In terms of the present system the search proceeds in a similar manner whether recognition or recall is the mode of test; the difference lies in the size of the examination subset in the two cases. Once information is recovered from LTS, however, the decision process involved in response generation may be somewhat different for recognition and recall. In a paired-associate design, the search will begin with an attempted recognition of the stimulus, with the decision whether to continue the search dependent upon a positive stimulus recognition (Martin, 1967). Hypotheses which ascribe different retrieval mechanisms for recognition and recall are not necessary. In both recognition and recall the presented stimulus will be sorted into an LTS area, and a search initiated there. In the case of recognition, this search can be quite limited, perhaps consisting of an examination of a single image. In the case of recall, the stimulus may be recognized with little search needed, but the necessity for recovering the response may entail a larger search, although "larger" might imply only examination of two to five additional items (Shiffrin, 1968).

CONCLUSIONS

The theory outlined here is descriptive; we have attempted to present a theory of memory in fairly general terms and to demonstrate for certain commonly studied variables how the theory can be applied. It is beyond the scope of this paper to present specific quantitative models that follow from the general theory and apply them to data, but such models have been set forth elsewhere and applied successfully: in continuous paired-associate learning experiments where the variables examined included the number of intervening items, rankings of responses, second-guessing, proactive interference effects, intrusions, and latencies (Shiffrin, 1968); in free-verbal recall where the variables examined included list length and presentation time (Atkinson & Shiffrin, 1968a); and in paired-associate memory tasks where the variables include list length, confidence ratings, and response times (Atkinson & Shiffrin, 1965; Phillips, Shiffrin, & Atkinson, 1967). Despite these successes, we wish to emphasize that the theory is still in an early formative stage, and awaits application to a wider range of problems. For example, it is not yet known whether the theory can be extended in an elegant way to account quantitatively for the interference phenomena observed in a typical list-structured task. Whatever the fate of such applications, the present theory serves the purpose of providing a general framework within which many of the specific quantitative models known to the authors may be placed, including all of our own work. In addition, we hope that this report will lead to a more detailed consideration of memory input and output mechanisms, especially the memory-search process.

REFERENCES

Atkinson, R. C., Brelsford, J. W., Jr., & Shiffrin, R. M. Multiprocess models for memory with applications to a continuous presentation task. *Journal of Mathematical Psychology,* 1967, 4, 277-300.

Atkinson, R. C., & Shiffrin, R. M. Mathematical models for memory and learning. Technical Report 79, Institute for Mathematical Studies in the Social Sciences, Stanford University, 1965. (Republished: D. P. Kimble (Ed.), *Proceedings of the third conference on learning, remembering and forgetting.* New York: New York Academy of Science, in press.)

Atkinson, R. C., & Shiffrin, R. M. Human memory: A proposed system and its control processes. In K. W. Spence & J. T. Spence (Eds.), *The psychology of learning and motivation: Advances in research and theory,* Vol. 2. New York: Academic Press, 1968. (a)

Atkinson, R. C., & Shiffrin, R. M. Some speculations on storage and retrieval processes in long-term memory. Technical Report 127, Institute for Mathematical Studies in the Social Sciences, Stanford University, 1968. (b)

Bernbach, H. A. Decision processes in memory. *Psychological Review,* 1967, 74, 462-480.

Binford, J. R., & Gettys, C. Nonstationarity in paired-associate learning as indicated by a second guess procedure. *Journal of Mathematical Psychology,* 1965, 2, 190-195.

Bjork, A. Learning and short-term retention of paired-associates in relation to specific sequences of interpresentation intervals. Technical Report 106, Institute for Mathematical Studies in the Social Sciences, Stanford University, 1966.

Bousfield, W. A., & Cohen, B. H. Clustering in recall as a function of the number of word-categories in stimulus-word lists. *Journal of General Psychology,* 1956, 54, 95-106.

Bower, G. H. A multicomponent theory of the memory trace. In K. W. Spence & J. T. Spence (Eds.), *The psychology of learning and motivation.* Vol. 1. New York: Academic Press, 1967.

Brelsford, J. W., Jr., & Atkinson, R. C. Short-term memory as a function of rehearsal procedures. *Journal of Verbal Learning and Verbal Behavior,* 1968, 7, 730-736.

Brelsford, J. W., Jr., Shiffrin, R. M., & Atkinson, R. C. Multiple reinforcement effects in short-term memory. *The British Journal of Mathematical and Statistical Psychology,* 1968, 21, 1-19.

Cofer, C. N. On some factors in the organizational characteristics of free recall. *American Psychologist,* 1965, 20, 261-272.

Cohen, B. H. Recall of categorized word lists. *Journal of Experimental Psychology,* 1963, 66, 227-234.

Dallet, K. M., & D'Andrea, L. Mediation instructions versus unlearning instructions in the A-B, A-C paradigm. *Journal of Experimental Psychology,* 1965, 69, 460-466.

DaPolito, F. J. Proactive effects with independent retrieval of competing responses. Unpublished doctoral dissertation, Indiana University, 1966.

Deese, J. *The structure of associations in language and thought,* Baltimore: Johns Hopkins University Press, 1966.

Estes, W. K. The statistical approach to learning theory. In S. Koch (Ed.), *Psychology: A study of a science.* Vol. 2. New York: McGraw-Hill, 1959.

Feigenbaum, E. A. Information processing and memory. In *Proceedings of the fifth Berkeley symposium on mathematical statistics and probability, 1966.* Vol. IV. Berkeley: University of California Press, 1966.

Greeno, J. G. Some attempts to locate associative information. Technical Report, Department of Psychology, Indiana University, 1967.

Harley, W. F., Jr. The effect of monetary incentive in paired-associate learning using an absolute method. *Psychonomic Science,* 1965, 3, 141-142.

Hellyer, S. Supplementary report: Frequency of stimulus presentation and short-term decrement in recall. *Journal of Experimental Psychology,* 1962, 64, 650.

Hintzman, D. L. Explorations with a discrimination net model for paired-associate learning. *Journal of Mathematical Psychology,* 1968, 5, 123-162.

Keppel, G. Retroactive and proactive inhibition. In T. R. Dixon & D. L. Horton (Eds.), *Verbal behavior and general behavior theory,* Englewood Cliffs, N. J.: Prentice-Hall, 1968.

Kintsch, W. Memory and decision aspects of recognition learning. *Psychological Review,* 1967, 74, 496-504.

McGovern, J. B. Extinction of associations in four transfer paradigms. *Psychological Monographs,* 1964, 78 (16, Whole No. 593).

Mandler, G. Association and organization: Facts, fancies, and theories. In T. R. Dixon & D. L. Horton (Eds.), *Verbal behavior and general behavior theory.* Englewood Cliffs, N. J.: Prentice-Hall, 1968.

Martin, E. Stimulus recognition in aural paired-associate learning. *Journal of Verbal Learning and Verbal Behavior,* 1967, 6, 272-276.

Melton, A. W. Implications of short-term memory for a general theory of memory. *Journal of Verbal Learning and Verbal Behavior,* 1963, 2, 1-21.

Melton, A. W., & Irwin, J. M. The influence of degree of interpolated learning on retroactive inhibition and the overt transfer of specific responses. *American Journal of Psychology,* 1940, 53, 173-203.

Millward, R. An all-or-none model for noncorrection routines with elimination of incorrect responses. *Journal of Mathematical Psychology,* 1964, 1, 392-404.

Murdock, B. B., Jr. The serial position effect of free recall. *Journal of Experimental Psychology,* 1962, 64, 482-488.

Norman, D. A. Toward a theory of memory and attention. *Psychological Review,* 1968, 75, 522-536.

Osgood, C. E. Psycholinguistics. In S. Koch (Ed.), *Psychology: A study of a science.* New York: McGraw-Hill, 1963.

Phillips, J. L., Shiffin, R. M., & Atkinson, R. C. Effects of list length on short-term memory. *Journal of Verbal Learning and Verbal Behavior,* 1967, 6, 303-311.

Pollio, H. R. *The structural basis of word association behavior.* The Hague: Mouton, 1966.

Postman, L. The present status of interference theory. In C. N. Cofer (Ed.), *Verbal learning and verbal behavior.* New York: McGraw-Hill, 1961.

Rumelhart, D. E. The effects of interpresentation intervals in a continuous paired-associate task. Technical Report 116, Institute for Mathematical Studies in the Social Sciences, Stanford University, 1967.

Runquist, W. N., & Farley, F. H. The use of mediators in the learning of verbal paired-associates. *Journal of Verbal Learning and Verbal Behavior,* 1964, 3, 280-285.

Schnorr, J., & Atkinson, R. C. Repetition versus imagery instructions in the short- and long-term retention of paired associates. *Psychonomic Science,* 1969, in press.

Shiffrin, R. M. Search and retrieval processes in long-term memory. Technical Report 137, Institute for Mathematical Studies in the Social Sciences, Stanford University, 1968.

Sperling, G. The information available in brief visual presentations. *Psychological Monographs,* 1960, 74 (11, Whole No. 498).

Thompson, W. J. Recall of paired-associate items as a function of interpolated pairs of different types. *Psychonomic Science,* 1967, 9, 629-630.

Tulving, E. Subjective organization in free recall of 'unrelated' words. *Psychological Review,* 1962, 69, 344-354.

Tulving, E. The effects of presentation and recall of material in free-recall learning. *Journal of Verbal Learning and Verbal Behavior,* 1967, 6, 175-184.

Underwood, B. J. Interference and forgetting. *Psychological Review,* 1957, 64, 49-60.

Underwood, B. J. Stimulus selection in verbal learning. In C. N. Cofer & B. S. Musgrave (Eds.), *Verbal behavior and learning: Problems and processes.* New York: McGraw-Hill, 1963.

Wickelgren, W. A., & Norman, D. A. Strength models and serial position in short-term recognition memory. *Journal of Mathematical Psychology,* 1966, 3, 316-347.

(Received February 2, 1968)

FOOTNOTES

[1.] Preparation of this article was supported by a grant from the National Aeronautics and Space Administration, and is an outgrowth of ideas first developed in two earlier reports (Atkinson & Shiffrin, 1968b; Shiffrin, 1968). This paper, in combination with papers by Atkinson and Shiffrin (1965, 1968a), represents an attempt to formulate a general schema within which to analyze memory and learning.

[2.] Now at Indiana University. Requests for reprints should be sent to Richard C. Atkinson, Institute for Mathematical Studies in the Social Sciences, Ventura Hall, Stanford University, Stanford, California, 94305.

21 'Superstition' in the Pigeon

B. F. Skinner, Indiana University

First published in *Journal of Experimental Psychology,* 38, 168-172 • Manuscript received June 5, 1947

To say that a reinforcement is contingent upon a response may mean nothing more than that it follows the response. It may follow because of some mechanical connection or because of the mediation of another organism; but conditioning takes place presumably because of the temporal relation only, expressed in terms of the order and proximity of response and reinforcement. Whenever we present a state of affairs which is known to be reinforcing at a given drive, we must suppose that conditioning takes place, even though we have paid no attention to the behavior of the organism in making the presentation. A simple experiment demonstrates this to be the case.

A pigeon is brought to a stable state of hunger by reducing it to 75 percent of its weight when well fed. It is put into an experimental cage for a few minutes each day. A food hopper attached to the cage may be swung into place so that the pigeon can eat from it. A solenoid and a timing relay hold the hopper in place for five sec. at each reinforcement.

If a clock is now arranged to present the food hopper at regular intervals *with no reference whatsoever to the bird's behavior,* operant conditioning usually takes place. In six out of eight cases the resulting responses were so clearly defined that two observers could agree perfectly in counting instances. One bird was conditioned to turn counter-clockwise about the cage, making two or three turns between reinforcements. Another repeatedly thrust its head into one of the upper corners of the cage. A third developed a 'tossing' response, as if placing its head beneath an invisible bar and lifting it repeatedly. Two birds developed a pendulum motion of the head and body, in which the head was extended forward and swung from right to left with a sharp movement followed by a somewhat slower return. The body generally followed the movement and a few steps might be taken when it was extensive. Another bird was conditioned to make incomplete pecking or brushing movements directed toward but not touching the floor. None of these responses appeared in any noticeable strength during adaptation to the cage or until the food hopper was periodically presented. In the remaining two cases, conditioned responses were not clearly marked.

The conditioning process is usually obvious. The bird happens to be executing some response as the hopper appears; as a result it tends to repeat this response. If the interval before the next presentation is not so great that extinction takes place, a second 'contingency' is probable. This strengthens the response still further and subsequent reinforcement becomes more probable. It is true that some responses go unreinforced and [p. 169] some reinforcements appear when the response has not just been made, but the net result is the development of a considerable state of strength.

With the exception of the counter-clockwise turn, each response was almost always repeated in the same part of the cage, and it generally involved an orientation toward some feature of the cage. The effect of the reinforcement was to condition the bird to respond to some aspect of the environment rather than merely to execute a series of movements. All responses came to be repeated rapidly between reinforcements - typically five or six times in 15 sec.

The effect appears to depend upon the rate of reinforcement. In general, we should expect that the shorter the intervening interval, the speedier and more marked the conditioning. One reason is that the pigeon's behavior becomes more diverse as time passes after reinforcement. A hundred photographs, each taken two sec. after withdrawal of the hopper, would show fairly uniform behavior. The bird would be in the same part of the cage, near the hopper, and probably oriented toward the wall where the hopper has disappeared or turning to one side or the other. A hundred photographs taken after 10 sec., on the other hand, would find the bird in various parts of the cage responding to many different aspects of the environment. The sooner a second reinforcement appears, therefore, the more likely it is that the second reinforced response will be similar to the first, and also that they will both have one of a few standard forms. In the limiting case of a very brief interval the behavior to be expected would be holding the head toward the opening through which the magazine has disappeared.

Another reason for the greater effectiveness of short intervals is that the longer the interval, the greater the number of intervening responses emitted without reinforcement. The resulting extinction cancels the effect of an occasional reinforcement.

According to this interpretation the effective interval will depend upon the rate of conditioning and the rate of extinction, and will therefore vary with the drive and also presumably between species. Fifteen sec. is a very effective interval at the drive level indicated above. One min. is much less so. When a response has once been set up, however, the interval can be lengthened. In one case it was extended to two min., and a high rate of responding was maintained with no sign of weakening. In another case, many hours of responding were observed with an interval of one min. between reinforcements.

In the latter case, the response showed a noticeable drift in topography. It began as a sharp movement of the head from the middle position to the left. This movement became more energetic, and eventually the whole body of the bird turned in the same direction, and a step or two would be taken. After many hours, the stepping response became the predominant feature. The bird made a well defined hopping step from the right to the left foot, meanwhile turning its head and body to the left as before.

When the stepping response became strong, it was possible to obtain a mechanical record by putting the bird on a large tambour directly connected with a small tambour which made a delicate electric contact each time [p. 170] stepping took place. By watching the bird and listening to the sound of the recorder it was possible to confirm the fact that a fairly authentic record was being made. It was possible for the bird to hear the recorder at each step, but this was, of course, in no way correlated with feeding. The record obtained when the magazine was presented once every min. resembles in every respect the characteristic curve for the pigeon under periodic reinforcement of a standard selected response. A well marked temporal discrimination develops. The bird does not respond immediately after eating, but when 10 or 15 or even 20 sec. have elapsed it begins to respond rapidly and continues until the reinforcement is received.

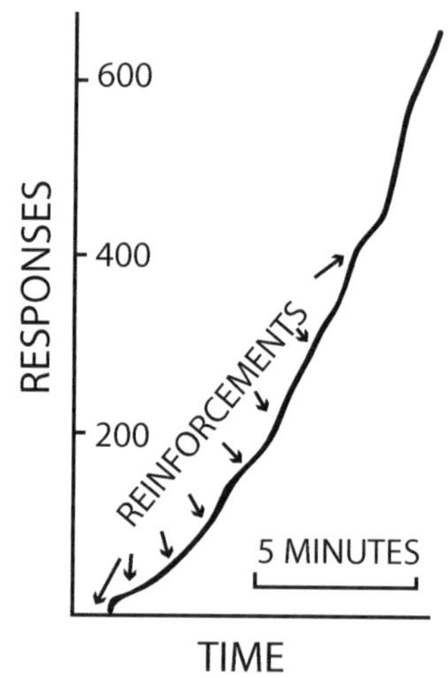

Fig. 1. 'Reconditioning' of a superstitious response after extinction. The response of hopping from right to left had been thoroughly extinguished just before the record was taken. The arrows indicate the automatic presentation of food at one-min. intervals without reference to the pigeon's behavior.

In this case it was possible to record the 'extinction' of the response when the clock was turned off and the magazine was no longer presented at any time. The bird continued to respond with its characteristic side to side hop. More than 10,000 responses were recorded before 'extinction' had reached the point at which few if any responses were made during a 10 or 15 min. interval. When the clock was again started, the periodic presentation of the magazine (still without any connection whatsoever with the bird's behavior) brought out a typical curve for reconditioning after periodic reinforcement, shown in Fig. 1. The record had been essentially horizontal for 20 min. prior to the beginning of this curve. The first reinforcement had some slight effect and the second a greater effect. There is a smooth positive acceleration in rate as the bird returns to the rate of responding which prevailed when it was reinforced every min.

When the response was again extinguished and the periodic presentation of food then resumed, a different response was picked up. This consisted of a progressive walking response in which the bird moved about the cage. [p. 171] The response of hopping from side to side never reappeared and could not, of course, be obtained deliberately without making the reinforcement contingent upon the behavior.

The experiment might be said to demonstrate a sort of superstition. The bird behaves as if there were a causal relation between its behavior and the presentation of food, although such a relation is lacking. There are many analogies in human behavior. Rituals for changing one's luck at cards are good examples. A few accidental connections between a ritual and favorable consequences suffice to set up and maintain the behavior in spite of many unreinforced instances. The bowler who has released a ball down the alley but continues to behave as if he were controlling it by twisting and turning his arm and shoulder is another case in point. These behaviors have, of course, no real effect upon one's luck or upon a ball half way down an alley, just as in the present case the food would appear as often if the pigeon did nothing - or, more strictly speaking, did something else.

It is perhaps not quite correct to say that conditioned behavior has been set up without any previously determined contingency whatsoever. We have appealed to a uniform sequence of responses in the behavior of the pigeon to obtain an over-all net contingency. When we arrange a clock to present food every 15 sec., we are in effect basing our reinforcement upon a limited set of responses which frequently occur 15 sec. after reinforcement. When a response has been strengthened (and this may result from one reinforcement), the setting of the clock implies an even more restricted contingency. Something of the same sort is true of the bowler. It is not quite correct to say that there is no connection between his twisting and turning and the course taken by the ball at the far end of the alley. The connection was established before the ball left the bowler's hand, but since both the path of the ball and the behavior of the bowler are determined, some relation survives. The subsequent behavior of the bowler may have no effect upon the ball, but the behavior of the ball has an effect upon the bowler. The contingency, though not perfect, is enough to maintain the behavior in strength. The particular form of the behavior adopted by the bowler is due to induction from responses in which there is actual contact with the ball. It is clearly a movement appropriate to changing the ball's direction. But this does not invalidate the comparison, since we are not concerned with what response is selected but with why it persists in strength. In rituals for changing luck the inductive strengthening of a particular form of behavior is generally absent. The behavior of the pigeon in this experiment is of the latter sort, as the variety of responses obtained from different pigeons indicates. Whether there is any unconditioned [p. 172] behavior in the pigeon appropriate to a given effect upon the environment is under investigation.

The results throws some light on incidental behavior observed in experiments in which a discriminative stimulus is frequently presented. Such a stimulus has reinforcing value and can set up superstitious behavior. A pigeon will often develop some response such as turning, twisting, pecking near the locus of the discriminative stimulus, flapping its wings, etc. In much of the work to date in this field the interval between presentations of the discriminative stimulus has been one min. and many of these superstitious responses are short-lived. Their appearance as the result of accidental correlations with the presentation of the stimulus is unmistakable.

22 The Myth of Mental Illness

By Thomas S. Szasz (1960)

First published in *American Psychologist,* 15, 113-118

My aim in this essay is to raise the question "Is there such a thing as mental illness?" and to argue that there is not. Since the notion of mental illness is extremely widely used nowadays, inquiry into the ways in which this term is employed would seem to be especially indicated. Mental illness, of course, is not literally a "thing" - or physical object - and hence it can "exist" only in the same sort of way in which other theoretical concepts exist. Yet, familiar theories are in the habit of posing, sooner or later - at least to those who come to believe in them - as "objective truths" (or "facts"). During certain historical periods, explanatory conceptions such as deities, witches, and microorganisms appeared not only as theories but as self-evident *causes* of a vast number of events. I submit that today mental illness is widely regarded in a somewhat similar fashion, that is, as the cause of innumerable diverse happenings. As an antidote to the complacent use of the notion of mental illness - whether as a self-evident phenomenon, theory, or cause - let us ask this question: What is meant when it is asserted that someone is mentally ill?

In what follows I shall describe briefly the main uses to which the concept of mental illness has been put. I shall argue that this notion has outlived whatever usefulness it might have had and that it now functions merely as a convenient myth.

MENTAL ILLNESS AS A SIGN OF BRAIN DISEASE

The notion of mental illness derives it main support from such phenomena as syphilis of the brain or delirious conditions - intoxications, for instance - in which persons are known to manifest various peculiarities or disorders of thinking and behavior. Correctly speaking, however, these are diseases of the brain, not of the mind. According to one school of thought, *all* so-called mental illness is of this type. The assumption is made that some neurological defect, perhaps a very subtle one, will ultimately be found for all the disorders of thinking and behavior. Many contemporary psychiatrists, physicians, and other scientists hold this view. This position implies that people *cannot* have troubles - expressed in what are *now called* "mental illnesses" - because of differences in personal needs, opinions, social aspirations, values, and so on. *All problems in living* are attributed to physicochemical processes which in due time will be discovered by medical research.

"Mental illnesses" are thus regarded as basically no different than all other diseases (that is, of the body). The only difference, in this view, between mental and bodily diseases is that the former, affecting the brain, manifest themselves by means of mental symptoms; whereas the latter, affecting other organ systems (for example, the skin, liver, etc.), manifest themselves by means of symptoms referable to those parts of the body. This view rests on and expresses what are, in my opinion, two fundamental errors.

In the first place, what central nervous system symptoms would correspond to a skin eruption or a fracture? It would not be some emotion or complex bit of behavior. Rather, it would be blindness or a paralysis of some part of the body. The crux of the matter is that a disease of the brain, analogous to a disease of the skin or bone, is a neurological defect, and not a problem in living. For example, a *defect* in a person's visual field may be satisfactorily explained by correlating it with certain definite lesions in the nervous system. On the other hand, a person's *belief* - whether this be a belief in Christianity, in Communism, or in the *idea* that his internal organs are "rotting" and that his body is, in fact, already "dead" - cannot be explained by a defect or disease of the nervous system. Explanations of this sort of occurrence - assuming that one is interested in the belief itself and does not regard it simply as a "symptom" or expression of something else that is more interesting - must be sought along different lines.

The second error in regarding complex psycho-social behavior, consisting of communications about ourselves and the world about us, as mere symptoms [p. 114] of neurological functioning is *epistemological.* In other words, it is an error pertaining not to any mistakes in observation or reasoning, as such, but rather to the way in which we organize and express our knowledge. In the present case, the error lies in making a symmetrical dualism between mental and physical (or bodily) symptoms, a dualism which is merely a habit of speech and to which no known observations can be found to correspond. Let us see if this is so. In medical practice, when we speak of physical disturbances, we mean either signs (for example, a fever) or symptoms (for example, pain). We speak of mental symptoms, on the other hand, when we refer to a patient's *communications about himself, others, and the world about him.* He might state that he is Napoleon or that he is being persecuted by the Communists. These would be considered mental symptoms only if the observer believed that the patient was not Napoleon or that he was not being persecuted[sic] by the Communists. This makes it apparent that the statement that "X is a mental symptom" involves rendering a judgment. The judgment entails, moreover, a covert comparison or matching of the patient's ideas, concepts, or beliefs with those of the observer and the society in which they live. The notion of mental symptom is therefore inextricably tied to the *social* (including ethical) *context* in which it is made in much the same way as the notion of bodily symptom is tied to an *anatomical* and *genetic context* (Szasz, 1957a, 1957b).

To sum up what has been said thus far: I have tried to show that for those who regard mental symptoms as signs of brain disease, the concept of mental illness is unnecessary and misleading. For what they mean is that people so labeled suffer from diseases of the brain; and, if that is what they mean, it would seem better for the sake of clarity to say that and not something else.

MENTAL ILLNESS AS A NAME FOR PROBLEMS IN LIVING

The term "mental illness" is widely used to describe something which is very different than a disease of the brain. Many people today take it for granted that living is an arduous process. Its hardship for modern man, moreover, derives not so much from a struggle for biological survival as from the stresses and strains inherent in the social intercourse of complex human personalities. In this context, the notion of mental illness is used to identify or describe some feature of an individual's so-called personality. Mental illness - as a deformity of the personality, so to speak - is then regarded as the cause of the human disharmony. It is implicit in this view that social intercourse between people is regarded as something *inherently harmonious,* its disturbance being due solely to the presence of "mental illness" in many people. This is obviously fallacious reasoning, for it makes the abstraction "mental illness" into a cause, even though this abstraction was created in the first place to serve only as a shorthand expression for certain types of human behavior. It now becomes necessary to ask: "What kinds of behavior are regarded as indicative of mental illness, and by whom?"

The concept of illness, whether bodily or mental, implies *deviation from some clearly defined norm.* In the case of physical illness, the norm is the structural and functional integrity of the human body. Thus, although the desirability of physical health, as such, is an ethical value, what health is can be stated in anatomical and physiological terms. What is the norm deviation from which is regarded as mental illness? This question cannot be easily answered. But whatever this norm might be, we can be certain of only one thing: namely, that it is a norm that must be stated in terms of *psycho-social, ethical,* and *legal* concepts. For example, notions such as "excessive repression" or "acting out an unconscious impulse" illustrate the use of psychological concepts for judging (so-called) mental health and illness. The idea that chronic hostility, vengefulness, or divorce are indicative of mental illness would be illustrations of the use of ethical norms (that is, the desirability of love, kindness, and a stable marriage relationship). Finally, the widespread psychiatric opinion that only a mentally ill person would commit homicide illustrates the use of a legal concept as a norm of mental health. The norm from which deviation is measured whenever one speaks of a mental illness is a *psycho-social and ethical one*. Yet, the remedy is sought in terms of *medical* measures which - it is hoped and assumed - are free from wide differences of ethical value. The definition of the disorder and the terms in which its remedy are sought are therefore at serious odds with one another. The practical significance of this covert conflict between the alleged nature of the defect and the remedy can hardly be exaggerated.

Having identified the norms used to measure [p. 115] deviations in cases of mental illness, we will now turn to the question: "Who defines the norms and hence the deviation?" Two basic answers may be offered: (a) It may be the person himself (that is, the patient) who decides that he deviates from a norm. For example, an artist may believe that he suffers from a work inhibition; and he may implement this conclusion by seeking help for himself from a psychotherapist. (b) It may be someone other than the patient who decides that the latter is deviant (for example, relatives, physicians, legal authorities, society generally, etc.). In such a case a psychiatrist may be hired by others to do something to the patient in order to correct the deviation.

These considerations underscore the importance of asking the question "Whose agent is the psychiatrist?" and of giving a candid answer to it (Szasz, 1956, 1958). The psychiatrist (psychologist or nonmedical psychotherapist), it now develops, may be the agent of the patient, of the relatives, of the school, of the military services, of a business organization, of a court of law, and so forth. In speaking of the psychiatrist as the agent of these persons or organizations, it is not implied that his values concerning norms, or his ideas and aims concerning the proper nature of remedial action, need to coincide exactly with those of his employer. For example, a patient in individual psychotherapy may believe that his salvation lies in a new marriage; his psychotherapist need not share this hypothesis. As the patient's agent, however, he must abstain from bringing social or legal force to bear on the patient which would prevent him from putting his beliefs into action. If his *contract* is with the patient, the psychiatrist (psychotherapist) may disagree with him or stop his treatment; but he cannot engage others to obstruct the patient's aspirations. Similarly, if a psychiatrist is engaged by a court to determine the sanity of a criminal, he need not fully share the legal authorities' values and intentions in regard to the criminal and the means available for dealing with him. But the psychiatrist is expressly barred from stating, for example, that it is not the criminal who is "insane" but the men who wrote the law on the basis of which the very actions that are being judged are regarded as "criminal." Such an opinion could be voiced, of course, but not in a courtroom, and not by a psychiatrist who makes it his practice to assist the court in performing its daily work.

To recapitulate: In actual contemporary social usage, the finding of a mental illness is made by establishing a deviance in behavior from certain psychosocial, ethical, or legal norms. The judgment may be made, as in medicine, by the patient, the physician (psychiatrist), or others. Remedial action, finally, tends to be sought in a therapeutic - or covertly medical - framework, thus creating a situation in which *psychosocial, ethical,* and/or *legal deviations* are claimed to be correctible by (so-called) *medical action*. Since medical action is designed to correct only medical deviations, it seems logically absurd to expect that it will help solve problems whose very existence had been defined and established on nonmedical grounds. I think that these considerations may be fruitfully applied to the present use of tranquilizers and, more generally, to what might be expected of drugs of whatever type in regard to the amelioration or solution of problems in human living.

THE ROLE OF ETHICS IN PSYCHIATRY

Anything that people *do* - in contrast to things that *happen* to them (Peters, 1958) - takes place in a context of value. In this broad sense, no human activity is devoid of ethical implications. When the values underlying certain activities are widely shared, those who participate in their pursuit may lose sight of them altogether. The discipline of medicine, both as a pure science (for example, research) and as a technology (for example, therapy), contains many ethical considerations and judgments. Unfortunately, these are often denied, minimized, or merely kept out of focus;

for the ideal of the medical profession as well as of the people whom it serves seems to be having a system of medicine (allegedly) free of ethical value. This sentimental notion is expressed by such things as the doctor's willingness to treat and help patients irrespective of their religious or political beliefs, whether they are rich or poor, etc. While there may be some grounds for this belief - albeit it is a view that is not impressively true even in these regards - the fact remains that ethical considerations encompass a vast range of human affairs. By making the practice of medicine neutral in regard to some specific issues of value need not, and cannot, mean that it can be kept free from all such values. The practice of medicine is intimately tied to ethics; and the first thing that we must do, it seems to me, is to try to make this clear and explicit. I shall [p. 116] let this matter rest here, for it does not concern us specifically in this essay. Lest there be any vagueness, however, about how or where ethics and medicine meet, let me remind the reader of such issues as birth control, abortion, suicide, and euthanasia as only a few of the major areas of current ethicomedical controversy.

Psychiatry, I submit, is very much more intimately tied to problems of ethics than is medicine. I use the word "psychiatry" here to refer to that contemporary discipline which is concerned with *problems in living* (and not with diseases of the brain, which are problems for neurology). Problems in human relations can be analyzed, interpreted, and given meaning only within given social and ethical contexts. Accordingly, it *does* make a difference - arguments to the contrary notwithstanding - what the psychiatrist's socioethical orientations happen to be; for these will influence his ideas on what is wrong with the patient, what deserves comment or interpretation, in what possible directions change might be desirable, and so forth. Even in medicine proper, these factors play a role, as for instance, in the divergent orientations which physicians, depending on their religious affiliations, have toward such things as birth control and therapeutic abortion. Can anyone really believe that a psychotherapist's ideas concerning religious belief, slavery, or other similar issues play no role in his practical work? If they do make a difference, what are we to infer from it? Does it not seem reasonable that we ought to have different psychiatric therapies - each, expressly recognized for the ethical positions which they embody - for, say, Catholics and Jews, religious persons and agnostics, democrats and communists, white supremacists and Negroes, and so on? Indeed, if we look at how psychiatry is actually practiced today (especially in the United States), we find that people do seek psychiatric help in accordance with their social status and ethical beliefs (Hollingshead & Redlich, 1958). This should really not surprise us more than being told that practicing Catholics rarely frequent birth control clinics.

The foregoing position which holds that contemporary psychotherapists deal with problems in living, rather than with mental illnesses and their cures, stands in opposition to a currently prevalent claim, according to which mental illness is just as "real" and "objective" as bodily illness. This is a confusing claim since it is never known exactly what is meant by such words as "real" and "objective." I suspect, however, that what is intended by the proponents of this view is to create the idea in the popular mind that mental illness is some sort of disease entity, like an infection or a malignancy. If this were true, one could *catch* or get a "mental illness," one might have or *harbor* it, one might *transmit* it to others, and finally one could get *rid* of it. In my opinion, there is not a shred of evidence to support this idea. To the contrary, all the evidence is the other way and supports the view that what people now call mental illnesses are for the most part *communications* expressing unacceptable ideas, often framed, moreover, in an unusual idiom. The scope of this essay allows me to do no more than mention this alternative theoretical approach to this problem (Szasz, 1957c).

This is not the place to consider in detail the similarities and differences between bodily and mental illnesses. It shall suffice for us here to emphasize only one important difference between them: namely, that whereas bodily disease refers to public, physicochemical occurrences, the notion of mental illness is used to codify relatively more private, sociopsychological happenings of which the observer (diagnostician) forms a part. In other words, the psychiatrist does not stand *apart* from what he observes, but is, in Harry Stack Sullivan's apt words, a "participant observer." This means that he is *committed* to some picture of what he considers reality - and to what he thinks society considers reality - and he observes and judges the patient's behavior in the light of these considerations. This touches on our earlier observation that the notion of mental symptom itself implies a comparison between observer and observed, psychiatrist and patient. This is so obvious that I may be charged with belaboring trivialities. Let me therefore say once more that my aim in presenting this argument was expressly to criticize and counter a prevailing contemporary tendency to deny the moral aspects of psychiatry (and psychotherapy) and to substitute for them allegedly value-free medical considerations. Psychotherapy, for example, is being widely practiced as though it entailed nothing other than restoring the patient from a state of mental sickness to one of mental health. While it is generally accepted that mental illness has something to do with man's social (or interpersonal) relations, it is paradoxically maintained that problems of values (that is, of ethics) do not [p. 117] arise in this process.[1] Yet, in one sense, much of psychotherapy may revolve around nothing other than the elucidation and weighing of goals and values - many of which may be mutually contradictory - and the means whereby they might best be harmonized, realized, or relinquished.

The diversity of human values and the methods by means of which they may be realized is so vast, and many of them remain so unacknowledged, that they cannot fail but lead to conflicts in human relations. Indeed, to say that human relations at all levels - from mother to child, through husband and wife, to nation and nation - are fraught with stress, strain, and disharmony is, once again, making the obvious explicit. Yet, what may be obvious may be also poorly understood. This I think is the case here. For it seems to me that - at least in our scientific theories of behavior - we have failed to *accept* the simple fact that human relations are inherently fraught with difficulties and that to make them even relatively harmonious requires much patience and hard work. I submit that the idea of mental illness is now being put to work to obscure certain difficulties which at present may be inherent - not that they need be unmodifiable - in the social intercourse of persons. If this is true, the concept functions as a disguise; for instead of calling attention to conflicting human needs, aspirations, and values, the notion of mental illness provides an amoral and impersonal "thing" (an "illness") as an explanation for *problems in living* (Szasz, 1959). We may recall in this connection that not so long ago it was devils and witches who were held responsible for men's problems in social living. The belief in mental illness, as something other than man's trouble in getting along with his fellow man, is the proper heir to the belief in demonology and witchcraft. Mental illness exists or is "real" in exactly the same sense in which witches existed or were "real."

CHOICE, RESPONSIBILITY, AND PSYCHIATRY

While I have argued that mental illnesses do not exist, I obviously did not imply that the social and psychological occurrences to which this label is currently being attached also do not exist. Like the personal and social troubles which people had in the Middle Ages, they are real enough. It is the labels we give them that concerns us and, having labelled them, what we do about them. While I cannot go into the ramified implications of this problem here, it is worth noting that a demonologic conception of problems in living gave rise to therapy along theological lines. Today, a belief in mental illness implies - nay, requires - therapy along medical or psychotherapeutic lines.

What is implied in the line of thought set forth here is something quite different. I do not intend to offer a new conception of "psychiatric illness" nor a new form of "therapy." My aim is more modest and yet also more ambitious. It is to suggest that the phenomena now called mental illnesses be looked at afresh and more simple, that they be removed from the category of illness, and that they be regarded as the expressions of man's struggle with the problem of how he should live. The last mentioned problem is obviously a vast one, its enormity reflecting not only man's inability to cope with his environment, but even more his increasing self-reflectiveness.

By problems in living, then, I refer to that truly explosive chain reaction which began with man's fall from divine grace by partaking of the fruit of the tree of knowledge. Man's awareness of himself and of the world about him seems to be a steadily expanding one, bringing in its wake an ever large, *burden of understanding* (an expression borrowed from Susanne Langer, 1953). *This burden,* then, *is to be expected and must not be misinterpreted.* Our only *rational* means for lightening it is *more understanding,* and appropriate *action* based on such understanding. The main alternative lies in acting as though the burden were not what in fact we perceive it to be and taking refuge in an outmoded theological view of man. In the latter view, man does not fashion his life and much of his world about him, but merely lives out his fate in a world created by superior beings. This may logically lead to pleading nonresponsibility in the face of seemingly unfathomable problems and difficulties. Yet, if man fails to take increasing responsibility for his [p. 118] actions, individually as well as collectively, it seems unlikely that some higher power or being would assume this task and carry this burden for him. Moreover, this seems hardly the proper time in human history for obscuring the issue of man's responsibility for his actions by hiding it behind the skirt of an all-explaining conception of mental illness.

CONCLUSIONS

I have tried to show that the notion of mental illness has outlived whatever usefulness it might have had and that it now functions merely as a convenient myth. As such, it is a true heir to religious myths in general, and to the belief in witchcraft in particular; the role of all these belief-systems was to act as *social tranquilizers*, thus encouraging the hope that mastery of certain specific problems may be achieved by means of substitutive (symbolic-magical) operations. The notion of mental illness thus serves mainly to obscure the everyday fact that life for most people is a continuous struggle, not for biological survival, but for a "place in the sun," "peace of mind," or some other human value. For man aware of himself and of the world about him, once the needs for preserving the body (and perhaps the race) are more or less satisfied, the problem arises as to what he should do with himself. Sustained adherence to the myth of mental illness allows people to avoid facing this problem, believing that mental health, conceived as the absence of mental illness, automatically insures the making of right and safe choices in one's conduct of life. But the facts are all the other way. It is the making of good choices in life that others regard, retrospectively, as good mental health!

The myth of mental illness encourages us, moreover, to believe in its logical corollary: that social intercourse would be harmonious, satisfying, and the secure basis of a "good life" were it not for the disrupting influences of mental illness or "psychopathology." The potentiality for universal human happiness, in this form at least, seems to me but another example of the I-wish-it-were-true type of fantasy. I do [*] believe that human happiness or well-being on a hitherto unimaginably large scale, and not just for a select few, is possible. This goal could be achieved, however, only at the cost of many men, and not just a few being willing and able to tackle their personal, social, and ethical conflicts. This means having the courage and integrity to forego waging battles on false fronts, finding solutions for substitute problems - for instance, fighting the battle of stomach acid and chronic fatigue instead of facing up to a marital conflict.

Our adversaries are not demons, witches, fate, or mental illness. We have no enemy whom we can fight, exorcise, or dispel by "cure." What we do have are *problems in living* - whether these be biologic, economic, political, or sociopsychological. In this essay I was concerned only with problems belonging in the last mentioned category, and within this group mainly with those pertaining to moral values. The field to which modern psychiatry addresses itself is vast, and I made no effort to encompass it all. My argument was limited to the proposition that mental illness is a myth, whose function it is to disguise and thus render more palatable the bitter pill of moral conflicts in human relations.

REFERENCES

Hollingshead, A. B., & Redlich, F. C. *Social class and mental illness.* New York: Wiley, 1958.

Jones, E. *The life and work of Sigmund Freud.* Vol. III. New York: Basic Books, 1957.

Lancer, S. R. *Philosophy in a new Key.* New York: Mentor Books, 1953.

Peters, R. S. *The concept of motivation.* London: Routledge & Kegan Paul, 1958.

Szasz, T. S. Malingering: "Diagnosis" or social condemnation? *AMA Arch Neurol. Psychiat.*, 1956, **76**, 432-443.

Szasz, T. S. Pain and pleasure: *A study of bodily-feelings.* New York: Basic Books, 1957. (a)

Szasz, T. S. The problem of psychiatric nosology: A contribution to a situational analysis of psychiatric operations. *Amer. J. Psychiat*, 1957, **114**, 405-413. (b)

Szasz, T. S. On the theory of psychoanalytic treatment. *Int. J. Psycho-Anal.*, 1957, **38**, 166-182. (c)

Szasz, T. S. Psychiatry, ethics and the criminal law. *Columbia law Rev.,* 1958, **58**, 183-198.

Szasz, T. S. Moral conflict and psychiatry. *Yale Rev.,* 1959, in press.

FOOTNOTES

[1] Freud went so far as to say that: "I consider ethics to be taken for granted. Actually I have never done a mean thing" (Jones, 1957, p. 247). This surely is a strange thing to say for someone who has studied man as a social being as closely as did Freud. I mention it here to show how the notion of "illness" (in the case of psychoanalysis, "psychopathology," or "mental illness") was used by Freud - and by most of his followers - as a means for classifying certain forms of human behavior as falling within the scope of medicine, and hence (by *fiat*) outside that of ethics!

[*] *Classics Editor's note:* In the original *American Psychologist* text the word "not" appears at this point. Dr. Szasz has informed me, however, that it "was a typo, which [he] corrected when [he] reprinted the piece, e.g., in *Ideology and Insanity*" (personal communication, 2002).

23 Conditioned Emotional Reactions

By John B. Watson and Rosalie Rayner (1920)

First published in *Journal of Experimental Psychology*, 3(1), 1-14

In recent literature various speculations have been entered into concerning the possibility of conditioning various types of emotional response, but direct experimental evidence in support of such a view has been lacking. If the theory advanced by Watson and Morgan [1] to the effect that in infancy the original emotional reaction patterns are few, consisting so far as observed of fear, rage, and love, then there must be some simple method by means of which the range of stimuli which can call out these emotions and their compounds is greatly increased. Otherwise, complexity in adult response could not be accounted for. These authors without adequate experimental evidence advanced the view that this range was increased by means of conditioned reflex factors. It was suggested there that the early home life of the child furnishes a laboratory situation for establishing conditioned emotional responses. The present authors have recently put the whole matter to an experimental test.

Experimental work had been done so far on only one child, Albert B. This infant was reared almost from birth in a hospital environment; his mother was a wet nurse in the Harriet Lane Home for Invalid Children. Albert's life was normal: he was healthy from birth and one of the best developed youngsters ever brought to the hospital, weighing twenty-one pounds at nine months of age. He was on the whole stolid and unemotional. His stability was one of the principal reasons for using him as a subject in this test. We [p.2] felt that we could do him relatively little harm by carrying out such experiments as those outlined below.

At approximately nine months of age we ran him through the emotional tests that have become a part of our regular routine in determining whether fear reactions can be called out by other stimuli than sharp noises and the sudden removal of support. Tests of this type have been described by the senior author in another place.[2] In brief, the infant was confronted suddenly and for the first time successively with a white rat, a rabbit, a dog, a monkey, with masks with and without hair, cotton wool, burning newspapers, etc. A permanent record of Albert's reactions to these objects and situations has been preserved in a motion picture study. Manipulation was the most usual reaction called out. *At no time did this infant ever show fear in any situation.* These experimental records were confirmed by the casual observations of the mother and hospital attendants. No one had ever seen him in a state of fear and rage. The infant practically never cried.

Up to approximately nine months of age we had not tested him with loud sounds. The test to determine whether a fear reaction could be called out by a loud sound was made when he was eight months, twenty-six days of age. The sound was that made by striking a hammer upon a suspended steel bar four feet in length and three-fourths of an inch in diameter. The laboratory notes are as follows:

One of the two experimenters caused the child to turn its head and fixate her moving hand; the other stationed back of the child, struck the steel bar a sharp blow. The child started violently, his breathing was checked and the arms were raised in a characteristic manner. On the second stimulation the same thing occurred, and in addition the lips began to pucker and tremble. On the third stimulation the child broke into a sudden crying fit. This is the first time an emotional situation in the laboratory has produced any fear or even crying in Albert.

[p.3] We had expected just these results on account of our work with other infants brought up under similar conditions. It is worthwhile to call attention to the fact that removal of support (dropping and jerking the blanket upon which the infant was lying) was tried exhaustively upon this infant on the same occasion. It was not effective in producing the fear response. This stimulus is effective in younger children. At what age such stimuli lose their potency in producing fear is not known. Nor is it known whether less placid children ever lose their fear of them. This probably depends upon the training the child gets. It is well known that children eagerly run to be tossed into the air and caught. On the other hand it is equally well known that in the adult fear responses are called out quite clearly by the sudden removal of support, if the individual is walking across a bridge, walking out upon a beam, etc. There is a wide field of study here which is aside from our present point.

The sound stimulus, thus, at nine months of age, gives us the means of testing several important factors. I. Can we condition fear of an animal, e.g., a white rat, by visually presenting it and simultaneously striking a steel bar? II. If such a conditioned emotional response can be established, will there be a transfer to other animals or other objects? III. What is the effect of time upon such conditioned emotional responses? IV. If after a reasonable period such emotional responses have not died out, what laboratory methods can be devised for their removal?

I. The establishment of conditioned emotional responses.

At first there was considerable hesitation upon our part in making the attempt to set up fear reactions experimentally. A certain responsibility attaches to such a procedure. We decided finally to make the attempt, comforting ourselves by the reflection that such attachments would arise anyway as soon as the child left the sheltered environment of the nursery for the rough and tumble of the home. We did not begin this work until Albert was eleven months, three days of age. Before attempting to set up a conditioned response we, as before, put him through all of the regular emotional [p.4] tests. *Not the slightest sign of a fear response was obtained in any situation.*

The steps taken to condition emotional responses are shown in our laboratory notes.

11 Months 3 Days

1. White rat suddenly taken from the basket and presented to Albert. He began to reach for rat with left hand. Just as his hand touched the animal the bar was struck immediately behind his head. The infant jumped violently and fell forward, burying his face in the mattress. He did not cry, however.

2. Just as the right hand touched the rat the bar was again struck. Again the infant jumped violently, fell forward and began to whimper.

In order not to disturb the child too seriously no further tests were given for one week.

11 Months 10 Days

1. Rat presented suddenly without sound. There was steady fixation but no tendency at first to reach for it. The rat was then placed nearer, whereupon tentative reaching movements began with the right hand. When the rat nosed the infant's left hand, the hand was immediately withdrawn. He started to reach for the head of the animal with the forefinger of the left hand, but withdrew it suddenly before contact. It is thus seen that the two joint stimulations given the previous week were not without effect. He was tested with his blocks immediately afterwards to see if they shared in the process of conditioning. He began immediately to pick them up, dropping them, pounding them, etc. In the remainder of the tests the blocks were given frequently to quiet him and to test his general emotional state. They were always removed from sight when the process of conditioning was underway.

2. Joint stimulation with rat and sound. Started, then fell over immediately to right side No crying.[p.5]

3. Joint stimulation. Fell to right side and rested upon hands, with head turned away from rat. No crying.

4. Joint stimulation. Same reaction.

5. Rat suddenly presented alone. Puckered face, whimpered and withdrew body sharply to the left.

6. Joint stimulation. Fell over immediately to right side and began to whimper.

7. Joint stimulation. Started violently and cried, but did not fall over.

8. Rat alone. *The instant the rat was shown the baby began to cry. Almost instantly he turned sharply to the left, fell over on left side, raised himself on all fours and began to crawl away so rapidly that he was caught with difficulty before reaching the edge of the table.*

This was as convincing a case of a completely conditioned fear response as could have been theoretically pictured. In all, seven joint stimulations were given to bring about the complete reaction. It is not unlikely had the sound been of greater intensity or of a more complex clang character that the number of joint stimulations might have been materially reduced. Experiments designed to define the nature of the sounds that will serve best as emotional stimuli are underway.

II. When a conditioned emotional response has been established for one object, is there a transfer? Five days later Albert was again brought back into the laboratory and tested as follows:

11 Months 15 Days

1. Tested first with blocks. He reached readily for them, playing with them as usual. This shows that there has been no general transfer to the room, table, blocks, etc.

2. Rat alone. Whimpered immediately, withdrew right hand and turned head and trunk away.

3. Blocks again offered. Played readily with them, smiling and gurgling. [p.6]

4. Rat alone. Leaned over to the left side as far away from the rat as possible, then fell over, getting up on all fours and scurrying away as rapidly as possible.

5. Blocks again offered. Reached immediately for them, smiling and laughing as before.

The above preliminary test shows that the conditioned response to the rat had carried over completely for the five days in which no tests were given. The question as to whether or not there is a transfer was next taken up.

6. Rabbit alone. The rabbit was suddenly placed on the mattress in front of him. The reaction was pronounced. Negative responses began at once. He leaned as far away from the animal as possible, whimpered, then burst into tears. When the rabbit was placed in contact with him he buried his face in the mattress, then got up on all fours and crawled away, crying as he went. This was a most convincing test.

7. The blocks were next given him, after an interval. He played with them as before. It was observed by four people that he played far more energetically with them than ever before. The blocks were raised high over his head and slammed down with a great deal of force.

8. Dog alone. The dog did not produce as violent a reaction as the rabbit. The moment fixation occurred the child shrank back and as the animal came nearer he attempted to get on all fours but did not cry at first. As soon as the dog passed out of his range of vision he became quiet. The dog was then made to approach the infant's head (he was lying down at the moment). Albert straightened up immediately, fell over to the opposite side and turned his head away. He then began to cry.

9. The blocks were again presented. He began immediately to play with them.

10. Fur coat (seal). Withdrew immediately to the left side and began to fret. Coat put close to him on the [p.7] left side, he turned immediately, began to cry and tried to crawl away on all fours.

11. Cotton wool. The wool was presented in a paper package. At the end, the cotton was not covered by the paper. It was placed first on his feet. He kicked it away but did not touch it with his

hands. When his hand was laid on the wool he immediately withdrew it but did not show the shock that the animals or fur coat produced in him. He then began to play with the paper, avoiding contact with the wool itself. He finally, under the impulse of the manipulative instinct, lost some of his negativism to the wool.

12. Just in play W. put his head down to see if Albert would play with his hair. Albert was completely negative. Two other observers did the same thing. He began immediately to play with their hair. W. then brought the Santa Claus mask and presented it to Albert. He was again pronouncedly negative.

11 Months 20 Days

1. Blocks alone. Played with them as usual.

2. Rat alone. Withdrawal of the whole body, bending over to left side, no crying. Fixation and following with eyes. The response was much less marked than on first presentation the previous week. It was thought best to freshen up the reaction by another joint stimulation.

3. Just as the rat was placed on his hand the rod was struck. Reaction violent.

4. Rat alone. Fell over at once to left side. Reaction practically as strong as on former occasion but no crying.

5. Rat alone. Fell over to left side, got up on all fours and started to crawl away. On this occasion there was no crying, but strange to say, as he started away he began to gurgle and coo, even while leaning far over to the left side to avoid the rat.

6. Rabbit alone. Leaned over to left side as far as possible. Did not fall over. Began to whimper but reaction not so violent as on former occasions. [p.8]

7. Blocks again offered. He reached for them immediately and began to play.

All of these tests so far discussed were carried out upon a table supplied with a mattress, located in a small, well-lighted darkroom. We wished to test next whether conditioned fear responses so set up would appear if the situation were markedly altered. We thought it best before making this test to freshen the reaction both to the rabbit and to the dog by showing them at the moment the steel bar was struck. It will be recalled that this was the first time any effort had been made to directly condition response to the dog and rabbit. The experimental notes are as follows:

8. The rabbit at first was given alone. The reaction was exactly as given in test (6) above. When the rabbit was left on Albert's knees for a long time he began tentatively to reach out and manipulate its fur with forefingers. While doing this the steel rod was struck. A violent fear reaction resulted.

9. Rabbit alone. Reaction wholly similar to that on trial (6) above.

10. Rabbit alone. Started immediately to whimper, holding hands far up, but did not cry. Conflicting tendency to manipulate very evident.

11. Dog alone. Began to whimper, shaking head from side to side, holding hands as far away from the animal as possible.

12. Dog and sound. The rod was struck just as the animal touched him. A violent negative reaction appeared. He began to whimper, turned to one side, fell over and started to get up on all fours.

13. Blocks. Played with them immediately and readily.

On this same day and immediately after the above experiment Albert was taken into the large well-lighted lecture room belonging to the laboratory. He was placed on a table in the center of the room immediately under the skylight. Four people were present. The situation [p.9] was thus very different from that which obtained in the small dark room.

1. Rat alone. No sudden fear reaction appeared at first. The hands, however, were held up and away from the animal. No positive manipulatory reactions appeared.

2. Rabbit alone. Fear reaction slight. Turned to left and kept face away from the animal but the reaction was never pronounced.

3. Dog alone. Turned away but did not fall over. Cried. Hands moved as far away from the animal as possible. Whimpered as long as the dog was present.

4. Rat alone. Slight negative reaction.

5. Rat and sound. It was thought best to freshen the reaction to the rat. The sound was given just as the rat was presented. Albert jumped violently but did not cry.

6. Rat alone. At first he did not show any negative reaction. When rat was placed nearer he began to show negative reaction by drawing back his body, raising his hands, whimpering, etc.

7. Blocks. Played with them immediately.

8. Rat alone. Pronounced withdrawal of body and whimpering.

9. Blocks. Played with them as before.

10. Rabbit alone. Pronounced reaction. Whimpered with arms held high, fell over backward and had to be caught.

11. Dog alone. At first the dog did not produce the pronounced reaction. The hands were held high over the head, breathing was checked, but there was no crying. Just at this moment the dog, which had not barked before, barked three times loudly when only about six inches from the baby's face. Albert immediately fell over and broke into a wail that continued until the dog was removed. The sudden barking of the hitherto quiet dog produced a marked fear response in the adult observers!

[p.10] From the above results it would seem that emotional transfers do take place. Furthermore it would seem that the number of transfers resulting from an experimentally produced conditioned emotional reaction may be very large. In our observations we had no means of testing the complete number of transfers which may have resulted.

III. The effect of time upon conditioned emotional responses. We have already shown that the conditioned emotional response will continue for a period of one week. It was desired to make the time test longer. In view of the imminence of Albert's departure from the hospital we could not make the interval longer than one month. Accordingly no further emotional experimentation was entered into for thirty-one days after the above test. During the month, however, Albert was brought weekly to the laboratory for tests upon right- and left-handedness, imitation, general development, etc. No emotional tests whatever were given and during the whole month his regular nursery routine was maintained in the Harriet Lane Home. The notes on the test given at the end of this period are as follows:

1 Year 21 Days

1. Santa Claus mask. Withdrawal, gurgling, then slapped at it without touching. When his hand was forced to touch it, he whimpered and cried. His hand was forced to touch it two more times. He whimpered and cried on both tests. He finally cried at the mere visual stimulus of the mask.

2. Fur coat. Wrinkled his nose and withdrew both hands, drew back his whole body and began to whimper as the coat was put nearer. Again there was the strife between withdrawal and the tendency to manipulate. Reached tentatively with left hand but drew back before contact had been made. In moving his body to one side his hand accidentally touched the coat. He began to cry at once, nodding his head in a very peculiar manner (this reaction was an entirely new one). Both hands were withdrawn as far as possible from the coat. The coat [p.11] was then laid on his lap and he continued nodding his head and whimpering, withdrawing his body as far as possible, pushing the while at the coat with his feet but never touching it with his hands.

3. Fur coat. The coat was taken out of his sight and presented again at the end of a minute. He began immediately to fret, withdrawing his body and nodding his head as before.

4. Blocks. He began to play with them as usual.

5. The rat. He allowed the rat to crawl towards him without withdrawing. He sat very still and fixated it intently. Rat then touched his hand. Albert withdrew it immediately, then leaned back as far as possible but did not cry. When the rat was placed on his arm he withdrew his body and began to fret, nodding his head. The rat was then allowed to crawl against his chest. He first began to fret and then covered his eyes with both hands.

6. Blocks. Reaction normal.

7. The rabbit. The animal was placed directly in front of him. It was very quiet. Albert showed no avoiding reactions at first. After a few seconds he puckered up his face, began to nod his head and to look intently at the experimenter. He next began to push the rabbit away with his feet, withdrawing his body at the same time. Then as the rabbit came nearer he began pulling his feet away, nodding his head, and wailing "da da". After about a minute he reached out tentatively and slowly and touched the rabbit's ear with his right hand, finally manipulating it. The rabbit was again placed in his lap. Again he began to fret and withdrew his hands. He reached out tentatively with his left hand and touched the animal, shuddered and withdrew the whole body. The experimenter then took hold of his left hand and laid it on the rabbit's back. Albert immediately withdrew his hand and began to suck his thumb. Again the rabbit was laid in his lap. He began to cry, covering his face with both hands. [p.12]

8. Dog. The dog was very active. Albert fixated it intensely for a few seconds, sitting very still. He began to cry but did not fall over backwards as on his last contact with the dog. When the dog was pushed closer to him he at first sat motionless, then began to cry, putting both hands over his face.

These experiments would seem to show conclusively that directly conditioned emotional responses as well as those conditioned by transfer persist, although with a certain loss in the intensity of the reaction, for a longer period than one month. Our view is that they persist and modify personality throughout life. It should be recalled again that Albert was of an extremely phlegmatic type. Had he been emotionally unstable probably both the directly conditioned response and those transferred would have persisted throughout the month unchanged in form.

IV. "Detachment" or removal of conditioned emotional responses. Unfortunately Albert was taken from the hospital the day the above tests were made. Hence the opportunity of building up an experimental technique by means of which we could remove the conditioned emotional responses was denied us. Our own view, expressed above, which is possibly not very well grounded, is that these responses in the home environment are likely to persist indefinitely, unless an accidental method for removing them is hit upon. The importance of establishing some method must be apparent to all. Had the opportunity been at hand we should have tried out several methods, some of which we may mention. (1) Constantly confronting the child with those stimuli which called out the responses in the hopes that habituation would come in corresponding to "fatigue" of reflex when differential reactions are to be set up. (2) By trying to "recondition" by showing objects calling out fear responses (visual) and simultaneously stimulating the erogenous zones (tactual). We should try first the lips, then the nipples and as a final resort the sex organs. (3) By trying to "recondition" by feeding the subject candy or other food just as the animal is shown. This method calls for the food control of the subject. (4) By building up "constructive" activities around the object by imitation and [p.13] by putting the hand through the motions of manipulation. At this age imitation of overt motor activity is strong, as our present but unpublished experimentation has shown.

INCIDENTAL OBSERVATIONS

(a) Thumb sucking as a compensatory device for blocking fear and noxious stimuli. During the course of these experiments, especially in the final test, it was noticed that whenever Albert was on the verge of tears or emotionally upset generally he would continually thrust his thumb into his mouth. The moment the hand reached the mouth he became impervious to the stimuli producing fear. Again and again while the motion pictures were being made at the end of the thirty-day period, we had to remove the thumb from his mouth before the conditioned response could be obtained. This method of blocking noxious and emotional stimuli (fear and rage) through erogenous stimulation seems to persist from birth onward. Very often in our experiments upon the work adders with infants under ten days of age the same reaction appeared. When at work upon the adders both of the infants' arms are under slight restraint. Often rage appears. They begin to cry, thrashing their arms and legs about. If the finger gets into the mouth crying ceases at once. The organism thus apparently from birth, when under the influence of love stimuli is blocked to all others.[3] This resort to sex stimulation when under the influence of noxious and emotional situations, or when the individual is restless and idle, persists throughout adolescent and adult life. Albert, at any rate, did not resort to thumb sucking except in the presence of such stimuli. Thumb sucking could immediately be checked by offering him his blocks. These invariably called out active manipulation instincts. It is worthwhile here to call attention to the fact that Freud's conception of the stimulation of erogenous zones as being the expression of an original "pleasure" seeking principle may be turned about [p.14] and possibly better described as a compensatory (and often conditioned) device for the blockage of noxious and fear- and rage-producing stimuli.

(b) Equal primacy of fear, love and possibly rage. While in general the results of our experiment offer no particular points of conflict with Freudian concepts, one fact out of harmony with them should be emphasized. According to proper Freudians, sex (or in our terminology, love) is the principal emotion in which conditioned responses arise which later limit and distort personality. We wish to take sharp issue with this view on the basis of the experimental evidence we have gathered. Fear is as primal a factor as love in influencing personality. Fear does not gather its potency in any derived manner from love. It belongs to the original and inherited nature of man. Probably the same may be true of rage although at present we are not so sure of this.

The Freudians twenty years from now, unless their hypotheses change, when they come to analyze Albert's fear of a seal skin coat - assuming that he comes to analysis at that age - will probably tease from him the recital of a dream which upon their analysis will show that Albert at three years of age attempted to play with the pubic hair of the mother and was scolded violently for it. (We are by no means denying that this might in some other case condition it). If the analyst has sufficiently prepared Albert to accept such a dream when found as an explanation of his avoiding tendencies, and if the analyst has the authority and personality to put it over, Albert may be fully convinced that the dream was a true revealer of the factors which brought about the fear.

It is probable that many of the phobias in psychopathology are true conditioned emotional reactions either of the direct or the transferred type. One may possibly have to believe that such persistence of early conditioned responses will be found only in persons who are constitutionally inferior. Our argument is meant to be constructive. Emotional disturbances in adults cannot be traced back to sex alone. They must be retraced along at least three collateral lines - to conditioned and transferred responses set up in infancy and early youth in all three of the fundamental human emotions.

FOOTNOTES

[1.] 'Emotional Reactions and Psychological Experimentation,' *American Journal of Psychology*, April, 1917, Vol. 28, pp. 163-174.

[2.] 'Psychology from the Standpoint of a Behaviorist,' p.202.

[3.] The stimulus to love in infants according to our view is stroking of the skin, lips, nipples and sex organs, patting and rocking, picking up, etc. Patting and rocking (when not conditioned) are probably equivalent to actual stimulation of the sex organs. In adults of course, as every lover knows, vision, audition and olfaction soon become conditioned by joint stimulation with contact and kinaesthetic stimuli.